For Niall
with the la

Black Elk e Elijar

THE FOUR ASCENTS

THE FOUR ASCENTS

Part Two

of

The Two Roads Trilogy

Eliza White Buffalo
with Nicholas Black Elk

authorHOUSE

AuthorHouse™ UK Ltd.
1663 Liberty Drive
Bloomington, IN 47403 USA
www.authorhouse.co.uk
Phone: 0800.197.4150

© *2013 by Eliza White Buffalo with Nicholas Black Elk. All rights reserved.*
Cover art by Bernie Cargill. All rights reserved—used with permission.

This story is based on my experiences with Black Elk and my soul family

No part of this book may be reproduced, stored in a retrieval system, or transmitted by any means without the written permission of the author.

Published by AuthorHouse   06/11/2013

ISBN: 978-1-4817-9495-4 (sc)
ISBN: 978-1-4817-9496-1 (e)

Any people depicted in stock imagery provided by Thinkstock are models, and such images are being used for illustrative purposes only.
Certain stock imagery © Thinkstock.

This book is printed on acid-free paper.

Because of the dynamic nature of the Internet, any web addresses or links contained in this book may have changed since publication and may no longer be valid. The views expressed in this work are solely those of the author and do not necessarily reflect the views of the publisher, and the publisher hereby disclaims any responsibility for them.

CONTENTS

Acknowledgements ix
Prologue xiii
Introduction: Rose... xvii

PART ONE: RISE AND FALL

Chapter One: The Father's Dream 3
Chapter Two: The difficult path..20
Chapter Three: The holy path 32
Chapter Four: The Order of Delphi 56
Chapter Five: The Challenge..71
Chapter Six: The search for Philo....................................96
Chapter Seven: The fall from grace 118

PART TWO: THE VISION

Chapter Eight: The Six Grandfathers................................... 147
Chapter Nine: Death and resurrection 165
Chapter Ten: The four ascents.. 173

PART THREE: SO SHALL IT BE ON EARTH

Chapter Eleven: The second ascent...................................... 189
Chapter Twelve: A quest for knowledge 204
Chapter Thirteen: Remember who you are 219
Chapter Fourteen: The third ascent 230
Chapter Fifteen: Escape from the black road........................... 243
Chapter Sixteen: The choice 258
Chapter Seventeen: The fourth ascent...................................... 268
Chapter Eighteen: Heaven on Earth 275

About the Author.. 295

*This book is
dedicated to Flaming Rainbow
who seeded the dream
with Black Elk*

ACKNOWLEDGEMENTS . . .

I wish to say thank you to many people who had a part in the creation of this book. My special thanks to all of those who listened to hours and hours of past life stories, especially:—

My husband and soul mate: Thank you for your support, patience and acceptance of the demanding process that writing this book has been. Thank you for the years of love and deep friendship we have shared together, not only in this lifetime but throughout our souls' journey on earth. I love you, darling; I always will.

Lu Jones: I met Lu many years ago and we quickly recognized that we are sisters, soul family. When we met I was still very much in the shadow of my life. Lu helped me to heal. She helped me to have faith in and to love who I was, and to follow Black Elk's guidance with more clarity and passion than I had ever done before. The Two Roads Trilogy might still be an item on my must do list if it weren't for Lu, who channelled the format of the first book for me, giving me the push I needed to begin. Thank you, dear Lu. I love you.

Stephen Oliver: I first met Stephen in 2008. And gosh! Was I excited! Black Elk had been telling me of his entering my life for many years before that. Stephen has helped me greatly on my journey with The Two Roads Trilogy and I know he will be with me throughout the birth of book 3. Stephen, thank you for all the hours of research and computer stuff . . . you know I can't stand that gunk. I love you.

Gusta Peters: Black Elk often shows me a person's face when they are to come into my life for divine purpose; Gusta is one such person. When we were finally drawn to each other's side by Spirit, we began to enjoy a loving and honest relationship. I have shared much with Gusta who loves unconditionally, understands divinely, and has great compassion for all of God's creatures. Gusta, thank you for being such a great friend, and thank you for all the hours of proof reading and encouragement. I love you.

David Pieters: I met David and his wife, Nancy when they came to Ireland to visit with Gusta. I fell in love with them both immediately. David has proved to be a source of transformation for me. I love you, David. Thank you for being there and for helping me to get the story straight.

Nancy Pieters: Nancy, you know we are especially fond of you. Thank you for being so good to me. You are truly beautiful. I love you.

Reggie.Jameson: I first met Reggie 15 years ago. Reggie introduced me to energy healing. It was a delight for me to express my true essence for the first time in many years. He continues to be close by, always willing to be a source of light. Thank you, Reggie, I love you.

Matthew Lennon: Thank you, Matthew, for the months and months of healing energy you channelled. Thank you for all your guidance and wise words. And thank you for your 'special feature' in this book. I love you.

Peter Shearer: Thank you Peter, for all the lovely meetings we have enjoyed. Thanks for all the treatments you gave so lovingly. I cherish every one of our special chats.

Tommy Suggs: Tommy is the author of *From a Student's Notebook volumes 1-4*. He has been a source of strength and grace for me in this past year I have known him. Tommy, your books are great; a wonderful guide to the essence of native spirituality. Thank you so much for all you have done so that *this* book is the best it could be. I love you.

Jonette Crowley: Thank you, Jonette for all you have done for me. In particular, thank you for reading the first draft of the manuscript and for the valuable and constructive review of it. I love you.

Bernie Cargill: Thank you, Bernie for the beautiful piece of art that now graces the cover of this book. I love you.

My deepest respect and gratitude goes to Black Elk and his son, Ben Black Elk, for guiding me, loving me, and awakening me to my divine purpose. Thanks to you both and to John for sharing the dream.

Related books:

Eliza White Buffalo with Nicholas Black Elk . . . *The Two Roads,* part one of the two roads trilogy.
John G Neihardt . . . *Black Elk Speaks*

Recommended reading:

Jonette Crowley . . . *The Eagle and The Condor*
Tommy Suggs . . . *From a Student's Notebook* series
Cathleen Hulbert . . . *The First Lamp*
Gary R Renard . . . *The Disappearance of The Universe & Your Immortal Reality*

PROLOGUE

This book is a follow up from my first book, *The Two Roads,* what I wrote with the help of my spirit guide, Nicholas Black Elk. Those of you who have read *The Two Roads* will be somewhat familiar with who Black Elk is. For the benefit of those of you who possibly have never heard of Black Elk, I shall briefly outline who he is and what his relationship to me is.

Black Elk was born a Lakota Sioux Indian, near the Black Hills of South Dakota, in 1863. When he was nine years old he had a great vision. It was a very beautiful and spiritual vision. In this vision, six grandfathers representing the Powers of the Universe showed him many things. They showed him two roads he would walk with his nation. They gave him gifts of healing and knowledge, and they showed him that he would walk on earth for four ascents with these gifts. It is my understanding that the four ascents signified, amongst other great things, that his soul would live on earth for four more lifetimes counting his. The life I am living in this present day, is the fourth lifetime; the fourth ascent. Black Elk and I are individual parts of the one original soul. He dwells within my spiritual being. It is from there that he speaks and I listen. In this manner I channel his words from his higher realm of consciousness.

Throughout my life I have connected with Black Elk. With his guidance I have recalled many of the incarnations my soul has had; this book is based on these memories and on what Black Elk has told me about the journey of the soul. In the context of our linear time frame, the journey begins at the point of creation and continues throughout our history to the present day.

In 1931, whilst still alive, Black Elk told his life story and his vision to a soul brother, John G Neihardt. John wrote Black Elk's words in a book. That book is *Black Elk Speaks* by John G Neidhardt. Now, Black Elk retells the vision from the higher understanding he has from where he is now in the spirit world; it is an understanding conveyed by the story of this book. In my experience of writing this book I connect with the part of my soul that is Black Elk. I sit with pen in hand or at my computer, and I empty my own thoughts out of my mind. When the first words are placed into my thoughts by Black Elk I begin to write them down. And so the process begins; as the words flow into my thoughts I write them. The words in this book have been written to a large degree as they were given. I have changed or moved some of

Eliza White Buffalo with Nicholas Black Elk

them about somewhat for the purpose of making them more like a story form but they are very much as authentic as they were spoken by Black Elk to me.

At the back of the book you will find a table. The first column shows the many characters from the first book, *The Two Roads*. These characters are based on the many souls my soul has incarnated with throughout its journey on Earth. They have all had many lifetimes in which they have experienced being different bodies, different personalities. In the other columns you will see just who these different personalities were in each lifetime represented in the course of the story. I suggest you familiarize yourself with the table before reading the story as it will give you an understanding of the continuity of each soul.

Eliza White Buffalo

There are two roads in life.

*One is a vertical road which
leads to Truth, Spirituality, and Love; a good red road that
uplifts us and brings us happiness.*

*And there is a horizontal road,
a road leading nowhere, a road of fear, powerlessness
and despair.*

*And where these two roads meet
is a holy place where peace is all around.*

*It is the place of power
from where the soul makes its ascension, its journey home.*

INTRODUCTION

Rose

Ireland 2009

It's five in the morning. The sun has just risen over the top of the forest that stretches across the mountain next to my home. I have been sitting here on the sofa in my prayer room, meditating as the sun came up. I got up extra early this morning. I didn't want to sleep through dawn today. It's a very special day for me and my daughter, Grace. Last June we met for the first time since she was born thirty years ago. She had been taken from me at birth and handed over to a childless couple in England to take as their own daughter. I had yearned for her for years, never knowing where she was or how to begin to look for her. Then, about six weeks ago there she was. The spirit world had led me to her, to the very place where she lives in England with her fiancé John. I am a psychic channel for my spirit guide, Black Elk, and I was giving an audience in the town where Grace lives, and there she was, just as Spirit said she would be. Apparently she had been searching for me. She and John had been here in Ireland, to the place she was born, even to the very spot. I was close by all along and never knew. I guess the timing just wasn't right for us to meet then. But we have now, and she and John have come to Ireland again to visit me at my home. And today is our big day; today she will publicly announce that she accepts me as her mother by taking the name Grace in a special naming ceremony. Her adoptive parents gave her the name Melissa, Lissy for short. It's a lovely name to be sure, and Lissy is a lovely girl but I know her in my heart as Grace and when I spoke that name to her she felt like I did, that there is no other name for her but Grace.

"Oh Rose, it's as if I chose the name before I was born," she said to me then, and I had to agree. It seems that Lissy, or Grace, also has the gift of connecting with Spirit. I have been connecting with the spiritual realms all my life. It wasn't easy for me growing up but the connection with Spirit made such a difference to my childhood. I had been sexually and emotionally abused. It was how Grace came to be conceived. I was twelve years old, just turned thirteen when I gave birth to her. I am happy that she had a good upbringing with two loving parents. Somehow, I don't think she would have had that if she had stayed with me. Joyfully, now I can give her all the love in the world. I can surround her with joy and hope, for I may have experienced a terrible beginning to my life, but with the love and help of Black Elk I have risen out of pain and into joy.

It's almost five thirty am now. My husband Jack and sons Ollie and Jerry won't get up until seven. I hug myself with happiness because this morning, like no other morning before, their sister Grace is with us. Emma will be here for the ceremony too which is wonderful. Emma is Jack's twenty year old daughter. She is so happy for me, bless her. I have loved her since she was four years old when I met her father. Jack, my soul mate, has loved me for what feels like forever and I have loved him. He is part of my soul family, two groups of beautiful souls that I have incarnated with over and over since our first appearance on Earth. A lot of them will be here today for the ceremony. Grace is a very special member of the soul family and they all delight in our reunion. None can be happier for us though than Black Elk for my happiness is *his* happiness; my joy is *his* joy. Almost six am now. I will connect with him before I start the day. I have a feeling that today shall be special in more ways than one.

∞∞∞∞∞∞∞∞∞∞∞∞∞∞∞∞∞∞∞∞∞∞∞∞∞∞∞

Black Elk is speaking: "Rose, you do not know how you feel to me at this moment. You have no idea of the love that I feel for you. The scared waters of the good red road flow within the canals of my being which is your being too. Oh Rose, how close the canals are that flow within your being! It is my being."

I take several more deep breaths. The canals are open and I feel the waves coming through; wave after wave of life-giving water. It is the sacred water of the good red road that flows through me. It is the consciousness of Source, the spirit of the Father that floods my being waking every cell and resurrecting me from the shadows of darkness.

"I love you too Black Elk," I whisper. "I feel the sacred waters flowing within. It lifts me into a better place; a place where I know who we are."

"And who do you say we are Rose?" encourages Black Elk.

"We are Eliza. *I Am* Eliza, a child of Beloved Source," I reply.

"It is so! The native peoples know this; that we are children of the sky who is our father and the earth who is our mother. We are one with them in the holy place where the two roads meet. If you remember the vision you will know that the four ascents begin in the holy place. From there we walk both roads in balance. The waters of the good red road sustain us on our journey upwards and through the power given to us by Beloved Source, the power to destroy and to make live, we resurrect our earthly beings into the light of Heaven. It is the prophecy; it is the Father's Dream, Heaven on Earth."

Black Elk is referring to the prophecy of harmony and wholeness that he was shown in his mighty vision when he nine years old on Earth. He saw two roads in life, a difficult earthly road and a good spiritual road, and where the two roads met was a holy place of balance and wholeness. From that place he saw four ascents stretching far upwards towards a world of harmony amongst all beings. When I was a child I had glimpses of the vision, which he showed to me. He would say to me, *As I have danced upon the earth so shall you.* He meant that I would continue with the prophecy.

"I used to believe that the prophecy was something given to only you by the Sacred Parents," I tell him now, and not for the first time. "I realise now that not only was it given to you but to all living creatures. Why even a rose begins its life in the darkness of the earth and makes its way through stages to blossom in the beauty of wholeness."

"Yes," Black Elk agrees, "And even the rose has its thorns, its shadow. Remember what I said, it is only through walking both roads in balance that we come to know the wholeness of who we are."

"But, Black Elk, even now I am often reluctant to walk the black road," I tell him thinking of all those times that I spent in the ethereal temples of the universe. "Even now, I yearn to escape and fly away to the higher realms where I feel a sense of elation. Why even when I was a child I lived for the times we spent together on *The Green.*" When I was a child I escaped my terrible life by travelling with the help of a motherly spirit called May to a place in the higher realms, in the spirit world. It was called *The Green.* There I would meet with Black Elk. He taught me a lot in those days about spirit and about who I was. It didn't make sense of the awful things I endured on earth but it did help me to have courage. It gave me hope and a sense of identity that I clung onto for survival in those terrible times.

"And it is that very child that is your salvation, White Buffalo," Black Elk replies reminding me to come into the centre of my truth and not to indulge in depressing thoughts. Black Elk has called me White Buffalo Woman for years now, but recently he has taken to calling me Rose, which is my Christian name.

"Of course, you are right as always!" I agree, laughing at myself.

Black Elk laughs with me. He has not forgotten what it is like to be on Earth. Last year, I wrote a book, *The Wounds of the Shaman*. In that book I explained how the inner wounded child is our true messiah. The child comes to the world in purity with the spark of Beloved Source alive within the heart. That spark never perishes. It is infinite and is the hope and salvation that Black Elk and I know to be the Christ Consciousness. The wounds that result from the fearful black road (from the difficulties of the earthly life) when destroyed and resurrected by the sacred waters of the good red road (the spiritual life) are the means by which we climb the four ascents. We quite literally raise them into Heaven. This is the holy ascension which takes place in our hearts, in that holy place where the Child is one with the Father and the Mother, the three supreme beings in one, and that One is Beloved Source.

"The four ascents are four steps of the return to Source," Black Elk reminds me now. "Rose, you have tasted that wholeness in the holy place in your heart space, and you know the four ascents of consciousness arise from there. You also know that the return to Source is a journey that the soul makes over many incarnations on the earth plane."

"Aye, as we learn our earth lessons," I add.

"Yes, we learn through our physical domain, through our earthly experience; we learn who we are, and we make choices."

"Oh aye, choices . . . I learned the hard way that it is our choices that determine our experience. You told me once I had the power to choose all along. I know now that in every moment there is an opportunity for choice. I do try to choose light every time, you know, but it's not always easy. Sometimes I am so tempted to choose what feels good to my shadow self. It's like I am torn in two; like I have an inner battle going on most of the time."

"I understand, Rose. That is the nature of the two roads," Black Elk says calmly. "It is called duality. It belongs to the physical plane. I have moved beyond the physical plane, therefore I do not feel duality, but it is my job to help *you* to move beyond duality too. The reason you feel this duality within you is to help you to empower yourself. The more you empower yourself the more you move closer to absolute wholeness wherein there *is* only power."

"And I empower myself by choosing light?" I add.

"Exactly, by being centred in the holy place, which is in your heart, of course, you are in the perfect place to make the right choice. When you are in the holy place you can see both roads clearly. And so, you are able to see the consequences of either choice. This is empowerment, my dear Rose. Now, I said the soul makes the four ascents of consciousness over many incarnations.

The Four Ascents

This is another way of saying that full empowerment is reached over many incarnations or lifetimes."

I thank Black Elk. I am grinning inside and out because I know he is about to teach me great things. "I feel a lesson coming on," I tell him with a giggle.

"Hmmm, let us begin then," he laughs. "Okay, so here we are, you and I. You know me to be your twin flame, the Father essence of your soul."

"I do."

"And I am here in the spirit world and you are there in the physical world."

"Aye."

"And here you are making the four ascents into your awareness of Spirit, into the awareness of power; in other words, on the journey back to Beloved Source."

"Aye, I understand."

"And you understand we are Eliza, a child of Beloved Source?" he asks.

"Aye, And Eliza is the soul," I add.

"Eliza is the soul, yes. But, who *is* Eliza. Is she you and me? Or is she much more than that? Consider this . . . if the soul incarnates many times in order to make the journey home, then it will have many lifetimes, and in each lifetime it will have a new body, a new personality. Now, I have gone before you, or so it seems that way in the passing of time. I have lived my life and I have now come to the part of the soul's journey where I no longer have to live on the physical plane and learn the lessons of duality. But I *did* live on the earth, as you are now, *and* as many others have done too."

"I understand," I tell him eagerly. "The memories I have of other lifetimes, such as being Maria in Mexico, and of being in The Order of Delphi in Ancient Greece, are two such examples of the soul being incarnated at a particular time on Earth."

"That is so, my dear Rose, my White Buffalo Woman," he replies. "And you were shown much of this journey by the Master Hilarion, in the ethereal Temple of Truth."

"I saw it in the Emerald Flame of Truth," I nodded. My heart is beating quicker; it means Black Elk is lifting my consciousness up into a deeper trance like state. This is the state of consciousness that enables me to travel into the spirit world and see and hear with spirit.

Black Elk pauses until I adjust to this altered state of awareness, and then he continues, "The soul, Eliza, has been on Earth many times. All souls spring from the well of Source like droplets from a lake. They make their way back again by splitting themselves up into even smaller droplets. These droplets live on the physical plane, each learning aspects of itself that will enable it to make its way back to the wholeness of that one original droplet. Do you understand?"

"I do. All souls come from God, and each soul splits itself up into many individual souls. The individual souls bring themselves back to wholeness of the original soul by learning through their lifetime."

"That's it." Black Elk smiles and sends another huge wave of love throughout my being. I relax even more into a deep trance. "And so, my dear Rose, you see that you are a droplet of water that is part of an original droplet from the lake of Beloved Source I, like many before me, have found my wholeness which means that I am now one with the original droplet, the original soul."

"And I am still working my way towards that wholeness," I add.

"Yes . . . well done. Now, the journey of the soul seems like a long journey in the passing of time. The soul will incarnate a part of itself many times in order to bring that part back to itself in wholeness. And so you can be sure that your soul has lived on Earth many times as a person other than who you are now. You can be sure that just as you have an individual spirit, each of those persons also has an individual spirit which is part of your original soul; and so each spirit has contributed to the ascension of the soul back to the lake, back to its Beloved Source. When you feel the truth of who you were in those lifetimes, for example when you remember being Maria in Mexico you are actually tuning in to the original soul which holds the memories of each of its individual life experiences; you are tuning in to the part of the soul which remembers being Maria."

"Wow! Yes, I understand that, I *feel* it.

"Great! And so this is the perfect moment to begin. I am taking you on a journey into the memory of your original soul. I will show you many lifetimes experienced by the individual parts of the soul. I will show you only what you need to know and I will also add a few things here and there so that you can get a better understanding of the journey. Lie back now Rose, relax, your family won't awaken until we are done."

Moving from my meditation position, I grab a rug from the back of the sofa, and wrapping it around me for warmth I lie back flat on the sofa. I am ready to begin. My breathing is slow and shallow and I soon drift off into my inner vision. Black Elk's voice is low and distant as he leads me into a spiralling feeling. Round and round I go, deeper and deeper into trance, deeper and deeper into my inner world. A loud shooshing noise echoes in my ears for a bit and then settles down into a low drone. Pictures begin to flash into my inner sight as the room I am lying in seems to drift further and further from my awareness. Very soon, the pictures settle down and just as I had seen in the Emerald Flame of the ethereal Temple of Truth, a kind of video begins to play. I feel myself enter into the video as if it were happening to me right now. I feel I am right at the beginning of my existence. Nothing seems to have gone before for I feel nothing. I *am* nothing.

∞∞∞∞∞∞∞∞∞∞∞∞∞∞∞∞∞∞∞∞∞∞∞∞∞∞∞∞

In the beginning there is nothing. I am nothing. Yet . . . I *am*. I desire to be. The desire is great. I *am* desire. I am a zillion particles of desire yet I am nothing. I am infinite desire devoid of expression. I am darkness. And I say "Let there be light."

Now there is light. I am light. In the light I know that I am nothing yet I am all there is. I am light and I am darkness. I am Heaven and I am Earth. I am two yet I am one. I am *One*.

I look upon the earth and I say, "Let there be water" and there is water, and, "Let there be green," and the waters are divided by dry land and it is good. All over the earth there are waters and green. There are trees and growth, and on these are many coloured fruits and herbs and I see that they are good. I rejoice in the heavens for the earth is good and beautiful and she is my *Self*, She is my left hand.

With my right hand I send a voice and I say, "I am a great light. I am spirit. Let the great light shine one on my right hand and one on my left hand and let them light the earth. I am the sun and the moon. I am two yet I desire to be many, and so I say, "Let there be many."

Now I am many. I am a zillion particles of my Self burning brightly in the heavens. I am stars. I am stars and great lights in heaven and I am beautiful, and I am waters and green on earth and I am beautiful. And I rejoice. On my right hand I am light and I am beautiful and on my left hand I am darkness and I am beautiful. I am Beauty.

I desire to know my Self on Earth, and so I say, "Let Heaven be on Earth." I come down into the waters and I am many different swimming creatures below the green. I come down over the waters and I am many winged creatures that fly above the waters and the green. I rejoice for it is good and

I say, "Let every creature multiply." And I swim in the waters and fly in the skies and I multiply in my likeness.

I desire to walk upon the green, and so I say, "Let there be four-leggeds and all manner of creeping creature to move over the green." *Now* I walk upon the green breathing life from my being, and I swim in the waters breathing life from my being, and I fly in the skies breathing life from my being. I am life. I am the swimming ones and the flying ones. I am the crawling ones and the four-legged ones. I sustain my bodies with the life in the waters and the skies and with the fruits and herbs of the land, and I am happy.

I am in Heaven and I am on Earth. In the heavenly light I know all and I see all. I am all there is. I am many. Yet in my earthly darkness I know my Self to be one *of* many instead of one *and* many. I am too far from the light to see my wholeness, and so I say, "Let me come closer to the light." Now I am closer to the light and I see that I am many and that I am one. I walk on two legs and I breathe into my Self so that I may live and know who I am. I am man on my right hand and I am woman on my left hand.

Because I know who I am I love my Self. I love my waters and my green, I love my swimming self and my flying self, I love my crawling self and my four-legged self, and I love my two-legged self. Because I love my Self I take good care of my Self and I nourish my Self. I feed my Self with the good fruits and herbs of the earth. I feed my bodies, my children. I cleanse their bodies with my waters. I am their mother. I am Mother Earth. Because I love my children I take good care of them and I nourish them. I feed them with the living breath of my being. I feed my children and I cleanse their bodies with my spirit. I am their father. I am Father Heaven. I am Mother Earth and I am Father Heaven. I am Body and I am Spirit.

My sons and daughters walk the earth and they are happy. They care for my waters and my green and they care for the swimming ones and the flying ones. They care for the crawling ones and the four-legged ones. They take good care of all their relatives. I rejoice for I am many on the earth and I am many in the heavens.

And so it is that I am one with many faces. And each of these faces is my Self in my wholeness. In one quarter of my wholeness I am my breath, *air*, and here my children find wisdom, and in another quarter of my wholeness I am my path, *water*, and here my children learn trust. In a third quarter of my wholeness I am my spirit, *fire*, and here my children find enlightenment and in a fourth quarter of my wholeness I am my body, *earth* where my children gain power. I am North, South, East, and West. I am four quarters of my Self, and

The Four Ascents

in each of these quarters I have three faces. I am the Father and the Mother and I am the spark of my creation, my Holy Spirit.

I am four and I am three times four. I am twelve yet I am one. I am many in Heaven and on Earth and yet I am one . . . I am one . . . I am one and yet I am nothing. I am all things and yet I am nothing. I am desire longing to be . . . I Am . . .

. . . In the beginning there is nothing. I am nothing. Yet I am. I am infinite desire devoid of expression. I am desire longing to be. My father says, "Let there be light" and I am two. I am light and I am darkness.

I am two and I am one. I am a star. I am Osiah from the constellation Serabe meaning awareness and purity of placement. I am a star created by my father in the beginning.

Now my father says, "Let Heaven be on Earth." In the temple of my being there is a big upheaval and my right hand is separated from my left hand.

My mother says, "Come to me." She is clothed in the golden ruby light that is the Self and she sings. As she sings she becomes all manner of earthly life and her song breathes this life into itself until I am made over into her likeness.

Now I am rock. I see that I am rock limited in a hard dense world. I feel myself as one yet there is a strange discord in my being. The world changes and I am a large swimming being in the waters of Earth. I begin to feel the discord as loss, and the world is dark and full of yearning for . . . what? What is this strange yearning for? I feel a pull on my consciousness. This strange yearning is pulling something closer to my being. Oh that I could know what it is that I long for! I would surely be happy.

The world changes again and I am above the waters moving swiftly through the skies. I feel a great light on my back and I like it. I see the green land below and I make my home there. It is good. I am crawling upon the dry lands of earth with the light on my back and I nourish myself with the earth's bountiful pleasures. Still the yearning is great and the pull is stronger and the world changes more and more, and as it changes I become all manner of creatures living on the earth. I have four legs and I can run fast and catch prey for my sustenance.

Now I stand on two legs and I begin to reflect on the feelings that I have. The yearning is great now and I am beginning to know what I am missing. I walk the earth now as a human being. I know there is another place for me, an ancient place. It is a way of being that I yearn for. It is wholeness of being and the great loss is my right hand. I yearn for my right hand, that twin flame of my being. He is the Father Flame and I am the Mother Flame. Together with the spark that gave me life on Earth, my Holy Spirit, we are one, the great I Am.

Oh what bliss it is to know who I am once more! And to remember that once I was whole with my right hand one with my left hand. I send a voice to my sacred parents and I say, "Mother, Father, I am your child. I come to you now for help. Take my hand and lead me home where I can be one with you. Light the three-fold flame in my heart, the flame of Faith, Hope and Charity. I know this to be the Father, the Mother and the Holy Spirit. Only then can I truly be at home."

And my parents reply, "My child, I am proud of you. For four ascents you must walk the earth reflecting my Self. Then you shall be with me in Heaven and your brothers and sisters all over the universe shall rejoice for they shall know that they are with me in Heaven."

∞∞∞∞∞∞∞∞∞∞∞∞∞∞∞∞∞∞∞∞∞∞∞∞∞∞∞∞

The pictures of the video begin to merge into bright colours pulsing with intensity, and I rest in a deep state of trance. The video is over for now.

"Rose, Rose," I hear. "Black Elk is speaking. "You have seen how the soul came to be, how it was created. You have understood that the soul is one with Beloved Source; the soul, the I Am within your being, is one with Source. You have seen how the soul came to Earth from the stars. You understand that the soul is on a journey back to the stars, and eventually back to oneness with Source. What happens next is the story of your journey on Earth and how you became lost in the wilderness and were found again to be reunited with your starry home."

Then the colours form pictures once again and the video plays again. I find myself in a sweet smelling meadow.

Part One

RISE AND FALL

CHAPTER ONE

The Father's Dream

Atlantis

When a being comes to Earth for the first time it is the responsibility of those already here to help them integrate with their new bodily domain. The call comes very quickly. I project my thoughts into my sister's mind, "There are beings from the Pleiades in the temple, Sister. I am being called to assist them with the integration."

"As am I," my sister replies.

She and I are sitting among the long grasses that grow by the banks of the little stream in the west meadow. This is the first meadow created by the masters when we arrived here in Atlantis. Already she is a dear loving friend to us humans, providing us with a place to sit and enjoy the rays of the great lights and to listen to the bubbly voices of the stream telling of happenings in the upper meadows. Above us the winged beings fly from tree to tree and sing in the branches of tales from the skies. There are times my sister and I simply sigh with the trees as the air pushes through them causing them to bend. Lately they have taken to sudden shudders and their yellowing leaves drop to the grass below. My sister and I have just this moment been discussing this and we are wondering if the trees, like us, are missing their heavenly home, wherever that might be. I am from the constellation Serabe and my sister is from Sirius. In the temple now are many from the Pleiades and we must go to them because they will be feeling excited and nervous all at once. We, like everyone else here in Atlantis, have learned quickly that feelings can leave one unbalanced if allowed to gain control over our higher being.

I rise to my feet and notice that the grass I have been sitting upon has flattened into the earth. It looks so pitiful. "Oh beautiful green grass!" I think, and clasping my hands together in a beseeching manner. I send the words to the grass with my mind, "I have been dismissive of my training." I ought to have been more mindful of my body weight, and now I have crushed you. Please forgive me." I place one hand over the flattened grass and I focus with my mind until the grass is once again tall and cheery and waving about in the breeze. I am forgiven.

My sister smiles and offers me encouragement. "Dear one," she projects to me, "you are to be responsible for your solid form. Do not rebuke yourself but learn from this experience that which will help you to grow in oneness with the earth." She rises from her grassy seat and the tall grass that was beneath her bounces up and sways with its family, happy to have been of service.

We begin to walk towards the temple holding each other's hand. This physical touching thing feels wonderful and the priests have told us that it can do no harm to the experiment to enjoy our new sense of touch as long as we give it our full awareness and not forget who we really are. The priests and the masters remind us every morning at sunrise and every evening at sundown of the intentions of this great plan. It is of course to be totally present on earth, keeping the awareness of our heavenly origins. They will no doubt give the preliminary projection once more to these new arrivals in the temple.

My sister and I quicken our step as the call to the temple comes again. On the way we join with many others who are to assist the newcomers and I have to mindfully resist the excitement that is rising up within my body. I have not learned yet to house the intensity of such feelings without being overwhelmed by them. I know of many others, mostly from Serabe, who are finding this lesson particularly difficult. Still I am sure we can do this for had we not the ability, we would never have been selected for this elite experience in the first place. I send a projection to my sister, "Do you still think of Sirius dear sister?"

"You know I do," she replies.

"Do you ever think of the moment of separation?" I ask her.

"No! There is no gain in dwelling over that. You know the masters have lain down that we are not to yearn for our other halves as if they were left behind but to focus on the wholeness within." My sister has felt my moment of lapse and she grasps my face in her hands. She holds me gently yet firmly just as she gently but firmly projects into my mind and my heart the message that all is well, that I am whole and that I have everything that it takes to complete this awesome task.

"Thank you sister," I reply, and then I hesitate. Oh! She will surely feel my hesitation.

She does and as usual she remains calm and understanding. "Come this way," she projects into my mind. She leads me towards a grassy area where there has recently been displayed a magnificent water fountain with room on its stone circumference to sit comfortably. She sits down and pulls me down to sit alongside her, looking around in case any one has seen us leave our path and perhaps has noticed my unrest. Deciding we are alone, she pours huge amounts of compassion into my heart and commands my attention. "There is something amiss with your integration," she projects. "I feel it now and it feels raw as if it is an open wound which cannot be healed; cannot be healed that is unless you go back to the separation procedure and let it go" She looks deep into my being and for the first time ever I feel a reluctance to be here on earth. She sees it. It is reflected in her eyes, a loss, a yearning for home.

"Forgive me, Sister. I have no desire to pull you down to this level," I project into her mind.

She breathes deeply bringing her attention into her heart; into the centre of her being. Immediately I feel her attention detaching from my energy, from me. Well it is best that she does. After all, what is the gain in her losing her composure as well and the both of us being struck off the experiment?

"You cannot lower the vibration of my energy, Sister," she projects compassionately, "No-one can do that except me and I do not choose to align with any lower vibration."

I bow my head to her wisdom. "Of course, Sister," I reply. "That is the correct way. It's just . . ." Oh what am I doing now? Do I really think that I have the right to project such negativity into my sister's pure mind?

"*Speak* it . . . use your earthly voice," comes her projection.

I lift my head and take a few moments to remind my throat how to project sound. We are all taught this ability when we first arrive but there is never any need to use it except for experience and maybe now that my thoughts would be potentially dangerous for another. Sometimes I feel it would be easier for me if I were from Sirius too because those beings are so strong in their minds. I have yet to know of one of *them* to be sent off the experiment. I think like so many of the others who have gone home, that if I should fall so low as to jeopardise the plan, then I would volunteer to go home and allow another the opportunity to experience this wonderful earth.

"You know that you cannot hide your negativity from the priests. They will see it as soon as you enter the temple, for in there nothing is hidden," adds my sister with her own earthly voice. She does it so well.

"It is almost full moon anyway," I reply, also with voice, "and we shall be called to the Great Assembly in the upper meadow. Perhaps I should wait. They shall surely offer me counselling once they see my discord."

"That is true," my sister agrees, "but let us first try a little counselling of our own. Tell me what is it that ties you to the separation procedure?"

I think about her question. What is it that ties me to the separation procedure? I am not sure I know. Perhaps if I relate my memory of the procedure I will chance upon the cause of this imbalance. I begin to speak but I am distracted by a strange buzzing insect. It is akin to the bees but much smaller. There has been an increase in the appearance of these creatures of late and I have heard tales of people being 'bitten' by them. It is all very strange and interesting. I saw one of these creatures just yesterday and . . .

"Sister!" My sister's voice breaks through the silence outside my mind. It startled me to the fact that my mind itself is not in silence. Oh how difficult this task is becoming! "Sister, you are Osiah from Serabe, and you are infinitely aware of who you are. Be present here and now," my sister states affirmatively.

"I am sorry, Sister," I respond "Thank you for pointing out my folly." Her gentleness caresses my being and I feel my self becoming more centred as my mind relaxes and quietens. "Thank you, Sister." I take a deep breath and begin my story, and as I do I feel her once again detach her energy from mine. She is so mindful of the law. "I shall begin when I first knew the Father's dream," I tell her, "Let Heaven be on Earth! What an amazing plan! Already, action was being taken in Lemuria to facilitate this awesome plan. I had gone there with the entire energy of Serabe. I was simply Osiah like all females from my star origins, and my brothers from my constellation were simply Amir, and we were enjoying our freedom of movement and will. But it was so easy there. There wasn't any reason to be distracted, in any way, from who we are because there wasn't any thing there to distract us. We simply knew that we are the One, the great I AM. Oh yes! As in many other worlds there was the visual concept of many beings but never did we have to contend with this intense illusion of separateness. We knew we were one with each other just as we were one with Source, with the Sacred Parents. We knew about Earth of course. The Sacred Mother often told us stories of Earth and all her children upon it. She told us of the huge bodies of water and the green that runs over the face of Earth. Then she told us of the separation procedure. At first we couldn't understand the implications of this. How could we? We had never known anything other than wholeness."

I hesitate now to reflect on the awareness of wholeness. How good it feels! If only I could hold on to this awareness and still maintain my connection with Earth. My Sacred Parents would be so proud of me. They tell me that I must walk this path for four ascents and then I will come home to be with them in Heaven. But if I cannot experience this path whilst remaining fully present upon it then what gain would it be for I would only be bringing half an experience back to them? Of course, the priests have lain down the law in the temple, and the law states that the four ascents must be gained in full awareness otherwise the homecoming will be delayed. But I am once again allowing my mind to wander. My sister is waiting patiently for my story to resume.

"So when the Father's dream was spoken our Sacred Parents called us into total communion with Source," I continue. "We were told of the separation procedure, and then it was happening. It was most strange that experience as I recall. Did you not think your separation procedure was strange? For the first time I could feel my self to be in a somewhat solid form. Of course, it wasn't as solid a form as we are now, but it was altogether new to me and I liked it . . . at first."

"At first?" my sister asks.

"Yes, I believe so," I reply. "I liked it at first but there was a strange sensation that came with it and it is not until this very moment that I know what that is."

"What is it?" she asks.

"It is as if I did not fully agree to this experiment; as if a tiny little piece of my consciousness was reluctant to leave Lemuria."

"You are mistaken," she suggests. "How could you agree to the experiment and feel that way? It is not possible in the higher temple. What you describe is a malady of *this* world. Do you not see how some of the poor unfortunate souls who have fallen are questioning their will like that?" I contemplate her words. She's right of course . . . and I do not want to be one of them.

"Oh, Sister!" I exclaim. "Please lead me to the temple where I shall plead for counselling. I do declare I am not ready to go home just yet. I believe I can do this and all I ask is for healing."

"It is yours," she says. "First though, you must finish your story."

I stand up and calm my being, bringing my awareness into the inner centre. Soon I am ready to resume my story. "I felt as if I was lying down," I tell her, describing how I had felt during the separation procedure, "And what I was lying on felt to be what we know now to be rock. You know that hard grey substance that we sometimes find when we dig into the earth; the gardeners speak of it often?"

She nods. "I have seen it in the nurseries," she says. "It must be the most solid form I have seen yet."

"I was lying on rock, and as I looked with these new sensory eyes, I saw myself lying on another piece of rock. This is the strangest part yet; on that other piece of rock was what appeared to be a masculine form of me whilst I was a feminine form. I was split into two forms. Is this what you experienced?" I ask.

"I shall not say for I have fully detached from the procedure," she replies.

"Of course you have, and I have not. Perhaps that is why I am not such a successful participant. Your mind is so strong."

"Your mind is the Father's mind also," she reminds me, "therefore it is perfect. It is your heart energy that you have an imbalance with."

"That is so for it is there that I feel the imbalance. When I lay in two forms on that rock the Mother took form and she was tremendous. What beauty! The earth does not display Her beauty absolutely. How could it? By taking on such dense form one loses ones essential emanation, does one not?" I suggest.

"It is still there but I agree, it is not so easily perceived," is the reply.

I nod indicating that I find that to be the way it is, and I continue, "She was so beautiful, *is* so beautiful" I say remembering how the mother looked to me. "She wore a gown that displayed in living form all things of nature. Her light shone from my twin forms and it was as red as the blood that runs in our bodies. I felt I was one again; I was one with her and with my feminine and my masculine self. And then in one incredible moment which I cannot describe only to say that it haunts me still, I was separated into two once again. The separation deepened as my masculine self vanished from my senses and I felt my self lowering into a world between there and here."

"Dear Sister! How difficult that sounds!" My sister is beginning to understand now where my unusual feelings emanate from. "I believe that was not *my* experience," she tells me. "I have never heard of such a world. That moment you spoke of, that you cannot describe, I have spoken with counsellors who describe that feeling as trauma. It is when the soul wills a certain precipitation or manifestation but the new lower will resists. What manifests is something that lies between the Father's holy will and the lower will."

My sister's compassion comes flooding into my being and I am grateful for such a blessing. I remember the first time I saw her. She was standing alone in the temple, following her constellation's preliminary ceremony, and I recognized in her the colour of the mother's light, that deep bright red. I know I emanate the golden ray of the father, and so I thought our union to be beneficial to the experiment. I was correct because we balance each other so well. That is until I began to have problems with my integration. Now it seems that her superior intellect has forced me down into my heart where I can heal this trauma energy of the separation procedure. I do not know why she is not a healer in the temple for she has the mind and heart of any great healer, yet her duty is to be of service to the newcomers, integrating them with the ways of the earth and with their senses.

"Sister," I say, "Thank you for being such a good teacher for me. You have my love, you know that."

"I feel it," she replies smiling. "It is pure, as is your mind energy. They will be your salvation and will ensure that you complete the experiment successfully."

I thank her and add, "I will continue with my story and then we shall proceed to the temple for we shall be missed presently if we do not hasten. Now, in this new world was all that you see here but not just as beautiful. I think I was still in Lemuria, yet I perceived otherwise. It was as if all was created by reluctance . . . or resistance as you so aptly put it. I was already feeling this loss of my other half and I beseeched the Sacred Parents for understanding. The Parents sent a messenger, a golden being of light, to me. And The Parents spoke through the messenger saying, 'My child, I am proud of you. For four ascents you must walk the earth reflecting my Self. Then you shall be with me in Heaven. And your brothers and sisters all over the universe shall rejoice for they shall know that they are with me in Heaven.' Then the messenger gave to me a shining gem. It was multi-faceted and emanated a red light with streaks of gold. The messenger said, 'Take this stone. It is the power of the Sacred Parents. You shall carry it with you throughout your journey. When you have completed your task, when you are ready to come home, the Red Stone of Power will sing and a prophecy will be released. Hold it in your heart centre until then.'

"What about my right arm? I asked the messenger.

And the messenger replied, "Everything you need is within the Red Stone of Power. As long as you remain in the centre where the stone is held, then you shall know wholeness. This world you see around you has been created by you. You are destined to walk between worlds from now until the Red Stone sings and the prophecy is released.'

"With those words, the messenger left and I found myself once more lying on a bed of rock. This time however, I lowered and lowered until I found that I *was* rock. I experienced myself as this hard dense form yet at the same time I was aware of my true essence. I felt trapped, yet the more I focused on my lightness, the lighter I became in form. I experienced myself in the waters as certain kinds of mammal and fish and then on the land as small crawling creatures and then as four legged fast moving creatures. I have an explicit memory of being one of these grazing creatures who so generously provide us with their produce. And all the time I yearned for this loss that I now know to be my right arm. And then I called upon my Sacred Parents once more, and again the message came that I was to remain on earth for four ascents. Now it all seems as if it were only one moment of eternity in which I dreamed that I was all those creatures. And now I am here in Atlantis, participating in the experiment I volunteered for."

"And what about the Red Stone of Power?" asks my sister. "Where is it now?"

"It is here," I reply, holding one palm to my heart centre. I feel the stone throb beneath my palm and its throbbing becomes a message in my mind: *All is well!*

"All is well," my sister echoes the stone. She touches my face and the stone leaps in my heart in response to her wisdom.

"All is well," I repeat. All is very well indeed as my sister and I teleport to the temple where our duties as Atlanteans await us. We are Atlanteans, compassionate, mindful, loving beings from across the universe, gathered here as a community, living the dream of the Father, to be Heaven on Earth.

∞∞∞∞∞∞∞∞∞∞∞∞∞∞∞∞∞∞∞∞∞∞∞∞∞∞∞∞

"Hasten, Sisters," our brother projects into our minds as we enter the side door of the temple. "The preliminary projection is almost done." We are very fond of this particular brother. He is from Serabe as well and we know him to be Amir of course, just as I am known as Osiah. However, there is no need to label our identities here on Atlantis for we are all one as Atlanteans. I am feeling centred and balanced now. How great a healer my sister would make! Our brother leads us to a seat to the right of the door, and we sit, quietly asking for forgiveness for our tardiness. The high priestess turns her head and glances at me. In that one glance I know we are forgiven and I know that she knows that it was because of my indulgence that we are tardy. I tune into the projection she is giving to the congregation.

"The four ascents you will experience as follows," comes the high priestess' projection into our minds. "The first shall be into the fifth centre of power which you will find located in the throat area. Your guides will point out this area to you but it will be your responsibility to ensure that you attend all the classes regarding this area. You will learn to use speech as a way to communicate. You may of course communicate as normal, but it is simply an exercise in which to experience the full form of your bodies and their senses. There are five earthly or physical senses. These are sight, hearing, touch, taste and smell. These you will learn in your lessons also. Now, as I have said, the first ascent is into your throat centre. The second ascent is into your brow centre. This area is located above the throat, here." She points a finger to a spot between her eyes. "You will discover that this area houses your original sight but of course it is the physical sight that we wish to experience. The third ascent is into your higher temple or what will be known as the crown. Once again it shall be pointed out to you and you will learn all about these areas in your classes. When you have fully integrated your physical experience with these three centres, then you will make the fourth ascent easily. The fourth ascent is into the power centre above your head. You will find that it houses the energy of the Monad. We call it the Monad but essentially it is your star origins. That may seem a little difficult to understand since you know that you still *are* that being in whole, but believe me the physical dimension has distractions everywhere that pull your consciousness down to a level where it is actually possible to *forget* who you are. Many of you will experience episodes of forgetfulness. It may begin with the fading of your natural abilities, but please do not worry; there are priests and healers as well as counsellors available here at the temple should you experience any of these maladies. The council, the masters, and I, as well as the other priests and priestesses here in the main temple, thank you profoundly for your participation in this experiment. As you proceed you will discover that you have made a very great decision. Many times in the past this experiment has failed, but now we are certain that everyone here has the ability to succeed where our predecessors did not. If at any time you feel that it is for the greater good, then we have the facility to send you back. Your experiences here will of course be wiped from your consciousness."

As the preliminary projection comes to a close I look around at the beings from the Pleiades. What beautiful souls these newcomers are! The high priestess finishes her projection. It normally causes a little ripple of imbalance amongst her audience, and yet every one of these beings here remains centred harmoniously with the others as one perfect entity. And what an entity they are! My sister and I are truly blessed to be given the opportunity to assist with

Eliza White Buffalo with Nicholas Black Elk

their integration. On Serabe, the ray of truth was focused upon, so here on Atlantis it is the power that Osiah and Amir emanate. I think about the words my sister spoke to me: *Your mind is The Father's Mind, it is your heart energy you have an imbalance with.* I must focus now using the power I have been given by the Father to raise my heart energy to that of the Mother. These Pleiadeans have obviously come on the ray of divine love so their focus is the Mother Energy. I feel them to be the Mother in all her beauty and serenity. If I balance myself with them just as I do with my sister, then I should succeed.

Suddenly, a projection comes from my sister, "Sister, these souls are pure love. I feel so drawn to them. We shall harmonize well, don't you think?"

"You harmonize well with all," I reply, "I would that I was as well balanced as you."

"You are, Sister, you are," she smiles.

Our brother is still standing by the side door and I think he may have been tuning into our conversation because he projects right into the middle of it. "Sister, did you not manifest from Sirius?" he asks. "Is not the focus there the ray of service? I feel it appropriate for you to serve us all by introducing your newcomer to our little group."

"How naughty of you!" my sister retorts with laughter.

I laugh at her laughter and our brother laughs too as he walks over to us. "Oh!" he exclaims using his voice when he is close enough for us to hear it. "I shall never tire of laughter. Is it not the greatest gift our parents have given us here on Earth?"

"It is indeed, Brother," I reply, also using my voice, "but let us not over indulge ourselves because we are attracting quite an interest." It is true. Many of the newcomers seem bewildered as they have never experienced sound like this. I have no doubt, when they begin to learn to use their physical sound they also will welcome laughter as a great gift.

"Hush now," our sister projects, "we are to be assigned to our charges."

We each centre our attention in our hearts once more and are led to our newcomers. I see a wonderful emanation of the love ray before me, a brother. He sends a powerful projection of love to me and I feel myself lifting into the higher temple. I note that I must train myself to stay grounded otherwise I cannot fully experience Earth.

The Pleiadean receives my thoughts. "We have been instructed to master the art of grounding before we arrived in the temple," he projects into my mind. "Allow me to help you as it is something that I discovered I do well."

"Thank you, I shall accept your help," I project back to him.

The Four Ascents

"We are committed also to serve Earth and all upon her. You have my infinite service, Sister," he continues.

"And you have mine. Let us proceed to the classrooms where you will learn much about how to exist on this planet," I suggest to him.

I teleport to the classrooms instead of walking because my charge will not have used his new legs much and I desire that he is at ease with his new abilities. It would not do to overwhelm him at this early stage. He follows me immediately and I begin the procedure of introducing him to the concept of placing his body in a structured gathering. "The lessons shall be given thus," I project.

As the day proceeds he grasps the new concepts very easily and I am somewhat amazed at the serenity he attains whilst doing so. It is evident that the beings of Pleiades are highly functional. I wonder how it came to be that we Atlanteans have lowered our function so much.

"We have been told that the manifesting of one's energy automatically pulls the consciousness down so that one can appear cloudy," the Pleiadean projects to me. "I see that you have become quite cloudy in areas, especially in the heart energy. We have been informed of the concept of emotions and what they can do to us. You are experiencing these emotions, are you not?" he asks.

I answer his question with admiration, "You are correct my brother. Truly, I have been affected by emotion from the moment of separation. Detachment from my emotions is the law I desire to master fully, and if I cannot, then I shall return home but I do so desire to succeed in this experiment."

"You will." He smiles which surprises me since he has been here less than one day and already he is expressing pleasure in a physical motion. "I am learning from you as we interact," he explains with his voice.

I am amazed. "But I have not taught you how to use your voice. You are amazing indeed!" I exclaim.

And to my utter astonishment he actually laughs out loud. Many of the other Atlanteans notice, and at once he is crowded by sisters and brothers, all eager to congratulate and encourage him on his success. I have never met such an amazing being before on Atlantis. As I ponder this I rise into the higher temple where I have a vision of him making a vow of service to me. In return, I pledge to join with him in body as well as in spirit. And I see before us many more beings that will come to Earth as a result of our union. With the vision over, I return to my centre and smile as the last of the congratulators leave him to his integration lessons.

"We shall beseech the council when I have completed my lessons and we shall ask that we are joined in service to Earth," he projects warmly into my mind. He has obviously seen my vision. What a being!

"I agree," I reply warmly. The Red Stone of Power leaps in my heart.

∞∞∞∞∞∞∞∞∞∞∞∞∞∞∞∞∞∞∞∞∞∞∞∞∞∞∞∞∞

"Brother, Brother!" I project to Amir when I take my charge's leave this evening. My brother is off somewhere having fun. I shall have to project more mindfully, "Brother! May I speak with you? Where are the others? May we gather in the west meadow?"

"Greetings, Sister!" I receive, "I am picking strawberries at the moment. They taste wonderful. Is it not the most wonderful taste the parents have blessed us with?" Dear Amir, his enthusiasm is wonderful.

"Dearest Amir, how I love you!" I project to him in return. "Your enjoyment of this experience is equalled to none and I love you so because of it."

"As I love you, my dear Osiah. I shall be in the west meadow when you arrive and I shall have with me a basket of these wonderful berries. Be with you soon."

"With you soon," I reply.

I call to the others as I walk slowly to the meadow. I desire to walk instead of teleport because I am teaching myself to stay firmly grounded and I find that it helps to walk barefooted on the green grass. The others are all there when I arrive and I see one of the newcomers with them too, a sister. *The others* is a phrase I use when I mean the little group of seven souls who all seem to balance each other well. There is my sister from Sirius and beside her a brother from Sirius also. My two brothers from Serabe are there. With me they make up three from our planet. And along with them there are our two brothers who had been selected from the old experiment. They are two of the many souls who did not fall into the lower will and they have been selected to help us as priests in the present experiment. I had no awareness of there having been previous experiments on Atlantis before I arrived here, so it was all the more honouring to know that I and my brothers and sisters had been selected to make it work this time.

Amir walks to greet me, holding the berries in his hand. "Thank Heaven you have arrived, Sister," he projects into all minds here, "I was almost tempted to eat your share."

"Thank you, Brother," I reply taking the berries and handing him back half of their quantity. Amir need not inquire as to my actions. He knows that I never receive anything without giving a share back to the universe. I had handed him back seven berries which is precisely the amount needed so that each of my company can receive one more each. I didn't count them.

Amir doles them out and is thanked profusely by all. "I suppose you shall take the remainder to your abode and share them there?" he asks me. He knows my ways so well for we have make an agreement to assist each other's progression, and so we study each other's intentions carefully.

"That is my intention, yes," I tell him. "I know these particular berries are abundant in the gardens but I find that the act of sharing their nourishment honours them all the more. They are such a lowly creation, they deserve to be exalted. Any way, it is the nature of the Mother, is it not?"

"It is," my other brother Amir projects as he joins us. "Osiah" he says, "there will come a time when *you* shall be exalted and you will teach many souls of this nature of sharing."

This brother Amir is a prophet and a visionary. He works in the temple as a healer. He also works between the high priestess and the masters. His contribution to the experiment is to hold the channel open for the masters to receive their instruction. I don't understand what he meant by saying I would be a teacher. When each soul arrives on Atlantis it is given its duties for the duration of the experiment. I am to assist souls with their integration, help them to implement the earthly concepts; the council has never communicated to me the duty of teaching or indeed that I shall be exalted.

"Do not be disturbed sister," Amir The Prophet tells me. "I see many more earthly domains for you and it is there that you shall be exalted."

"And the teaching?" I ask.

"You carry the prophecy in your heart centre, dear one. When you are ready you will know what to do," he tells me.

Heaven! The Red Stone of Power is leaping once again within my heart centre. Thrice today it has reminded me of its presence.

My brother continues, "Also at that time, you shall be identified in a word. I shall sound that word now so that you may fully manifest your true self." In my heart the stone is leaping still. It is speaking of truth. I bow to my brother to acknowledge this truth.

"Blessings, Brother" I project.

He bows and then stands upright as he sounds clearly, "Ee . . . li . . . zaa!"

"And so it is," I proclaim.

As I walk with my two brothers, Amir towards the little group of kindred souls I notice that the prophet holds his head low and walks meekly, a little behind me. The others smile and project their love to me as I approach. I send my love to them all and to the newcomer. Her person may be a stranger to me but I know her soul to be of Beloved Source. It still amazes me every time I meet with a newcomer and I realise how much I have diluted with Earth. If it were not for them and for the priests and priestesses of course, I perhaps might lose myself entirely. Should that be the case, then I may as well be that rock and serve my sacred parents thus as more deserving souls walk upon my being.

"You are my brother's guide I see," projects the newcomer to me. She refers to my charge. "He tells me he is to make an earthly union with you."

"It is so!" I reply.

Amir The Prophet opens his arms wide and projects to all, "Please friends, let us project openly to all for the sake of our new sister here. Sister of the Pleiades, you are most welcome to our little group of kindred souls. We have chosen each other carefully for one very special reason. If you study our energy fields you will see why." The seven of us stand in a line for the Pleidean to look. She finds this very amusing and I laugh at our earthly behaviour.

"Forgive our silliness," I project, "we are so adapted to our earthly eyes. At times we forget that the pure ones have no need for us to *show* our bodies."

"I see that you have much music in your soul. Your brothers here also have the same tune as you," the Pleiadean projects in response to my explanation, "only they express their song through the crown and the brow. You express through the throat."

"You have learned these new concepts quickly, Sister, well done," comes in Amir The Prophet, "what else do you see from the rest of our group?"

"You, Sister," the Pleiadean projects, acknowledging my dear sister from Sirius "you express your self through the heart, and your brother here, he expresses through the solar plexus." My Sirius sister and her star brother bow to her in respect.

I laugh again. "And tell us, Sister," I ask her, "what of our beloved two here; pray, tell us what you see from them."

She smiles at the two from the old project and projects, "I know of these two from my home planet. Greetings, Brothers." They bow to their kin. "Allow me to give news of home," she says to them. "There is much celebration there for your success. You are truly great and I only pray that you shall grace me with your wisdom so that I too will do great things." Then she turns and gazes at me. "Sister," she projects, "in your two friends here you will find the grounding ability that you aspire to, for they both are fully grounded on earth in the first two power centres."

Everyone smiles at me; they are aware of my doubt in my ability to succeed. I smile at my folly and this begins a ripple of laughter, firstly from my new Pleiadean sister, then spreading to the others; and when I think it appropriate to cease laughing, my brothers Amir burst into loud guffaws, causing us to laugh all the more. I do not think that I have ever experienced or heard such prolonged laughter. It feels wonderful to be so rapt in this beautiful sound. It takes one right down into the body and holds one there until one fights for breath, and the most wonderful thing about it is that it does not cloud one's consciousness as it grounds; rather, it lifts one up whilst firmly grounded in the body. Surely this is something I should do more often for I have never experienced such a bodily joy.

"Oh Dear Sister!" I speak with my voice forgetting my manners, "how shall I thank you for such a wonderful lesson in grounding? I declare, I shall never feel ungrounded again. Not now that I have such a powerful tool to avail of."

Then, pertaining to the energy of this earthly moment, my new sister uses her voice for the first time on Earth and she says, "Thank *you*, Sister, for teaching me to use my earthly throat centre." Wow! We seven gasp in amazement at how quickly she has learned to speak. It is no wonder to us now how our two sisters from the old experiment had succeeded where others failed. Pleiades must be an extremely functional constellation.

"Let us make a circle," Amir The Prophet speaks loudly to everyone.

We hold each other's hands, forming a circle around our new sister, and we sing our welcome to her as we dance around her. Singing is so much closer to our nature than speaking and we intend to create a circle of pure love around her that will show our appreciation of her gracious presence. The energy is building and soon we see the circle enfolding her in love. In response to this gift she reflects it back to the seven, lifting us and aligning us in one. After an eternal moment of bliss we lower our consciousness once more to the earth and we drop our hands to our sides. All remain silent for a few minutes until a tiny little hummingbird comes into the circle and hovers there. It seems to applaud and affirm the wonder of our union.

"What beautiful colours the little bird displayed!" I exclaim. The bird is gone now, flying off to some other deserving being some where on Atlantis.

With it will go the message that we so knowingly hold in our hearts which is that all is one in the glory of the Sacred Parents.

"Beautiful," echoes the Amir The Prophet, "just as *we* are even more beautiful in our union than we are in separation." He pauses while we agree silently to this truth and then he proclaims to us all, "Friends, we chose each other because we desired to form an intimate network of support for each other. We have discovered that by unifying our beings we form a perfect expression of the divine attributes of Beloved Source. And just as we individually reflect Source in our wholeness, so we now discover that as a sevenfold expression of Source we are even more powerful. It is in this way that we will succeed upon the earth, and in doing so we shall attain the Father's dream, to be Heaven on Earth."

He finishes his projection and hush prevails for a while. Then in unison, we show our appreciation of his wisdom with applause. I watch as our new sister copies our motion of bringing our hands together in this way. What blessings we have received today! Oh, wonderful, beautiful Mother Earth. How blessed we are to be your children!

The applause lessens and our new sister speaks. "Friends" she says, "You have honoured me greatly. We beings from Pleiades have seen many worlds. For infinity we have worked with various life forms throughout the universe. When we received the call from Earth we were more than happy to assist in this project. Truly, of all the planets we have helped evolve this is the most beautiful expression of the Mother. It is an awesome task indeed to be an earthly being and to so willingly agree to all the limitations it can involve. Yet we have had the honour of *seeing* Earth's future and I am happy to say that Heaven will in all its glory, *be* on Earth." She pauses while we all applaud again, and then she continues, "And so, we have been sent here to be physically among you so that we can assist you in whatever way you shall need us to." She looks around with her earthly eyes at us seven and at the beauty of our surroundings. "This is a beautiful planet. Here on this green meadow with its lush grasses and running water, I have been honoured such that I shall hold dear in all ways this place, this circle of love, and especially the union that is you seven. I vow here and now, that I shall remain close to this union until you accomplish your task."

∞∞∞∞∞∞∞∞∞∞∞∞∞∞∞∞∞∞∞∞∞∞∞∞∞∞

And so the pictures fade and merge into beautiful colours once again. The video is done for now. And Black Elk speaks . . .

"Rose, you have seen how the soul has come to Earth. Beloved Source, Creator has spoken and sent forth the word: Let Heaven be on Earth. And the word became flesh. The word became flesh and the word sounds throughout the universe, and the sound is Eliza, one who climbs the heights of Heaven reflecting the mind of Beloved Source. And so the soul begins her journey back to Source. She groups with other souls, other children of Beloved Source, and together they work to bring the truth of Heaven onto Earth. This togetherness reflects the oneness of all souls in their Father, Beloved Source. You have witnessed the unrest that the soul feels when she remembers the oneness with Source but feels separated from Source too. In this next part of the story watch and understand how that illusion of separation becomes more powerful than the memory of oneness."

CHAPTER TWO

The difficult path

The video plays on and the story continues . . .

The group is complete. As we each go our separate ways this evening, we each in our own hearts and minds will hold dear the beauty and blessings that our gathering has brought to us. I think of our new sister and I send a wave of gratitude to the Sacred Parents for such wonderful grace. Her brother, my charge, comes into my mind as I walk along the outer path of the community. I feel somewhat neglectful of him, yet at the same time I am in awe of his and his kin's amazing mind energy and their beautiful hearts. I am not in the least bit surprised when in response to my thinking of him, he teleports directly in my path. "Blessings, Sister!" he projects to me.

"Blessings, Brother!" I lower my head to him. He puts his hand beneath my chin and lifts my face to look at his.

"If we are to be joined in earthly union then I deem it inappropriate for you to place your honour beneath mine," he says. "Pray, do not bow to me for I am your servant until we return to our Beloved Source."

We walk together along the outer path until we come to the upper meadow where a circle of standing stones has been placed there by the masters. "This is where we gather every time the moon is full and when she renews herself," I tell my charge as I walk to the centre of the circle where a glowing white pedestal is humming lowly. "The Focus Stone is removed from the temple by The Crystal Keeper and placed here on this pedestal. See how it still vibrates from its contact with the Stone?"

"I do," he replies, "And does the Focus Stone activate all these other stones also?"

"One hears them hum but they never glow like the pedestal here. I believe this is composed of much lighter particles, plus it comes in direct contact with the Focus Stone which is composed entirely of clear quartz crystal. The masters use it in the temple to communicate with the Master Crystal in the Higher Council. I believe there is at least one Focus Stone on each island of Atlantis, but there are twelve in total plus the Master Crystal. It is where the masters get our direction and instruction from before they pass it to the priesthood, who in turn passes it to the people."

"And why is the Focus Stone placed here during gatherings?" he asks me.

"Well, it focuses the lights of the stars in its centre, and then reflects them out around the circle. Each group from each constellation is positioned around the circle so that they receive the emanations from their own constellation."

"And so they re-aligned with the constellation's vibration?" he asks.

"Exactly!" I reply.

He walks to the north end of the stone circle. He is tuning into the energy there.

"This is where the beings of the Pleiades position themselves," he states with certainty.

"That is so."

"And Serabe? Where do they position themselves?

"Right here where I stand now," I answer him with a smile, "We face north."

He walks to me and I take his hands in mine. Feeling the sensation of my fingers caressing his, he smiles back at me. "What is the procedure on Earth for a physical union?" he asks, his eyes twinkling with light. They have attracted my senses, and just as the beauty of the meadow flowers so lovingly remind me of oneness, so now this man's eyes penetrate my being, filling me up with love and the sense of wholeness I have missed since the separation procedure. *Be careful* my heart is whispering to me, but I ignore it.

"Firstly, we go before the High Inquisitor tomorrow and we ask for his blessing on our betrothal," I respond softly, my head bowed. "After that we engage in our physical union through the lower chakras. We humans have access to what is named as sexual energy. Essentially, it is pure life force stored in the lower body. During the earthly act of lovemaking it is released and provides a slipway for a soul to come to Earth through the earthly body of the female."

My charge looks at me as one who is keen to learn as much as possible about the successful physical union. Naturally, it is how any one of us would feel. In Lemuria, did I not express my desire to experience this kind of union? I desire, like so many to be a physical channel for others to come to Earth. However, having witnessed so many other unions result in temptations and perils for both parties, I am now aware that it is quite possibly the biggest task of them all, and that without constant vigilance it could result in major limitations to the soul. However, as I now gaze lovingly into the eyes of my charge I see only purity and strength. We *shall* be successful. I feel it in my heart, and with my voice I ask "Is this what you desire?" My heart skips a beat when he replies softly that it is.

Just now, The Crystal Keeper teleports to the circle and appears beside the pedestal. She and I are well known to each other. We have even discussed the potential of forming a group of seven. She is already one of seven, as I am, but we feel that a common group will be beneficial to both of us. "Blessings!" she bows slightly to us and we return the gesture.

"Blessings, Sister!" we project in unison.

She turns to our new brother. "You arrived today, Brother, did you not?" she projects.

"That is so," he replies, "and I find it most beautiful."

"Indeed. I am to prepare the circle for the ceremony tomorrow. There is to be a special ceremony to mark Earth's orbital journey around the sun. We have noticed that as she begins to lean away from the Great Light, Nature appears to wither and die. During the colder times she appears to sleep. Nothing grows as she sleeps but when Earth once again turns to face the Great Light she wakes up and appears to come alive and blossom once again."

"And so the circle of life and death continues," I add, bowing to The Crystal Keeper. She goes about her duty and we say farewell and walk back to the outer path.

"Pray, explain to me what death is," my betrothed asks me.

"Death is an illusion of the human perception," I tell him. "It is when a being appears to be gone, to be no more, to have died. Although the spirit still perceives that being, it is only in pure form and not in material form. Many humans have died in this way, and although they are still in pure form their loved ones feel the absence of their physical forms so deeply that they create a malady of the heart. Many have had to receive healing from the temple because of this malady."

"But surely, their loved ones would have agreed with them that they were ready to return home. Why the imbalance?" he asks.

"One of the limitations of incarnation is the concept of attachment. The lower mind can become attached to the physical presence of another. When that physical presence is no longer there, the attachment creates strong emotion which in turn creates an imbalance."

My betrothed is somewhat bewildered at the concept of attachment. In due course he will come to witness this in others, if he can maintain his clarity enough not to fall into the illusion himself. "Those poor creatures" he says with compassion streaming from his being, "When we make our union we shall focus on reality. In that way we shall best be able to assist them in regaining clarity."

The Red Stone of Power leaps in my heart. It signifies that my betrothed has spoken in honour and that our union shall be clear and true. But immediately, a strange thought appears in my mind. *It shall not be so, for already you have become attached to him,* says a lower will within me. Its words pierce my heart and my mind powerfully and I feel something creep its way into my being. It is dark and ugly and it catches my breath and quickens my heart beat. It smells of decaying matter like the leaves that lie beneath the trees, drained of all sustenance. It attempts to grip me completely in its power but I shall not succumb to it. I know it is an illusion of this world and no illusion is a match for my light. So, I straighten my back and focus on the threefold flame in my heart, the twin Mother/Father flame burning brightly with the spark of Beloved Source, and in a moment I regain my composure. Centred in the secure knowledge of the *Self,* I project to my brother that all is well.

"Thank you for teaching me of this limitation," he says. I bow to him and again I wonder if he can remain detached from any dark limitations that may threaten our union. We begin our walk back towards the community. As we walk, neither of us notices the sudden appearance of many biting bee-like creatures swarming around the stone circle.

∞∞∞∞∞∞∞∞∞∞∞∞∞∞∞∞∞∞∞∞∞∞∞

The sun has not yet risen, but I have. I tossed and turned about on my cot all night long. I wonder did I sleep at all. My mind was so busy, thinking of my betrothed and our proposal to the High Inquisitor. In the food hall I fix myself a goblet of warm cow's milk and honey. I carry it to my cot where I settle back in the warm covers. I thought a lot about my betrothed, during the night. I thought a lot about The Crystal Keeper also. I imagine it must have been the wonderful experience with the others that got me thinking about the proposed group with the Crystal Keeper. Last night the stars were especially beautiful, more beautiful than I have seen them yet from Earth. I found myself gazing at the Pleiades more and more, wondering what it is like there from whence came my betrothed and the amazing being who gave of herself so lovingly, vowing to serve our group until we are ready to return to Beloved Source. And as I gazed at the Pleiades my heart filled with the great

Eliza White Buffalo with Nicholas Black Elk

compassionate emanations coming from there, my brow centre glowed, and I heard the Father's word: *There will come two beings who, along with your betrothed and three others that are presently incarnate on earth, will make up the six souls that are destined to join with you as a sevenfold expression of Source. The Crystal Keeper is one of those incarnate. Both your groups will work to ground the light of Heaven on Earth, and just as the others have been blessed with a guardian spirit from Pleiades, so will a spirit be assigned to guard the second group. You will know him by his sound and his sound shall be Artamor.*

I was utterly amazed. I am amazed yet, at the gentle way the Father unfolds His will upon us. Such wisdom and such beauty! I shall enjoy relaying the Father's word to my betrothed and to The Crystal Keeper. Two more beautiful souls from the Pleiades, and a guardian spirit as well. What joy awaits us!

The morning unfolds with the gentle rhythm it began. Before long I find myself standing side by side with my betrothed before the High Inquisitor in the Inquisition Chamber. It is the High Inquisitor's duty to inquire from the High Council if our union is for the greater good of the Atlantis Project. Having confirmed that it is, he proceeds to prepare us for the task we have chosen.

"As representative of the High Council," he states, "it is my duty to inform you of the task that you have chosen and to remind you of your devotion to the sacred path that is the four ascents." And addressing me, he projects, "You have had ample time on Earth to experience the temptations of the flesh and of the lower mind. The illusion of power and attachment to power can be extremely dangerous to the project. Any limitation can cause the soul to be stuck in the lower body indefinitely, and it would take much healing and enlightenment for that soul to rise up into the light again. This has been the downfall of Atlantis from the very first project. However, we are aware this time of these limitations and so we shall succeed with careful implementation of The Law."

"The Law? You mean the higher will?" I ask him, no longer understanding what is meant by the law.

"Yes," he replies. "The High Council has received instruction from the twelve arch beings of Beloved Source. The Holy Will has spoken and instructed the arch beings to preside over the earth project, focusing through the twelve rays, certain commandments. These commandments are the Holy Will of Beloved Source, known as The Law."

The High Inquisitor does not reply but looks at me with compassion. I turn to my betrothed for the answer . . . nothing! Why don't they answer me? I turn my thoughts inwards and attempt to answer myself. The Red Stone of Power will surely answer my question. But the stone is silent. I listen for a whisper; wait for a tiny leap that tells me what I wish to know . . . nothing. What is worse is the creeping feeling from last night reminding me once more of its desire to take me into its gripping power.

"Pleiadeans have implemented The Law within many civilisations," my betrothed projects to me seeing my discomfort. "It is the cloudiness of your heart centre that prevents you from accessing the knowledge that was conveyed to you in Lemuria."

Oh goodness! My heart is beginning to beat very fast and my head feels strange. I find it difficult to bring my awareness to the experience of Lemuria. Oh heavens! What nature of energy is this that I cannot lift my awareness any higher than the quickness of my heart beat and the dryness of my throat?

The smell of decay fills my senses as the lower voice I heard in the stone circle speaks again of my failure. *You have forgotten the will of the Father,"* it taunts, *"The Law is lost to you forever. How can you survive now that you are no longer one with Him?*

"Who *are* you?" I utter. My voice sounds low and weak. There is a pitch to it that I have never heard before. It grates through my throat centre causing it to close in on itself. I attempt to project to my company for help but I cannot do even that. I will have to speak again, allowing that awful pitch to be felt rubbing and grinding away at my being. I open my mouth and manage a low grating sound, "Brothers, help me! It is attacking my being." All around me this alien creature is creeping. Its dark heavy energy is clouding my sight now. Just as the High Inquisitor and my betrothed both reach out to me, their words are lost in the darkness and I feel myself to be falling in circles. Down and down I spiral until I come to rest on a soft surface.

∞∞∞∞∞∞∞∞∞∞∞∞∞∞∞∞∞∞∞∞∞∞∞∞∞∞

I feel somewhat more settled, though all around me are strange images. The alien energy must have created these images because I know I haven't created them. They pop in and out of my vision. Some are of the sisters and brothers in my life but they are mostly images of my betrothed. He is smiling with those beautiful eyes, and as I smile back the space around me brightens and I can see where I am. I am in the lower meadow, my favourite meadow where the trees and the long grass and the merry little stream all dance in the beauty of Mother Earth. Only now they are not dancing. They seem detached from me. I look to the sky to see the birds swooping overhead. They sing and although I know their song sings to my heart, I do not hear their lyrics. It's as if I have forgotten how to listen.

"I have fallen" I whisper sadly to the birds. "But where am I?" I ask the trees. I flop down upon the long grass and plead to the stream. "My body is here," I tell it. "This awful alien energy that has taken me over is here, but where am I? I'm not here. All that is left is this shadow of my holy self."

The stream trickles and bubbles over the smooth stones that lie upon its bed but I do not hear its voice. I am somewhere else. I am lost, lost forever in the lower limits of my being. I hang my head and I am not surprised to feel water run from my eyes, down my face and fall to become one with the stream. I hear a buzzing noise. *The bees!* I think hopefully. *They will know where I am.* But when I look I see only the strange biting creatures swarming in and out of a tree trunk. The sight of them sends a chill up my spine and causes my heart to thump wildly.

I imagine I hear the lower will deride me. *Ha! They have lured you into my trap,* it seems to say. It sounds fearfully like my own voice.

Suddenly I hear another voice, "Eliza!" it says brightly. Who was that? I heard a voice, did I not? Perhaps it was the bubbling of the stream. "Eliza!" There! I heard it again. It was not the stream.

Standing up I look around for someone, anyone who may have spoken to me and perhaps can help me find my way to my holy self. But there is no-one here but me. Perhaps hearing a voice that is not there is a malady of the limited world.

"Eliza!" says the voice a third time, "Turn around."

I turn around to see a road stretching out far beyond where I stand. I see no end to this road. I turn back, and behind me the same road stretches far beyond in the opposite direction. I begin to walk along the road towards where I think the voice came from. Soon I see a light in the far distance. It shines so brightly and hope fills my thoughts. If I can reach that light I will surely be whole again. I walk and walk for what seems to be hours. Hours turn into days and still I do not reach the light, yet it shines on just as brightly as it always does. The hope in my thoughts begins to wither and before long it turns into despair. Why can I not reach the light? What is wrong with me that the light remains aloof? Having lost all hope I stop walking, and I sit down upon the long road. Where did I go wrong? There is no answer.

Then the memory of my betrothed's words comes into my thoughts: *It is the cloudiness of your heart centre that prevents you from accessing the knowledge conveyed to you in Lemuria.*

"That's it!" I proclaim out loud, "The cloudiness of my heart centre." My heart beats fast again and I feel the now familiar creeping energy attempt to overpower me, to tell me that I am lost. But I know; oh how I know! I am not lost at all. It is the cloudiness of my heart centre that prevents me from accessing my true self. I *am* here. I just have to find myself. I stand up and lift my voice to the sky, "Father, Mother! I am here. I am your daughter. Hear my voice. Oh Dearest Parents! Never again shall I allow myself to feel lost. I understand now about illusion. Show me the way, Beloved Source. Dispel this illusion from my heart, and show me the way back to wholeness."

Immediately the mysterious voice speaks again and I recognise it this time as the voice of Beloved Source. It is the voice of my Sacred Parents. "Eliza! Turn around my child," They say.

I look around me, and there is the road stretching far ahead with the light glowing brightly in the distance. I turn again and the same road stretches far ahead in the direction I have come from. I turn again, but this time I only make a quarter turn and to my surprise, I see a second road stretching far ahead. I see that it crosses over the first road where I stand, and it stretches far beyond in the opposite direction. I look to the north of this road and to my immense joy I see that there in the distance is shining another light. It is red and gold and is coming closer to me as I open my arms to welcome it. The closer it comes to me the brighter the world becomes. Soon all the world is red and gold and my heart floats in heavenly bliss as I find myself back in Lemuria. The golden messenger of light that spoke to me then stands before me once more holding the Red Stone of Power. He is projecting The Law to me.

"What about my right arm?" I hear myself ask again.

"Everything you need is within the Red Stone of Power," the messenger repeats. "As long as you remain in the centre where the Red Stone of Power is held, then you shall know wholeness. This world you see around you has been created *by* you. You are destined to walk between worlds from now until the Red Stone sings."

Oh how I thought I would never forget those words! But for a short while, I had. Here I am in a world I have created through the cloudiness of my heart. It is a world of illusion, of limitation and yearning of the heart. Where once joy flowed freely from the Source, this lower will, this alien energy creeps its way throughout until I no longer even know that I am present.

The messenger stands before me yet with the Red Stone in his hands. "You are in the centre, Eliza," he says, "where the two roads meet."

"Is this the heart?" I ask hoping that the cloudiness had gone.

"Yes, the heart," the messenger confirms. "The road you have walked for days is a road of difficulties. It is the earthly road, strewn with limitations and shadows. As long as you walk only this road the light you see will always be elusive to you because it is merely an illusion of salvation that promises wholeness. But it will never be. Only here in the centre where the two roads meet, can you hope to know your wholeness which is pure spirit in an earthly body. It is the balance of both roads."

The messenger leans toward me and places the Red Stone of Power in my heart space. I feel its familiar joyful leap and I smile. As I do so the messenger steps aside revealing that there, stretching far ahead of me is the second road. Some way along the road I see a star. "It is the monad, the star origin," the messenger tells me. Further along the road, beyond the star, there is a light so beautiful and captivating that I wish to go there immediately. "Beloved Source," the messenger says smiling. "Eliza, you have a choice. You can walk this good road and return to your original essence that is of Beloved Source, or you can choose to walk both roads. Remember, it is only by doing so that you fulfil the Father's dream of Heaven on Earth."

Oh sweet wholeness! What bliss it would be to feel this once more! "The Father has spoken," I say to the messenger, "Let Heaven be on Earth."

"It is so!" the messenger replies. "Now the vision is done!"

∞∞∞∞∞∞∞∞∞∞∞∞∞∞∞∞∞∞∞∞∞∞∞∞∞∞∞∞

Amir The Prophet drops his arms to his sides. Immediately a dome of blue light that he had been holding over my being fades and goes. A loud hum that had been sounding within the light goes too. I realise that I had been surrounded by a healing dome. In the silence I feel the vision; it is warm within my heart, its wisdom and knowledge fast becoming part of my conscious awareness.

"You have been in trance for over three days, Sister," Amir projects into my mind. "According to the High Council, only the highest visionary can

The Four Ascents

sustain trance level for that length of time. Yet the priests have not declared your role to be so. Pray, why is that?"

"I resisted it until now, Brother," I reply realising now my true contract with Earth. "I admit that in the separation procedure I was reluctant to fully incarnate, hence the imbalance of the heart. And so I struggled with my integration. Then the imbalance took over. It was like . . . . like . . ." I am finding it very difficult to define the alien energy I had experienced, "It was like nothing that is good," I tell Amir. "Can you conceptualize an energy that is not good?" He looks at me with compassion in his eyes. Of course he cannot conceptualize an energy that is not good.

"Dear Sister, *all* is good," he says reassuringly. "All that seems to be otherwise is but an illusion of the lower mind. It does not exist."

"Yes! Yes, that is it," I reply with enthusiasm. "What I experienced was an illusion, yet it can seem so real. It seemed to creep throughout my being, poisoning and dispelling all awareness of myself until I actually believed myself to be lost."

"That is the illusion I speak of," he says compassionately. "Many on Atlantis have fallen in this way. It is difficult to perceive at first. But then the Self begins to cloud over with what feels to be an alien presence. Of course, there is no presence other than the One, so it is evident that this alien energy is created by the lower mind. In other words, it is illusion. The lower mind creates this illusionary presence to such a degree that the person begins to identify with it. They wander about in the wilderness constantly searching for the Self, for a part of them that they feel is lost. So many have fallen to this limited existence that the High Council now recognises this illusion as a real limitation of the earthly life. They have named it fear. Fear, my dear Osiah, is what you felt overpowered by."

"Fear?" I repeat. "It is such a small word for something that can seem so powerful. It seems laughable now. I cannot, at this moment, imagine what it even felt like. It is alien to all that I know I am."

Amir just smiles. "Because you are love," he says. "Love is all that is; and now you have experienced the illusion of not being who you are, you have experienced the absence of love. You have experienced the illusion of fear."

I fall silent for a few moments. I am trying to remember what it felt like to be in the illusion of fear. I cannot. I am love and love is all there is. Amir puts his hands on my shoulders and a stream of pure life-force strengthens the flow in my being. He smiles and adds, "Though here you are. You stand before me fully present. Well done, Sister, you are to be congratulated. It is

29

Eliza White Buffalo with Nicholas Black Elk

an awesome task to walk the path of limitation and return to tell of your experiences."

The path of limitation . . . Amir's words remind me of the road of difficulties from my vision; there was the road of difficulties and the good road that cross over in the centre. It is the good road that leads to healing, to wholeness. Oh! The Red Stone of Power is leaping with joy within my heart space.

Speak Eliza it is saying. I open my throat, and from the wisdom and knowledge of the vision I speak the truth of my heart, of the power that lies within.

"The road of limitation is a difficult road" I proclaim. "But we must walk that road if we are to be fully present on Earth. It is by walking that road that we learn of our adversity, of that which we are not which is the illusion of fear. It is by knowing our adversity that we conquer it. Thus, by walking the difficult road, we gain great power; it is the power of knowledge. But do not be mislaid, for we must also walk another road, a road that crosses over the difficult road; it is a good road that leads to awareness of the Self. You have said, Dear Brother, that whilst in the illusion of fear the being constantly searches for the Self. I can tell you now, that unless that being comes to the centre where the two roads meet, he cannot know the Self. He will wander the lower world, always following some illusion of the light, but he will never reach it. Not until he goes within, to the heart within, to the centre. Only then will he know the Self, and by this enlightenment he can be whole upon the earth."

I stop speaking and Amir and I look at each other for a moment. I see the light of understanding in his eyes. I spoke the truth. "My Dear Osiah, it is so!" he affirms.

"Call me Eliza, Dear Brother. I am to walk the two roads over four ascents. And so it is that across the universe I am known as Eliza, one who climbs the heights of Heaven, reflecting the mind of Beloved Source."

∞∞∞∞∞∞∞∞∞∞∞∞∞∞∞∞∞∞∞∞∞∞∞∞∞∞∞

There the video stops. And Black Elk speaks . . .

"My Dear Rose, the heights of Heaven ascend like a staircase. With the heart of the Mother and in communion with the Father, Eliza must climb reflecting the truth of Beloved Source. So shall the word grow revealing The

Father's desire . . . Let Heaven be on Earth. Rose, in the last part of the story you witnessed how the soul has fallen from a state of Divine Grace. You understand that the separation she believes in so much is but an illusion. She must wake up and know that she is *one* with Source. You witnessed how she rose from her fall to begin her ascent again. She was sent a mate for her soul, another soul who will remain with her as she journeys on Earth. He will not forsake her, and even though at times the illusion will cast a shadow over truth, he will reflect this to her and her to him so that together they will come into the light, and together they will return to Source. This is how it shall be for all souls that group together in oneness. That oneness shall carry them all home to oneness with Beloved Source. In this next part of the story you shall see how the soul is incarnate in a different life, a different personality called Phoenix. She is still the same soul, though her spirit is individual. Remember the droplet from the lake of Source? Each droplet is a soul and the soul splits into individual spirits in order to learn on Earth. This new spirit is of the original soul. She is still Eliza in the wholeness of her being."

CHAPTER THREE

The holy path

The video plays on, and so the story continues . . .

I find myself in Ancient Egypt

I look out from the chamber window. The sun is still hidden below the horizon and the oasis is bathed in a half light. The only sound is the low rhythmic breathing of my beloved as he slumbers on our bed of soft down. It is the one luxury we allow ourselves. Ever since the high priestess, Elmara called us to the temple we have sworn ourselves to a life of humble service. I am her personal handmaiden and I look after her every priestly need. I am to be at her side whenever she needs me. Still I have lots of time to be alone since she spends so much of the day in meditation. The rest of the time I am mindful of her needs as she carries out her priestly duties. I sit close by and listen to her words of wisdom as she teaches her young students in the ways of the priesthood, their eager faces lit up with the light of Elmara's holy emanation. Perhaps if I serve her well she will deem me fit to be inaugurated as a priestess. I desire to serve her well for in doing so I serve my Sacred Parents in Heaven. Each morning I stand before their heavenly glory on Earth and under the rays of their great earthly light rising in the sky I send a voice heavenwards and I pray, "Father, Mother, You say I must walk the earth in four ascents. I asked for you to show me the way. Elmara can teach me the four ascents in the temple. Oh Father Heaven! Mother Earth! If this is the way for me then only say it is so and Elmara will announce my inauguration."

This morning the great light has not yet shown its glory and I turn to view my beloved; my dear Seth, he is so wise and so knowledgeable. His grandfather was one of the last priests on Atlantis, and Seth has carried forth his spiritual power and knowledge, as did his father before him. Seth chose to lead a simple life many years before he met me. As a teenage boy he told his parents that he was going to go out into the world alone and speak to the masses of sleeping souls of their godly origin. He would take with him only the robes he wore and the sandals on his feet, and he would speak the words his father and grandfather had spoken to him. For as long as he could remember they had spoken to him of who he is and the kingdom that awaits him. And then he met me, and his dream of teaching the world alone became a dream of service to it through another, through me. Oh how he believes in me! How he believes in my ability to transcend the realms of my being!

I study his beautiful face now as he lies in dreams. They must be good because his mouth is turned up at the corners in a smile. I wonder what he is dreaming of. Perhaps he dreams of the lands far away where so many human beings dwell in their sleepy state of awareness, far from the Land of the Gods. I know it has long been his desire to serve those unfortunate beings and to teach them the way of the Sacred Parents; yet he seems content to remain as servant of the High Priest, never asking for more than has been laid down for him. I on the other hand would give anything to ascend this life and know once more the joy of our heavenly home. Or perhaps he dreams of our union as lovers. Perhaps he relives the moment when our eyes met and we each craved the other's presence in our lives. He murmurs and turns over in his sleep and I no longer see his beautiful countenance. It is softer now, bronzed and lined with age. When we first met it was chiselled and strong. His smooth skin stretched over his powerful features, flawless and glowing with youth and determination. Amber eyes flickered and glowed with the spark of life as they looked down into my own, also amber but with less ferocity. He said that when he first looked deep into my eyes he saw my soul and it was beautiful.

"You reflect the infinite love of the Sacred Parents," he had said then. "I see in your eyes the kingdom of Heaven." And when he had said this he bowed low at my feet and proclaimed, "From this moment on I am your faithful servant. I vow to protect you, even if I must carry your load on my back. I shall be a plinth on which you shall stand tall so that the world may see the glory of the Sacred Parents and know the Kingdom of Heaven."

"Why is it my love that so many are clothed in forgetfulness?" I had asked him. "Why don't the Sacred Parents call to them and rouse them from their sleepy ignorance?"

He had taken me lovingly in his arms and from his deep well of knowledge he spoke as one who had long waited to speak his truth. "Phoenix, my heart, the Sacred Parents *are* calling to them," he had told me then. "When you speak the purity of your sound is the Sacred Parents calling. When you sing the world listens in awe to the glorious chorus of heavenly voices singing, 'children, turn to the light and you shall find me there with open arms waiting to welcome you home,'"

I had listened to his words with bewilderment. How can it be that he embellishes me so with such godly attributes when my Sacred Parents themselves have said that I am not fit to enter their kingdom just yet? I had lowered my head to speak my next words so that he might not see the unrest written in my eyes, but as I spoke I could feel his admiration smiling down upon me, tainted only with an air of amusement.

"I pray in the mornings when the Great Light shows his face over the horizon," I said. "I pray to the Sacred Parents and I ask that I may come home. The answer is always the same. I must walk the earth in four ascents before I find my heavenly home. In the temple Elmara teaches of the four ascents of the inauguration. I listen as she is teaching her young students and I understand that what she teaches is what the Sacred Parents speak of. If only I could be inaugurated into the priesthood then I shall be able to gather the world in my arms and take it with me as I go home to my Parents."

That was what I said and it's what I truly believed but Seth had not entirely agreed with me. He looked at me, wide eyed with amusement and curiosity. "Your childlike faith is commendable," he had said, "but why would you think that you will do this where Elmara and the other priests and priestesses have not?"

And I answered, "My Sacred Parents have told me. They have said that when I come to be with them in Heaven my brothers and sisters all over the universe shall know that they are with their Sacred Parents in Heaven."

He had kissed the crown of my head then and held me tighter than before, and the words he said to me resonated within my soul so powerfully that I knew he spoke the truth. "Phoenix," he said, "it is not your way. The four ascents that the Parents speak of are four lifetimes on the earth. Each lifetime you will rise up one step of the ladder closer to Heaven. Each step shall be the equivalent of one ascent of the priesthood. The priesthood is honourable and it is a great service to the Sacred Parents and to humankind but it will not change your path. When you have reached the fourth ascent you will understand what the Parents mean when they say that your brothers and sisters will know that they are with their Sacred Parents in Heaven."

"I have been on the earth I feel a long time as life other than what you now see before you," I told him. "I feel the pull to my heavenly home yet I know now that it is my Parents' plan for me to realise the Kingdom of Heaven here on Earth. Here is where I must be, and if my Parents say it will be another three lifetimes then so be it."

"But beware, Phoenix, because if you fall along the way, you will begin the four ascents again. How long you are on the earth is decided by your ability to stay clear and focused on your purpose."

I had rested my head on Seth's strong chest and I was thankful that he had vowed to serve me on my journey. The road ahead seemed long and arduous. I had overheard Elmara teaching that the student must be mindful of many temptations that lie along the four ascents. To surrender to any one of these temptations would mean a fall from grace and the climb then would seem insurmountable. I remember sighing, long and deep.

"Fear not my heart," Seth had whispered lovingly into my ear. "The way ahead is set down for you and it is my place to warn you of any danger. I shall not fail you."

Dear Seth. That had been so many years ago when we both were young and passionate and we dreamed of rousing the unfortunates with our reflections of heavenly glory; but passion fades with age and the years take with them our dreams. Now the only dream I have left is to be a priestess and even that seems so very much unreachable. I suppose it feels like a wild hope I have held on to for much too long. And poor Seth, he gave up his plans to go out to the other lands and speak of his knowledge so that he could be by my side. He believes in me, that I am destined to lead the earthly nations in the way of the light. But I am impetuous and I think that I can live it all now when I barely know what it is to be human. If Seth is correct and he will live aside me for the next three lifetimes then I shall have ample time to embrace my humanness and accomplish the dream while I climb each ascent of the ladder to my heavenly home.

∞∞∞∞∞∞∞∞∞∞∞∞∞∞∞∞∞∞∞∞∞∞∞∞

This morning I walk up the white steps to the temple in a dream like manner. The world is much more liveable in this state of awareness. There are times I can dream myself off to invisible worlds where there are the most amazing colours, and the gold that is there is not contained in hard cold statues like these new idols of the gods, but is fluid and permeable and lifts one up into a heavenly state. When I am there, rapt in that golden energy, I feel the love and wisdom of the Heavenly Father. The ecstasy that fills my being could never be compared with the lesser ecstasy of my lovemaking with Seth. And when I walk by the banks of the great river, and let my hands brush against the hanging acacia and papyrus grasses releasing their powerful aroma, I let my mind wander to the depths of Earth where it is cool and refreshing. Then I feel the compassion of Mother Earth gently caressing my cares away. I ought to be more self controlled but like a child breaking away from her mother's hand I run and twirl and lift my face to the great light. I am so full of joy I wish to shout it forth and let the great river carry it throughout the land for all to hear. Elmara has found me often in this rapturous state of joy and has often advised me to control it.

"Phoenix," she has said often, "if you are to aspire to the priesthood then you ought to learn to contain your emotions. Quietism and piety are the qualities of the priestly soul."

As I near the temple now I am mindful of being still but oh! How can I contain my joy when this very moment a flock of wild geese are flapping into the sky calling to me of freedom? I smile slightly and lower my head reverently so that none can see my indulgence.

"Good morning, Phoenix" says Rahtu as I pass him in the colonnade. Rahtu is one of Elmara's young students. He is a bright boy with a mass of black curly hair and piercing brown eyes. His parents work on the river bank as merchants but he does not wish to go into the family business and instead has a strong pull towards the priesthood. He had to pass many tests before he was eligible for the student life but pass them all he did and now he is on the forth ascent of his inauguration. I like Rahtu, yet I am a little cautious of him for he often is dismissive of an acceptable level of familiarity between a young boy such as he is and a woman of my advanced years. In my experience the youth of today are all too much led by their masculine desires and the increasing power of the god, Osiris, God of the Underworld.

"Good morning Rahtu," I say keeping my head lowered for fear that he would see my thoughts. I may have reservations about him but not once has he said or done anything to add credence to them. Indeed, his family are honourable people and I have shared pleasantries with his mother when meeting her in the marketplace. She is quite a lady and would not be out of place amongst the ladies of the palace. Rahtu is an exemplary son who has been taught the proper decorum between men and women. How proud his mother was when we talked of his inauguration!

I put Rhatu's familiarity down to my friendly interaction with his mother and I pause for a while to silence my thoughts before entering the outer temple. Elmara has requested that I meet her this morning in her quarters for she has something to discuss with me regarding a matter within the temple.

I hope I am to assist her with the daily communions with the great sun god, Ra. Elmara knows of my undying love for the Heavenly Father's great light, and perhaps she has deemed me worthy of being in the presence of the holy shrine of Ra. She has never required an assistant before for this duty but since the passing of one of our elder priestesses her duties have increased in number and press heavily on her respite.

As I stand before the doors of the temple I find myself grinning with joy so I chide myself for my obvious lack of self control. "Phoenix, be quiet!" I silently tell myself. Oh where is the piety of my youth? Where is the heavenly quietude that Seth witnessed within me? Can it be that in my advancing years I have descended from my path rather than risen upon it? I have failed myself and more importantly I have failed dear Seth. His life has been futile with me.

My hand rests upon the door opener. It is a little golden sculpture of Khepri. I caress the sculpture willing Khepri's strength and dedication to the great light to enter through my hand and into my heart and mind. Khepri is represented as a dung beetle for he rolls the great light along the sky tirelessly just as a beetle rolls the dung. Just then the door pushes back against my hand and I am startled out of my reverie. I jump back and stumble on the stone pavings. As my head hits the floor I yell out for Seth but it is Rahtu's worried face that I see now before me; his voice I hear calling my name, and it is his hands I feel holding my head as I drift out of consciousness into a strange land far away from the temple . . .

. . . The wind is cold and slaps at my skin with dampness such as one gets following bathing. It has a strange smell as if it is laden with salt and it assaults my nostrils with its coarse acidity. I wrap my shoulder clothing about me for warmth as I gaze out across a great river. It is so wide that I cannot see its far-off banks and its waters come crashing into this bank with fierce strength. I look to the sky for the solace of the great light but even *he* lies behind an endless cloak of grey. I gasp as I look around me at land that is rugged and rocky and I fear I am so far from home I will never see Seth again. The earth is green everywhere and it rises in mounds, some of which, although far-off, seem to rise to the heights of the great pyramids.

How did I get here? Have I been carried off in my sleep? Perhaps the gods are displeased with my lack of piety and have chosen another path for me. I drop to my knees and cannot prevent the tears from stinging my eyes. "Seth! Seth!" I shout, "I am here. I am here." But no-one is coming. My voice is lost in the wind. Panic rises up in me but I realise that there is only one thing for me to do; I must quieten myself and pray to the Sacred Parents for help and understanding. "Father, I am your child," I pray now. "Hear my voice. I find myself in a strange land far away from my beloved. Help me please. Give me your understanding so that I may know why I am here. Give me your help so that I may find my way home again. My life, my heart belongs to you. I have nothing left to give to you for your help, but I trust that through your holy love for me you will grant me what I ask."

As I finish my prayer, the vast greyness in the sky opens up a little and the Sun shows his powerful face. I have been heard. I lift my countenance to the light and drink in the warm compassion offered while I listen so still with my heart as the answer is given. *My child,* speaks the beautiful sound of the Heavenly One, *I am proud of you. Your heart you have given to me and your life in devotion to my holy path. One approaches who will challenge your will. If he fails to take you then you shall achieve the third ascent."*

A great roar sounds from the heavens and water falls from the sky amidst the rays of the sun. Despite my desolate situation I smile and receive the offerings of the Heavens. Then, kneeling upon the ground I place the palm of my hand on the grassy earth and pray, "Mother, thank you for your bountiful care. My Father has said that one is approaching who will challenge me. Should I succeed I shall achieve the third ascent. My Father has granted me the grace and strength to succeed. I ask you to grant me the physical strength I need to endure this land and this test."

And the answer arises in my heart, "*You shall have what you ask.*"

I rise now from my kneeling position and pull my shoulder clothing around me tighter. It is so cold here I must find warmth and sustenance. A short distance in front of me I discover a sandy path. As my feet follow the earth's guidance the sand feels good beneath them, and although my body shivers with this unaccustomed climate, my feet are warm and happy for they feel they are walking on sacred ground. I have only walked a short distance and already the earth is rising into one of the smaller mounds. It reminds me of climbing the steps to the temple and I find my self anticipating something wonderful at the top. Like a child I give in to my pleasure again. I feel my Sacred Parents so close to me and yet my indulgence is not reproved. My playfulness heightens as I run the final climb to the peak of the mound.

I can hear my Parent's voice in the wind encouraging me. "*Play, Phoenix, play,* they tell me. *I have placed you upon the earth to play my child. It is your signature song. Never rebuke my joy for it is my gift to you and the music by which you shall sing your way home."*

Oh joy of joys! How free it feels to be given permission to follow my heart. I lift my arms to the sky in praise. "Father, Mother," I cry out, "You are everything there is; all the gods are nothing before you. You have made all things in Heaven and Earth. How great you are! And now you bestow on me this gift of freedom. It fills me with such a force that can only be likened with your goodness. Surely it shall carry me through the task ahead. Ask anything of me oh Great One and it is yours. I bow before you, your humble servant."

And as I lower my gaze from the skies, with eyes closed I give myself over to the Holy Oneness. In this spiritual quietude I see the land around me. But instead of the rugged cold terrain I experience a myriad of colours that wisp and merge to form rocks of knowledge and mounds of wisdom. Blues and pinks dance about me and touch my skin pulling my senses into the dance with them until I no longer feel I am separate from this world at all but that I am interlaced with all there is. The air is warm and pleasing and as I touch each wonderful formation I merge with its being. I am rock; I am grass; I am a mighty mound of earth as old and wise as the great sage in the sky. There is a myriad of purples forming before me and I reach out my hand to experience them. In my palm tiny little purple energies are coming together to form small round balls. A sweet smell reaches my nostrils and I breathe it in deeply.

And now I open my eyes. The rugged landscape has returned and in my hand I am holding a sprig of purple berries. They smell so good. Realising that I am hungry, I place one berry tentatively into my mouth. It tastes wonderful: sweet and satisfying. I consume every last one sending my gratitude to Mother Earth. Oh how good I feel now when such a short time ago I was frightened of this place!

Suddenly a strong gust of icy wet wind blows around me and I feel a chill pass along my spine. The challenger must be coming because I hear people close by. Their voices are carried by the wind which warns me of their approach. And now, here they come, three, no five people. Oh, how strange they look! Their clothing is thick and more suitable for this climate than my light temple robes. As they approach I see that they have spotted me and they halt to discuss my presence. There is one man that I can make out. His hair is long and covers his chin. I have seen men like this before among the traders who pass along the great river but I have never seen hair that colour. It has a reddish glow to it that reminds me of firelight. The others appear to be women. Their heads are covered with shawls and they are much smaller in stature to the fiery haired man. He carries a staff. I think perhaps he is a holy man because only the High Priests and the Pharaoh are worthy enough to carry such a staff.

Oh, where are you Seth? I think, as the man approaches me with a proud masculine stride. He is indeed a great man. *Where are you my love?* I think again. How was I dropped here so far from my protector?

I raise my hand to my throat as the giant man reaches the peak of the mound. My mouth is dry and my heart beats wildly, yet I still can feel the force of my Father's power and the warm strengthening sustenance of the berries in my belly, and I know without a shred of fault that I am a match for this awesome being.

"Good day, My Lady," he says coming to a stop not a chariot's length away. "May I have the honour of knowing your name and where you hail from?"

He smiles widely with his mouth and although his manners are gentle his eyes portray to me an inner fire. I cannot speak. Already he has won the first part of the challenge. He has captured my senses in his eyes. Those eyes are familiar somehow. I have seen that look before.

"Oh, holy land of our fathers . . . It is Rahtu! Those eyes belong to Rahtu," I tell myself.

The memory of Rahtu's hands on my head comes into my mind and I feel myself once more losing a grip on my consciousness. The world blackens and I feel like I am falling down into a deep dark chasm. I feel I am in the underworld. All around there are fires, huge blazing terrifying fires. On the red hot rocky ground numberless cobras hiss and spit their fatal venom at unseen victims. I breathe deeply but the hot thick air attacks my nose and throat and chokes the life from my lungs. I fear for my life but I must be strong. I must focus on the power given to me. I straighten my back and lift my head and with the power of The Sacred Parents I stand resilient to my surroundings. At once I am lifted from that dire pit of evil. I find myself once more on the mound with this man somewhat lessened before me. No longer does he instil awe in me. He seems to have lessened even in stature. The power within me is ablaze now, burning with the same ferocity of the fires of the chasm, and from within me the compassion and wisdom of my Parents looks now upon this pitiful creature.

He speaks again. "If you do not inform me of your place then I shall assume you are here without just cause," he tells me, "and I warn you, this is my land and all on it belong to me." I understand his words. I know he desires my female body and I know he would take it with or without my consent.

"I shall not go with you," I announce.

"Do you know who I am?" he demands to know but I don't answer him. "I am Duncan, son of Deismut, the greatest man of Scotland ever to stake these shores of Erin with his mighty sword and staff."

I listen to him calmly and then reply, "I know who you are and again I say I shall not go with you."

This man who would have my body, who would have my mind, he shall not succeed. He shall not devastate my body and soul. He shall not be responsible for my descent into the lower world. I have seen his world now and it has shown to me the fruits of error. It is a world of instant gratification of the lower body and of thick suffocating desires that will serve no purpose but to pull one further and further from Heaven.

He takes a strong hold on my arm prepared to pull me along where he wishes to go but my stillness startles him and he lets go looking deep into my eyes. I see a small boy now, lost and lonely and afraid of the world around him. My heart glows with compassion for his plight. I feel my inner power silently telling him to let go, let go of all your fears and worries. Give them to me and I shall lift you up from the den of tortured souls to a place of light and inner peace. "I shall not go with you," I repeat calmly. This pitiful creature, this once great man lowers his gaze and walks meekly away from me. I have passed the challenge. As I watch my challenger disappear from view, the rugged landscape once again merges into a myriad of colours. I close my eyes and breathe in their harmony. Suddenly I am home . . .

. . . "My thanks brother-in-law," I hear Seth's voice say. "She is coming back to us. You are a great healer indeed and I shall see to it that you are paid handsomely for your kindness."

"I do not require payment for my devotion to my sister's well being," replies my brother Ames' voice. "It is enough that she comes out of this unharmed. Let us pray that it is so."

I hear them talking back and forth and I am pleased that their concern is only for my well being; my lovely Seth and my dear brother, Ames. I keep my eyes shut so that I may savour this moment. Thank heavens I am away from that cold land and that pitiful creature that challenged me with such might. I pray that he finds peace. I wonder what Seth and Ames would say if I tell them where I have been and of the amazing way in which my soul sang to the Sacred Parents. I fear they will say that I have been dreaming, so I hug the memory to myself and choose to remain silent.

Eliza White Buffalo with Nicholas Black Elk

"Phoenix?" It is Ames that is speaking.

"Phoenix? Phoenix, My Love?" comes Seth's voice.

They're calling me. I should relieve them of their burden. "Seth! Ames! I utter smiling at each in turn.

"Oh thank heavens, My Love!" exclaims Seth clasping my hand to his lips, "I feared you were gone from me."

"Never," I assure him.

"Ames has healed you with his herbs and magic potions," he says, and he turns to Ames. "I shall be forever grateful to him."

Ames seems pensive. He gazes at me with that inner knowing that only he can profess to. Many of the priests of the temple display the gift to a lesser degree but Ames has had this gift since he and I were children and none has ever displayed it with the same power and with such humility of spirit as he does. "You were gone a long time, Phoenix, and I saw you there," he tells me. "Then I knew when you were returning; you came in a spiral of colour."

"Oh Ames!" I gasp. "I dream not. But I was in a land far away. It is a cold land where the river stretches far beyond any natural banks. Great mounds of land reach as high as the pyramids into a grey sky."

"I know," he replies, "I saw that land and the giant man who helped you."

Helped me? Surely he is mistaken, but Ames is rarely mistaken. "How can he have helped me Ames?" I ask him. "He attempted to pull me into the underworld with him but I overcame his awesome might." My head is paining me and I feel tired. I really ought to sleep now but I cannot rest until I know how it could be that that both fearsome *and* pitiful creature had helped me in some way.

But Ames only adds to the confusion. "There is something that I should have told you a long time ago, but I never did," he tells me. "I confess I am guilty of neglecting my duties. Forgive me, Sister, and I shall make things right as soon as you are rested. For now though, you must sleep." Ames seems truly troubled by this neglect whatever it is. I am so tired, but how am I to rest with so must intrigue? But I must. Lack of self-control is not my only folly. In honesty, I must add impatience to that, but oh! I am so full of questions.

"Ames, you cannot go from here without an explanation," I insist. "What must you tell me? How did that man help me?"

"Hush now, My Love," whispers Seth stroking my head, "please don't upset yourself. Rest now and you can talk with Ames later. That is my word."

"But Seth . . ."

The Four Ascents

"Your husband is right, Phoenix," Ames agrees. "Best do as he says and we will talk later."

∞∞∞∞∞∞∞∞∞∞∞∞∞∞∞∞∞∞∞∞∞∞∞∞∞

I open my eyes. Ames' healing has been successful and I feel refreshed and energetic. The rays of the sun are beaming into my chambers so strongly that I decide it must still be midday. Sitting up in bed I realise that someone is sitting on the window seat. I have to squint to see who it is that now rises from their sitting position and is coming towards me. It is Elmara; her youthful slender body glides across the room and in her dulcet voice she greets me. "Ah, you are awake at last," she says. "I did think you were attempting to sleep for the whole of Egypt." She smiles warmly, and at once I am blessed with her godly emanation.

"Elmara! How wonderful that you bless me with your company! But where are Seth and Ames? They were here before I closed my eyes. I can't have been sleeping long for it is still midday."

She laughs and strokes my greying hair. "It is midday indeed" she says. "You are correct my dear old friend. However, it is midday on the second day of your sleep. I thought you would never wake up and I was so looking forward to our meeting."

"What? You mean I have been asleep for a full day?" I ask, astonished. She laughs again and rises to go to the door of my chambers. I watch as she opens the door and speaks to a young maiden before turning to come back to my bed.

"I have ordered some food for you, dear friend," she says. "You must allow *me* to tend to *you* for a change."

"Elmara!" I exclaim, "I cannot do such a thing. Please, give me a moment and I will be up and ready to serve you as is my duty." But she wags one finger and insists that I stay in bed. I feel quite foolish but there are times when one simply does not argue with Elmara. So we settle to discussing the events of yesterday. I think of Rahtu. "My goodness!" I exclaim. "Rahtu must know that I am well. It was he who came to my immediate assistance." As I speak I feel a strange knowing within that Rahtu has helped me more than I profess to remember.

"Rahtu is aware of your well-being," says Elmara with a giggle. "Of that we can be sure because the young maiden who should by now have brought your food has no doubt related the good news to him." I must look confused

43

for she adds, "I believe he and she are in a romantic entanglement. It is quite amusing actually and I confess to being more interested than I ought to be. Rahtu, as you know, has been walking out with young Edina for quite some weeks now. She is the daughter of the fish monger on the south side of the market. Do you know who I speak of?" I nod, eager to hear of Rahtu's romance. Elmara laughs again. "Well, the little maiden here," she continues, indicating the maiden that had waited outside the door, "I think her name is Ahmose. She is very taken with Rahtu although she is four years his junior; and I believe Rahtu has professed an interest in her too. Ha ha ha ! I hear the two girls have had strong words for each other and have ordered Rahtu to choose between them, would you believe."

"Ha ha ! Only Rahtu could have gotten into that predicament," I laugh. "I must say, he does love female company."

"Ha ha ha!" laughs Elmara. "To the dismay of his poor father indeed, for he would have him choose a wife and settle into the family business."

"Yes," I agree, still laughing, "But I have spoken with his mother and she is so proud that he has been called to the priesthood. I do not think though, that he neglects his path in any way. It obviously comes first, before any beautiful maiden."

"I agree, I agree." Elmara breathes deeply whilst searching my face. Then she grins at me as if she has wonderful news to give. I cannot stand the suspense.

"What?" I insist.

"Speaking of the priesthood," she begins. "Our planned meeting yesterday was secretive, I confess. But I wanted to surprise you for I know how long you've desired this day." She pauses to ponder her next words.

"For Heaven's sake, tell me" I push her excitedly.

"I shall be honoured to announce your inauguration, if indeed it is what you truly desire," she says to my amazement.

"Oh joy of joys!" I exclaim. "Do you mean it? Do you really mean it? I am to be inaugurated?"

She is highly amused at my question. "Ha ha, ha ha!" she laughs. "My dear old friend, how long have you patiently waited for this day? And now you question your just reward?"

I am delighted, so very happy, but Elmara's words trouble my delight and cause me to doubt that I am worthy. "You say, Elmara, that it is my *reward* to be inaugurated? I ask. "How unfortunate then that you feel like that, for

I would prefer that the priesthood was my calling and not my reward. You speak as if I am a child who is to be indulged for good behaviour."

"Phoenix, listen," she replies. "Yes, your patience is to be rewarded. Indeed, it is a virtue of the godly, but that is not the reason for my decision. If you feel that the priesthood is the path for you then that is the only reason necessary. Do you feel it is your path?"

She looks at me with concern. Perhaps she is wondering now if she is mistaken in her decision. After all I have questioned my path since Seth said all that time ago that the priesthood was not my way. The four ascents I must live upon the earth are to be four lifetimes, not four ascents of the priesthood; but is not the priesthood an honourable path to lead? Is it not the best way I can serve my Sacred Parents in Heaven? And what about my vision? In that the Sacred Parents have said that I *am* on the holy path.

Elmara has noticed my hesitation and her eyes portray what her mouth cannot say. "If you have the calling you would know the answer to that question," she states quietly. My dream at last . . . but something has changed since my vision and I must be true to that.

"Alas, Elmara, now that this wonderful day has come, I find myself questioning if it is indeed the best way for me to serve my Sacred Parents. The Sacred Parents know I am devout and that I desire to serve. It's just . . . . well, I believe they want me to follow a different path."

Elmara listens to me and closes her eyes to contemplate my words. She may not agree with me but I must be true to my heart, and my heart tells me that I question the place of the gods when it comes to the heavens for I can only worship one true god and that is my Heavenly Father and Mother. As one, they are my god and the home of my soul.

"There are many ways to serve the Heavenly Parents," says Elmara, "but you are what you are, my dear friend, and I would have you no other way. You must follow your heart, but if you change your mind I shall be in my quarters. Now, let me hunt down that young maiden with your food. I fear she has fed it to Rahtu as a bribe to choose *her*."

"Ha ha!" I laugh but what a strange feeling I have! It is as if I am freed from invisible ties that had bound me to the temple and to the gods for all eternity. It is a good sensation. I feel the power of the Father in my being and the love of the Mother nurturing and encouraging me. I know I have chosen correctly.

"I shall return." waves Elmara as she leaves.

Eliza White Buffalo with Nicholas Black Elk

∞∞∞∞∞∞∞∞∞∞∞∞∞∞∞∞∞∞∞∞∞∞∞∞∞

I tell Ames of my decision regarding the inauguration. He is not as surprised as I thought he would be. Perhaps he knows me better than I know myself. He has come to see me about what he said yesterday, about how he has something to tell me, something he ought to have told me before now. Seth had been dining with us both in our chambers but he discreetly left me alone with my brother. I must admit, I feel quite excited and I can hardly wait to hear what Ames has to say.

We begin by saying some prayers together. We beseech the Sacred Parents to grant us clarity and openness of mind as we discuss this important matter. By the time Ames is ready to begin talking I feel uplifted once again, just as I was today with Elmara and just as I was in the far-off land. My Parents are good to me, of that I have no misgivings; they grant me what I need to keep looking forwards on their holy path.

At last, Ames is beginning. "Phoenix, my sister," he says. "For many years now I have been aware of my path in life. It is a good path which leads to The Sacred Origins in the stars." He watches my reactions for a moment before continuing. "As you know, you are my sister. I have no other sister but you." He pauses again.

"I know, Ames," I say, wondering where he is going with this. "I am your sister and you are my brother. Now that our parents have passed away we are all that remains of our family."

"But you are not only my earthly sister, Phoenix," he replies. "You are my *heavenly* sister or what I call my *star* sister. We come from a constellation of stars created by our Heavenly Father in the beginning."

Shivers are tingling up and down my spine and my breath slows into a deep sigh of recognition for what Ames is saying. "Why are you speaking these words to me, Brother," I ask him, "whilst all the time I feel that I already know what you say is so? In fact, I feel that I know what you will say next."

"You know because you have never forgotten where you come from," he replies. "The Father and The Mother have always been with you. You are their child, a star made up of the spirit of the Father and the body of the Mother. Are you following me?" he asks.

I *think* I am following him . . . at least I *feel* I am. But I feel there is more. "Yes" I decide. "I follow you. I understand that I was once a star, their child; but there is something else, something that has niggled at me all my life." I pause for I am not quite sure I believe I am saying these things. I feel quite light, like I am floating but with my feet upon the ground.

"What is that?" Ames asks encouraging me to feel my way.

"I feel I was once two," I tell him. "Not two people but more like two parts of me, and now I feel only one, yet I yearn for the other."

"You *are* two," he says triumphantly. "In a way," he adds, "two parts of your *self* which is one soul. One part is the feminine which is now incarnated upon the earth as the being who is Phoenix; the other masculine part resides with the Father in spirit."

"Oh bless the heavens! I know what my dream is about," I exclaim.

"Tell me your dream, Phoenix."

And so I relate to Ames the dream I have been having ever since I can remember. "So many times I dreamed that I am in a temple with a lover who is part of me," I begin. "Only it is as if we are two bodies. The Mother comes in and covers us with a red light which becomes who we are. The next thing I am aware of is, I am rock. I forget about my male love and it is only when I become Phoenix that I begin to feel his absence once more."

"And what does that feel like?" Ames asks with obvious interest. His voice has taken on a higher tone and his eyes are twinkling like the stars.

"Like I am pulled with a magnet towards him as he is to me. I shall never be complete until I feel that oneness again with him," I say.

"That is because he *is* you and you are he," he explains, grinning from ear to ear. "You are twin flames, two flames of the one soul. *You* are the reflection of *him* in spirit, and when you are in spirit you are reflected by *him* on earth. The soul is in balance at all times, half masculine energy from the Father and half feminine energy from the Mother. It is only when you come to earth and fall into the realms of forgetfulness that you tend to create imbalance and you yearn for your counterpart to make you feel complete."

I listen to all of this with a deep knowing that it is truth. It is the wisdom of the Father that Ames speaks. Of that I have no doubt. Yet there is one more thing I am curious about. "I know you speak the wisdom of the Father, Ames, but I do not understand fully. Why do we seek that completeness then in another soul, just as I know I have sought it in Seth and he in I?" I ask.

And Ames explains, "We are not fully conscious of who we are. It is as if we are unconscious and we are only dreaming. Everything about us that is manifest is but an illusion. Reality lies in our spiritual realms, in our heart space within. It is where the flame of the Father is one with the flame of the Mother. It is when we balance the Father energy and the Mother energy *consciously* within our spirit that we are whole. Until then we unconsciously seek our twin flame in other souls. We find it reflected in one such as Seth; this is known as our soul mate, and although our twin flame or our soul's twin can be incarnate on earth at the same time as us we will only join with that twin when we are ready to. And when that happens, it will reflect your wholeness within, which was there all along."

This explains a lot, especially how I feel about Seth. I explain my feelings to Ames. "When I first met Seth, all those years ago, I believed that I had always loved him. I felt that *he* was the missing part of me," I say. "As the years went on I realised that although he is a huge part of who I am, he is not that missing part. He fulfils me as a husband, yes, but spiritually I still yearn for my twin flame."

Ames studies my face, probably trying to determine what his next words should be. "You felt that way about him, Phoenix, because you *have* loved him before," he tells me.

His answer increases my deep sense of knowing that all of this is real. "It is true," I acknowledge. "But tell me how that can be because I have known it to be true since the moment I first saw him, and he will tell you the same thing, that he has loved me always. Yet how can that be when we had never met before?"

And Ames continues unhesitant. As he speaks my heart seems to acknowledge the truth with tiny leaps of joy amidst a deep peaceful rest. "Phoenix," he says gently and with much wisdom, "you have listened to many reports of Atlantis and of the brave souls who crossed the unknown to be here in the land of Egypt. Seth's grandfather himself claimed to arrive here up the great river from the ocean. He claimed that the entire civilisation of Atlantis lies now beneath the water; none of us know for sure, even *he* has no vivid memory of what indeed happened. But he felt it, and that is the difference between knowing and not knowing. When one *feels* truth, then one knows. He knew that the memory of him being a priest on Atlantis was real because he felt it."

"Just as I *feel* that I have loved Seth before," I add.

"Exactly. But not only do I believe that Seth's grandfather was on Atlantis, but I believe that we all were on Atlantis at one time. Elmara was there, and Rahtu was there; he was our star brother too." Ames pauses, perhaps not sure of his words or perhaps to note my reaction to them. I feel the latter and urge him to continue. "You and I were brother and sister," he goes on. "I mean star brother and sister, and Rahtu was our star brother too. There were many from

The Four Ascents

our constellation there. There were others from many different constellations. Seth was there. Where he was from, I don't know, but he and you loved each other then."

"I know," I reply. "I feel it stronger now than I ever did. And I feel he is from the Pleiades. It was the first time we knew each other, though we were destined to be joined in body."

My memory is serving me well. I am remembering something else though, something very significant to who I am . . . . but what is it? "There's something else Ames" I say hoping he will clarify it for me. "What was it I did, or saw? I had a vision then, did I not? Just as I had yesterday only . . . oh what was it?"

I search Ames' face for an answer but although I can see some recognition in his eyes he doesn't seem to remember what it was either. Oh my heavens! Something is jumping within my heart space. It is urging me to remember. *Listen*, it says, *remember*. I stare into Ames' eyes, my breath bated with expectancy, but to no avail. My attention shifts from him to me, to whatever it is in my heart that is making such a stir within me. I listen. *Remember*, it says again, *remember*.

When I next lift my gaze to meet Ames' we seem to simultaneously share a memory of a moment from another time, a moment in which we both recognised the truth. He speaks it now just as he did then, "You carry the prophecy in your heart, Phoenix," he almost whispers.

"The Red Stone of Power," I add.

My whole being starts to shake with power. I remember I had a vision. It was about a prophecy and how I am to walk the earth in a sacred manner. It is the path laid down for me by the Sacred Parents. I remember I shared the vision with Ames. Was he really my star brother? And Rahtu . . . was he my star brother too? Does *he* know of the prophecy, the Red Stone of Power? Overwhelmed with emotion I put my hands to my face and cry. As each tear falls from my face the peace within my heart returns and grows stronger and stronger until I am completely still within. The Red Stone of Power seems to rest within my heart space, glowing red and gold.

There is absolute silence now in the room. Ames has stopped speaking his mysterious words. There is a silence within me also. My mind has ceased its endless questioning and is content to rest for a moment. That moment seems like an eternity of contentment, of peace, of utter nothingness. I feel myself as if I float in this nothingness, yet within the nothingness I still exist, as something so essential to my being that I feel that everything exists *only*

Eliza White Buffalo with Nicholas Black Elk

because of this powerful energy. It is I, it is who I am and . . . and . . . yes! It is the star. But wait . . . . this is who I am. I *am* this powerful energy that is nothingness. I know that much . . . . and there's more. Awareness is lighting up my being as if a torch has been lit within me. It shines brightly and powerfully, quickening my understanding and at last I know . . . I am eternity. I am the Source of all life. I *am* my Sacred Parents. The joy that I have given myself permission to be comes flooding into my being. Oh wonderful, uplifting, rapturous joy! What bliss it is to be joy!

I barely see Ames any longer. What I see before me is simply another expression of my true self, another expression of knowing and of joy. How long has he felt the anguish of silencing such rapture? I feel compassion for him, for me. The compassion swells and strengthens until I feel it too is who I am; I am Love reaching forth into every particle of my being, all-embracing and healing. I *am* Love. I am Joy and I am Love. I float for a few more moments of eternal joy and love. Then I feel my consciousness come closer to my physical body and mind and I begin to see Ames once more; my brother, my amazing star brother. I open my eyes and breathe. I had not realised that my eyes were closed or that my breathing had become so minimal that I was barely moving. Ames is sitting before me. He is smiling and in his eyes I see the beauty of the knowledge he has so powerfully opened my awareness to.

"Ames," I whisper.

The sound of my voice accentuates the awesome silence and I pause. There is no need for words. All communication, all interaction has never been as pure as in this silence. I close my eyes once more and cry. I feel Ames' hand touch mine and his message is loud and clear: all is well! Several minutes pass as I allow my tears to trickle from my eyes, down my cheeks and fall from my jaw onto my lap. I have no desire to prevent their journey. They feel so appropriate. They are releasing me from all that I knew before; before I awakened to the beauty and knowledge of who I am; before I awakened to the prophecy in my heart. One day when I am ready, when I have climbed the four ascents, the Red Stone of Power will sing within my being. When that happens the prophecy will be fulfilled and I will be in my heavenly home.

It is Ames who breaks the silence. "Phoenix," he says. His voice seems strange. "Phoenix, I know you understand what I have said to you. I could have spoken those words years ago but I felt that you were not ready. Forgive my restraint, Dear Sister. I felt that you were too impetuous with your dreams of becoming a priestess. Recently I see that you are much calmer and

The Four Ascents

accepting of your place and path in life and it seems I am correct for you have refused the inauguration."

I rise from my seat and walk about the room. My brother is correct, I have always been impetuous. I had wanted nothing else but to be inaugurated. I desired to serve my Sacred Parents in what I thought to be the most honourable and holy way possible. The desire had consumed me until I had lost myself entirely in that one dream. But now . . . oh how I have been transformed! I know myself now to be how I truly am, my true identity as a child of the Source. I am the perfect form of a marriage between the Heavenly Father and the Earthly Mother. I am them and they are I, and I know no more honourable nor holy way of serving them than to be who I am right now in this present moment.

There is a knock on the door. It opens and Seth comes quietly into the room. I go to his side and take his hand, and kissing him gently on the cheek I turn to Ames. "I *am* accepting of my path, Dearest Brother" I say with the utmost clarity. "It is here, alongside my husband."

∞∞∞∞∞∞∞∞∞∞∞∞∞∞∞∞∞∞∞∞∞∞∞∞∞∞∞∞

It is late but we've only just eaten our evening meal. I have invited Ames to join us in a special celebration meal because he has brought so much to us these past two days. Why, if he was not such a great healer I might have wandered that lower world for all eternity. And today he has shown to me not only the *higher* realms of my being but the beauty of my true identity and my holy path. Seth has noticed a change in me and he looks at me often this evening with fresh wonder and admiration just as he did all those years ago. We are sitting on the roof of our house. The moonlight shines softly across the space offering us ample light as we cool down from the heat of the day. I sit closer to Seth and breathe in his warm masculine aroma. It fills me with a feeling of security I so often seek from him. "May we discuss that man in the cold world so far away?" I ask Ames.

"Tell me about him," says Ames.

I picture the giant man in my mind. "He looked at me with a passion in his eyes that I have seen before in another's eyes," I say.

"In whose eyes?" asks Seth, "Tell me whose eyes you speak of and I shall pluck them out." We all laugh because we know that Seth merely jests of his jealousy.

"Actually, you will both be surprised because I speak of Rahtu," I tell them.

"Rahtu?" repeats Seth, "the young student in the temple who assisted you when you fell?"

"That is he." I pause, expecting more interest in Rahtu but there is none.

"Please continue," says Ames.

"His eyes seemed to pull me into them until I no longer had the power to speak or indeed move," I relate. "Before long I found myself in a dark fiery underworld; it was terrible. There were cries of anguish from many who were being consumed by the flames of that world. The air was thick and I struggled to breathe, and all the time I thought I was dying."

"It *is* a kind of death," says Ames, "and one that many human beings have not come back from. They exist, yes, in a kind of sleeping consciousness. I call it the long sleep."

Seth sits up straight with interest and joins in the conversation. "My grandfather taught me of that form of existence when I was still a young boy," he tells Ames. "Phoenix and I know them as the unfortunates and we pray that some day we will rouse them from this 'long sleep' as you so aptly name it, and remind them of who they are and where they come from. I suppose we hope they will wake up and . . . I don't know . . . be truly alive again I suppose . . . in their true identity."

I look up into Seth's face and I notice how alive he seems when he speaks of his truth in this way.

"Your grandfather was a great man and a wise soul" Ames remarks.

"That is so," Seth affirms nostalgically.

"I have often wondered why your father and mother chose such a humble life for you. Why did you never go into the priesthood yourself?" Ames asks him.

"Heavens, Ames!" is the reply. "Do I really need to tell *you* of the blessings of a simple life?"

"Of course you don't," Ames replies bowing his head to Seth. "Forgive me for questioning your humility of spirit. It was not my intention."

"I know that, Dear Brother-in-Law," Seth reassures him, "but once more I fear we have wandered from the topic to be discussed. Phoenix?"

"There I was in a pit of burning passion," I say, continuing with the account of my vision. "It was the kind of passion that one might associate with the lower bodily urges and the instant gratification that one seeks when enthralled with those urges. There was no hope for a more heavenly way of being except for that which my Sacred Parents had so generously bestowed on me just moments before. It was that which my salvation was."

"Explain," says Seth knowingly pulling me closer to him.

"Oh, My Love! It was that which you saw in my eyes so very long ago when we first met; the grace and beauty of the heavenly state. It uplifted me and told me that I could transcend that terrible world, and I did. Not only that but when the then less powerful creature insisted that I go with him, I not only refused but I reduced his threat to that of a mere handmaiden. He turned and meekly walked away from me."

"It's obvious," says Ames explaining, "You reflected his light. You brought the essence of the Sacred Parents out in him so powerfully that he understood in that very moment that he also had a desire to exist in a higher way of being; in the higher way of being that he had originally fallen from."

"You mean that he was sleeping, or unconscious, in this long sleep that we spoke of, and what Phoenix did awakened him?" Seth asks.

"To a degree I suppose," replies Ames; "enough to give him a glimpse of who he really was anyhow. He may not even have recognized this truth in you but he did *feel* something powerful in you. You did him a great justice, Phoenix."

I don't quite understand what my brother means. "But I thought you said that *he* had done *me* the justice. *He* had helped *me*," I say reminding my brother of what he said when I first came to from my unconscious vision.

"He did," Ames replies. "Just as *you* reflected to *him* the light within him, *he* reflected to *you* the darkness of your lower body, the lower realms. Had he not done so you could easily have fallen into them unknowingly and then you would be no better off than those unfortunates who sleep the long sleep."

I suddenly understand and Ames must see that in my face because he smiles and adds, "We help each *other* on the path. I have no doubt that your soul is connected with his in an agreement that you would do this for each other. That poor soul was floundering in the darkness before you came to him, and *your* soul was likely in danger of falling before *he* came to *you.*"

"I understand," I say, "just as it was always your place to awaken me to our star origin, so was it his place to awaken me to the darker realms of my being."

"Yes, Phoenix, that's it," Ames says, excited that I have grasped what he is telling me. "And it was *your* place to awaken him to the path of his soul which is to come up out of his sleepy awareness and reach for the heights of heaven. In this way he will come to know his star origin."

"Good heavens!" I yawn sleepily, I am worn out.

Seth laughs at me. "He intended to keep you from sleep not send you into it," he laughs.

"Very funny, very funny, Brother-in-Law" laughs Ames too. "Seriously though, I should go. My sister has had a tiring two days and she needs her rest. I'll say goodnight then."

"Goodnight Ames."

"Goodnight, Dear Brother," I yawn.

Seth and I retire to our chambers. It is not long before I am dreaming in peaceful slumber. In my dreams I come before a being of golden light. We are in a strange world where nothing seems to be solid. I know this world to be called Lemuria. The golden being is speaking to me, directly into my mind, like telepathy, I suppose.

"Phoenix," the being says to me, "you have climbed the second ascent. Your Sacred Parents are proud of you. You feel the Red Stone of Power glow within your heart centre, and you express that which is holy. Now you must walk the earth with the power of the third ascent. By bringing that power always into the centre you will open your earthly perceptions to the knowledge and wisdom of the Father and the Love of the Mother. Good speed child."

∞∞∞∞∞∞∞∞∞∞∞∞∞∞∞∞∞∞∞∞∞∞∞∞∞∞∞∞

The video comes to a stop again. And Black Elk speaks . . .

"My Dear Rose, the soul has ascended the first two rungs of the stepladder to Heaven. It is time for her to step out of the illusion. Only in this way shall she make the ascension into her heavenly home. Oh how she is loved! Dear Eliza . . . she springs from the loins of Source like the cub from the wild cat. Free and playful, she runs and prances, leaps and pounces. She sucks milk from the breast of the Mother and touches the spirit of the Father's breath. She must be like the wild cub that knows no fear. She must trust in the Mother for her sustenance. She will not forget her. She must walk with the Father in faith. He will not forget her. She must be like the human child that takes the hands of its parents, trusting and knowing that all is well, all is provided. Rose, you have seen how Phoenix has been given a vision, a premonition if you like. She has been shown that she belongs with the Sacred Parents and that she is firmly on The Holy Path. She realizes that she is to be challenged. All souls are challenged, Rose. It is how we learn on the earth

The Four Ascents

plane. For what purpose does experience serve if not to learn about truth, about reality? And what good would that experience be if it did not reveal to us the duality of the earthly being? It is by revealing to us what is illusion that we come to know what is real.

You have also seen how the members of the soul group reincarnate into the same lifetime and come together to assist each other along the holy path. In this next lifetime, Eliza is incarnate as an eighteen year old girl called Demetria. Demetria is arrogant and eager to be exalted above others. She feels the evolutionary progress of her soul that had been made in the previous lifetime, that of Phoenix. Remember that Demetria, like Phoenix, is but an individual spirit, a new expression of the soul, Eliza. However, Demetria's earthly personality, which merely houses this temporary soul, is causing a limitation to it; to its progress on the holy path. Let us see how Demetria deals with the upcoming challenge. Will she choose the way of her spirit, or will the illusion of her arrogance overpower her causing her soul to fall a second time?"

CHAPTER FOUR

The Order of Delphi

The video plays on, and so the story continues . . .

I find myself in Ancient Greece

'*It is dusk on the seventh day and Apollo is in his temple. On the eighth day he will ascend in glory amidst trumpet blasts and choirs of heavenly voices. All those who heed his word shall be exalted. Many in the Order of Delphi shall be anointed with fire, the living spirit of the mighty god to whom they have devoted their lives. When the great sun god rises on the morn of that day the dream will be fulfilled and Heaven will prevail on Earth. Praise be to the gods! This is the word of Athena, Goddess of Truth and ruler of the Temple of Truth.*'

I take my leave from Eumelia; she has served us well since taking her place on the seat as the Oracle of Delphi. Today she channelled for me. She knows that her reward lies in the heavenly state, her inner cella. I am to be exalted according to the law of the gods. I am to make the ascent into the eighth house of the soul. There I will commune with the gods and they will guide my spirit to my heavenly home. Through Eumelia, the Holy Pythia, the great Sun God, Apollo declared that I have served him well. I have risen up the first three ascents on the stepladder to Heaven and now I am to expect to rest for a while in the higher temple of my being; there I will be taught to make the final ascent wherein I achieve the inner cella.

I sit down on one of the marble benches inside the columned porch. This temple was built hundreds of years ago by the light beings that fled here from the doomed continent of Atlantis. In its cella, its inner chamber, there stands a beautiful marble statue of Apollo and an equally beautiful one of Pallas Athena who has presided over the temple since its beginning. Deep within the cella, between the two statues, there is a grand altar on which the Flame of Truth burns tirelessly. The flame was taken here from the original Temple of Truth on Atlantis. Its emerald green hue inflames the heart and mind of any person willing to be true to them selves. All day and throughout the night also, people come to pray to Apollo and to Pallas Athena, and to offer their gratitude for blessings bestowed upon them. The Flame of Truth will always enlighten any deception that may be brought in with them. No-one enters the temple unless they are prepared to distinguish truth from error. This current priesthood was established over two hundred years ago, but it goes back for generations before that. We work to keep this dispensation, not only for Greek men and women, but for all that desire to know truth.

I smile smugly and hug myself as I look out across the city. The sun is setting in the west, over the peak of Mount Pernassos. The peak is glowing red and purple in the quake of the sun's rays. I have often wondered how it would feel to stand there on the top of the world with everything spread out below me. I think that I should feel like it will when I make my final ascent into Heaven. I have always been a dreamer. My father has often declared that I ought to be more mindful of my day to day duties, telling me that I serve the gods better if I keep my mind on earthly things. He had chosen a potential husband for me three years ago, Philo, a wealthy farmer. Father presented him to me on my fifteenth birthday but I had greatly disappointed him by announcing my desire to join the order. I could not possibly take a husband. I knew I was called by the gods, to serve them and mankind through the holy order. But Philo is wonderful, and if I *were* to marry then I feel it would be to him. As it is, I am not to marry but to devote my efforts to learning from Pallas Athena herself. Philo is determined to wait for me, until I am ready to be a wife to him. He loves me so much. At times I feel stifled by his attentions, although he has been a wonderful aide in my priestly lessons. If it were not for Philo I may never have ascended so quickly. He is my source of worldly affairs. He keeps me grounded with his earthliness whilst giving me the freedom I need to explore the spirit. Although for one so grounded on Earth he is very spiritual also. He teaches me about the natural world, often reminding me that I am of the earth also and not only spirit. He talks often of a father/mother god. He calls his god Father Heaven/Mother Earth. He says that true power is in the wisdom and love that comes from knowing that we are all sons and daughters of this one true god.

"This is the knowledge that our ancestors in Atlantis held," he told me; it was a short time after we met. Already we had become firm companions. We could say anything to each other as we seldom disagreed, but that one day, we did. We were lying on our backs on the rocky hillside, watching Philo's goats as they grazed happily unaware of the debate that had begun amidst their human company.

"Then why did the ancestors not bring that knowledge with them when they came to Greece?" I had asked him. "Could it be that they were wrong, and that over the years righteous people have learned the truth which

Eliza White Buffalo with Nicholas Black Elk

is that all the gods and goddesses are equal. We have a duty to them, Philo. You cannot go about saying loosely that there is only one god. It is highly disrespectful. And which do you say is the one true god? How could you favour one against the others?"

"I don't," he replied.

"You just said that there is only one, so which one is it?" I insisted. "Surely you're not discarding them all?"

I was upset. Philo was speaking against all that I knew to be true. I knew what I wanted to do with my life. I was going to be a priestess in The Order of Delphi. I was going to serve under the direction of Pallas Athena and Apollo, and in doing so I was going to fulfil a dream I had ever since I was a small girl. I still have this dream in which I am walking a long road. I walk and walk for days before a great golden god comes to me and tells me that I will walk another road. He shows me a road that leads to the heavens, and tells me that my place is in the temple, in the centre where the two roads meet. Philo does not understand, I think. He says that it is a dream and dreams aren't real. He says that what is real is his love for me. I do love Philo. In some ways it feels like I have always loved him. But I know my dream is real and that it is bigger than love.

The sun drops quickly now behind Pernassos. It will get cold; I hate the cold. It seems to weaves a dark magic into my life, penetrating my skin and wrapping its icy fingers around my heart. It brings with it horrible, stinking thoughts, thoughts that are not in keeping with a priestess such as I. They reek of dark places and giant red men that breathe fire, destroying all goodness of life until all that remains is the stench of death. In these places the gods are overthrown by the dark lords of night. I do not want these thoughts that seek to destroy me, but lately they have come in the coldness of the night air. Something is approaching I fear, something bad.

Philo's words come back to my thoughts now as I set off walking to the warmth and safety of my father's home. I had asked him which of the gods he deems to be his one true god. His answer was that all of them together portray his father/mother god in His/Her wholeness. I think he tried to say that none of the gods is worthy of being the one true god on their own, but that together their collective attributes form one perfect whole, one god. Sometimes I wonder how it is that I could love a man who speaks such wicked things. I often wonder if Philo, in his confusion, will bring upon me this terrible thing I feel coming closer and closer; yet I need him near me and he needs me.

When I reach the door of my father's house I discover it is locked. *That's strange*, I think, *My Father's door is never locked.* I rap loudly on the wood. "Father, Mother!" I shout, "It's me, Demetria."

The door opens and my father pulls me inside by the fabric of my dress. "Hush, Demetria," he whispers. He sticks his head a little through the doorway and glances left then right before closing the door quietly.

"What?" I utter. The hairs on the back of my neck tingle as a dozen fearful thoughts race through my mind.

Father puts his finger to my lips. "Hush" he whispers again, and pulls me into the dining room. Around the table sit four other gentlemen; Mother is serving wine to them. She beckons to me to join her, which I do, quietly following her to the cooking area.

"Mother, what in the name of the gods is going on?" I ask her. "Why is the door locked and why did Father pull me in so roughly, insisting that I hush?" I keep my voice low. The tingling to the back of my neck warns me that this is serious. Anyway, Father has guests so it would be rude to be heard.

"Demetria, My Dear," Mother replies almost tearfully. "The entire city is in fear. All are urged to remain indoors and lock their houses. Even here in the acropolis we may not be safe."

"Great Zeus!" I exclaim, "What can it be that threatens us so?"

"Demetria!" Mother is surprised at my casual use of the great ruler's name. "Your Father would not be pleased at such language. If it were not for your upcoming graduation I would report you instantly. As it is, I will be happy when you finally achieve your aims for then you can focus on marriage and raise a good family."

"Mother, tell me what is wrong," I urge her, ignoring her assumptions.

She takes my hand in both of hers. "My Dear, metics have arrived in the city," she tells me keeping her voice low so that Father won't hear her. "At first the merchants were excited but then . . . oh dear! I was there myself. Your father wanted me to purchase some of that new incense he likes. Well, I decided to take Eusebius with me to carry back some grain, you know. Anyway, thank the gods that I did for I would have feared for my life."

She puts her hand to her chest and breathes deeply, eyes closed as she shakes her head in a dramatic gesture. I do not like this side of my mother. She can be so strong when she needs to be. This portrayal of weakness is a falsehood. I urge her to sit and take a sip of wine. I am a dutiful daughter and I will always forgive her little idiosyncrasy.

"What has alarmed you so, Mother Dear? Surely, you are not frightened of a few metics? What do they bring? Fine wines, silk?"

"You did not see them, Demetria," she says dramatically. "They are not the usual metics that come to trade; they are huge men with manes of hair as red as could be."

"Oh Great Zeus!" I exclaim again. This time it is I who clasps my chest, my breath caught in my throat. The giant red men! The lords of night!

"I know," Mother responds, thinking my reaction is similar to hers.

But how can I tell her that I have dreaded the arrival of these men? How do I say that I have thought of them often, wielding their dragon's breath upon any unfortunate being that wanders into their lair? But it seems now that they are the ones to come amongst us. Oh, will anyone be safe? "The temple Mother," I blurt out in panic. "We must seek refuge in the temple. I must tell Father. I must tell him that we are not safe here. We must go to the temple."

"No, no dear," she replies pleased that she got the desired reaction to her report of the metics. "Your father is this moment discussing a plan with his peers. Let *them* decide what is best."

I look to the table where my father is deep in discussion with the four men. Does he know what manner of evil has come into our city? It is likely that I am not the only one to predict the onset of this threat.

Against Mother's pleas not to, I dash to the table and interrupt the conversation, "Father, what manner of man is this with red hair and fire for breath? Will they indeed overthrow the gods?" I demand to know.

All five men gaze at me in astonishment. It is not appropriate for a daughter to interrupt her father like this, especially when he is entertaining such important government figures. I don't know their faces but I am quite sure they are government men because Father is the Oligarch, one of the esteemed rulers of the city.

Father speaks first, "Daughter, what are you saying? No man can overthrow the gods. Where did you get that idea from? And fire for breath? Are you ill?"

For the first time I contemplate the idiocy of my thoughts. Hearing me speak them aloud has thrown much needed common sense into the mix. "Forgive me, Father," I relent, "indeed I am well. I am a little tired perhaps. I don't know what I'm saying."

The Four Ascents

"You are pardoned, my dear," Father accepts. "And please, do not allow the situation to cause you such distress. Until we know what manner of man we are dealing with we shall remain cautious, but there is no need whatsoever for conjuring up insane fears. These men are likely to be harmless. As it is, they have given no-one cause to think otherwise, but you are advised to keep your distance, for now at least."

"But we ought to be prepared, ought we not?" I ask him anxiously.

"If you leave us to our discussion, we may just be able to make preparations," he replies somewhat angrily.

I say no more; I have been outspoken as it is. To question the government's ability to keep us safe would be unforgivable. Reluctantly, I go to the courtyard to pray. Perhaps the gods will help me to make sense of this. Father and his peers return to their discussion and Mother returns to her serving.

Entering the courtyard I see our slave, Eusebius, there mixing wine. He has been with my family since before I was born. Father bought him for two kraters of fine wine. When I was little I amused myself with playing tricks on Eusebius. I would hide among the branches of the olive trees in the grove beside our house, and when he came to pick olives I would make a noise like a snake. It was fun to see his expression when he realised it was only me hiding there. I liked him immensely. Mother and Father didn't like me to distract him from his duties but he was always a willing playmate, forgiving my childish pranks and occasionally teaching me about the stars in the night sky. Recently, he met a young woman slave from the city. Her name is Xanthe and I think they must be very much in love because he has implored me to coerce Father into buying her.

Eusebius bows to me now as I approach him, keeping his head low as Father insists. "Oh dear Eusebius, do not hide your face from me," I say to him. "I like to see the light in your eyes." At once he lifts his head and his entire face is smiling. "I must say, I have never seen you look so happy" I tell him. "May I assume that you have seen Father and that he has agreed to have Xanthe here?"

"He has, thanks to you, My Lady," he replies, "although it is not the sole reason for my happiness."

"Oh! Pray tell."

"Xanthe's mistress has agreed to sell her on the condition that she and I are to be married." There are tears glistening in Eusebius's eyes. He simply cannot hide his joy and he knows there is no need to hide it from me.

"Great Zeus! How wonderful! I shall insist that you have the best servant's wedding imaginable." I tell him. I am genuinely happy for them.

"Thank you, My Lady, thank you. Xanthe and I would be honoured," he says with his head low.

"The honour shall be mine. Dear Eusebius, you deserve happiness. I shall pray for you both in the temple." He lowers his head again and bows slightly. "You are dismissed Eusebius," I tell him. "I wish to pray."

"My Lady."

I watch him as he leaves. He was my only childhood friend. He does not know how precious he was to me then. "Eusebius!"

He stops and turns, the smile etched into his face, "Yes, My Lady?"

"Eusebius, do you remember how I used to play tricks on you when I was a little girl?" I ask. "Do you remember how I would hide in the olive trees and pretend to be a serpent?"

"Why, yes My Lady, I do," he says trying to hide a grin.

"You were always so mild with me. I must have given you many reasons to be upset but you never once hinted at my behaviour to my parents, did you?"

"You did not upset me, My Lady," he replies.

"You are gracious, indeed. Thank you; that is all."

He turns to go then pauses and addresses me again. "If you would be so kind as to pardon my insolence, My Lady," he says, his head bowed.

"Yes?"

"I think it is *you* that is truly gracious, My Lady. Ever since you were a child I have noted your grace. It's just that . . ." He pauses, not sure if he is being too bold. He lifts his head and gazes at me. The gaze seems to penetrate my entire being. It is a gaze I often see in the face of my dear friend Eumelia. It is a knowing gaze that only the likes of a gifted oracle possesses. How does a lowly slave come to have that very gaze? Could it be that Eusebius possesses the gift of prophecy also? If so, then how unfortunate for him is his fate of birth.

"Pray, continue," I beg him.

"There was always something about you," he says much braver now. "At times, in the olive grove when I was lost in thought, it would occur to me that you are vulnerable in this world. And I often thought that you have a great mission ahead of you. I see it now as I look at you."

The Four Ascents

I feel keen to encourage him. "What do you see, Eusebius?" I ask.

"I see two roads that you will travel so that you can fulfil a prophecy you have held since the beginning of time," he replies to my astonishment.

His words fill my heart with warmth and I feel a presence leap within me; it means that he speaks of truth. He has indeed the same gift as Eumelia. It is my turn now to lower my face. I bow to him as I do to Eumelia, honouring his gift. Poor Eusebius, he cannot cope with this reversal of roles. He fumbles with his tunic and backs away from me.

"No Eusebius, please don't be afraid," I reassure him. "It's just that I wish to honour your words. Father shall not hear of this, I assure you. It's just you and me, not as servant and mistress but as two human beings acting on their truth."

"I . . . I do not wish to be disrespectful, My Lady." He keeps his head low.

"You're not," I assure him. "It is I who wishes for you to be candid with me. Please tell me more. I do so wish to know what you see."

"I fear you will not like what I say," he bravely tells me.

"Say it anyway. I will not hold you in disdain."

He lifts his head and gazes deep into my eyes. I feel the hairs on the back of my neck tingle for the second time this evening. "My Lady, I fear that you are mistaken in your choice of life," he begins. "The Master Philo cares for you greatly. I feel that perhaps you will travel the two roads with more integrity of who you are, if you should agree to be his wife."

Great Zeus! I have never known a servant to be so bold in his opinion. Yet every breath in my body knows what Eusebius says is true. Am I on the wrong path? Perhaps Father is correct; I *should* marry Philo. And what of this prophecy? How did Eusebius know of my dream of two roads? After a few moments silence, during which Eusebius drops to his knees with his head held as low as possible, and I pose a hundred questions in my mind, I take his hands in mine and raise him up to face me.

"Arise, My Dear Eusebius," I say, "do not fear retribution for your candour. I asked for your thoughts and you delivered with honesty and bravery. I shall think about your words for I feel them to be sent from the gods. You have served me well. Thank you."

"My Lady."

He leaves me to pray but I cannot; my mind is full of questions about roads and prophecies, mixed with giant fire-breathing men with red hair. Instead, I return to the dining room where Father and his peers are still deep in discussion and Mother has a platter of food waiting for me. After I eat I ascend the stairway to my chambers. My bed has been made ready by Eusebius and he has left a gift for me on my headrest. It is an olive leaf. I tenderly press the leaf to my smiling lips. I cannot believe that a slave has touched my heart so much so that I feel love for him. I disrobe and don my night wear.

"It's not a romantic love though," I say to myself as though I needed to justify my feelings. "It's a love that one would have for a brother or a sister. It's the kind of love I have for Jason. Jason is Eumelia's assistant; he is a priest of the order also. He oversees the proceedings of the oracle, interpreting the messages for the public and so forth. "Jason would have you in the temple, if he knew of your gift" I say to the olive leaf, although my words are meant for Eusebius.

I settle into my bed and hug the covers to my face. Today Pallas Athena had spoken the will of Apollo, God of the Sun. He has declared that I am to be exalted, risen up in spirit to the House of the Gods. There is no greater honour that can be bestowed upon me. All my life, I have desired to serve the gods. How much more I can do for them when I am under their direct instruction! I am proud of myself, of what I have achieved in just three short years in the temple. I *should* be proud. Not many eighteen year old girls have risen to my status, although Apollo has stated that I have done this over three lifetimes on earth. I think that must mean that each of the three years I have been in the guidance of Pallas Athena is akin to one whole lifetime of service. I *am* special indeed. And now even Eusebius says I am, though he is but a mere slave and I am a priestess. A prophecy is what he said; I have held a prophecy since the beginning of time. I won't tell Eumelia and Jason about this; they would not understand but try to convince me that I ought to be more humble. Modesty is a virtue I have perfected within myself but to deny my importance entirely would be a travesty of justice. What was it Eumelia said to me just this evening before I left?

"Demetria, you are very dear to me," she said, "but I see a side of you that I fear would not please the gods at all. The gods are great, you know that, and we are but mere servants. For a servant to claim importance above others and align themselves with greatness that only the gods have earned the right to is like the slaves putting themselves alongside their masters."

"You don't understand Eumelia," I had replied, "to me, Eusebius is a friend. I don't feel more important than he is. I simply follow the rules of service. It is the same with the gods. I follow the rules of service, and I am always ready to be of service, but I also acknowledge that they are rewarding me for that. I am chosen by them to be an example of righteousness for all mankind. I feel I have earned that right, have I not?"

"You have served well," she said to me. "I cannot argue with that. You are indeed on the path of the righteous, but please, Demetria, allow me to steer you on that path, for it is my deepest concern that you will be challenged very soon. I do not wish to see you fall."

"Do not be unnecessarily concerned," I told her. "Has not Athena herself channelled through you that I am to be exalted?"

"Yes," she replied. "But Demetria, you are not separate from the whole. It is the order that is to be exalted. Remember, what you do affects the others and vice versa, and as one we will be exalted."

"Jason disagrees with you," I said adamantly. "He and I spoke only this morning, and he agrees that I have earned the right of passage into the eighth house."

"Jason is correct, and even though he is to be amongst those to be exalted, he would not have pertained to that, did he?" Eumelia asked me then.

"No, he did not," I replied.

"Because," she explained, "he sees himself as one of many small pieces of the whole. There is none of us chosen above the others, Demetria. Do not let your thoughts delude you."

"Eumelia is such an enigma, at times," I had said to myself then. "Even now when she ought to be glad for me, she reduces my honour to nothing. Yet I know she loves me and that she means well. Perhaps she will learn from my example". I bade her farewell then before I retreated from the oracle chamber. As I closed the chamber door she had called after me.

"It's a long way to fall, Demetria."

To be honest, now I am feeling quite disturbed by Eumelia's words. Oh, the injustice of it all! Why did all this stuff have to come up now just before my graduation? If I was in the city now I would reach for one of those red men and march him to the temple, if only to prove to Eumelia that I am ready, that I have the purity and strength of spirit to overthrow any threat to the temple and the gods. I shall *not* be challenged. I am so upset that I find it difficult to rest.

When sleep finally comes I dream I am in a gorgeous meadow. Buttercups and daisies creep over the lush green grass. There are stones, huge big stones about waist high sticking up from the ground. The air is so still and warm. It is not a stifling heat though; more a crisp clean atmosphere that is neither too hot nor too cool. I walk aimlessly about the meadow, touching each stone as I meet it. They are set in a circle with a central plinth. I go to the centre and sit upon the plinth; it feels warm under my body. One would expect to feel coolness from stone. On closer inspection I note that it is not stone but a substance I am not familiar with. In the night sky the Pleiades shine brilliantly down upon the meadow. I know them well, for Eusebius has taught me much about the stars. But what is *this* star? I have never noticed its presence before. To the north of the Pleiades a star is shining, far out-glowing the millions of others in the sky. It seems to be glowing brighter and brighter. I actually feel its warm emanations on my face. I feel anticipation, like I am waiting for a voice to speak within my mind.

When a voice does speak however, it comes from behind me. I turn to see a man standing there. How did he get here so quickly? There was no-one here a moment ago. The man says, "Eliza", just like that, just Eliza.

"Who are you?" I enquire. "Why do you call me Eliza?" He seems somewhat familiar.

"I am Amir from Serabe," he tells me, "and you are Osiah, known as Eliza upon the earth. I come to caution you of the road ahead."

"Why?" I ask. "What is so wrong about the path I have chosen?" I am still a little angry, but this man is stirring up other emotions within me too, feelings of sadness and loneliness. Tears spring to my eyes.

"Be not afraid, Eliza," he says. "All is well in our house but I wish to remind you of our conversation in the temple." What? When did I meet this man in the temple? I seem to recognise him, but I would know if he was a priest of the order. It is strange though and I feel that maybe he speaks of a different temple.

"When did we meet before? What did we talk about?" I ask him.

"We spoke of the prophecy," he replies. "The Red Stone of Power dwells yet in your heart space. If you wish to honour it you would do well to come to the centre where the two roads meet. Only there will you find that you are truly exalted and yet, you are no greater than a grain of sand."

Amir's words resonate in my heart. I know that he speaks from truth; yet I do not feel pleasure in the acknowledgement of the prophecy. I do feel sad and lonely and terribly afraid. With tears streaming from a broken heart I hold out my arms to the messenger and implore him.

"Please, I have erred," I implore. "Show me the way so that the prophecy will be complete."

"You have a choice, Eliza," he replies compassionately. "You always have a choice. You can return to Serabe where you exist forever in peace, but forsaking the Father's Dream which you envisioned. If you choose however, to stay on Earth, you are more than capable of fulfilling the prophecy. In order to do so you will walk the long road of difficulties. It is there that you will gain the understanding you need to fully be present as a godly being on Earth. You have walked the good road for three ascents but is only by walking both roads that we achieve the Father's Dream."

Amir looks at me now with understanding and compassion, and I feel that I will never cease crying; my heart is broken and my spirit is bruised. "I need to heal, don't I?" I ask.

He smiles tenderly in response and reaches out a hand to me. I hold out my own hand and he places in it, an olive leaf. I sniff loudly, tears wetting the leaf as I place it to my lips, and Amir places his arms about me and holds me tight while I sob unto his shoulder.

"Be not afraid, Eliza," he says. "Today you shall enter the house of God. I love you, My Sister." Something in the tone of his voice is so familiar, and when he once more gazes with compassion into my eyes I recognise the giver of the olive leaf. It is Eusebius. It is his spirit.

"Forgive me, Brother," I say to him, "my error has been great. From this moment on I will walk the road of difficulties. It will be made easy because I have you. In your great wisdom you will guide me on the path until we walk home together, hand in hand."

"It is so," he affirms. "And remember, where the two roads meet the place is holy; there you will find your respite. Good speed!" And in a glance, he is gone. I look to the star which I now know to be Serabe, still shining brightly upon me, and as the warmth of its emanations lessens it dims and disappears from sight. It takes with it my messenger, or at least a part of him, for he is still with me on Earth, the only friend I had when I was a lonely and spoilt little girl, my meek and wonderful Eusebius.

∞∞∞∞∞∞∞∞∞∞∞∞∞∞∞∞∞∞∞∞∞∞∞

"It was Atlantis," Eumelia says knowingly.

"Do you think?" I sniffle. I wipe my runny nose on the kerchief she gave me some twenty minutes before when I began to tell her about my dream.

"I know it was," she replies. "Amir is a soul that you knew in a past lifetime in which you were on Atlantis."

Eliza White Buffalo with Nicholas Black Elk

"But he was so like Eusebius; it was as if it were him" I insist.

"It was, but then he was called Amir. Oh my dear Demetria, you are so sweet but you have so much to learn before you are ready to serve as High Priestess. Amir was correct, you do have a long road ahead to travel. You are about to embark on that journey; how you do that is up to you."

"What do you mean, Eumelia? Am I not to graduate?" I ask her.

"Of course you are to graduate, you have earned it. You know, the soul is multi-faceted; there is still so much we do not know about who we are, and what we are capable of. It is alright channelling from the gods and it is a worthy thing, yes. But there are realms of spirit that even the masters have not yet traversed. Who are we to say what fulfilment is and what is not. Personally, I feel that when we achieve the inner cella it is only the beginning; we have a long way to go then."

"Perhaps you are correct," I say to her. "I *will* graduate; then I shall not make the same error I made before. This time I will know my weakness and be ready to overcome it at every point." I give Eumelia a grateful smile; she is so good to me.

"And your weakness is?" she asks.

"Forgetting my place, which is with Philo as well as the priesthood; both roads" I add.

"Be careful," she tells me. "The challenges come in disguise. We must be alert." She gives me a sisterly hug just as Jason enters the hall where we are sitting. He instantly notices my tear stained face.

"What ails you, Demetria? Are you ill?" he asks.

"I'm fine, I'm fine," I reply, brushing his concerns away.

Jason stands before Eumelia and me. He is a huge figure; I have never noticed before just how tall he is, and strong. His stature portrays a strength and protectiveness to me that I have never perceived until now.

"Jason?"

"What is it my little songbird?" he asks. He calls me his little songbird because when I first came to the temple I constantly hummed with happiness that I was here.

I smile as his warm concern fills my heart, lifting my mood immediately. "Why do you look after me so much?" I ask him. "There are many young ones in the temple, yet none of them can boast of having your constant support as well as the brotherly love you so readily bestow on me, even though I don't deserve it."

The Four Ascents

"What is this?" He is taken aback a little at my sudden change of attitude. He looks to Eumelia who simply smiles and nods to him. I see the light of understanding come upon him. They have obviously been discussing my path before this.

"Demetria, listen to me," Jason says. "We are all here to help and serve each other on our individual paths. Some of us are connected in ways that only the gods fully know. I am here, simply to be of service to them and to mankind. I feel that it is in the course of that service to watch over you and Eumelia here. We three ought to stay together because that is the power we profess to have on earth."

"Oh Jason, I don't understand," I moan.

"You will, Dear One, you will. Now, what are all these tears about my little songbird? Tell me, tell Jason."

And so I relay the dream once more. It is beginning to make more sense to me and I see by my friends' reactions that they too are recognising a holy wisdom in it. "You have been given a gift, Demetria" Jason tells me now that I'm done. "I knew this when I first saw you" he says. "But it's a responsibility that's far beyond your years. Some day you will be ready. Until then though, you have a long way to go with many challenges along the way. Be prepared, Dear One, because I fear that the biggest challenge is nigh."

"That's what Eumelia said yesterday," I tell him. "Do you remember Eumelia?"

"Yes," she smiles, "I do. Now, Demetria, Jason, we have important discussions to attend this morning regarding these strange metics that have arrived. We must make haste else we will keep the others waiting."

∞∞∞∞∞∞∞∞∞∞∞∞∞∞∞∞∞∞∞∞∞∞∞∞∞

The video stops playing. And Black Elk speaks . . .

"My Dear Rose, you understand how Demetria had separated herself from her spirit. And once again the soul, Eliza was given divine assistance. She was shown that she has a choice in every moment. We must walk both roads if we are to fulfil the Father's dream of Heaven on Earth. And it is a balance that is achieved only in the holy place where the two roads meet. Demetria must walk the difficult path now; it is the only way she can consciously know her true reality. And in becoming conscious of her true Self she will rise again on the four ascents.

Eliza White Buffalo with Nicholas Black Elk

And The Red Stone of Power . . . ah yes! How powerfully the crystal heart calls! Watch now, Rose, and see how the crystal heart calls to Demetria. She must listen to her heart; listen to its whispers, not to its proclamation. She must listen to its quietude, not to its majesty. She must listen to the gentle whispers of the crystal heart lest she slips on the highest rung. It is a long way to fall. It is a long difficult road that is clothed in darkness. Oh, how dark her path shall seem to her to be! Yet the Light is always with her. How near The Father is to her! He is closer than the breath in her lungs. He is closer than the blood in her veins. He is closer than the hairs on her head; he has counted every one. How close He is! Yet she acts as if she is a million miles from Him.

And so I tell you now, Dear Rose, be not afraid. Step aside from the fear that you create. It is part of the great illusion that slips over your eyes. Look behind the illusion. Flip it over and gaze upon the face of God. You are His child. You are His word. Eliza, Eliza, He is calling to you."

CHAPTER FIVE

The Challenge

And so the story continues . . .

We open the door to the conference chamber; most of the seats around the outside of the room are filled. We take our places and await the remaining few who have still not arrived. There is much murmuring among the forty or so priests and priestesses. In fact, it is so noisy that the high priest, Hermetius is leaned to hush us with the sounding of the gathering bell.

The room falls silent. All eyes are on Hermetius, our high priest, counsellor and primary healer. He is a man of middle years, a little younger perhaps than Jason and Eumelia. Still quite handsomely featured, he is tall and always perfectly poised. He took the vow of chastity as a young graduate and to this very day he remains steadfast in his aims. I have only been in the priesthood for three years now and I cannot count the amount of young chelas who have been heart broken, every one of them thinking that she would be the one to attract the favour of this majestic beauty. I study his face closely now as he sits high upon the dais. The heavy white drapes behind him accentuate the glossy black of his hair and beard. His priestly robes hang loosely with gold ornaments and are held with the symbol of Asclepius, a golden serpent. Asclepius is god of medicine, and none is equal to Hermetius in the knowledge of herbs and potions.

"How many of us are missing?" he asks of his assistant, Thucymus, who replies that four of the chelas are absent. I look around at the empty seats, trying to discern who they are. Two young faces come to my mind, yet I do not know their names. I wonder what manner of priestess I would make if I cannot even make it my duty to acquaint myself with the younger students. But then, I have adhered myself so closely with Eumelia and Jason, and I feel that it is because I am not familiar with youth about me. As far back as I can recall my only friends have been Mother and Eusebius. There was a young boy once, when I was perhaps eight or nine years old. He was the son of a rich merchant who came to stay at our home for a short while. I don't think Eusebius liked him much since the boy abused him at every opportunity.

Poor Eusebius did not complain, but I know that he went to bed some nights nursing several cuts and bruises. I did not like that boy, probably more for what he did to my lovely servant, but also because he would pull on my hair just to see me cry.

"Can any of you explain the absence of these four chelas?" asks Hermetius in a loud voice. There is a low murmur but no-one stands to answer the question. The bell is sounded again. Hermetius will no doubt announce the beginning of the conference. I watch as he raises the scroll and clears his throat. However, before he can utter one word, the door slams open against the posterior wall, the noise reverberating around the chamber. Everyone is silent as we watch a young soldier stride insolently up the middle of the room; long, noisy strides, his tunic swishing and his metals clanging as he proceeds. He stops before Hermetius and pulls a scroll from his tunic. Hermetius, in his trained state of composure, does not react to this display of disrespect, but nor does he sit in its presence. Rising to his full height, he towers above the unwelcome intruder who now reads aloud from the scroll.

"I have come under instruction from the House of Pluto," the soldier reads. "It is to be announced that the Temple of Athena shall be of service to the House of Pluto by hosting a special banquet that is to be in gratitude to the three sails of traders that have recently harboured. The traders have brought many rare and valuable substances that will be of great benefit to the people of the city."

Of great benefit to the House of Pluto, I think scornfully, *and to the dark wizards that hide their ungodly magic behind its once esteemed identity*. A sudden murmuring of disagreement and shaking of heads tells me that my company agree with my thoughts. The House of Pluto was once a valuable source of comfort to all. Priests there were trained in the art of easing the grief of loss of loved ones. Pluto is God of the Underworld. He along with Persephone was a constant source of counsel and respite in times of hardship. But when these dark wizards took over several years ago, the priests of the house slowly began to succumb to the level of dark, banal and sometimes outright wicked spells of the wizards. They keep up the persona of aide to the grieving and heart-stricken, but behind the scenes everyone knows that evil lurks.

The priestess sitting to my right leans towards me and whispers in my ear, "If you ask me, Pluto has left His house a long time ago." I nod in agreement and strain to hear what the soldier is saying now. It is something about the

The Four Ascents

many wonderful herbs and medicines that can be used for the healing of many ailments.

The murmuring eventually quietens. Hermetius is about to speak. "On what authority do you make this announcement?" he demands to know from the young soldier.

"On the authority of the Oligarch," the soldier replies.

Immediately, outrage sweeps throughout the room. I am shocked. I cannot accept that the Oligarch, headed my own father, would serve the House of Pluto.

Thucymus jumps to his feet. "Your Grace," he implores Hermetius, "this cannot be. It is widely agreed upon that the House of Pluto be nothing more than a den of iniquity. Surely the Oligarch would not bend to the demands of such blatant adversity?"

"Silence, Thucymus," replies Hermetius without as much as a raised tone. His poise is to be admired and respected. It does not go unnoticed by the soldier, who is now not as seemingly arrogant and forthcoming as he was. "What is your name?" Hermetius asks him.

"Daniel, Your Grace," he replies with his head bowed.

Much more fitting, I am thinking. The soldier kneels. He looks around the room nervously, perhaps looking for back up from a hidden comrade. I notice that he is very young; not yet eighteen, I should think. I feel sorry for him. I wonder if he is lonely.

"Daniel, who was it that dispatched this announcement in your keeping?" Hermetius asks him with a kind voice.

And Daniel replies, "The Lord Perikles, Your Grace."

There is another outburst of condemnation. Many turn to look at me; some with accusation already written in their faces. Lord Perikles is my father, leader of the Oligarch. But no! I will not accept that Father is in league with the dark ones. I stand and stare at the young soldier who is now, like everyone else, staring at me. I search his face for a glimmer of untruth, but I find none. He is a young honest boy, merely conveying a message, a message of outrageous demands from one who is elected to lead and guide us, always with our best interests at heart; from my own father, who listened to my excited tales of the order knowing all along that he was in league with its enemy. I think about the way he tried to deter me from my path, insisting that I marry Philo. I was not much older than this boy I see before me now, this innocent and vulnerable soul. I wonder how much of my father's precious gold has lured the allegiance of the Athenian Army.

Eliza White Buffalo with Nicholas Black Elk

The boy looks into my eyes. I feel he beseeches me to speak for him. It is a disgrace; the responsibility should not fall on him; this poor boy, manipulated by those who ought to mould him into a brave warrior for freedom and not merely a pawn for wrong doing. I take courage from my promised graduation, and I present myself before Hermetius. All eyes are on me as I take the scroll from the boy's hand. There in my father's handwriting are the words announced by the brave young soldier just moments before. I recognise my father's signature. I feel no shame. Nor do I feel hurt. My memory flashes to the night before and my father and his comrades sitting around the table, deep in discussion about the metics. I recall how he had pulled me roughly through the door, frightened that someone would be watching the house. I suppose he was concerned that his secret little world would be discovered. Great Zeus! In our own house, how could he? Still, I am his daughter, and I shall defend his honour.

"Do you have something to say, Sister Demetria?" The high priest asks me.

"I have, Your Grace," I reply proudly. "I wish to say that in my father's defence, I have never been inclined to suspect that he may be in league with the House of Pluto. In fact, I am not entirely convinced that this situation is as it seems. If I am permitted, I would ask that Your Grace grant me leave to question my father on the matter."

The room is deathly quiet and my words hang in the silence; no-one, not even Hermetius, is willing to acknowledge their meaning. As people slowly exhale, they silently pray that Hermetius will grant me leave. They want me to go, taking with me the young soldier and leaving them to the luxury of dismissing the past few minutes. I look at Hermetius, usually so tall and mighty, but there is a weakness showing now about him. I see it as I would see those strange thoughts in my head. I see a dark energy creeping its way around Hermetius' body, wriggling a path into his middle. As I watch him perspire and hesitate, the weakness rapidly becomes powerful until Hermetius stands now, not so tall, not so mighty.

He speaks; his voice sounds different, low and fearful, "Let us hear what the Great Athena has to say on the matter," he decides. He looks about the room. "Sister Eumelia? Where is Sister Eumelia?"

"I am here, Your Grace," responds Eumelia, approaching the dais and coming to stand shoulder to shoulder with me. She touches my hand with hers and I am comforted. She will not judge me, or my father. A wash of love for her floods from my heart and warms the air.

The Four Ascents

Behind me, the young soldier begins to breathe. I had not noticed that he was not until this moment. I look to Hermetius and silently ask again to be dismissed. He nods at me, and I give a small bow before turning to go. As I pass by the boy I whisper to him that he may follow me, and without a glance sideways I proceed down the lengthy room and quietly exit. The boy lets the door slam noisily behind us.

"Pardon me, Miss, er . . . My Lady . . . . er . . ." he stutters, not sure how to address me or indeed, if he is dismissed even.

"Sister," I say, feeling sorry for him.

"Sorry, Sister. Pardon me, Sister, but I must report back to erm . . ." He is red-faced and has obviously realised who I am.

"You may be excused," I tell him, "thank you."

Oh the poor boy! He backs away from me until he reaches the door to the porch; then he makes a fumbled exit. It is all that I can do to contain my amusement. After a few moments, giving him time to put some distance between himself and the temple, I exit to the porch. I see him beyond. He is going in the direction of my father's house. An idea comes to me. If I follow him and stay hidden from sight, then I may discover exactly who it is that he is reporting back to. It may not be Father after all. Perhaps someone has betrayed him and copied his signature, pointing the responsibility in his direction. It is midday and I will be expected in the classroom shortly but this is much too good an opportunity to pass over. I shall make my excuses later when I have reported that Father is not in league with wrong doers.

So I set off following Daniel. Perhaps he will take a turn away from my Father's house before long. Alas, he does not, but leads me straight home. I hide in the olive grove, and watch as he knocks on our wooden door. From where I am, I can see who opens it; it is Eusebius. Words are exchanged which I cannot hear, and then Eusebius goes back into the house leaving Daniel standing outside. I try to get a little closer to the house but I am forced to crouch behind some shrubbery when Father appears at the door. My heart sinks. So, it is true. It *was* Father who sent the messenger. Some words are being exchanged, and now . . . Great Zeus! They are walking this way.

I keep low and dash back into the thicket of the olive trees. I shall need a good place to hide, and quick. Looking around frantically, I see nowhere. The tree trunks are too narrow to shield me. I shall have to do climb up. Without thinking I choose a tree and immediately begin to scale its trunk. I haven't done this since I was a child but it seems I have not forgotten the technique. Before long I am securely hidden in the leafy branches of the tree. Just in

Eliza White Buffalo with Nicholas Black Elk

time, for here comes Father. But it is not Daniel who is with him but a large man. Who can this be? They come closer. The man's hair is a strange colour, and I must say he looks quite strangely dressed. Great Zeus! It has to be; it's one of the metics. As the gods would have it, they stop just a little short of the very tree I am in; just within hearing distance. Perfect!

"You say the merchandise is in a safe place," Father is saying. "How can I be sure that it is good if you won't allow me to know where it is?"

"You have to trust me," replies the stranger in a rather burly voice. "When I have payment secured you will have your precious plant. Anyway, it is in the custody of that priest, what's his name? What is it for anyway?"

Good heavens!, it seems that this stranger who has brought to our city what it is that the House of Pluto wants, does not know himself what he carries. It could be that he is ignorant of whatever evil the dark lords have planned for his freight. Just another pawn, I suppose. I study his appearance as he speaks. His hair really does seem to be of a reddish colour, his beard too. He looks quite youthful despite a weather-beaten face. It is difficult to ascertain his height from above but he must at least be a foot taller than Father. Given that Father is considered to be of above average height that leaves the stranger in the 'unusually tall' bracket. Strange that I don't feel frightened of him, especially since my thoughts of late have turned to dark places where men like this breathe fire and the righteous are overthrown by dark lords. His voice, in a way reminds me of Hermetius. It has such presence that I feel somewhat commanded by it. He is speaking of sailings and weather; sailor's tales I think, but I am not altogether listening to his words but to the awesome sound of his voice. It surrounds me with awe, fills me with awe. I have never before felt such intoxication. I think I am drifting off somewhere in my mind. I had better be careful lest I fall from this tree and be discovered as an eavesdropper as well as hurt myself.

Father's angry voice startles me back to reality. "Just who do you think you are?" he demands angrily.

And the stranger replies haughtily, "I am Duncan, son of Deismut, the greatest man of Scotland ever to stake the shores of Erin with his mighty sword and staff. You will honour the agreement made between us. If you do not then I shall . . ."

But I cannot hear the rest of that sentence. The stranger's words are lost to me. They fade into oblivion as my heart thumps so wildly inside me that I hardly can breathe. I think I am about to pass out of consciousness. Just at the crucial moment I am able to have enough presence of mind to hold on to the tree, securing my body in its boughs. The world seems to spin as I drift further and further away. Faces pop in and out of my inner vision, faces of people from a long time ago. They are loving, concerned faces. They speak to me . . .

. . . "Phoenix! Phoenix!" they say. "Where are you?" As I watch, unable to communicate with them, they change. Who are they and why do they call me Phoenix? Now they are the faces of Eusebius and Philo. Why do they too call me Phoenix? Another face appears; it is the stranger. I feel myself drift further into another land. It is so cold here and the wind blows through me, chilling me. But no chill will ever again match what I feel now as I hear those same words that were spoken just moments ago: *I am Duncan, son of Deismut, the greatest man of Scotland ever to stake these shores of Erin with his mighty sword and staff . . .*

Reality drifts back into my consciousness. I am awake, slumped against the tree trunk. As I begin to contemplate what I just saw and heard terror takes me, and I know that this strange man is no stranger to me. Somehow, somewhere, perhaps in some other time when I was called Phoenix, I met this giant man before. I feel we battled with each other, he attempting to pull me into darkness and me overcoming his powerful magnetism. But I don't feel so powerful now. I am a mere undergraduate, innocent of the world and men like this. How can a vulnerable priestess possibly overcome such force? Down below me the same man is sitting on the ground with Father opposite him. Dear Athena, please don't let them stay there too long. My mouth is dry and I fear they will hear my frightened panting. I close my eyes and pray, "Dear Athena, help me. Oh Merciful Gods, help me." An image of Philo comes into my mind and I desperately plead, "Oh One God of All! Philo knows you to be the only god. Please come to my aid. Do not allow this terrible creature to take the piety I have studied so long to obtain."

When I open my eyes, the men are getting to their feet. I hold my breath and wait. Yes! Thank the gods! They are leaving the grove. I wait several minutes to ensure that they are back in the house, and then I descend from the tree and make my way shakily through the back of the grove.

Safely on the other side, a good distance from sight of the house I sit down upon a tree stump to rest. Beside me a little stream trickles its way down the hills towards the city. There it runs into large pools where the city dwellers bathe and wash their robes. Up here in the acropolis, the water is purer, pure enough for me to drink. I kneel on the grassy bank and cup my hands in the cold water. Then I bring them up to my mouth and sip the refreshing coolness. The sun is shining down brightly upon the hill. Soon its warmth and the refreshing water have a relaxing effect on me and I lie back upon the grass and close my eyes.

"Hello, My Lady. You have decided to come out of your hiding place I see."

I jump to my feet, startled by the unexpected voice. Here before me is the stranger, tall and awesome. I back up a little from him and my foot slips into the trickling stream. I do not remove it but step through unto the other side.

"I was not hiding, I shall have you know," I reply in an unmistakeably frightened voice.

The man's eyes widen in surprise and then his face softens. "Forgive me, My Lady," he says in a low softer voice yet with the same magnetic quality. "It was not my intention to startle you or to frighten you in any way. I was merely amused when I noticed you high in the branches. It was quite a surprise to see such a beautiful woman in such an unlikely place."

Great Zeus! What boldness! What outright insolence! "Do you know who I am?" I demand to know. Immediately my words seem to me to be spoken before in my meeting with this man. Only I think that perhaps they were *his* words, not mine, and I am now simply repeating them. How strange but how right it feels!

"No, but I'm sure you will enlighten me," the stranger replies.

So, he is arrogant as well as insolent. I will not tell him who I am. I shall however, insist on knowing who *he* is and why he is consulting with the government of this city. He said his name was Duncan. As I look at Duncan now, I see in his eyes a glint of amusement, but also an unmistakable kindness that I had not expected. His hair really is a fiery red.

"Why is your hair so red?" I ask thoughtlessly.

He laughs and his eyes crinkle up around the corners; the glint in them sparkles, white and silver. I feel such a fool, a silly girl with a crush on the local farmer's hand. The merchant's son had eyes like this and *he* laughed at everything I said. I remember I was quite angry at him for that, but I was secretly flattered that he found me interesting. I fear my face is now as red as Duncan's hair.

"Well now," he replies to my odd question, "where I come from most have hair of this colour. It is quite a blaze, is it not?"

I blush again. "And you come from Erin, is that correct?"

"You heard me say it, and it is true. Do you know where that is?" he asks me.

The Four Ascents

"Of course I do," I reply proudly. "I will have you know that my father has provided me with the very best teachers available."

"And your father is . . . ?"

"That is none of your business," I retort curtly. I glance towards the olive grove as I speak. How terribly, awfully obvious! He will work it out.

He does. "Ah! I see" he says with a smirk. "Father is Lord Perikles. So you were hiding from Father then?"

"I told you, I wasn't hiding," I insist. Oh dear! I feel so embarrassed and childish; it is obvious that I was hiding. But what will he do about it? Will he go to Father and tell him that they have been overheard, and by his very own daughter of all people?

Duncan holds his hands up in front of me in a gesture of submission. "Look!" he says, "We have gotten off to a bad start. Don't worry. I won't say a thing of your little tree time. Let's start again." He bows low to me. "Good day, My Lady, I am Duncan, son of Deismut."

How gracious of him to save my embarrassment like this! I find him suddenly very interesting and I am drawn to his witty charm and twinkling green eyes. He is not so terrifying at all.

"And you are?" he asks after a long pause in which a hundred questions race through my mind.

I want to know who he is, what he is like, what it would feel like to touch that red hair, what it would feel like to be kissed by that red mouth. Oh, I know Philo loves me deeply but right now I want to be loved by this strange, fascinating creature. "I am Demetria . . . Demetria of Perikles," I tell him, my heart thumping against my chest.

"Well now Demetria of Perikles," he says "it is an honour to make your acquaintance."

"And yours, Duncan, son of Deismut," I reply.

"Would Demetria of Perikles do me the honour of walking with me?" he asks.

Yes please, I think, but I say, "I am needed at the temple. I am a priestess there."

"It is on my way. Come, walk with me," he says offering me his arm. "It is not every day that I have the pleasure of such loveliness."

I blush again and look to my feet. Should I ask about the merchandise? Would it be too bold? I decide it is too good an opportunity to waste. Taking his arm, I ask him, "Duncan, pray tell me, what manner of plant is it that you bring to my father?"

Eliza White Buffalo with Nicholas Black Elk

"I can truthfully say that I do not know," he replies, not taking his gaze from my eyes. "Only that it is grown by the Erin folk in secret. Its name and origin is quite a mystery actually. Some say it is grown by the little folk but I don't know about that."

"The little folk?" I ask looking ahead of us.

"Fairies, leprechauns, that sort of thing."

"But that's nonsense, is it not?" I ask, pretending to be interested in the flowers that grow alongside the path; anything to keep from meeting his gaze.

"Don't let any of my men hear you say that," he says. "They would swear by the existence of the little folk. Did you not hear me tell your father of all the difficulties I had on my journey here? These men don't sleep unless the little folk say so. We had to ride the winds only when it was permitted, and lower our oars so as not to disturb the elementals of the seas. It's all very serious according to the Erin folk."

"Goodness!" I exclaim, thankful for an opportunity to giggle. "And so the plant is grown by the little folk, is it? And I suppose they must have given their permission for it to be shipped here to Greece?"

"Exactly," he says, laughing too. "I had to wait for three whole moons before I was allowed to set sail and I must wait for the new moon before I can embark on my return. Even then, if the elementals deem it impertinent to set sail I may be stuck here for all eternity, ha ha!"

"Ha ha!" I laugh at the idea but the thought of spending eternity with this man near sends tingles up my spine. I notice that when he laughs his green eyes sparkle even more. His teeth are very white. But I must not get distracted from my task. "I wonder what the plant is used for?" I ask him, feeling more comfortable. "Is it for medicine, do you think?"

"If you think that then you are innocent indeed," he tells me. "I believe its properties can be used for medicine, but I know that it's normally used for something quite different." So he does know what he delivers after all.

"And what is that?" I ask.

He stops walking to look at me properly, taking in my whole appearance. I feel naked before him and I blush again. "It has a strange effect on one, if taken by the mouth" he says, continuing to walk. "It gives one hallucinations and a 'high' experience that is said to be not of this world. If I am correct, then many have taken it in the hope of transcending reality only to lose their mind in the process."

"Why do you suppose the House of Pluto would want it?" I ask trying to trick him into talking about the dark lords' activities.

The Four Ascents

But he is too clever for me. "I'm sure I do not know why *anyone* would want it, let alone this House of Pluto you talk of. What is the House of Pluto anyway?"

He is not going to indulge my questioning. I try a different tactic. "No-one" I say, dismissing their involvement. "I was just wondering who would Father possibly be purchasing this plant for. What would he want of it himself if not to have it made into medicine for distribution to the local healers? I said the House of Pluto for they have many healers amongst them."

I may have asked too many questions because he suddenly stops walking, and holding my uncomfortable gaze for a moment he says, "My Lady, it pains me that I cannot satisfy your curious mind, and alas, we have come to the end of our walk. I must go this way. I bid you good day, My Lady. I hope we shall meet again. Farewell!" He bends and takes my hand in his. Bringing his lips down upon my hand he plants a tender kiss upon the soft skin. Shivers tingle up my spine and my tummy flutters with hidden wings.

"Farewell Duncan" I utter, "Until we meet again." And with a grin and a twinkling of his eyes, he is gone. I watch him walk away. He turns and waves and I wave back, smiling broadly.

I almost run back to the temple I am that excited. I feel so alive and breathless with joy. Could this be true love? Is this what Philo feels for me? I can't imagine so. His love is protective and solid. His love keeps me on the ground, not like this. I feel if I am not tied down soon I will fly off the face of the earth. I reach the temple in a dream. The doors are all closed firmly. I skip to the private quarters where Jason and some of the higher priests live. Everywhere is firmly shut. Eumelia's chambers are on the east side of the campus; I run there and rap loudly upon her door. Jason opens it.

"Where have you been, Demetria?" he asks immediately. "We've been looking for you every where we could think of. We even went to your home but your mother said she hadn't seen you since this morning. We were worried about you, silly. You seemed so upset about the announcement in the temple."

"Oh Jason, *dear* Jason, I'm fine, really I am," I pant breathlessly. "Give me time to get in and I will tell you where I've been."

"I must say, you're in a much better mood than I expected," he says. "Could it be that our little graduate in the making is learning to accept what is?"

But I am too rapt in my excitement to play teacher and student. Pushing past him, I get straight to the point. "I have a lot to tell you" I say, entering the sitting area. Eumelia is there with Hermetius and Thucymus. Everyone is so solemn. Eumelia and Jason are demanding to know where I've been and

Thucymus is staring into a goblet of wine. By the way he is lolling on the chaise it seems he may have drunk several goblets full already. I glance at Hermetius. He is holding his head low, avoiding my gaze. Poor Hermetius, this is as much a blow to him as it is to me.

"Demetria, you must tell us exactly what you know," demands Eumelia.

"Indeed, pray tell us, for then we can quash the nasty rumours that have started regarding your part in all this," adds Jason. He doesn't look at me when he speaks but to the floor, red faced. Eumelia looks near to tears. What in the name of Zeus!

"What?" I ask them, confused. "What rumours do you speak of? What do you mean by my part? Surely you don't think I would know anything of this?" There are tears in Eumelia's eyes and she turns to look at Hermetius. "Your Grace! Pray tell me what is wrong" I continue, imploring Heremtius to look at me. He remains awkwardly silent and keeps his gaze averted. "Your Grace, please speak to me. Jason, you believe me don't you? I would never have anything to do with The House of Pluto, you know that."

Jason takes my arm and ushers me onto the chaise next to Thucymus. He kneels at my feet and looks into my face inquiringly. "Demetria, we need to know where you have been and who you have spoken to," he says solemnly. "We've been looking for you ever since you left the temple with the young soldier who announced . . . you know."

"But that is exactly what I've been trying to tell you Jason," I reply impatiently. "I followed Daniel . . . the soldier . . . to see where he'd go . . . . to see who he would report back to. I had hoped it wouldn't be but it was . . . it was Father. I kept close by and well . . . it was Father who sent him on his way. But there was another man there too."

Jason glances at Hermetius who is suddenly alert and attentive. Now that I have their attention I go on, though I am somewhat nervous. "They went into the olive grove to talk, and I heard. I heard every word they said . . . well, most of it."

"Were you *with* them?" asks Jason, not wanting to believe I could be involved.

"I . . . er . . . I was . . . hiding . . . in a tree. I climbed a tree and hid in the branches."

"What?" he chuckles, "you were up a tree?"

"In the name of the gods," declares Eumelia, "you could have been hurt. Are you alright?"

The Four Ascents

"I'm fine, I'm fine, don't fuss," I tell them. "Why do you always have to treat me as if I'm useless? I'm quite skilled at climbing those trees. I did it all the time when I was little."

"Sorry, go on," says Jason. I turn to Hermetius who holds my gaze for a moment before looking to the floor.

"It was one of the metics," I go on, watching Hermetius' reaction carefully. He glances up at Eumelia, and then rises to walk to the other side of the room where with folded arms he stands facing the wall. Something is not right. Why did he glance at Eumelia like that when I mentioned the stranger? Why won't he look at me?

"What did they say, Perikles and the metic . . . what did they say?" Jason's face is kind as he speaks. He smiles. "It's alright my little songbird. No-one is accusing you of anything. We just need to know what is going on."

"For all our sakes!" adds Eumelia, anxiously. I continue, really nervous now.

"Father wanted something that the metics have brought with them; a plant of some sort, and Duncan wouldn't give it until Father had paid his men for their trouble" I tell them.

"Duncan?" asks Jason.

"The stranger; he's Duncan of Deismut, from Erin. Well, he's Scottish but he went to Erin with his father many years ago" I explain.

"How do *you* know who he is?" asks Hermetius in a loud impatient voice. Jason gives him a look that says, *be careful.*

"He . . . he told me," I stutter.

Again Jason warns Hermetius to be careful with a cautionary glance. Then he turns back to me. "What do you mean, he told you?" he asks me. "*When* did he tell you? Where you there at this meeting? Did you *speak* with this man and your father?"

"No, I was up the tree. I told you." My nervousness increases and I defend myself. "Why won't anyone believe me? I have nothing to do with the matter, nothing at all."

"We do believe you, Demetria," Jason calmly replies, "but you're not making yourself clear. When did the stranger tell you his name?"

"When the meeting was over; Father had gone into the house and I was in the upper meadow by the stream at the back of the olive grove. The stranger must have seen me go there and followed me." I am careful not to call Duncan by his name again and I won't tell them that he knew I was there the whole time. "He came up behind me and spoke," I go on. "I must say, he

Eliza White Buffalo with Nicholas Black Elk

startled me at first but then he seemed nice. He told me he was from Erin, Duncan of Deismut . . . . and," I hang my head before saying, "I told him I was Demetria of Perikles."

"What!" roars Hermetius, making me jump in my seat. His face is red and he is now pacing up and down the room waving his arms angrily. I can't imagine how he ever came to be like this. I have never seen him any other way but calm and poised. Does he know more about this matter than it first seemed? He can't possibly think I'm to blame, can he? He darts towards me and grabbing Jason, he almost throws him to one side in order to reach me.

In a heartbeat Eumelia leaps between us. She takes hold of his arms and speaks calmly and firmly. "Your Grace, don't do this," she insists. "You know Demetria is innocent. Isn't it obvious? She has no idea what is going on, and you're scaring her. Now stop it this instant!"

Hermetius stares at her, breathing heavily, then backs off. He sits down again and hangs his head in his hand, rubbing his forehead. "Arhh!" he groans frustrated, "What in the name of the gods are we to do now? I fear that all is lost."

"We don't know that Your Grace," Eumelia answers him, "and Demetria is here now with us." She waits for Hermetius to look at her before she continues. "What can possibly happen? She's safe with us."

"Very well then," he relents. "But we must discuss where we go from here. She can't possibly go back to her father's house."

Suddenly, Thucymus, who is sitting beside me, takes my hand and jumps up pulling my arm. "She'll come with me," he slurs. "I'll look after her for you, Your Grace."

"No, leave me alone. I'm going nowhere with you," I struggle. I pull my hand free, and demanding to know what is going on, I turn to Hermetius. "Your Grace, I'm sorry if I appear insolent, but you have to tell me what on earth is going on," I demand. "*Why* would I not be safe? Who or what would threaten me?" But Hermetius doesn't answer me.

Jason sits down beside me where Thucymus had lolled moments before. "Leave us, Thucymus," he orders him. When Thucymus closes the door behind him Jason puts a brotherly arm around my shoulders and pulls me into an embrace. "Please don't fret," he croons, "trust me. I wish to keep you safe from the metics is all. None of us know what they are capable of."

"But Duncan is lovely," I explain. "Really he is. And his men are just a bunch of simple Irish peasants. They have no idea of what they are involved in and I'm quite sure Duncan hasn't either. He doesn't even know what the plant is for, the one that he carried."

"Perhaps, although I doubt that he is that innocent," Jason says. "He couldn't be that naïve, and until we know what his real business here is we have a duty to insure your safety, what with your father being involved especially. Now don't look at me like that. We all know that Perikles wouldn't put you in danger but it may not be in his power to keep you safe if . . . well, anyway, I just want to know that you're safe."

"Why doesn't she stay *here*?" suggests Eumelia, "I'll look after her. Lord and Lady Perikles will not suspect a thing. We can say that it is in preparation for the graduation."

"Did anyone follow you here?" Hermetius asks in a tone more in keeping with his usual manner. I relax a little, leaning against Jason. I find myself wishing it was Philo I was leaning against, my lovely, safe, dependable Philo. All the excitement of my meeting with Duncan is gone. It is only Philo that I want now. What is love anyway? When the dream ends and the darkness creeps around us, all we want is to know that someone is there, and Philo will always be there for me; I have no doubt about that.

"No-one," I reply to Hermetius.

"That's settled then," declares Eumelia, "you will stay with me. Your Grace, I promise I will not leave her side until all this is over."

"And if the words of Athena come to pass?" Hermetius asks.

"Then I shall stay with her and bring her home. I will not lose her, Your Grace. I promise."

"We both do," adds Jason. Hermetius bows to them both in turn, then to me.

"Let it be so," he says. "I bid you farewell." He opens the door and leaves. Eumelia goes after him.

"Your Grace!" she calls, "Thucymus! It might be a good idea to insure his discretion. I fear the wine may have loosened his tongue, and you know what he's like."

"Indeed," Hermetius calls back to her. "Farewell Sister. May the gods be with you, with you both."

"And with you, Your Grace," she replies.

∽∞∽∞∽∞∽∞∽∞∽∞∽∞∽∞∽∞∽∞∽∞∽∞

It's a beautiful morning, though Eumelia and I walk so quickly to the temple that its beauty is wasted on us. Last night I questioned her incessantly.

I wanted to know what was going on. There has to be more to this than a mere distrust of the metics. Still, many people *are* frightened. But now I know different. I have spoken and been quite familiar, to my shame, with their leader. I am quite charmed by him actually. I lay awake last night in a strange bed, thinking about a strange man with fiery red hair and twinkling green eyes. I must admit, I was too excited to sleep. I wonder if I will chance upon him today. Or perhaps he will make it his intention to chance upon me. Oh, how wonderful that would be! I lay awake wondering about the strange vision I had of meeting with him before. I have convinced myself that he has nothing to do with the giant red men of my vision. I have to have known him in my dreams once, perhaps when I was little and lonely. Perhaps he was my handsome warrior who had come on a golden chariot to whisk me away to a magical land. So maybe I have concocted the fearful vision from confused memories of a dream. Or perhaps I knew him when I was on Atlantis. Perhaps like Eusebius, he is from another lifetime when I was Eliza and he was my handsome lover. Eumelia says that we incarnate again and again with the same souls. If that is true, then I would have known Philo in that lifetime too. Was he my protector then also?

I glance at Eumelia. She has been unusually secretive since the horrible meeting last night. She refused to answer any of my questions and insisted that I hush. "It's for your own good," she kept saying.

"Eumelia?" I begin now.

"Demetria, I cannot answer your questions," she replies impatiently. "You know that. If you want to ask Hermetius today then that is your choice but please do not ask me to disobey his orders."

"I'm not asking about that," I tell her. "I want to know about reincarnation. Do you think I knew Philo in another life?"

"Demetria, please . . ." she replies impatiently. "There is no time for idle talk today; we must hurry. His Grace wishes to call a conference this morning and I want to speak with him before it starts."

"What's the conference about? Has he decided to shelter the metics? Perhaps he has no choice. If he wants to . . ."

Eumelia almost shouts, "Demetria, hush! I don't want to hear any more questions. Didn't you listen to one word Jason said about acceptance?" Here they come again about acceptance; you don't need to question *why* things happen in your life, they keep saying; you just have accept them and know that everything happens for a reason. Try not to be upset, they keep telling me; all is in divine order. But Athena herself wouldn't have the patience I've had so far.

"For the love of the Gods, Eumelia, I have a right to know what's going on under my very nose," I insist angrily.

I stop walking and hold her still, waiting for an answer. How can she expect me not to be angry when everyone knows my business but me? How can she expect me to just accept that and act as if all is perfect? Well it's not perfect. It's far from perfect, and I *am* angry. I am furious, and I *will* ask Hermetius. No, I will *demand* that he tell me what is going on.

Eumelia shrugs out of my grip and walks on without a word. I follow her, a little ashamed now at my outburst. Where was the piety in that? Hermetius and Jason are waiting for us in the temple porch when we arrive. Sheepishly, we greet them good morning.

"Sister Demetria, may I see you in my chamber first thing?" Hermetius asks me. I bow my head to him, meaning 'as you wish'. We all walk in silence into the temple and I follow Hermetius to his chamber on the east corridor. "Sit down please" he says when he has closed the door behind us. I sit on a cushion on the floor. Hermetius goes into the food hall and returns with two goblets of pomegranate juice. He offers one to me.

"Thank you," I utter nervously, taking the goblet from him. I sip the juice as I watch him place another cushion on the floor in front of me and sit down on it cross legged. He sips his own drink and then places the goblet on the floor. Folding his arms, he stares at me, lost in thought. His expression is worrisome. It seems he is nervous, perhaps uneasy with what he is about to say to me. This new Hermetius does nothing to dispel any fears I may have about recent events. The old Hermetius would have put me at ease solely with his calm, poised demeanour. I am that on edge my heart is beating quite fast and my mouth is dry. I sip the juice again, then gulp it down in one go before placing the goblet on the floor beside his.

"Demetria," he finally says, "I have thought long and hard about last night's meeting. It must have been quite confusing for you."

"Yes, Your Grace, and I . . ."

"No, No, let me finish," he says. "What I have to say is that you conducted yourself with considerable poise given the circumstances. As you know, that is a quality I admire. I only wish that I had behaved with an equal decorum, but I fear I did not, and for that I am most sorry. Please forgive me."

Eliza White Buffalo with Nicholas Black Elk

"Er . . . yes, of course." I keep my eyes lowered to his goblet of juice. I could do with that right now. I wonder what he would say if he knew how I had lost my temper just a short time ago.

"In light of your piety and maturity in this matter," he continues, "I feel that you deserve to know what I do. Sister Eumelia and Brother Jason know of this also and so it is appropriate that they join us." He rises and goes to the door. Opening it, he moves aside for Eumelia and Jason to enter. They must have been waiting outside the door. I say nothing. I am content that I am to be told everything. They have simply obeyed orders from Hermetius, and for that they should be admired, not rebuked.

Seeing the manner in which I am sitting Eumelia throws down some more cushions, and she and Jason sit. Hermetius goes to fetch more juice and returns with a pitcher full and two more goblets. Having poured a generous measure for every one of his guests, he sits once more cross-legged before me. "Some time ago I had a dream" he announces. I dreamed of dark times in the future. In these dark times the Temple of Truth is in ruins. The statues of Apollo and Athena are destroyed and their help is lost to all. People run amuck, following their own individual gods. There is much joviality. They eat like wild beasts and give in to temptations of the flesh. All over the city there are orgies. Husbands lie with others' wives, and no-one even knows that they are living lives of debauchery." He pauses a while, shaking his head in dismay, then continues, "If it were but a foolish dream, I would rest easy, but some two moons ago I was called to the Oracle. The Lady of Delphi, the Great Athena wished to speak to me. What was spoken through the lips of our Sister Eumelia that day will haunt my every breath until Athena speaks again and tells me that all is well. She spoke of you, Demetria, and of a tragedy that will be of your making. I believe that time is now and that is why we must keep you safe." Hermetius' voice begins to wane and he looks to Eumelia to help him, "Sister, I pray that you relay the prophecy as it was given to you."

The prophecy; surely not my prophecy, I am thinking in panic. I shift my position on the cushion. No, my prophecy is good. It is one of harmony and peace among all peoples. Besides, Athena would not have spoken it to Hermetius before *me*. Amir said that the prophecy remains in my heart and that I would be the one to fulfil it. Hermetius is wrong; it is my destiny to build, not to destroy.

Eumelia speaks now. "I am Athena," she begins to repeat Athena's words. "I am Truth, and I am proud of all my warriors of truth who speak in my name. I am proud and I love you, each and every one. You shall know that

The Four Ascents

there is one among you that will forsake my truth, though I love her and will always love her. On that day my temple will be overthrown by darkness and the world will no longer hear my word. She who you now see before you is soon to be challenged by a stranger in your land and she will fall from this house of grace. She will be blinded and struck dumb until her name is spoken by the Holiest of Holy."

When Eumelia finishes everyone is silent. In the space between us is an awkward pulling and pushing of energy, as each of us in our own fear try to make sense of the words just heard. For the others who have heard this before and have most likely made up their minds what it means, it must be deepening their beliefs, cementing what they have decided is the truth. For me though, it rattles my being like a wicked child with a toy. It un-grounds me to an extent that I feel I want to hold on to something safe for fear that I may be destroyed. Can this really be me that Athena has spoken of? Perhaps they were mistaken. Oh where is Philo now? This is the second time I have yearned for his presence.

I break the silence with a tiny voice, "Are you sure it was me that Athena spoke of?"

Eumelia answers "We both saw you in the flame," she says.

I look into each of their faces, silently commanding them to look at me. In each strained countenance I see the pain and anguish that they must have harboured since that day. I see their love for me etched clearly in lines of worry and tear stained eyes. I look at my goblet of juice and absent-mindedly lift it to my lips with a trembling hand. The juice feels alien to me as it passes down my throat and into my stomach. It lies in me like a weight causing me to gasp for breath. Frantically I search their faces for evidence of a mistake, for a tiny glimmer of hope that means they have the wrong person. I am to graduate, to be exalted into the house of the soul, not to fall into the lower realms where none are safe from the fires of hell. The fires of hell! Oh Great Zeus! I know what this is all about.

"No," I utter, shaking my head at them, "I won't let it happen."

"Nor I, child; I will protect you," Hermetius says, though he doesn't sound convinced that he can.

"But you don't understand," I tell him excitedly. "I saw this coming. I saw the red men."

"Red men? Saw what coming, Demetria?" asks Eumelia worried.

Taking a deep breath I ponder what I am about to tell them. Would speaking it make it more real? Will it actually make it happen? I _have_ to tell them. I have to tell them everything now. They are the only ones who can stop it. Oh why do I constantly see Philo in my mind? Can it be that he will keep me safe?

"Your Grace, grant me one favour?" I beseech him.

Hermetius nods to me, "Speak."

"May I have permission to go to Philo? I do not wish to disrespect the order, but I feel that he is the one to protect me from this."

But Hermetius replies, "Demetria, what can a farmer do that I cannot? No, you are safer here. Tell me what you saw coming."

But I won't give up. I mustn't give up. And so I beg, "Could we just have him here then . . . to be here with me? Jason could fetch him."

Hermetius looks at me as if I am losing my mind, but my mind is quite clear now. If I am to let this pass me over then I need Philo. Hermetius can see that I am not going to back down on this, and so he relents. He gets up and walks to a table, puts his goblet down there and picks up a little gong. Sounding the gong he shakes his head. He thinks I am lost in panic; that I don't know what I am saying or doing, but as long as I can get Philo to come to me, then that is all that matters, Hermetius can think what he likes.

I look to Eumelia and implore her, "Eumelia, *you* know what Philo is to me. I have often spoken to you of the protective way he loves me."

"*I* can protect you, Demetria," insists Jason. "I have said countless times how I am to watch over you and Eumelia here. Will I not suffice?"

"No, Jason," I reply. "I'm sorry, but Philo is different. You may watch over my spiritual needs but Philo keeps me safe physically. I don't know why, but I feel it is this, his physical protection, his earthly love for me that keeps me at his side. When I'm with Philo I feel that no matter what happens, no matter what worries or responsibilities I have, I can relax totally. When I'm with him he takes care of all my needs. I don't have to make any choices when he's there. If anyone can keep me from error it is he."

"You love him."

"Yes, yes I do, but . . ."

"But what?"

"It doesn't matter. Yes, I love him, and he loves me." *But what about Duncan,* I think to myself, *Am I not in love with him?* I ignore my thoughts. I want to tell them about the vision I had about the giant, red fire-breathing men and the dark lords who overthrow the gods, but before I can the door opens and Thucymus enters the chambers.

"Your Grace," he bows, greeting Hermetius. Thank heavens he is sober.

90

"Thucymus, I wish for you to fetch someone for me," Hermetius tells Thucymus. "Demetria, where is Philo to be found?" he asks me.

"He'll be in the market place, on the far eastern side," I reply. "He sells his pitchers of goat's milk from there."

"Thucymus," says Hermetius, "go to the east side of the market and locate Philo the goat farmer. Bring him here to these chambers. Tell him nothing of recent events or of why we would have him here."

"As you wish, Your Grace," replies Thucymus. He shoots a curious glance at me before leaving the room.

"Now, why don't you tell us what it is that you saw coming?" Hermetius asks me. He sits again on the floor. It is clear to see that he is tired and weighed down by the burden that has been placed upon him. He asks Eumelia to fetch him some wine even though it is yet early morning.

I feel somewhat guilty now, but not for the burden itself, for as yet I have erred none. I feel guilty for the added burden of placing certain conditions on him before I would respond to his inquiries, and for the terrible things I am about to relate to him. I clear my throat, and with some courage gained from the prospect of having Philo by my side, I tell of the dark vision. "For some time now," I begin, "I have felt cold within me and an alien being attacks me from within. When the sun goes down beneath the world I feel a damp chill run through my being, its icy fingers reaching into every sacred place within. I have terrible thoughts of places far away . . . only . . . ." I pause; the realisation that they may not be so far away sends chills through me. I shiver and wrap my arms about me.

"What is it, Child? What has upset you?" inquires Eumelia who has just re-entered the room and is setting a pitcher of wine down on the floor beside Hermetius.

"Oh Eumelia, you don't know what these places can be like," I tell her without explanation. "There is fire there; great big fires that burn with the stench of hot burning flesh, and giant red men that breathe fire, sending innocent souls to a hellish demise. Dark lords of the night fight with the gods and the gods are powerless before them. It is terrible, just terrible."

I cry, for the vision seems to be upon me and the terrible things I dreaded happening are destined to be mine. Athena has spoken. It will be as it is. If the love of my dearest Philo cannot save me now then all hope is gone, for me *and* for the temple. And it will be because of my failure to pass the unknown challenge that lies ahead. Oh I cannot bear the shame!

Jason takes my hand and hands me a kerchief. "Don't cry, My Little Songbird," he says kindly, "Here, dry your tears and give us a smile. It's a dream, that's all; you had a bad dream and it has filled your waking hours."

"It's not a dream, Jason," I sniff. "It's real. It's a vision, a foretelling of things to come; and it's not only coming to me but to all of us. Your Grace, did I not see that very same energy worm its way around you just yesterday morning? Did it not make a path into your being through your solar plexus? I saw it; it unnerved you, did it not? Tell me I'm wrong and then I will take sole responsibility for whatever fate befalls the temple."

"Demetria!" exclaims Eumelia. She will not hear me speak this way of our high priest.

I want to defend my words but I cannot; there is no excuse for speaking of Hermetius in that manner. He gulps down the last of the wine in his goblet. "No, Eumelia, Demetria is correct," he admits. "I cannot hide it. Not now, not from you who are my dearest companions. We ought to stick together in this awful time, not keep vital information from one another."

"But what are you saying, Your Grace?" Eumelia asks disbelievingly; "that *you* have felt this alien being? Has it invaded *your* thoughts? Jason and I are depending on you, Your Grace. How can we possibly keep Demetria safe if you are not well enough to guide us?"

"Calm down, calm down," he replies. "I have felt something yes, but I am still here, although I feel it should be as your peer. From now on we work as equals. It's the only way to overcome this alien energy. We shall face it head on, and by the power of the gods we shall demand that it go back where it came from."

Hermetius' words give me much needed hope and suddenly it becomes very clear to me; I know what it is that has threatened us and I know how it is to be stopped. "No" I declare. I stand up and say it again, "No. It's me that it wants. Athena has said as much and I am the one that saw it coming. It has come for me and *I* will face it. I can beat it!"

"What makes you think that? No, I won't permit you," says Hermetius, dismissing my words with a hand gesture which I ignore.

"I can," I tell him. "I know I can. It's my destiny. I chose it."

"What?" Hermetius exclaims.

Oh, the look on their faces when they listen to my tale about the two roads; as if they are seeing me for the very first time. "Here within me," I touch my heart space, "resides a power. It was given to me a very long time ago in another place. It is a red stone of power, a prophecy of harmony among all beings. Some day I will make that prophecy sing, but until then I must walk a long road. It's a road of difficulties. I *will* be challenged and at times I will feel that I cannot go on, but I will. This shall be one such challenge. But there is hope, for where the difficult road crosses with another, a good road of spiritual understanding, there is a place that is holy. This place resides within me where the red stone of power sits ready to sing."

"But Demetria . . ." Eumelia is worried.

"It is fine, Eumelia" I explain. "We know now that I will be challenged soon. I feel that the red men of my vision *are* the metics. They have brought something bad to the city. I know what it is I have to do. I must go to The House of Pluto and I must find that plant and destroy it."

"Demetria . . ." she pleads with me.

"Please, Eumelia, let me finish. I must destroy this plant or at least stop whatever it is The House of Pluto intends to do with it. If I succeed then I shall have overcome the challenge fulfilling one part of the prophecy. One day the red stone of power will sing. If I fail this challenge then according to Athena I shall fall from Grace."

Finally Eumelia gets to speak, "But if you fail you will fall into those very places that you fear; the fire and the . . . . no, Demetria, we cannot allow you to do this."

Dear Eumelia, she doesn't understand that this is how it will be; there is no other way. "I have a choice," I tell her, "but I have already made that choice. I chose to walk the road of difficulties. It is the only way for the prophecy to be fulfilled on earth. That is why I must do this, don't you see; this is all happening because of my choices. I was the one to create this and I will be the one to destroy it."

"You don't know that. You can't possibly know that," she says.

"I know," I affirm looking at each of them in turn, and I explain, "It was me that brought the red men upon us. When I first saw Duncan I knew. I was transported back to a time when he challenged me before. Maybe it was a vision of the future that I had in another time; it feels like that. But whatever it was then I had succeeded in overcoming his temptations. Now he has come again and he has brought this challenge before me. The thing is he's not alone. He has brought an army of red men with him. If I can only get by them and destroy the plant they brought to The House of Pluto then I will have beaten him for good this time." I look around at my company. I can see in their faces that they believe me.

"But what about the dark lords," asks Jason, "you will have to get by them too?"

"That's correct but I'll find a way," I reply. "Your Grace, you are very quiet. What say you?" I ask feeling, positive and in control.

"I have no objection," he replies to my relief. "You speak with honour and with integrity and so I give you my blessing and I wish you luck. It is our only hope."

"Thankyou. Jason, what do you say?" I ask.

Jason puts an arm around my waist, "Come here, My Little Songbird. Eumelia, come join us," he says to Eumelia. He reaches the other arm around her and embracing us both in this way he says, "I say that we three together can overcome any obstacle, any challenge that threatens us. You will not do this alone Demetria; Eumelia and I will help you. What do you say, Eumelia?"

"I say yes," says Eumelia. "I will go with you into The House of Pluto and together we will meet this challenge."

"And I will stay in the temple and be like a spy among the metics," adds Jason. I will probe and push and I will find what I can to aid you both. Maybe I can get my hands on the plant myself and if I do then I will destroy it without a moment's hesitation. And no matter if we find the plant or not these people will not succeed in bringing you down with them, Demetria. And do you know why? Because with your great love, Eumelia, and with my powerful faith, and with your gift of hope, Demetria, we are a trinity that can overthrow *any* dark power. Are these not the attributes of the heavens themselves? This powerful triangle shall be insurmountable to any darkness that dares to try. So from this moment forwards we shall remain united until our mission is done."

"Until the prophecy is complete," adds Eumelia.

"Until the prophecy is complete," says Jason.

The Red Stone of Power leaps within my heart space. "Until the prophecy is complete," I say.

∞∞∞∞∞∞∞∞∞∞∞∞∞∞∞∞∞∞∞∞∞∞∞∞∞∞∞∞∞∞

The video comes to a stop again. And Black Elk speaks . . .

"My Dear Rose, you have seen how the challenge presents itself. You understand that our greatest illusions are reflected in our world, in the faces and voices of those souls who work with us to lift us up. Remember

The Four Ascents

the time in Egypt, when the challenge was first presented? The dark illusion was overpowered in that instance, but like all great lessons, it comes again, seeming stronger, seeming insurmountable. If only Demetria can remain alert. If only, through the presence of her spirit, through the whisperings of her crystal heart can she consciously see what is before her. Spirit dwells within her and stands before her, a red giant, a messenger of hope. May she see the pride in his eyes; may she feel the lust in his loins and hear the illusion in his words. May she open her eyes of spirit so that she may see her pride, her fiery lust for exaltation. May she open her ears of spirit so that she may hear the illusion in her belief. Spirit stands before her, a simple goat farmer, a messenger of hope. May she see the love in his eyes; may she feel the magic in his loins and hear the truth in his words. May she open her eyes of spirit so that she may see her love, her magic; may she open her ears of spirit so that she may hear her truth. Spirit stands before her as two roads, one in light and one in darkness; both shall lead her to truth. She is given free will to choose which road she will follow, and as long as she comes to the holy place where the two roads meet she will know that she is not alone, for her beloved source is with her on her journey. And so, Rose, you have understood that the way the soul returns to Source is through the crystal heart. The Holy Spirit is born of the Father and of the Mother, and it is with constant attention to its truth that the path is made easy. Demetria is beginning to listen to The Red Stone of Power, her crystal heart. But she is still arrogant and refuses to see that the real challenge lies within. Watch now as the challenge increases in power, for the higher the soul climbs towards wholeness, the greater the temptation is to embrace the illusion of separateness."

Chapter Six

The search for Philo

And so the story continues . . .

"I won't wait any longer. I must sound the gathering bell before Lord Percius arrives," says Hermetius pacing the room.

It is gone midday and Thucymus has not yet returned with Philo. My shame is growing with every impatient step His Grace makes. Ever since he was thirty three years old Hermetius has held the seat of High Priest with poised dignity. His handsome stature and godly demeanour has until now never been challenged. But when I saw that alien energy worming its evil way into his middle I knew that he would meet this terrible thing. Just as I saw it coming towards me, I could see that it would also come to him. He is like me; or rather I am like him. I sculpted myself on him, the way he held his head high and never gave in to question about his priesthood. Now I understand Eumelia's caution when she told me that my pride would be my downfall. Just look at him now, pacing up and down the room like some poor distraught creature in a cage. Where is his great pride in himself now? What I see before me is a shadow of greatness; a frightened, godless creature, full of fear and uncertainty. Jason is twice the priest that he is, just as Eumelia is twice the priestess that I will ever make. But is it too late for poor Hermetius? Is it too late for me? Will Athena's prophecy come to be completed or is there hope that this trinity of power that is Jason, Eumelia and me can save our souls and our temple from eternal demise?

"That is it!" Hermetius decides. "I will sound the gathering bell. Demetria, you are to stay close to Eumelia and Jason, and speak to no metic. Before the day is done I fear the temple will be full of them."

"Eumelia," I whisper to her in the corridor on our way to the conference chamber. "Do you think we could skip the conference and go to look for Philo ourselves?"

"Don't be silly," she replies. "He will be here in time. Thucymus won't let his master down. Besides, we must attend the conference. If we are to beat this thing then we need to know every little detail of what the House of Pluto is planning."

The Four Ascents

"I'm not sure I trust Thucymus," I tell her. "You should have seen the way he looked at me when he left for the market place. And last night he was pretending to be much more intoxicated than he really was; I am quite sure about that. I was sitting beside him remember and I could feel the deception hanging there in the air."

"Are you sure it wasn't simply the fact that we were not telling you the whole story?" she asks me.

"No, I've felt that kind of energy before," I tell her. "A trader stayed at our home once with his young son. The boy was just a little older than me and I could feel how he was pretending to be so well mannered when all the time he was hatching ways of torturing me and poor Eusebius who didn't deserve such ill treatment."

"You never mentioned him before," Eumelia says with concern. "Did he hurt you?"

"Not much, but you should see what he did to poor Eusebius. It's the same evil I sense from Thucymus. I tell you, the man is not to be trusted."

Eumelia thinks about this for a moment. "We shall discuss it later with Jason," she decides. "Somehow, I feel our high priest is not up to such a discussion. Plus, I doubt very much that he will hear a word against his beloved assistant."

The conference chamber is packed when we enter. The entire priesthood is present, and the government. Before taking my seat I quickly surmise that Thucymus is here, sitting at the left of Hermetius as usual. Where is Philo then? Did he not find him? Surely he has not left again? No, Philo would never leave me when I need him. I glance at Eumelia, seated across the room with the other elders. She catches my eye and I can tell that she has also noted Thucymus' presence. The gathering bell is sounded and a hush falls over the room. As Hermetius rises to his feet I am astounded to see that sitting on his right hand side is Lord Percius. Lord Percius is High Priest at The House of Pluto. So he has got his wish then. Please don't tell me that Father is here too, but of course he would be, seated with the others from the government. Father is a proud and honourable man. He would never desert his duty because of a mere rumour. I strain my neck to look for him. Yes, he is here, proud and upright as usual.

Hermetius clears his throat loudly. I can hear the terror in his voice, "Ahem! I have called you all here today to discuss how we are to distribute the many goods that the three sails of traders have brought to our shore.

With us we have Lord Percius, representative of The House of Pluto, and Lord Perikles, our esteemed Oligarch. I trust that you will all give them a warm welcome." There is a round of applause as Lord Percius and Father both stand and bow. "By this evening our temple will be quite busy," continues Hermetius. "I apologise for any inconvenience this may cause but it will only be for a short time, I assure you. The traders, who have hailed from Erin I believe, will carry in bundles of goods that are to be distributed proportionately to the various homes and houses throughout the city. For now they will be stored in designated rooms within the counselling chambers. The doors are already marked with the seal of Pluto and no-one is permitted to enter within. Some of the traders themselves will be accommodated within the same chambers and will be permitted to avail of the temple food hall. Normal temple activities are suspended until further notice. However, the inner cella will remain available for supplication, so it is imperative that we have quiet respect for those in prayer."

I imagine that last remark was directed at Lord Percius and his metics. Hermetius takes a deep breath and continues, "Now, Lord Percius would like to say a few words and then you are free to go."

Hermetius takes his seat again, thankful that part is over. He slumps slightly in his chair; his head tilted downwards a little. I fear his strength has left him. I cannot blame him because The House of Pluto has a grand support within the city. With the Oligarch on its side Hermetius will have had no choice but to meet Lord Percius' demands. I must admit my own strength is beginning to wane, especially with the question hanging over Philo's whereabouts.

Lord Percius stands to a feeble applause. "Good day, friends," he begins, "it is a great pleasure to be here again, side by side with the great Hermetius here." He smiles but I don't imagine that any one reciprocates. "Ahem! Allow me to offer my sincere gratitude to you for the use of your beautiful temple. My friends, the sea men will of course conduct themselves with the highest respect for your piety as they will for my fellow priests who will be stationed throughout the temple to oversee the proceedings. One more thing, Lord Hermetius has been very gracious in offering us the use of this grand chamber for a banquet that will be held three days from now. It is in honour and gratitude to the three sails, for their courage and dedication to the long arduous journey they have endured and to raise their spirits somewhat for the embarking of their return journey to their own land of Erin. Now, before proceedings begin I introduce to you their leader and chief navigator, Duncan of Deismut."

The Four Ascents

At the mention of Duncan's name I sit up alert, my heart beating quicker. I had no idea that he was here. There is a cautious applause and a loud murmur spreads over the gathering. Duncan appears from behind Hermetius and makes his way to the front of the dais. His huge stature dwarfs the priests beside him. Many take in a sharp awe filled breath. I see Eumelia and Jason looking across at me discreetly. My heart seems to be in my mouth as I watch Duncan scan the room with those twinkling eyes, obviously looking for me. His eyes meet with mine and I drop my head for fear that all will see my attraction to him. Great Zeus! How can I ever hope to resist his challenge when I can barely resist those eyes? My heart is beating wildly. When I lift my head again I see that Eumelia is watching me. The look of worry on her face says it all. Oh Philo! Where are you, my love? The murmuring subsides. Duncan will no doubt speak in that deep resounding voice that already has caused me to take leave of my senses and be transported to other times, other worlds. I must keep it together. I must remain calm and poised. A glance at Hermetius tells me that he too is having doubts about my ability to remain calm in the face of this adversity.

"Good day, friends," Duncan begins with perfect delivery of our native tongue. *What a commanding voice! And with that foreign accent too!* I think dreamily to myself.

"It is kind of you to offer your hospitality to me and my men," he is saying. "Thank you! I am sure we will all get along together very well. A few of you I have met already."

He looks at me again and I feel a rush of panic blast through me. Some of the young female students at the back giggle. Eumelia stares at them and then sends a look of disapproval to me. I turn to gaze at Duncan. He is talking of preparations and requirements. I must say, this all seems very innocent, although I cannot forget about the strange plant that Father is so keen to have. Will it be stored here at the temple as well or does Father or Lord Percius have special plans for that? Duncan has finished talking now but instead of taking his seat again he walks off the dais and down the length of the room without as much as a glance in my direction. As he passes the girls at the back there is another giggle and a whispering among them. He shoots a quick smile at them and then disappears out through the door. My face is blazing red and the temper I so easily arose to this morning shows its ugly face once more. I am jealous, of course I am. And I am disgusted with my behaviour. Here I am, practically betrothed to a wonderful loving man, and all the time I cannot prevent myself from playing games of infatuation for this . . . this enemy . . .

and with such immature little students as well. I shall have to go outside and walk in the fresh evening air if I am to shake this nonsense before all here is witness to it. I rise to go. Eumelia sees and follows me.

In the corridor she turns impatiently to me and whispers, "Demetria, what can you be thinking of leaving the conference like that? I forbid you to follow that man."

"Forgive me, Eumelia, I could not bear another moment inside," I reply. "It is as if he has cast a spell upon me. I fear that all is lost for I cannot resist his charm let alone his challenge."

She glances around quickly to make sure we are alone and then she says, "Oh Demetria, child! What am I to do with you?" She looks out from the window, into the porch.

"I have no intention of following him," I reassure her, "although I must have some air. Walk with me?"

"The conference *is* done, I suppose," she says thoughtfully, "and I don't suppose we can do anything now until the metics begin to arrive anyway. Come let us go and look for Philo."

"Please the gods we shall find him well," I reply, thankful to be doing something active at last.

"What do you mean?" Eumelia asks. "Why wouldn't he be well?"

"Let us walk to the market place first and we shall find out" I suggest because unless my heart deceives me, Philo may be in danger. Why else would he refuse to come to my aid?

"Wait!" Eumelia says suddenly stopping and grabbing my arm. "We ought to let Jason know where we're going. He will be looking for us presently."

"Of course," I reply. I open the conference chamber door a little and peek in. Hermetius is speaking; his deep voice echoes into the corridor.

"Wait here" Eumelia whispers to me before disappearing into the room. I walk to the window and look through into the long colonnade. There is no-one there other than a large black raven hopping about between the stone columns. It senses me watching it and it looks at me as if to say *expect magic*, then it flaps away, cawing noisily and startling me out of my reverie. In the same moment a voice speaks from behind me.

"Good day, My Lady." I turn around to find Duncan standing here. His huge height towers above me and I am forced to look up. He is that close to me I can almost feel his hot breath on my head. I am so confused by how he makes me feel and I say the only thing I can think of.

Who *are* you?" I utter desperately. I immediately regret my emotional reaction. I feel like a tiny mouse cornered by a wild cat. But I shall not be pounced upon so savagely. I shall hold my head high and give him no indication of my plight. After all, I am a priestess of this temple and he is but a mere trader.

Grinning handsomely he says, "Who am I? Alright then, I am Duncan, son of Deismut, the greatest man of Scotland ever to stake the shores of Erin with his mighty sword and staff."

"Good evening, Duncan of Deismut," I reply haughtily. "As I recall, you used those same words at our previous meetings. This is the third time you have done so. Is it that you have so little to say for yourself that you must behave thus?"

"The third time My Lady? he asks curiously. "In my defence I declare that I know not what you speak of." He looks quite bruised at my attack.

So the wild cat is not so fierce, I think. I relax a little and manage a slight embarrassed smile. My eyelashes flutter and my voice wavers as I realise my blunder. Of course he has no memory of our first meeting in that other time.

"I . . . I . . ." I stammer. *Heaven help me.* "I fear I am mistaken. I was lost in thought, just now," I tell him. He smiles kindly, his eyes portraying nothing but admiration. Oh why must he be so agreeable? His smile widens into a grin as I wrap my outer robe about me. In my embarrassment I attack again. "You're laughing at me?" I blurt out.

"No, no, My Lady, I would never laugh at you though you *are* amusing. No, I was thinking how nice it would be if we could finish that walk," he says still smiling.

"I . . . well I . . ." I stammer again. Thank the Gods, I am saved; Eumelia and Jason have just this moment come into the corridor. Their eyes widen when they see my companion. My whole body relaxes and I let my breath out quietly, beckoning them to join us.

"We were just about to embark on our own walk" I tell Duncan, feeling braver.

"Ah, I see," says Duncan, "another time then?" Ignoring his request I introduce Jason and Eumelia to him.

"Friends, this is Duncan of Deismut as you already know of course. Duncan, allow me to introduce you to Brother Jason and Sister Eumelia."

"It's a pleasure to make your acquaintance Sir, Sister." He nods at each of them. He is quite the gentleman despite his roguish appearance.

"Pleasure, Sir," replies Eumelia. Jason simply nods.

"You are from Erin I believe," Eumelia asks Duncan.

"Aye, that I am Sister." I notice he doesn't call her my lady. There is a short silence between us. No-one speaks, and then to my dismay Duncan says, "I believe you are the famous Pythia, eh? The Oracle of Delphi, is that so?"

"That is so," replies Eumelia a little uncomfortably. She is not accustomed to being acknowledged thus outside of the holy chambers.

"Most fascinating," Duncan says to her though his eyes are averted to me. He turns his attention back to Eumelia. "I would be obliged if you'd grant me the honour of walking with you," he says to her. "I have a few questions myself that I would put to your gods, if I may." Great Zeus! Such audacity! Poor Eumelia is quite taken by surprise.

But Jason surprises us even more. He throws his arm around Eumelia's shoulders and declares, "We would be delighted to have you walk with us, Dear Sir, would we not, Ladies?"

We both nod, wondering what on earth Jason is up to. It soon becomes clear as we set off for the most direct way to the market place. "I guess you will be selling some of your goods in the market place then?" Jason asks Duncan as we walk. "You can lead us to the best qualities you have. It is so difficult to get nice fabric for example. The servants in the temple are always saying how difficult it is to keep our robes so white. Some bleached linen would be wonderful. Have you any linen with you, Duncan? I believe Irish linen is the best to be had."

"Och aye, we have indeed some beautiful linen," Duncan replies. "But I must correct you there, Brother Jason for although Irish linen is most fine, I do believe that Scottish cloth is much finer; the finest to be had."

"And your father is Scottish, is he not?" I ask. My stomach leaps into my breast as he winks at me cheekily. I lower my head so as my friends do not see my flushed cheeks.

"Aye, he is that, My Lady. You remembered."

I don't lift my head but I can see that Eumelia is looking at me very worried. I feel like a chastised child. What hope can I be when Duncan can reduce me to this with a mere glance? I shall focus on finding Philo, I decide.

"Scotland you say," says Jason, taking the opportunity to find out more about what Duncan knows. "And do they have such interesting herbs in Scotland too? I understand the ships are loaded down with all kinds of specimens, some rare I believe."

Jason is being very clever but I wish he wouldn't make it seem that I was the one to tell of the special cargo. Duncan smiles and thinks hard about his

The Four Ascents

reply which gives me time to shoot a warning glance at Jason who decides to add to his inquiry and maybe win Duncan's trust. "Our High Priest, Hermetius has eyes and ears everywhere my friend," he says. "But be not discouraged. Lord Percius' business can stay within his walls. I am merely interested in herbology in general."

Still Duncan remains cautious with his information. "Well" he replies at last, "I imagine that if you require a sample for your studies then Lord Percius' man could oblige. What's his name . . . Och aye! Thucymus."

"Thucymus did you say? He's what . . . Lord Percius' man?" asks Jason mirroring Eumelia's and my surprise.

"Well it seems to be him doing all the running about anyway. He and the priest met me at the docks" replies Duncan unaware of the significance of his disclosure.

"And did they take you to The House of Pluto?" asks Jason cleverly.

"Aye. I spoke to him there again, just this morning; a stout man, very short?" Duncan describes Thucymus, no doubt. Jason acts casual but he must feel as I do, shocked and angry.

"I know him, thank you," he says. "I shall certainly ask a favour. You say he was at The House of Pluto this morning? Was he alone or did he have company?"

Duncan is suddenly very wary of answering Jason's questions. After all, it is not in his best interests to cause ripples amongst his hosts. "Please Duncan," I plead, stepping into line with him and taking his arm which seems to please him greatly. "We are looking for someone and we feel he may have been with Thucymus this morning."

Duncan gives me a cheeky smile. He knows I only act this way to get the information we want, but that is fine; he is more than happy to play my little game. "He *was* with someone, aye; a man from the market" he tells me.

"Philo?"

"I believe that's his name, aye."

"And do you know where he is now?" I ask. Duncan creases his brow, studying my face. I suppose he is trying to work out what my interest in Philo is. Oh, what on earth was Philo doing at The House of Pluto!

"I don't know, My Lady," Duncan decides to leave me with. "And now if you will excuse me, I must be somewhere else. Good day, good friends." And with a short bow he leaves us to ponder over his sudden departure.

Jason watches as he disappears from view and then turns to Eumelia and me. "Let's go to the market anyway," he suggests. "Philo may be there now and if we're lucky he'll know more than we do about the plans of the dark ones.

"Oh no Jason," I protest, "Philo would never be involved with them. If he was there this morning then he was taken there against his will. I am sure of that." But Jason does not share my faith in Philo.

"Against his will?" he repeats. "Demetria, you can be so dramatic at times. Why would Thucymus take Philo to The House of Pluto against his will? It's ludicrous."

"I know Philo," I reply. "He may be a simple farmer but he would make a better priest than most at the temple. He is a good man, Jason, unlike Thucymus who I am beginning to suspect is heavily involved with this whole nasty business."

"Can't argue with you there," Jason agrees. "Lord Percius' man, eh! It is clear that he is to benefit from this secret shipment at the very least. But, Demetria, you must prepare yourself for the possibility that Philo is also in on it." I can hardly believe Jason can suspect dear Philo of any misdemeanour.

"How dare you speak of Philo in that manner" I blurt out in his defence. "Jason, you are very dear to me, you know that, but I will not allow . . ."

"Stop it, you two!" demands Eumelia.

Immediately, I regret my reaction. This is the third time I've lost my temper today. Some priestess I am! Resentment sticks in my throat like poison. Oh, I am losing track of my piety *and* my joy! Where is my joy? Where once there was joy now there is resentment and anger. Heaven help me! I begin to cry. Even now, when I have erred against my brother I think only of myself.

"Sorry, I'm so sorry," I cry. "I should not have argued with you. It's just, I am so in need of Philo and now it seems he may be held against his will." I can see that Jason definitely does not agree with my theory. However, I am quite convinced that something, something unfriendly at least, has prevented Philo from coming to me. Thankfully, Jason is so good to me he would never hold me in debt. Putting his arm around my shoulder he pulls me into his embrace. He hugs me so warmly that I stop crying and begin to feel more positive. "Let us go to the market, then," I sniff, "and hopefully we will find him there all smiles and full of surprise that I thought him in danger for one moment."

"We're fine then? The trinity is good?" Eumelia asks, raising my spirits. I link my arm with hers and give her the biggest smile I have.

The Four Ascents

"The trinity is good and ready for action," I tell her happily. Several minutes later we arrive at the market place. We search for a long time but Philo does not seem to be here. His stall is here, the milk going off in the heat. Two goats are tethered to the stall, panting with thirst.

"Why doesn't anyone think of giving the poor beasts some water?" Jason asks, lifting a large bowl from the stall. He walks to the stone fountain in the middle of the market place and fills the bowl with water. Then he comes back and places the bowl on the ground before the suffering goats. "Let's go to Philo's farm," he suggests, "Is it near, Demetria?"

"It's quite a way off, I'm afraid," I reply. "But he won't be there, Jason; he wouldn't go home and leave his milk sitting here in the heat to ruin, to say nothing of these poor creatures. No, if you ask me he never came back from The House of Pluto. Perhaps we should go there?"

"No, no we can't just arrive there and ask for Philo," says Jason. "Besides, it's getting late and Hermetius will be anxious to know our whereabouts. Let's go back to the temple first and then we can tell him what we know. We shall decide a plan then."

"Yes, let's do that," agrees Eumelia, eager to get out of the heat, "but first we should do something about these goats."

"Just let them loose," I tell her, "they'll go straight to the hills to join the rest of the herd." So we untie the goats and watch them canter off towards the hills. Then we quietly make our way back to the temple where we meet with an extremely agitated Heremtius and a temple full of hustle bustle. What a day!

∞∞∞∞∞∞∞∞∞∞∞∞∞∞∞∞∞∞∞∞∞∞∞∞∞

It is rather late now. Eumelia and I are at my father's house. I had to let my parents know that I am well and that I will be spending at least one more night with Eumelia. They were somewhat curious as to why but accepted that we have some temple affairs to go over, especially since we can't to that during the day what with the constant coming and going of traders and priests, to say nothing of the increased number of townsfolk coming through the doors, all eager to see what is going on. Eumelia and I decided not to question Father or indeed give him any indication that we are suspicious of The House of Pluto and the secret shipment he is so eager to receive. Has it already been received? Are Lord Percius and his dark priests this very moment concocting some evil potion or other that will be used for ill intent? Maybe even to conjure up some dark evil presence that they worship in secret? The rumours about The House of Pluto have been thrown about wildly this evening. People have gathered in huddles, gossiping about Lord Percius' plans. Some say that he intends to take over The Temple of Truth and that Hermetius is in league with him. Others are saying that there is a struggle in Heaven and that Apollo and Athena are in battle with Pluto and the gods of the underworld. There are even those who say that Lord Percius is within his rights to take over The Temple of Truth, since Hermetius has gone mad and is no longer fit to be High Priest of the market never mind The Temple of Truth.

Father has not mentioned today's events at all and Mother would never start a topic of conversation in front of him, and because we have decided to appear ignorant the matter has not been broached. After some twenty minutes of small talk and good manners I ask to be excused. "Father, Mother, if you will excuse me I could do with some air. It is quite hot inside, is it not?" I say. "Will you join me on a walk through the olive grove?" I ask Eumelia. "We may as well go on from there as we can take the route down the hill by the stream then verge off left towards the temple."

Out in the olive grove we see Eusebius and his lady friend, Xanthe. They make to move out of our path but I call to them, "Eusebius, Xanthe, stay there. I wish to speak with you." Oh lovely Eusebius! See how he smiles so; how happy he is! He is as bright as he was in my dream. A thought comes to me and I reach up to a hanging olive branch and pluck a leaf from it. Upon reaching him I hold out my hand, the leaf hidden in my closed fist.

"What is this, My Lady? Eusebius asks with a small bow. Xanthe curtseys. I notice she is quite pretty and I give her a smile and a nod.

"Hold out your hand and you will find out," I tell Eusebius in a childlike manner. He always brings out the joy in me.

He reaches out a palm and I place the leaf in it. Smiling, though a little embarrassed, he says, "Ah, a gift for a gift!" And he bows low.

"Please don't bow, Eusebius," I say. "Let me introduce to you my dear sister in spirit, Sister Eumelia."

He bows to Eumelia, "My lady."

"And who is this?" Eumelia asks him indicating Xanthe.

"Xanthe, My Lady," he replies.

"Xanthe and Eusebius are betrothed," I add. "I intend to give them the best servant's wedding there is. Eusebius, I'm glad I bumped into you. I wanted to ask a favour of you. It didn't occur to me to ask you until I saw

The Four Ascents

you just now, but it is clear to me that you shall be the one to help me with my problem."

Eumelia is looking at me with such a perplexed expression. She is no doubt thinking that I have taken leave of my senses in asking a servant to help me but I know what I am doing. If I cannot have Philo with me as I go into this challenge then I ought to have Eusebius. After all, he knows of the prophecy I hold in the Red Stone of Power and he has said that he will guide me along the long difficult path.

Xanthe speaks next. "The Mistress is in need of my assistance with the preparations for the banquet," she tells me with a curtsey. "If you have no need for me, My Lady, then I should proceed to the house."

"You may go Xanthe." She curtseys again and hastens off towards the house. "Xanthe, just a moment!" I hasten after her. "I want to thank you for being so good to Eusebius. He deserves to be happy," I say catching up with her.

"Yes, My Lady. He makes me happy too."

"You love him?" I ask.

"Yes, My Lady."

"And he loves you."

"Yes, My Lady."

"Xanthe, may I ask . . . how do you *know* that you love him? What is it that makes you so sure he is the one?"

"Well I . . ." Xanthe is quite abashed at my breech of proper conduct between mistress and servant. "It is not my place, My Lady," she says.

I sit down upon a tree stump. "Father had Eusebius cut this tree down when I was a little girl," I tell Xanthe.

She sits on the ground so that she is not higher than me. I am sure she must be rather perplexed at my behaviour but she respectfully listens to what I have to say whilst keeping her eyes to the ground.

"The branch I was sitting on broke," I explain. "I fell to the ground and hurt my leg. I was only six years old so I was quite distressed. The branch was rotten apparently. Upon further examination Father decided that the whole tree was poorly and he had Eusebius chop it down. Dear Eusebius, he was so kind to me when I fell. Mother was at the market place and Father was also in the city so Eusebius had to tend to me as best he could. And he was so gentle, so very kind. He held my bleeding knee with his hands and he sang to me. I'll never forget the way he sang to me or the soothing heat of his hands on my leg. He made me better with his gentleness, not just my leg but all of me. For

Eliza White Buffalo with Nicholas Black Elk

a long time after that I felt so happy. I remember thinking that when I would grow up I would marry Eusebius, and live happily ever after. But what did I know? I was just a little girl."

Xanthe blushes as she says, "He is very special. I knew that the moment I met him. I love him very much."

"But how do you *know* that Xanthe? Please tell me," I beg her.

"You are in love, My Lady?" she asks making sure she doesn't look at me.

"I don't know," I reply. "How do *you* know?"

"I know by the way he makes me feel when I am with him," she replies. "I know when he looks into my eyes and I think I will fly away, I am that light. My heart skips its beating and sings with joy just at a mere touch of his hand."

Dear Xanthe. She is so sweet. How her face lights up with the thought of her beloved. I wonder does she think of him all the time even when they are apart. Could it be that these same feelings I have for Duncan truly mean that I am in love with him. Is he the one? And what of Philo?

"But what about practical, down to earth things like dependability and strength of character? Don't they count?" I ask Xanthe.

"Well, I suppose those things are important," she tells me, "but when you are in love it is the excitement that you crave." She dares to glance at my eyes for a fleeting moment and she blushes profusely. "When he kisses you," she almost whispers, "and you feel that consuming passion within there is nothing else in the world that matters but that one person. It is as if he has cast a spell over you." She stops talking. Her entire face is grinning with memories of enchanting kisses.

I say nothing. There are no words to express my thoughts as my heart relates to her bliss. I am in love with Duncan of Deismut.

Xanthe is suddenly aware of the intimacy of the moment. She stammers an embarrassed apology for which there is absolutely no need, and she curtseys to me making to leave me.

"Xanthe, please, before you go . . . do you think it is possible to be in love with two men at once?" I ask her.

She doesn't have to think about the answer. "No" she declares without hesitation. "There can only be one."

"How do I know which one is the one?"

"He is the one that you are almost frightened to love," she replies. "He is the one that turns your world upside down."

108

My heart thumps wildly as I think of how frightened I am of loving Duncan. "Is that how it was for you?" I ask her.

"Yes, it was, still is," she says.

"And me?"

"If he is the one, truly the one," she replies, "then he will bring death to the world you know in such a way that you will never be the same person ever again."

∞∞∞∞∞∞∞∞∞∞∞∞∞∞∞∞∞∞∞∞∞∞∞∞∞

"Don't you see," I plead with Eumelia. "Having the family servant with me will make my story believable and Duncan will believe that it is Father's business that we wish to speak with Philo. If you or Jason comes with me as we first agreed it would look suspicious. Why would two priestesses come to The House of Pluto to look for a farmer? We must have Duncan take us in and we must have a credible reason for doing so."

"Fine, fine . . . it does make sense," agrees Eumelia reluctantly. "Only, I worry that you will be alone."

"But I won't be alone," I argue. "Eusebius will be with me."

"*I* won't be there," she moans, "and I promised Hermetius that I'd stay with you."

"Then do as I suggest and wait for me in the gardens. If I don't return after twenty minutes say, then come and ask for me. Say you need me urgently or something, and you were told that I had gone there to look for a family friend."

This seems to abate Eumelia's concern and she agrees to do as I suggest. At first she was set firmly against me involving Eusebius, especially when I said that we would go to The House of Pluto alone, but now she can see how it could benefit us. We had taken Eusebius here to her quarters to tell him of the plan. I don't know whose eyes opened wider with surprise, hers or his, when I told him of Father's involvement and what he has dealt for. Still, Eumelia is now aware of my plan and it is a good plan, I think. Eusebius and I will go to Duncan and ask that he accompany us into The House of Pluto. I shall tell him that Father has sent me to look for Philo; he has important business with him that concerns the family."

"My Lady, won't Master Duncan wonder why you think Master Philo is there," Eusebius asks me.

"Good question, Eusebius," I reply. "I shall have to say that Father believes him to be there. I am going to tell a lot of falsehoods I know, but there is no other way. I must find Philo and we must find out what that plant is used for and stop them in their tracks before they do any harm with it."

I don't tell Eusebius about the challenge. Oh! If it were just that we were to thwart the dark priests' plans then it would not seem so huge. It would be challenging enough to prevent them from destroying our temple but I must also deal with the personal challenge that Duncan presents. I don't even know what the challenge is yet so I need to be extra vigilant. And how am I to focus on finding one love when another more powerful one rather than keeping me safe, pulls the ground out from under my feet? Is that the challenge? Am I to deny this love?

"We shall go tonight," I tell Eumelia and Eusebius decidedly. "I do not wish to wait another moment without Philo by my side."

"Or do you mean Duncan?" a voice whispers in my mind.

"As you wish," decides Eumelia. "But first we must speak with Hermetius and Jason, and we must have some food. We have not eaten since this morning, remember."

"Oh yes! I was wondering why I was so hungry!" I exclaim. "I have been so engrossed in finding Philo I totally forgot all about food.

"You can't eat because you are in love with Duncan," whisper my thoughts.

"Eusebius, you shall eat with us and then we'll set off," I tell Eusebius.

"As you wish, My Lady," he replies.

At dusk Eumelia, Eusebius and I set off for The Temple of Truth. It is only a short walk away so we do not discuss anything on the way but remain silent, preparing ourselves for the task ahead. When we reach the temple the torches are lit the whole way along the colonnade. We open the main doors and enter into the corridor, ignoring two priests from the House of Pluto that are standing nearby. Eusebius stays a little behind me, his head low; he has been here before. Servants are permitted of course like everyone else, to enter the inner cella to pray, but he has been here with *me* before also. Not two weeks ago I had need of him to carry some produce for me into the priests' quarters. Then I had him stay close to me while I went to Hermetius' chambers to fetch some scrolls and wait for me while I delivered them to the counselling chambers. Eusebius is well acquainted with the halls of this temple.

The Four Ascents

"Eusebius, go to the counselling chambers," I order him now. "Do you remember where they are, where we delivered those scrolls, they kept falling out of your arms, remember?"

"Yes, My Lady. I know the way," he says.

"Good. I want you to go there. You should find some of the metics there. I want you to ask where you may locate Duncan of Deismut. If anyone asks who you are or what you want of Master Duncan you are not to mention me. You may say that you are in service of Lord Perikles though. If you are lucky enough to find Master Duncan then you shall tell him discreetly that you are my servant and that I wish to see him. Ask that he accompany you here to the corridor. Either way, you must return here to meet with us presently. Do you understand?"

"Yes, My Lady. You can rely on me," he says.

"I know. That is why you are here" I tell him with a smile. "Thank you Eusebius. Now make haste." He gives me a quick bow and disappears into the west corridor, leaving me and Eumelia alone.

"Well done," she says to me, giving me a big hug.

"What was that for?" I ask.

"For being so brave, and mature, and decisive. I have seen another side to you today, Demetria. I believe you are ready to meet this challenge. I have every faith in you."

"Oh Eumelia, you don't know how much that means to me," I respond with a grin. "Thank you, Sister, thank you very much indeed. And you're right, I won't let you down."

"*As long as Duncan does not let you down,*" the inner voice whispers fearfully.

"*I* know you won't" Eumelia says pointing to herself. "It is Hermetius that needs convincing," she adds. "Come on, let's go straight to Jason's room and we shall all three tell His Grace together as one."

Jason's room is on the east side near to Hermetius' chambers, so if we are quick Eusebius will not have to wait about for very long. We come to Jason's door and knock loudly. "Who is it?" we hear from within.

"It's us, Jason," Eumelia replies. The door opens and there stands Jason in his civilian robes. "What are you . . ." Eumelia begins to say but Jason interrupts her.

"Come in here quick, quick!" he urges us.

With the door closed behind us Eumelia says again, "Why are you in your civilian robes, Jason? You look like a pauper I have to say."

III

Eliza White Buffalo with Nicholas Black Elk

"Shh listen!" Jason insists. "We priests are being watched. The House of Pluto are everywhere. Did you not see?"

"Well we did see . . . ." Eumelia begins to say and is interrupted again.

"I can't go anywhere without one of them tailing me," Jason adds ignoring Eumelia's attempts to answer him. "I have been here hours now. I'm dressed like this because I intend to sneak out and make my way into the city. I don't believe they will have stored the plant here in the temple. It must either be at The House of Pluto or in the city somewhere, perhaps even in your father's house, Demetria."

"Oh!" I exclaim, clasping Eumelia's hand.

"Wait," she says, "If the priests are being watched then it's likely that we've been followed here. Those two at the entrance . . ."

"You've been seen?" asks Jason cringing.

"I tried to tell you," says Eumelia, getting a little impatient with Jason's interrupting. "There were two of the dark ones just at the entrance to the colonnade."

"Why would they be following us, Jason?" I ask him, "I don't understand why the sinister drama?"

"They obviously don't want any of us knowing what it is they are up to. They're keeping tabs on us," he replies.

"I don't know, Jason," I say. "Anyway, we must go now to Hermetius and tell him that my servant Eusebius and I are going into The House of Pluto this night."

"You're *what!*" he exclaims. I tell him the plan and Eumelia thankfully supports me.

Jason is no fool. He sees the benefit of it and he knows I will be safe with Eusebius. He's just not convinced about Duncan though. "He's shifty, Demetria," he tells me, "and he is the very one you should be avoiding, is he not?"

"I told you about the challenge, Jason. It's vital that I win over him. Running in the other direction will solve nothing. Besides, he's already heavily involved. We're bound to have to deal with him sooner or later; best that he's on our side, eh?"

"Hmmm, but be careful. And if you feel for one moment that he's dangerous stay as far away as possible." Jason is very suspicious of poor Duncan who seems much too kind to be dangerous.

As I contemplate this the voice in my mind whispers to me, "*He's jealous. Perhaps he's afraid that you'll start listening to Duncan instead of him,*" it sneers.

112

The Four Ascents

"Fair enough," I agree with Jason, ignoring the voice, "but I'm sure you're wrong about him."

"Let's hope so," he says, shrugging his shoulders.

"So, now to His Grace," I decide after a moment of awkward silence between us. I hope it isn't obvious to Jason that I love Duncan.

"Hermetius isn't there," Jason states. "He's gone . . . since this afternoon apparently. No-one has seen him or heard where he has gone, nothing."

"Well I'm not sticking around to look for him," I decide. "We go ahead with the plan without his permission. He already has agreed that Eumelia and I should go into The House of Pluto anyway. What difference does it make if it's Eusebius and not Eumelia?"

"All the difference in the world when he discovers you intend to have Duncan take you there," Jason replies somewhat defensively.

I ignore what he says and make to leave. I don't want to waste a single moment. I wonder has Eusebius found Duncan yet or does he know where he might be.

"You two go then," Jason relents. "You will be followed but at least it'll give me a chance to slip out. If I'm careful, I'll get as far as the inner cella without being seen. Then I can blend in with the city folk. Thank the gods the proceedings have attracted quite a crowd. I should be able to hide my identity easily. Go on then and may Athena go with you."

"And with you, Brother," Eumelia says.

"Find that plant," I add.

As we enter the corridor we catch a glimpse of someone quickly moving out of sight. We pretend we haven't noticed and proceed to the main corridor, chatting casually about the clear night it is and how the full moon looks so beautiful. I am quite sure our shadow has tailed us straight to the main corridor. As we walk along its torch lit length we spot Eusebius coming in on the west side, and glory be, Duncan is with him! My heart leaps into my throat at first glimpse of him and my hands are sweating and shaking so much that I am forced to hold them behind my back for fear that they would reveal my feelings. I stop Eumelia in our tracks for a moment and I whisper in her ear, "I dare say our shadow will leave us now that we are under the watchful eye of the dangerous Duncan," I tease her.

"Oh don't, Demetria," she chastises me impatiently. "I must admit I am that scared for you that I feel like calling the whole thing off. Perhaps I should go with you after all?"

"I'll be fine," I tell her with a much kinder tone. "Shh, here they come."

Duncan and Eusebius have spotted us and are now walking quickly towards us. Dear Eusebius, he has no fear when it comes to my protection. He always did everything in his power to keep me safe from harm's way.

"Greetings, Sisters," booms Duncan, his huge voice reverberating around the spacious corridor.

"Greetings, Sir," I reply in a much lower voice, "and thank you for coming to my aid. It is most kind of you."

Duncan pats Eusebius on his shoulder, beaming with profuse gratitude, "Your man here, great man that he is, informed me that you wish to speak with me. Now, I do not want you to be angry with him because I made him tell me what you want." He takes a step backwards and then bows low to me in a dramatic fashion. "Here I am, Beautiful Lady," he says. "I am willing to do whatever your heart desires. I will go to the end of the world for you, to the moon if it be your desire."

I hold on to Eumelia's arm as a short gasping sound breaks forth from my lips. Overhead, a raven caws strikingly to me, "Ma-gic . . . ma-gic!" it caws. Heavens! My legs have become all wobbly. I shall need to sit down or I might fall down.

"What is it, Sister?" Eumelia asks worriedly.

"I'm fine, Sister, I'm fine, a little faint perhaps" I tell her.

I look up at Duncan. He seems very concerned that I may be ill. Perhaps he is feigning concern. "Are you ill?" he inquires. "I shall go at once and fetch some water. Are you in need of a healer? I can run to the House of Pluto if you require." So his concern is genuine. Oh! It is amazing. How can he not know that his spell of love has cast me down?"

"No, no I am fine, Dear Sir," I reply. "Besides, we have healers here at the temple."

"Eusebius, go and fetch the sister some water please," Eumelia interjects, quite oblivious to Duncan's worried ramblings.

"Right away, My Lady," Eusebius says.

"Here, My Dear, come out to the garden where it is cool," Eumelia tells me. She helps me to my feet as Duncan stands by not really knowing what to do. Eumelia helps me to the garden where we sit on a stone rest.

"I'm fine, really," I insist, a little embarrassed at my lack of self control. Oh the way he spoke to me! And, oh the way he looked at me with those enchanting eyes! In that one magical moment I lost control. That raven, that mystical bird of the night was correct; it is indeed some kind of spell that this awesome giant has cast upon me. I don't think I will ever be the same again.

The Four Ascents

I look around, into the night of the garden. Even it is filled with an aura of magic. "Look, Sister," I say, indicating the garden. "Duncan, look around us. See the pond before us; see how the light of the moon glistens upon its surface. Is it not beautiful? You can look right into its depths. Something approaches from deep below. What is it? Can you see? It's an orb of light, is it not? See how it grows brighter. It's calling to the night."

"My Lady, are you alright? You seem quite dazed?" Duncan asks.

I look up into his green eyes; they shine as brightly as the orb of light approaching from the depths of the lake. "Do you not see the orb?" I ask him. "See how it rises from the depths of the water. Look, look around us. Do you not see how the trees bend low to its call?"

I stand up and listen in the silence of the night. There is a strange feeling in the air. "Listen," I whisper. "The breeze is whispering through the leaves. It's speaking of portents and destiny. Someone will die tonight; I can feel it. I hear it spoken in the trees. I see it in the still dark water. Yes, there will be death tonight." I shiver as the meaning of my words hang in the air around me. "Who will die, Eumelia?" I demand to know, "Surely not my darling Philo?"

"Demetria . . ." Eumelia utters in a small frightened voice. "Demetria, you are ill child. Please let me take you home and help you to your cot. Duncan shall call for a healer."

"I'm *not* ill I tell you. I was startled, that is all. That same bird frightened the breath out of me earlier today. Do you remember, Duncan? You spoke to me at that very moment."

"Yes, My Lady," says Duncan. "But please, allow me to run for the healer. Just tell me where to find him."

"I have no need for a healer, I tell you. Bring me Eusebius. He is the only healer I need. In fact, had he not been born a slave he would have been the best healer any temple could hope for."

"Eusebius?" Eumelia is quite surprised at my revelation.

"Oh My Good Sister," says Duncan to her, "with risk of sounding impertinent, just because a man is a slave does not mean he cannot have healing ability. Many of our men back home are wonderful healers."

"I am merely surprised since I have known Eusebius a long time and I have never known this about him," Eumelia replies. She is quite upset. I can hear it in her voice and I don't think it's only because of me but also because she has made up her mind that Duncan is not to be trusted.

Eliza White Buffalo with Nicholas Black Elk

Eusebius is back with my water. "Are you recovered, My Lady?" he asks, handing the glass to Eumelia.

"I am fine, Eusebius, thank you. And thank you for the water." He looks at me quite concerned. "I *am* fine, honestly," I repeat.

"I shall accompany you to your father's house," Duncan declares like it isn't up for discussion.

"What? No!" I exclaim, "I must find Philo tonight. What if it is he who is to die? I must find him. Eusebius, I want you with me, and you, Sir, you shall accompany me also. If that is alright," I add.

Eumelia is very quiet. I half expect her to insist that I go home but I also feel that she wants to discover exactly what Duncan's intentions towards me are. I find myself hoping that they are not exactly what she would like them to be. I cannot help but believe that Xanthe is correct and that Duncan is the one. I shall fight him no longer. Besides, I no longer believe that his love is the challenge but where it takes me to will determine my success or my failure. And now it seems that more is at stake than the temple. It seems that someone may die tonight. Whether or not I succeed may be the saving or the demise of that person.

"*What if that person is you?*" whispers the voice in my mind.

"*Better me than Philo,*" I answer it silently.

"If the sister agrees then I shall be happy to accompany you to find your friend," declares Duncan. He looks at Eumelia questioningly.

After a few moments deliberation during which she surveys me thoroughly and decides that I am not to be stopped, she relents, "I agree, but I shall come too," she insists. "I do not wish to leave her side in case she becomes ill again."

"That seems a wise decision," Duncan replies. "So then, we four will set off now for The House of Pluto. What if Philo's not there?"

"He's there," I tell him.

∞∞∞∞∞∞∞∞∞∞∞∞∞∞∞∞∞∞∞∞∞∞∞∞∞∞∞∞

The video stops again. And Black Elk speaks . . .

"My Dear Rose, you have seen how the challenge works, how temptation works. It seems to Demetria that she is stripped of her power when she loses her outer source of strength, Philo. Philo is Demetria's soul mate, remember, and so he is the perfect source of help to remove from her, thus seeming to

The Four Ascents

render her powerless. The challenge now seems insurmountable and Demetria flounders on the shore of her power, desperately clinging onto whatever lifeline is thrown to her.

The two roads are presented before her. One is dark and full of illusion, yet it will teach her much about who she is. The other is light and full of truth. It too will teach her many things. The veil of illusion is strong, as strong as Truth. Yet it is that illusion of powerlessness that will teach her what real power is: co-creation with Source, in love and in faith. It will teach her hope. And Rose, you must always trust in hope. Walk both roads in love, faith, and in hope. I am here with you along the way. I will never forget you."

CHAPTER SEVEN

The fall from grace

And so the story continues . . .

Jason wanders around the inner cella blending in with the city folk inconspicuously. Fortunately, neither anyone from The House of Pluto nor any of the metics are there. Brother Bruce is there though, standing next to the altar. Some one of the priests must be next to the Emerald Flame of Truth at all times. It was carried here by the forefathers from the original Temple of Truth on Atlantis. It is much too sacred to leave unguarded even for a moment.

Jason gives Brother Bruce a wide berth; best if he's not recognized by anyone. If he's seen talking with the priest it might give his identity away. He wanders around, keeping a close eye on everyone. He doesn't think anyone followed him from his chambers and it doesn't seem that he's being tailed now. Deciding this is a good a time as any he casually exits the cella, taking the arm of an old gentleman. To anyone nearby it looks as if he's one of the city folk with his elderly father. He opens the outer door for the elder and they step out into the colonnade and down the temple steps to the gardens. All the time Jason can clearly see two dark priests stationed at the top of the steps and one in the garden who seems to be somewhat bored with his duty and is now skipping stones across the lake, disturbing its stillness. Jason keeps his head bent low, making it seem that his attention is on the elder when it is really on the priests; where they are and what they are doing. He hopes that the disturbed surface of the lake is not a bad omen for tonight. He thinks of Demetria and Eusebius and wonders exactly where they are now. Did they manage to find Duncan? Could they be in The House of Pluto this very moment? Will they find Philo? Jason is not altogether sure that Philo is not an accomplice. Why else would he go there and not answer Demetria's call for help. Is he not supposed to be in love with her? On the other hand it seems that Thucymus is working for Lord Percius so what if Thucymus didn't tell Philo of Demetria's need for him? But then, would he have fetched him and taken him to The House of Pluto against his will? No, it seems that Philo must have gone there willingly.

The Four Ascents

The old gentleman pats Jason on the shoulder bringing him out of his thoughts. "Thank you son; I bid you good night," he says.

"Oh! Good night, Father. May Athena go with you," replies Jason.

A loud splash brings his attention back to the lake. Turning to look for an instant, he sees that the stone skipper has been joined by another man. It is too dark to see who it is but it may be one of the Irish metics. It doesn't seem to be one of the dark priests because he's not wearing a robe but seems to be wrapping a blanket around him whilst clutching a jug. Judging by the way the man is swaying the jug no doubt contains wine or mead. Jason crouches down behind the perimeter shrubbery in order to spy on the two men. The metic, if he is a metic, seems to be urging the other man to join him in his revelry. At first the priest waves a disapproving arm at him as if he is saying 'be off with you!' But then he glances up at the temple colonnade; to his two comrades stationed there. Obviously deciding they are unaware of him and his company, he relents and starts to walk with the drunken man along the garden path towards the exit and towards Jason.

"Sweet Athena!" Jason mutters to himself, looking behind him. Just to his right is a large palm tree. It will have to do. He darts behind the trunk and stands sideways to it, hopefully out of sight. Moments later he hears voices.

"Why all the secrecy anyway?" the drunken man is asking.

Jason stays very still, hardly daring to breathe. If he can follow these men and stay close to them without being seen he may hear something useful. *That voice*, he thinks, *it sounds familiar. Who could it be; definitely not a metic, it sounds like a local.*

The priest then says, "What secrecy? There's no secrecy."

"Then why all the guards? Surely the goods are not that valuable?" asks the drunken man. He and the priest have just come out through the exit to the grounds and are level with the palm tree.

Jason sucks in his breath and stands as straight as he can, his heart thumping so loudly in his ears that he can barely make out what the men are now saying. He just about makes out the words *the girl* and then he hears the drunken man say aloud with surprise, "What? What girl?" And then, as if he suddenly understands, he asks, "You can't mean Sister Demetria? But she's nothing but an arrogant little brat. Sister Eumelia, now she really *does* have a gift."

Jason covers his mouth with his hand in shock. He can hardly believe what he is hearing. So the plant is not the reason for all the secrecy. What on earth can Percius be plotting that involves Demetria? Is Athena's prophecy

119

Eliza White Buffalo with Nicholas Black Elk

more sinister than it seems for poor Demetria? Hermetius was right to be so concerned for her safety.

"Damm!" Jason mutters. "It seems I've gone and let her walk right into the lion's den. Where is Hermetius anyway?" he wonders for about the tenth time tonight. He creeps out from behind the tree and very stealthily follows the two men. He keeps his ear pricked and his robe close around his head.

The drunken man is talking now. If only Jason could know who it is. The voice is so familiar. "Let's sit here so we can have a bit of a swig," he is saying, "good mead this. And then you can tell me all about it."

Jason holds his breath for fear that the men will hear him. He watches them sit on a stone bench overlooking the city. They are quite high up here on the edge of the acropolis and the view is beautiful at night what with all the torches in the city. Crouching down bravely behind a nearby bush, Jason listens nervously. If someone comes along the path behind him he will be discovered.

"Ah! It's quite lovely from up here," says the familiar voice.

"It is! I never have much cause to come this way," was the priest's reply.

"How do you get down to the city then? These are the only descents," the drunken man asks.

"Oh, we have an underground descent that goes straight from The House of Pluto to the outer caves along the coast. Didn't you ever take that route?" says the priest much to Jason's great interest. It is exciting to him to learn that there *is* such a route, and what is more exciting is the hope that the mead is loosening the priest's tongue. Perhaps he will learn exactly what is going on. What a spot of luck!

"So what does old Percius want with young Sister Demetria then?" the drunken man is asking. "I tell you she has no extraordinary powers that I know of."

"She's supposed to be *very* powerful according to Lord Perikles," replies the priest. "And he should know her better than anyone. Besides, she's a virgin."

Jason shivers and shifts his position uncomfortably. What has being a virgin got to do with it? Most of the priests and priestesses have taken the vow of chastity. Besides, Demetria is only eighteen years old, barely more than a child.

The drunken man seems to be as uncomfortable with the priest's words as Jason is because he suddenly coughs nervously and looks all around him. He looks straight in the direction of Jason's bush but thankfully doesn't notice

The Four Ascents

a thing. Jason does though. The man has given him a full on look at his face. The drunken man is Thucymus.

"Percius' man," Jason mutters silently through gritted teeth, "the traitor."

Thucymus asks next what Jason also wants to know: "What has being a virgin got to do with it? And what does he want with Demetria's supposed power anyway?"

"Oh come on now," the priest begins sarcastically. "Don't tell me that you don't know about the ceremony. Sure haven't we all talked about nothing else since the first time? Mind you, this time will be special. A real mystic *and* she's a virgin. This time it will be perfect. The House of Pluto will never be the same again."

"What do you mean, Ignatius?" asks Thucymus suddenly sobering up. "Here, have some more mead."

Thucymus does not appear to like where this conversation is going at all and poor Jason is beside himself with worry. He peers through the bush, trying to get a glimpse of what this priest looks like but he can only just make out the side of his head. At least he knows his name's Ignatius.

"What in the name of the gods could he be talking about?" Jason asks himself. "Surely The House of Pluto does not intend to involve Demetria in their dark ceremonies? How did they know about her gifts of sight and prophecy? Her father wouldn't betray her like that, would he? But then, how involved is he with The House of Pluto? He did after all, receive the mysterious plant and he did give orders that the Temple of Truth should comply with Lord Percius' demands."

Ignatius, the dark priest takes a long swig from the jug and then looks at Thucymus with a smug grin. "The gateway to the hidden worlds of course," he slurs. "And guess who is first in line to assist old Percius on his way . . . yours truly" he says pointing to himself. "You are looking at High Priest in the making, old boy. When the gateway is opened, by our dear Sister Demetria of course, then old Percius will follow her into the hidden realms. He will then attain the holiness he desires and I will be declared High Priest while he goes on to bigger and better things. Then it's only a matter of time before it's my turn. I shall have to find a fresh virgin. It won't be easy finding one who's a mystic like Demetria though. She's supposed to be a real innocent you know. Would stop at nothing to get what she wants from the priesthood as well, and that goof Philo would do anything for her."

Eliza White Buffalo with Nicholas Black Elk

"Philo?" ask Thucymus. "I wondered why Percius had me take him to the temple." He looks around nervously again. Shock and repulsion for what he has learned is written clearly all over his face.

Ignatius finishes what's left from the jug and looks around for another one. "Not got any more?" he slurs.

"Sorry, but I know a great inn that's always open to me. We'll go in a minute. Did you say that Lord Perikles knows about all this?" asks Thucymus.

Jason listens intensely for the reply.

"Old Perry?" chokes Ignatius. "For the love of the gods, sure wasn't it him that started the ceremony in the first place?"

"Oh right, I forgot about that," lies Thucymus. "What was it he said about Demetria then? You tell it so well."

In the shrubbery Jason listens, sweating profusely with anxiety. At least it seems that Thucymus is doing his best to loosen the priest's tongue.

Ignatius gives up his search for more mead and is happy to tell more. *And why not*, he thinks to himself, *this slimy piece of work makes a great audience. When I'm High Priest I'll make him run to the ends of the earth for me. He'll get me my virgin mystic if it costs him his life.* He grins to himself as he imagines what it will be like.

"Ignatius . . . sorry . . . Your Grace," says Thucymus slyly. "Pray, what was it that Lord Perikles said?" Ignatius sits up as straight as he is able to, and with an air of authority he says, "Well, Old Perry is in the same mind about it as I am, isn't he? After all, *Lady* Perikles has been happy enough to oblige for years. It's time Demetria knows what's what; fluffing about in that Temple of Truth; time she grew up and became a real woman."

"And you're sure Perikles started the ceremony in the first place?" asks Thucymus.

"Wasn't it him who taught Old Percy what he knows?" slurs Ignatius. "Besides, he's not gone empty handed all these years, has he? You don't think he could afford to give the good lady all that jewellery with a mere government pay, do you? Anyway, you're doing alright out of this. Not having second thoughts are you?"

Thucymus just smiles and says something about the mead making him soft but the truth is he's feeling sorry he ever got involved with Percius in the first place.

"You foolish ass!" Jason silently hisses at him. "What on earth did Lord Percius promise him in return for his service?" he wonders. "How much did he get? He's just as mercenary as Perikles, selling out his own daughter for money. How long did Thucymus slither around Hermetius for? I must not waste another minute" he tells himself. "I must get to Demetria. Surely they don't intend to harm her? Oh Sweet Athena! Send your army of angels to watch over her."

∞∞∞∞∞∞∞∞∞∞∞∞∞∞∞∞∞∞∞∞∞∞∞∞∞

The Temple of the House of Pluto is not unlike the Temple of Truth. Along its front runs a long colonnade made from white marble. It is only when one steps inside the main corridor that one sees the difference. On its walls are hangings of macabre scenes; men and women writhing in pain, in places that are obviously meant to portray the underworld. Devils and demons strike them with pitchforks and throngs of fire. As our foursome walk the length of the deserted corridor I become quite distraught with fear. After all, these are the places of my dark visions.

To Eusebius' great surprise, I grasp on to his hand, holding Eumelia's with my other hand. But instead of pulling away, he smiles to himself. The act of me holding his hand in the face of fear seems somehow natural to him. "It is the way it should be," Eusebius tells himself. "Have I not always believed that I am her guardian spirit? That I was put in the service of Perikles just so that I can be near to her, to protect her, to teach her, and to show to her the ways of the spirit?"

Duncan is forced to walk in front of us, partly because we walk three abreast and take up the width of the corridor, and partly because only he knows the way to Lord Percius' chambers. We reach the chambers without once coming into contact with anyone else.

"It seems everyone is at *our* temple," whispers Eumelia to me.

"Who goes there?" comes a loud voice from the side.

We all jump with surprise as a large figure looms out of the darkness from the right. A guard seems to have appeared out of the wall itself. He glowers at Eusebius, recognizing the servant's attire, and his eyes fall to his hand grasped firmly with mine.

Duncan leans towards my ear. "Leave the talking to me," he whispers. And then he announces, "I am Duncan of Deismut."

My spine tingles at the strength in his voice as he says, "I am sure you have heard of me. And this is Sister Demetria and Sister Eumelia of The Temple of Truth. Sister Demetria has come on important family business. She and her servant here have been instructed by her father, Lord Perikles, to

Eliza White Buffalo with Nicholas Black Elk

locate a certain farmer by the name of Philo and bring him back with them. It is believed that Philo is here somewhere at the temple."

"That is correct," the guard replies scanning Eumelia and me with lustful eyes. Despite this, my heart leaps with hope because Philo is here.

"Come this way," says the guard. "He's in the food hall dining with Lord Percius."

The guard leads the way back where we came from and off to the right. He stops at a large wooden door. "Wait here" he says, and goes into the room closing the door behind him. Several moments later he reappears and tells us to enter. Duncan goes in first, then Eumelia, then me, and then Eusebius who is still holding tight to my hand. The food hall is hardly distinguishable from any other food hall, except perhaps that it is a little larger than most. In the centre is placed a large rectangular wooden table around which sit several men. I quickly pick out Philo sitting at the bottom of the table; opposite him is Lord Percius. Three priests who were deep in conversation fall into silence as our small party enters the room.

"Philo!" I call out.

I am immediately silenced by Duncan's large hand on my shoulder. "Quiet!" he whispers in my ear.

Philo leaps up from the table and hurries to my side. He notices Duncan's angry expression when I throw my arms around him, hugging him tightly. Ignoring Duncan, he puts his arm around my waist, holding me protectively. I am not so frightened now. Philo will protect me from any harm. I smile to myself smugly. I have Philo's arm around me, and I have Eusebius behind me, *and* I have Duncan to the right of me. What can possibly go wrong?

"My Lord!" Philo addresses the high priest, "It seems you have got her to come after all, even without my assistance. I cannot say that I am glad but it is a good thing that her elder, Sister Eumelia is here, for she is the Holy Pythia and will be able to dispel any notion you may have about Demetria being chosen."

"Chosen for what, Philo?" I ask, holding tighter to him. The idea of being chosen for anything important has me tingling with excitement. What can it be?

"It seems that Lord Percius is convinced that you possess paranormal powers," Philo tells me. "He has been asking me all sorts of questions but I have not betrayed you, My Dear."

Great Zeus! So my visionary gifts have caught the attention of Lord Percius? I study him now before us. He glances at me; only briefly so that he

124

gives nothing away of what he knows. It seems he is amused at Philo's attempt at gallantry. He laughs rudely, shooing his priests out of the room.

"Go on with you," he sneers, "leave me alone to entertain my guests. Guard, you stay here."

After the three priests leave and the door is firmly closed behind them, Lord Percius stops his feigned laughter and gestures to us all to sit down around the table. He walks about the room, his hands held behind his back in a haughty manner.

"I didn't like the sound of that smarmy git in the first place," I whisper across the table to Eumelia, who shakes her head meaning shh, don't cause any trouble. But I am not to be silenced. I have taken strength from the presence of my three protectors; Philo, Eusebius and Duncan.

Standing up, I make myself heard. "Lord Percius," I declare, "I have come under instruction from my father to locate Philo and bring him back with me. Now that I have found him I shall be on my way."

"Oh!" Lord Percius grins, "I must say your reputation does not do you justice at all. It seems you know full well what you want. And you are not afraid to speak your mind eh?"

"My disposition is no business of yours, Sir" I retort proudly. "If you will excuse us my company and I will be on our way."

"Stay where you are" Lord Percius shouts at us. "No-one is going anywhere." He takes a deep breath in and then out slowly, staring at me once more with feigned amusement. "Forgive me," he says much too sweetly. "I merely wish to speak with you alone about a matter which I feel will be of great interest to you."

"You shall not speak with Demetria unless I am there too," states Philo angrily.

"And me," declares Duncan, much to Philo's surprise.

Eumelia stands up and comes to my side. "If it concerns Demetria, it concerns The Temple of Truth," she states nervously. She has no intention of leaving me for a moment, particularly with this rude excuse for a lord.

Poor Eusebius! He listens to all of this with the silence and humility befitting a slave. He gives the high priest the respect his status calls for, even though all would agree that this supposedly holy man is nothing but a rude, abusive, possibly dangerous criminal. But somewhere deep inside Eusebius' being is a *true* and honoured holy man. It is *that* man that speaks now; that man that knows just how worthy and valuable a human being he actually is. That man stands up and walks to Lord Percius; he stands just a step from him, face to face, while everyone else in the room stares and listens in awe to what he has to say.

"I am Eusebius," he says in a holy voice. "I have come with the Lady Demetria to assist her and protect her. All her life I have endeavoured to protect her to the very best of my ability. And I have done this all ways. But not only am I to protect her because I am her earthly servant but also because, and more importantly, I am a servant of Heaven. In this way it is my heavenly duty to guide her, protect her, and love her as I would my own sister. I know what it is you want from her; I see it written in your soul. But hear me now for it will be a cold day in Hades, or should I say Pluto, when I permit you to lead her unwittingly along this road."

Eusebius' holy voice leaves a big silence behind it and Lord Percius is compelled by the very authority he professes to have, to agree to the holy man's terms.

"You shall have your audience for it is to be" Eusebius, the holy man continues. "But your audience shall not be one, but three, which is also written. The sister shall be accompanied by Sister Eumelia and since the third is not here, then Philo shall be present in his stead. In this way, Lady Demetria can feel safe to make any choice she wishes."

And with that Eusebius bows slightly to Lord Percius and sits once again at the table, the holy man within apparent for all to see. I look directly into his eyes and the Red Stone of Power leaps gladly in my heart space as I recognize the man gazing back at me. It is Amir, my star brother.

"Agreed!" Lord Percius states after another silence in the room. "Shall we retire to my chambers? It is much more comfortable there," he adds.

"This will do," states Philo, signalling to Duncan and Eusebius to go. "You may wait outside Eusebius," he says. Eusebius gives a small bow to Philo and then to me, and with a reluctant Duncan he leaves the room.

Lord Percius fumbles in his robes for something which he does not seem to find because he gives up the search and sits in front of the fire, facing the table and us around it who are waiting defensively for whatever it is that he wishes to say to me. The ungodly priest takes several deep breaths and then begins. "Sister Demetria," he says, deciding to be direct. "It has come to our knowledge that you are in possession of certain spiritual gifts. As a priestess, and since you are about to be inaugurated into the eighth house . . . Oh yes! I too have the gift of knowing, My Dear. Do you not think that the gods would honour the underworld every bit as much as the other worlds? Is not the underworld an intricate part of our universe?"

The Four Ascents

"It is not Pluto that I have a problem with, My Lord, but it is what is done in His name that I disagree with," I reply though I am very interested now in what Lord Percius has to say.

"No doubt you have heard the rumours that there are those among us that like to dabble in dark magic," he continues, smirking. "I can assure you that anything done in this temple under my supervision is done with honour for all the gods, not just Pluto. I am not a fool to think that wrong doing never happens within these sacred walls but you can trust that it is never intentional, nor may I add does it go so far that I do not hear of it."

"So how far does it go then, Lord Percius?" asks Eumelia.

He chuckles confidently. "Please! People! I feel we have gotten off to a bad start. It seems you are under the impression that I am not to be trusted. I am High Priest at this temple, you understand. I have the authority to banish anyone who even smells of wrong doing. In the same way I have the authority to *elevate* anyone that shows promise. One such as you, My Good Sister," he says to me.

My interest in his words doubles instantly. Is he saying that I could be high priestess, and that he would see to it? I glance at Eumelia who immediately sees what I am thinking of.

"Sister, you are to be exalted in The Temple of Truth, remember?" she tells me.

"Although Jason is adamant that I am not to be exalted any higher than the whole," I retort.

I turn my eyes away from Eumelia. I know that she would disapprove of what I'm thinking now, which is that if I were to be exalted beyond the peerage of the priesthood then surely I would be in a position to become the prophet I'm destined to be. One glance at Lord Percius tells me that here is a man that understands what it is to be ambitious; to want the very best for oneself. And he may be an insolent tyrant but he *is* able to clear the way for me.

"And what do you propose Lord Percius?" I ask to Eumelia's dismay.

"I propose that you do not be exalted in The Temple of Truth," he replies, "but as I was about to say before I was interrupted. Come here instead and work under the direction of Pluto. There is so much suffering and despair in this city. We need a high priestess that is able to be all things to these wretched souls. I must confess, I am but a man, albeit one with knowledge. But it is all very well having knowledge and truth, but what good is it without the power to use it. *Your* temple is worthy of the gods no doubt but when a person is left with only truth; left to cope with it in a life that perhaps is one

Eliza White Buffalo with Nicholas Black Elk

of loss and pain, then that truth is not much good to them without hope. *Hope*, My Good Sister is what you will be. You will be a light of hope shining in the darkness of their lives. All who look to you for guidance will receive what they need to lighten their lives. It is the gift of hope, My Good Sister that you will give to the world."

"Indeed that may be so," adds Philo, "but she can give this gift to the world from The Temple of Truth, can she not, from anywhere actually?"

"Of course," Lord Percius replies, "but where are the very souls that are most in need of her, not in The Temple of Truth. Nor are they in the mountains among the goats. You see, when a person is in despair and their soul is in danger of losing its way, then it is to the great god Pluto that they come with arms outstretched. It is *He* who promises solace and respite from their pain. They don't want to go to Athena or Apollo who will only instruct them to accept their pain and be brave. People want their suffering taken from their shoulders. They want to know, no, to *feel* that there is hope." And when Lord Percius has delivered his inspiring speech he turns to me and asks "Sister Demetria, can we depend on you to be our pillar of hope?"

Oh Sweet Athena! How I deliberate over the choice that has just been put to me! I rise and walk about the room, enquiring of each face as I go, silently asking them for their thoughts. If I were to accept Lord Percius' offer and be inaugurated into The House of Pluto I would no doubt be in the perfect position to help the masses. If I were to stay in The Temple of Truth, then yes, I would be exalted there also but perhaps not in a way that would show me to be special in any way. And I should be. Has not Eumelia been exalted for *her* gifts? The seat of the Oracle of Delphi is indeed an honour for anyone. I have the gift of prophecy. People should listen to me. I wonder what Philo would do with this gift. He would say that we are all as meek little children of the one father/mother god, and that it is enough to know that we are loved and cherished so we have no need to set ourselves aside from others. No, he would not agree with my yearnings. Looking away from him, I let my thoughts fall upon Eumelia. Oh well, she will no doubt say that I seek to align myself with greatness and that I will displease the gods. No, she will definitely not agree with me. I turn my thoughts to Eusebius and at the same time try to block out what is going on in the room. Tuning into him in this way I am saddened because I know that he would dismay of my choice.

"Dear Eusebius, or should I say Amir," I silently project into his thoughts. "I never want to hurt you but I fear that you are not with me on this. Surely

The Four Ascents

you were the one to speak of the prophecy? How can it be that now when the opportunity arises for it to speak you clearly are against me going forwards?"

Words come back to me as thoughts, as if by an answer, "Eliza, listen to me," they say. "The Red Stone of Power dwells yet in your heart space. If you wish to honour it you would do well to come to the centre where the two roads meet. Only there will you find that you are truly exalted and yet you are no greater than a grain of sand."

With my heart sinking, the face of Duncan comes into my mind. He is looking at me with adoration in his eyes and my heart lightens at the sight of him. Oh Duncan, what would you say? Tell me what I should do. As I see with my inner sight, he smiles broadly and with a wink of an eye he fills my saddened heart with breathless love and hope. I am decided.

"Lord Percius! You have just got yourself a new graduate," I state bravely, "Soon to be High Priestess?"

"Indeed," he replies, exuberant. "And there is no time like the present. The ceremonial chamber is set and ready. Welcome to the House of Pluto, Sister, or should I say Your Grace." Outside on the colonnade Eusebius' heart skips a beat. He sighs heavily, having silently perceived the choice that has sealed my destiny.

∞∞∞∞∞∞∞∞∞∞∞∞∞∞∞∞∞∞∞∞∞∞∞∞∞

It is midnight and the full moon is bright and crisp in the clear sky. The stars twinkle all about but the atmosphere is sullen and dreary. Duncan and Eusebius are alone in the torch lit colonnade, each one there for his own reason, determined to stay and wait even if he must wait until morning.

"Master Duncan, why don't you retire?" Eusebius asks after an hour has passed. "I must stay here as Master Philo requested but there is no reason for you to wait."

"Eusebius? Is that your name? Eusebius?" asks Duncan. Eusebius nods. "Well Eusebius, I can see that you are a loyal servant. And I can see that you think highly of the lady. You would do anything for her, would you not?"

"I would, Master Duncan. I would die for her if necessary," replies Eusebius.

"So would I, Eusebius, so would I," Duncan says. He gives Eusebius an intense look.

The slave studies Duncan's eyes and says, "Forgive me, Master, but my betrothed, Xanthe says that you and the lady are in love."

Eliza White Buffalo with Nicholas Black Elk

Duncan's heart leaps with joy. "She has been talking about me, and to her servants of all people, and she has spoken of love," he tells himself happily. He looks at Eusebius with curiosity. Who is this slave that speaks so boldly? "I watched you in there," he tells him. "The way you spoke to Lord Percius was as if you are not a slave or even a mere man. You commanded him with the words you spoke and the way you delivered them. That is not the force of an ordinary man but a man like no other. And I see how devoted you are to the lady, yet it is not as I love her, with a love that a man has for a woman, nor even with a love that a slave has for his mistress, but a love that is . . . that is . . ." He cannot find the word to define what he means.

"Divine?" Eusebius suggests.

"Yes," Duncan says slowly and he stares into the eyes of the slave again. Eusebius' eyes also seem to be divine. At this very moment they are shining as if they are two pools of crystal light. Duncan is rapt in them. To him the semi-darkness in the colonnade slowly disappears as the light from the slave's eyes seems to be intensifying. A little afraid, and with shivery tingles all over his body, Duncan asks "Who *are* you?"

Eusebius doesn't answer but smiles kindly and puts his hand on Duncan's head. Duncan's first thought is to pull away but instead of feeling anger or fear or even embarrassment, what he feels is something completely unknown to him yet at the same time it feels familiar; as familiar as coming home. Warmth surrounds him and he smiles. Tears sting his eyes and he lets them fall, not knowing or caring what they are about. Darkness falls over his vision. In that darkness a picture begins to emerge . . .

. . . Suddenly, there is a different land around them. Duncan finds himself standing with Eusebius in a sweet smelling meadow. What is that wonderful smell? Oh! It's strawberries; they are eating strawberries. And here comes Demetria. He rushes to meet her, full of happiness that he has strawberries to give her. She is so happy to see him; it is as if she radiates love to him. Eusebius joins them and talks with Demetria. Duncan cannot hear what they are saying but he feels that it is something of great importance. There is a bond between them, not as mistress and slave, but as peers in a common quest. He is part of that bond also. He watches Eusebius bow low to Demetria and call her by her name. But it is not Demetria he says. It is another name, a name that Duncan has dreamed of ever since setting foot on the shores of Greece. That name is Eliza.

The Four Ascents

The picture vanishes and he is standing on the colonnade with Eusebius before him, one hand on his head. Eusebius lowers his hand and smiles, "Now ask me the same question?"

Duncan has to think for a moment. Oh yes! "Who *are* you?" he asks again.

"I am Amir, he that you saw," is the reply.

"And Eliza? The woman I dream of . . . . she is Demetria?"

"Yes."

"Then if that is true she belongs with us, not in there" Duncan says pointing into The House of Pluto.

"That is so," replies Eusebius.

"If you knew this, why did you let her stay?"

"How am I to stop her? Besides, it is the path she has chosen," says Eusebius.

"It is true then that she possesses paranormal powers?"

"It is."

"And what you just did to me, she can do that too?" Duncan asks

"Perhaps," replies Eusebius.

"And me. What about me?"

"What about you?"

"In the . . . . the thing you showed me . . ."

"The soul memory," says Eusebius.

"In the . . . the soul memory . . . it was as if we three were bonded," Duncan tells him. "I didn't hear what you were saying to her but it is as if I know what it is anyway."

"And what is that?" asks Eusebius.

"That she has paranormal powers; that she is a prophet and so are you; that she possesses something of great value; is it that which Percius wishes to gain from her?"

"I believe so," Eusebius replies, feeling proud to hear Duncan speak like that. He wonders if he should tell him that he, Duncan, is *also* Amir, his star brother and that Demetria is their star sister, Osiah, known as Eliza upon the earth. He decides not to; Master Duncan is not ready.

"Then why on earth did you not stop her?" asks Duncan becoming irritated at Eusebius' short replies. "She belongs with us. Hell, she could be in great danger."

131

"She knows what she's doing," says Eusebius looking out across the darkness of the gardens. He won't say anything else just yet; Master Duncan is not ready to hear the truth.

Duncan could only stare open mouthed at Eusebius. He has never known a man like this before. As far as he knows, Eusebius may not even be a mortal human being at all. Could it be that he is a god, sent to show him the way? If this is true then does that make Demetria a goddess? He shivers profoundly and sends a silent prayer to his Celtic deity. "Help me to know what is right," he prays.

Suddenly he is grabbed from behind. He swings around to find Brother Jason there, panting heavily as if he had run a great distance.

"She *doesn't* know what she's doing," pants Jason, breathlessly. "She *is* in danger, grave danger perhaps."

"What!" Duncan and Eusebius exclaim together.

Duncan grabs Jason by his shoulders. "You must tell me immediately. What danger is she in? What are they going to do to her?" he demands to be told.

As Jason tells his story of how he followed Thucymus and the dark priest and how he overheard their conversation, Duncan's and Eusebius' eyes open wide in disbelief and fear of what may be happening this very moment.

"Quick, we have to get her out of there," urges Duncan running to the door of the temple. It is locked. He dashes to the other door at the opposite end of the colonnade. It is locked too. Swearing, he dashes back to the other men and grabs Jason by the shoulders again, shaking him. "Why did you let her go? When I met you today you wouldn't leave her alone for a second. Why on earth did you let her go in there?"

"Oh for goodness sake, can you not see that it was you I was keeping her from?" says Jason exasperated by Duncan's oafish ignorance.

"What? What harm would *I* do her? I love her," replies Duncan defensively.

"She is betrothed to Philo. She is supposed to be with him, not you," explains Jason.

"And she is *with* him now," interjects Eusebius. "Please, Masters, she does not need us to bicker between ourselves; she needs our help."

"You're right," replies Duncan, "and Philo *is* there. What can they possibly do to with him there? If he loves her half as much as I do, then she'll be safe."

"Although Sister Eumelia is with them also. We have to get to them. One man may not be enough," says Eusebius.

"Oh no, please don't tell me Eumelia is there too," groans Jason in despair. Then he remembers, "There *is* another way into the temple," he almost shouts excitedly, "the priest spoke about a secret passageway from the temple descending down to the caves at the shore. If we go to the caves we can find the passageway and come along it to the temple here."

"Of course," adds Duncan, already striding across the grounds to the exit. "And I know which cave it is because I came up that way with Lord Percius after he met us at the harbour."

"Why come that way?" Jason yells after him. He is suspicious and his intuition is telling him that there had to be an important reason for taking a metic such a strange route to the temple.

Duncan turns around and stares at him, wondering if he can be honest. "What the hell have I got to lose," he decides to himself. "And Demetria's safety is more important than a measly payment." He shouts back to Jason, "The plant you asked me about is in a hidden room along the passageway."

"It has to be what they intend to use for this ceremony," pants Jason, hurrying to catch up with Duncan. He beckons to Eusebius to hurry. "There's no time to lose," he tells him. "When we get there I want you to wait in the cave. If we don't come back with Demetria and Sister Eumelia within say thirty minutes or so, you must go and get help. I don't care who you have to tell but get help, understand?"

"Yes, Master Jason," obeys Eusebius. "But you *will* find them, and you *will* bring her out."

∞∞∞∞∞∞∞∞∞∞∞∞∞∞∞∞∞∞∞∞∞∞∞∞

The passageway is so narrow that we are forced to walk in single file. The guard is at the fore, then Percius, then me, then Eumelia, then Philo. Behind Philo, coming last is another guard. The chiselled out rock steps descend steeply in places and we cautiously hold on to iron grips that were one time hammered into the cracks in the rock walls. The smell of seaweed and salty brine comes wafting up the stairway. A distant roaring can be heard. It is the roar of the sea. We have been informed that we are going to the temple's special ceremonial chamber.

"How far down is this chamber?" shouts Philo so that Percius can hear him from the fore. "It seems we are almost at the coast."

Lord Percius had told us before we embarked on our downward journey that the chamber was underground. "It is designed to accommodate a select

Eliza White Buffalo with Nicholas Black Elk

few only and since this is an elite ceremony, nothing but the best will do," he had added.

Philo had been very concerned at the whole strangeness of it, but Eumelia had told him that most of these temples, especially in Athens, have secret rooms underground. "The powerful energies inside the earth are sometimes availed of for holy ceremonial intentions," she had told him.

No doubt Eumelia is wondering now what on earth Hermetius would say if he knew what I am about to do. I am wondering that myself. What *will* he say to me? What will he say to *her* when he discovers that she has stood by and watched me swear service to Pluto? And what if this is all part of Athena's prophecy? Will it be my fault if the Temple of Truth is brought to its knees, perhaps before Pluto Himself? What will become of Eumelia? Will Athena cast her wrath upon me *and* her as well?

Eumelia is indeed wondering about those very things. She is wondering if she should try to change my mind, but here in this passageway it is much too difficult to hold a conversation. She can barely keep her footing. "Besides, Percius is just ahead and would likely sway Demetria's mind even further towards his gain," she tells herself. She jumps and looses her footing when Philo shouts from close behind her. "Ouch!" she exclaims, cracking her ankle against the rock.

"Almost there," shouts Percius from the front.

"Are you hurt, Sister? Do you need assistance?" Philo asks Eumelia, having grabbed her waist to steady her.

"I'm fine," she replies bravely. "I think I've cut my foot though. Ouch! Oh no, I may have sprained it." The passageway is in darkness mostly. The only light is coming from an occasional torch in the wall. "I can't see it to tell," she adds as we come to an abrupt stop.

"It seems we have finally arrived," says Philo, angry with the crude way us ladies have had to walk. He shouts up to the fore, "Sister Eumelia has injured her ankle. She needs to sit down, now!"

There is no answer but immediately a door opens up in the rock and we are all ushered in one by one to a small room made out of a cave. Philo helps Eumelia to sit down on a short sedan. The only other furniture in the room is a high table that takes up the length of the wall opposite the door and a beautiful ornate carpet covering most of the rock floor. Incense is burning on the table but it is not enough to mask the putrid smell of rotting seaweed. Also on the table are several goblets and jugs. The air is freezing cold and damp.

I sit down beside Eumelia. "How bad is it?" I ask her.

"Not too bad, dear. Don't worry. I'll be fine," she replies rubbing her ankle and grimacing.

"Perhaps some ointments?" suggests Lord Percius. "Wait here," he says and then leaves. He seems to be acting very oddly. Actually, the whole thing seems strange.

"Where's he going?" I ask the guard, "To get some ointment?"

The guard doesn't answer. He leers at Eumelia's naked ankle. She covers it up post haste. After several long minutes I begin to wonder why Lord Percius has not returned. Philo is also finding this strange. He opens the door and the guard stops him from leaving with a firm grip on his arm.

"Unhand me," Philo demands. I have never seen him so angry. He struggles to pull away from the guard's grip but the other guard is just outside the door, and he pulls the door closed. We hear it being locked on the other side. "What is going on?" Philo demands to know, "You can't keep us here. Ladies, come on, we're leaving."

Eumelia seems only too eager to get out of the passageway into the night air. Clearly, she has been feeling uneasy for quite some time and now it seems we are to be held against our will. Ignoring the pain in her ankle she hobbles over to Philo. The guard lets go of his arm and stands back, sneering at the goings on.

Trying hard to stay calm, Philo addresses me still sitting on the sedan. "Demetria, come on," he orders me. "You can come back to the temple tomorrow if that's what you really want. But for now I am ordering you as your future husband, come with me. We should not have agreed to this madness in the first place."

I would very much like to agree with him for the thought of being held by these guards is not pleasant whatsoever but the thought of upsetting Lord Percius' plans may be worse. What if he changes his mind and gets angry at being messed about like this? I may never become High Priestess of this or any other temple. Perhaps it is just Philo that is being held unwillingly. Lord Percius is obviously desperate to have me as High Priestess and he knows that I want Philo with me.

"Demetria, I mean it," Philo pleads, "It's not good what's going on. We need to go, and now."

"He's right, Demetria," adds Eumelia. "Please come home now. I will come back with you tomorrow," she says.

Perhaps I *should* come back tomorrow. Anyway, if Lord Percius wants me so badly he will be happy for me to come at all. Surely it doesn't have to be tonight, although there is a full moon tonight; tomorrow it will begin to wane.

"Demetria, please . . . I have a bad feeling about this," pleads Eumelia looking very upset. I had best postpone.

"Don't fret, Sister. I'm coming," I tell her, as much to my own relief as to hers.

I turn to speak to the guard to order him to unlock the door but he is laughing a sneering wicked laugh that fills me with sudden dread. It reminds me of the evil entity that stalks me. Suddenly the tiny room is filled with that evil. It is here and it seems that I cannot get away from it, my loved ones as well. Trembling with fear I get up slowly from the sedan and edge over to Philo who is waiting to take my hand. I reach out to him but before I can touch him the door opens and Lord Percius is back. He bursts into the room carrying a jug of something to drink.

Philo tries to hold the door open but the guard outside is too quick and the door is shut tight again. "Sorry, Lord Percius," Philo says, trying to sound assertive, "We have changed our minds and will be on our way. If you want to speak with Demetria you can do so tomorrow."

"At the Temple of Truth," adds Eumelia quickly.

My heart is pounding. The evil in the room has increased now that Lord Percius is back. Oh Sweet Athena, have I been wrong? Have I erred so greatly that the very thing I wished to avoid has sneaked up on me in my ignorance?

"But the ceremony is ready," Percius replies.

I can barely hear him with the pounding of my heart. Panic stirs within me and I feel I might cry out. I try desperately to hold on to reality. Lord Percius' words seem distant and I strain to focus on them. It seems he is concerned about the ceremony.

"That's where I was," he is saying, "making sure it was fit for a priestess such as Demetria. What can have changed your mind so suddenly?" He looks at me with intense eyes and asks me, "you haven't changed your mind, have you, Sister?"

My throat is dry but I manage to speak. My voice sounds very odd. "Well . . . it's just that I'm not feeling too well and my poor sister here has really hurt herself. It is best if we take her home. I shall return tomorrow, My Lord."

"Sit down for a moment," Lord Percius suggests. "Philo, why don't you go back to the temple? My guard will go with you. In my chambers you will

The Four Ascents

find a small cabinet stocked with wrappings and ointments. Bring some back along with a staff that will be provided for Sister Eumelia. We shall wait until you return and then we shall proceed with the ceremony as planned."

Before Philo could argue he is being pulled through the door by the guard outside the room, and the door is shut tight behind him. Shouting and struggling, he is ushered violently up the steps. He manages to turn around and face his abuser but seeing a knife being held to his neck, he has no choice but to turn around and continue up the steps. From inside the tiny cave room Eumelia and I can clearly hear his protests. We listen ashen faced as they get further and further away until they can no longer be heard at all. Terrified, I grab Eumelia's hand and she stares at me, too scared to speak. It is clear that Philo has been taken away from us against his will.

Dear Athena, what have I done? What have I gotten myself into . . . and poor Eumelia as well? What is going to happen to Philo? Will he come back with a staff so that Eumelia can walk and we can get out of here? Or is Lord Percius so persistent that he now wants Philo out of the way? Why did I agree with this? Eumelia was right; I have allowed my proud ego to get in the way of truth. I should be punished for this. Perhaps I needed punishing all along. To drag my dear sister into this, and poor Philo . . . what kind of priestess am I? I am so angry with myself. How foolish and selfish I have been!

I turn my anger on Lord Percius. "Why do you force him to leave?" I demand loudly. "Why won't you allow us to leave with him? I don't understand. What on earth do you mean to do that you must keep us against our will?" Alas, the anger does not mask the fear and Lord Percius can plainly see that I am feeling helpless. He has won.

"I'm not forcing anyone to do anything," he replies coldly. "I simply do not like my well intended plans to be cast aside, especially when I go to so much trouble. Let me offer you both a drink. I have a nice juice here that my priests squeeze themselves. It is quite delicious and refreshing and it has a little something in it that will help to relax and comfort you."

The second guard ushers us back to the sedan. We sit down on it shakily. Lord Percius goes to the table, and taking two goblets pours from the jug he carried into the room. "Here, this will make you feel much better," he tells us. "It will ease your pain as well, Sister. I take it often for aches and pains. Try some, it's hot."

Eumelia takes the offered goblet and sips. She gives me a little smile and nods. It must be good. I take the goblet offered to me and sip. It *is* good, hot and comforting.

137

Eliza White Buffalo with Nicholas Black Elk

"Thank you," I mumble.

"You're welcome," he replies with a cold smile. "And don't worry about Master Philo. He'll be back presently."

We drink the juice, relaxing a little as the hot liquid comforts us. The air in the room begins to feel warmer as we relax but the evil entity is still lurking close by. I can feel it touching my cheek with its foul breath. Will Philo be back soon? "Dear Athena, go with him," I silently pray.

What I don't know is that this very moment Philo is being pushed roughly into a cave not too far from where we sit. I don't know that he will spend long anguishing days, freezing cold and starving, only to die there alone, frightened and very angry, angry at the man who pushed him roughly into his final destination, angry at the man who had ordered his fate, but most of all, angry at me, the woman he loved, whom he had sworn to marry and who led him to his demise while she loved another.

The room is empty now, except for me and my dear sister and the evil entity that is now screaming to me of its presence. There is a stench; perhaps it is its foul breath or perhaps it is my fear. Percius and his men have left the room. I watched them go through hazy eyes and a heavy head. The door had shut with a bang which echoed through my entire body. It is trembling yet. Inside my head a thousand creatures are crawling and eating away at my mind.

I can hear Eumelia calling to me. I hear her cry out for help but her voice gets more and more distant as the creatures get louder and louder inside of me. Is Eumelia feeling like this also? What was in that drink? Have we been poisoned?

Each time I try to stand the room spins around and around and I fall back onto the sedan. As I make it to my feet one more time I see Eumelia reaching out to me. Where is she? Is she on the floor? It is impossible to tell which way is up. I lift my arm, noticing that it feels heavy, and I reach in the direction of Eumelia's hand. Just as I touch it, as I feel Eumelia's comforting fingers coil around my hand in a tight grasp, a wave of nausea sweeps through me. My belly is heaving but I must make it to the door. I must get us out of here. The urge to purge my belly is too strong and I vomit. My legs give way at the same time so that I fall heavily to the floor. When my vision settles I see the frightened face of Eumelia coming rapidly towards me. There is a loud crack like a head being hit against the rock wall, then Eumelia's limp body slumps on top of me. With the last of my strength I attempt to push her off me, crying "Eumelia, Eumelia!" but my voice sounds strange as if it doesn't belong to me.

Eumelia does not hear me, nor do I any longer. Darkness closes in around us. My body starts to shudder involuntarily and I think I have let go of my bladder. It is so cold and so dark.

Suddenly, the reaching fingers of the evil stalker wrap themselves around me. Squeezing every last drop of consciousness from my body, it writhes its way into my middle. I lie powerless, feeling it move through my middle and up my spine to my neck. It reaches its powerful hands around my throat and tightens its grip. It will surely kill me. The fires of hell spring into life around me and with each involuntary inhalation, my throat and lungs burn with searing black smoke. Am I dying?

"Oh Mighty Gods, help us," I whisper painfully. "Father/Mother God, Philo has such faith in you. If you are real then come to his aid. Have him find us before it is too late. I regret that I was foolish. I regret that I thought only of myself. Give me a second chance so that I can fulfil the prophecy in humility and grace."

I cannot hold on to consciousness a moment longer; willingly, I let go. With tears of repentance soaking my face and ready to face what comes next, I finally give in. As I do so a soothing comfort washes over me and I feel a tiny cool breath enter my lungs. The last thing I see is Philo's angry face glaring at me from within the vanishing flames. And then it is over. I see nothing, hear nothing, feel nothing; there is nothing yet I still exist . . .

. . . For what seems to be a hundred years I continue to exist without light, without air, without sustenance. For what seems to be a hundred years I lie in this state, floating in nothingness. My soul rests in peaceful quiet, not having to strive, not having to wonder, not having to be, just being.

After what seems to be a hundred years I hear a voice. At first it is small and distant. Now it is louder and clearer. It is saying "Eliza" over and over. There is no mouth, just the voice, just that one word, Eliza. The one word becomes solid. It is rock. I feel the word within me. I *am* the word. The word is rock for what seems to be a hundred years.

After what seems to be a hundred years the word changes. It is becoming less solid. It is green and it grows and breathes in the sunshine. I feel the light on my face. Oh, how sweet that sunshine feels on my face! What bliss to be touched by the light of day! For what seems to be a hundred years I am the word. I am green, growing and breathing with the sun on my face. I feel the rain on my head. I drink in the wetness of the rain. It sustains me. It helps

Eliza White Buffalo with Nicholas Black Elk

me to grow, to reach higher and higher to the light of the sun. Oh that light! How wonderful it is!

After what seems to be a hundred years the word changes and I am flying high in the skies. I fly as close to the sun as I dare. How I love the sun! That precious light! I fly close to the sun for what seems to be a hundred years, filling my soul with light and joy. Then as the word changes again I come down upon the earth. The word roams the land and eats the green. It swims the oceans and sustains itself of its bounty.

After what seems to be a hundred years the word changes and it walks on two legs. I am the word and I walk the earth. I touch the trees and the green. I drink the waters and take pleasure in the sunshine. I reach up my arms to the light and send my roots deep down into the darkness of the earth, for I am the word. I am Eliza.

After what seems to be a hundred years I hear the voice again. The voice is calling another word. It is calling "Artamor". The other word gets louder and clearer until it too stands on two legs. It is he. He is the word. He too touches the trees and the green. He too drinks the waters and takes pleasure in the sunshine. He too reaches his arms to the light and sends his roots deep down into the darkness of the earth, for he is the word. He is Artamor. For what seems to be a hundred years Eliza and Artamor walk the earth. He walks a little ahead of me at all times, showing me, teaching me, reminding me of who I am. I am the word which came from Osiah in the constellation of Serabe, to be balance of matter and light upon the earth. He is the word which is Artamor. He has come to be a walking guide, a light for me to follow. He has come to walk alongside me, a source of wisdom as I walk a human path once more.

After what seems to be a hundred years I hear the voice again. It is calling many other words. The many words come down upon the earth and they are flesh around me. They speak to me of life and stories and of being human. Many words surround me. They have human faces and human names. They come close to me and blow on my face. Their breath feels like unrest. I look to the sun for its light and warmth. As I drink in the sustaining life the faces block my vision. From a distant space I hear several voices calling to me, "Eliza, Eliza." The voices call to me but as they come closer they seem to be calling something else. They seem to be calling "Demetria, Demetria."

One voice becomes a full human body and it is Eumelia. She reaches out to me smiling. Warmth and happiness pour from her smile like sunbeams and around her head is shining a beautiful rainbow. There is a golden thread of

140

The Four Ascents

sunshine joining her heart to my heart and as a great light within her bursts forth, my heart leaps with joy and love as the word is revealed. And the word is beautiful like the most glorious music of the heavenly spheres. The music fills my being with its celestial notes. They touch every living cell within me. My whole being comes alive at their touch. I become the music until there is no separation between it and me.

"I am The Crystal Keeper," says the spirit of Eumelia.

Amidst the ecstasy I suddenly feel a tug at my heart. Eumelia is moving away from me and as she does so, the thread snaps. I no longer hear the music within me but I still feel its notes caressing my being, soothing the anguish of separation. As I watch Eumelia drifting further and further away her light dims. Soon she will be gone from me but I do not feel sad because her music still lives in my soul.

Finding my voice once again, I cry out, "Forgive me, Eumelia." May you rest in peace, My Dear Sister, until we meet again."

The other voices are getting louder now. They are much closer. And as the feeling of unrest comes back I reach my hands to the sun for salvation.

"Demetria, Demetria," I hear. Anxious voices all around me. I can see the sun but I am so cold. I do not feel its warmth. As I reach towards its light, a cold nausea sweeps over me and I vomit. The taste is salty and putrid. I feel arms around my back supporting me as clear fresh water is poured over my face and down my throat. I swallow painfully and retch again, then open my eyes once more to appeal to the sun for its light and its hope.

"She's coming to," I hear as a face appears before me; it is my wonderful star brother, Amir.

"Amir," I whisper before allowing myself to close my eyes and rest upon the sweet smelling grass. At last I can feel the heat of the sun's rays. I smile, thankful for the respite and that my heavenly brother is here.

"Amir?" someone else is saying with surprise, "she called you Amir." I open my eyes again. That voice is familiar. Who is it? Oh, it is Amir, or is it Rahtu? "Rahtu" I say smiling at him. Then I speak again, "Duncan, you came for me."

"You're a bit confused, My Lady," says Duncan, "but you'll be fine. We got you just in time."

"Philo. Where is Philo? Did he get out? Is he here?" I ask hoarsely. I am starting to feel more alive now and in the present moment. I look at Duncan and try to work out why I called him Rahtu. I know that Eusebius is Amir but who is Rahtu? "Did you find Philo?" I ask again. There is no answer.

Eliza White Buffalo with Nicholas Black Elk

Both Duncan and Eusebius look at me blankly. "I was gone so long," I tell them. "It seemed like forever . . . but it can't have been . . . can it?"

Don't fret, Demetria," says someone behind me. Turning my head, I see that one other person is here. Someone who is looking almost terrified that I nearly died; someone who is so overwhelmed with relief at saving me that he cannot speak. It is someone who came from a constellation far away, the word that was made flesh so that he could be a walking guide for me as I walk the human path once more. It is Jason. He is the word; he is Artamor.

I smile warmly at him. "I should have known you would rescue me, Jason."

He looks into my smiling face and I see a tear roll down his cheek, followed by another, then another. He hangs his head, no longer able to hold them back. "We were too late," he sobs.

"I know," I tell him, "but she's happy. I saw her just now before I opened my eyes. She was smiling. And . . . oh she was so beautiful, Jason. She was the most beautiful music. I didn't know she was music."

"I did," he replies. "I did."

∞∞∞∞∞∞∞∞∞∞∞∞∞∞∞∞∞∞∞∞∞∞∞∞∞∞∞∞∞∞

The video stops again. And Black Elk speaks . . .

"My Dear Rose, you have seen how Demetria chose her path, and the road of difficulties has resulted in a fall from grace for her soul. The temple of the soul was overthrown and dwelled in darkness, just as Athena had spoken. For what seemed to be hundreds of years but in reality is a thought, a whisper in the eternal now, the individual soul descended into the womb of Mother Earth. With Her nurturing care and loving abundance, the soul crawled out of the depths of darkness to reach to the light once more. That is why once again, for four ascents the soul will climb the stepladder to the heavenly abode. Once again, it will know the two roads. In the stillness of the crystal heart, the holy place where the two roads meet, the soul will know her wholeness.

You have understood, Rose, that the word Artamor was sent forth into the world, and the word became flesh. You understand that Artamor is a soul sent into the world to be a messenger of truth. To Eliza he is a source of strength and protection. Artamor is Jason's soul. And Eumelia, she that sealed the resurrection from the depths, the one who is known as music will be a constant companion for him. With Demetria they have expressed their oneness with Source.

You have already seen and understood how souls form groups in order to reflect the oneness that is Beloved Source. And you understand, Rose, that the soul splits into individual souls and the individual souls are sent to the earth plane to learn and grow and return to wholeness with the original soul. *This* original soul, *Eliza*, has sent many individual parts of itself to the earth plane. These are the lifetimes that you have witnessed and many more besides them. This lifetime you are in now is one such lifetime. *You* are a part of the soul, Eliza, which you understand. So you must understand that the soul, Artamor is also splintered and part of it is living on the earth. In this last lifetime that individual soul was known as Jason. Eumelia is part of the soul that she reminded you of, The Crystal Keeper. Remember The Crystal Keeper from the lifetime in Atlantis?

You see, Rose, the souls stay together, lifting each other up and presenting lessons with which to grow. In the same way, Philo who you know to be Demetria's soul mate is indeed the original soul mate that came from Pleiadies. And in the same way Seth was Phoenix's soul mate in Egypt. And Duncan, is Rahtu from ancient Egypt, who is originally Amir from Serabe who shared such huge joy with Eliza on Atlantis.

Now, in this next part of the journey you will understand that it is I, Black Elk, who is incarnate on Earth. I am not going to show you my life story or the great vision that was given to me. I have shown you parts of the vision before. When you were a child you saw what you needed to see. So now I am going to tell you about my great vision. I am going to tell you what it means to me now that I am whole with the original soul. And I want you to respond to my telling of it.

So, you're going to feel a change now, from the high energy that is holding you in vision, to a lower energy where I want you just to converse with me.

I too am a part of the soul, Eliza, as I have explained to you. My experiences on Earth were a valuable piece of the journey just as yours are, and Demetria's were, and Phoenix's too. All the splintered parts of the soul come together in wholeness and it is in this way that the soul evolves and returns to Beloved Source. I am one with the soul. I am whole with the soul; I do not feel separate and I do not have to experience duality because I have risen the four ascents and passed into Spirit where I have been welcomed back into wholeness. The wholeness that you experience within your crystal heart is but an iota of what it feels like to be free from duality and totally one with

143

Eliza White Buffalo with Nicholas Black Elk

the soul. Yet you have had glimpses of this, I assure you. When I lift your consciousness up to a level where you can travel in the Spirit World, or when you sit in trance so that I may speak to others, you feel then a greater sense of what it is like for me.

So now I shall give you an account of the great teachings that were given to me when I was upon the earth."

Part Two

THE VISION

CHAPTER EIGHT

The Six Grandfathers

"My dear Rose, I speak to you now from the realms of the spirit. I am Nicholas Black Elk. Nicholas was the name given to me by the black robes of the church when I adopted the ways of the Christian. It was a good way for me then; it taught me much about the man called Jesus and what many call Heaven and Hell. I'm happy that I learned those ways for it taught me many things."

"And these are the things that you taught me in The Green, when I was a little girl?" I ask Black Elk.

"Yes, and much more, Rose. Oh! So much more. Then I spoke to you about the knowledge of those things; from their truth and beauty and from the truth and beauty of the Lakota way also. And now I can speak to you about them with so much more understanding of the knowledge of both ways, and not only of the knowledge of those two ways, but also of the knowledge which is alive within each and every one of you on Earth. It is the knowledge of your essential nature as spiritual and human beings. This knowledge knows no religious limits, not does it know separation of any kind. So before I begin, know this, I love you, I love all of you, and I will never forget you. We are all one in spirit. I cannot love myself without loving you."

"I understand that, Black Elk," I tell him. "I feel it when we talk, and when I look at you I feel love like no love I've ever felt before."

"I am pure spirit, Rose. Spirit is Love, therefore Love is all there is here. We will talk much about all there is, and you will learn a great deal from the vision, which we are about to discuss. Are you ready?"

"I'm ready," I say, focusing on the great sense of stillness in my heart.

"As I have always said, this is the real world, the spirit world, and the physical world is but a reflection of what is. It is you that brings this truth into the physical world through your being. In this same way and only way, my great vision is in the real world. Let it be reflected on Earth through your being. I will tell you now how it is in the other world. I will talk to you about the great vision's prophecy of oneness and harmony. And you understand that

Eliza White Buffalo with Nicholas Black Elk

it is the same prophecy held in The Red Stone of Power, the same prophecy that Demetria was aware of?

"I understand that, Black Elk."

"Good. I will talk to you about the prophecy so that you might consciously choose to bring it through your being to the physical world. And believe me, by choosing to do this, you *will* be choosing oneness and harmony for yourself and ultimately for your world. And so it is that from the knowledge and wisdom of *this* world, the world of spirit, I speak to you about the vision. I will tell it to you afresh and in the present tense, in the *now."*

"Why in the present tense, Black Elk, when it was in the past?" I ask.

"Good question; the answer is because it belongs to all of us. It is not only a vision that was given to me over one hundred years ago, but it is a truth that exists within each and every one of us *now.* You will have noticed that the story I am showing to you, the journey of the soul, is shown in the present tense, in the *now."*

I nod in agreement and tell him, "I felt as if it were happening right now, to me; as if I were the person in the story. I know you mean that all those people are expressions of my original soul and so it *is* me in a way; it's my soul."

"And you felt that you were present as each of those people," Black Elk encourages.

"Exactly!"

"That is because the now is all there is. The past does not exist, albeit in our linear memory. The future does not exist either except as a projection of our minds. Therefore the present moment, *now,* is all that exists. And it is now that you can bring the truth of the vision through your being to the physical world. It is now that this choice is available to you. And since now is eternal, this choice has always been, is now, and always *will* be available to you."

"Wow! I get that, I really get that!" I exclaim.

"Ha, ha, ha, ha," he laughs, and I feel the world laugh with him. "Oh by the way, I am going to ask you a question, and I want you to feel your way to the answer."

"Okay."

"Where is Little Buffalo?"

I'm not sure I even know who Little Buffalo *is,* but I do feel a sense of the soul whom Black Elk speaks of. So I tell him, "I *feel* him, Black Elk, I really do, but I don't know where he is. Will he be coming into my life again?"

The Four Ascents

"You'll see. But let me tell you this: when John Neihardt came to me on Earth. You know, when he listened to my telling of the vision and then he wrote *Black Elk Speaks* . . . I could see in John the one who was Little Buffalo. It seemed to me at the time that Little Buffalo was inside John. I know now that he and John share soul energy; do you remember we talked about this concept before . . . sharing soul energy?"

"I do. It was Uncle Gerry who first mentioned it to me."

"That is because Uncle Gerry shares soul energy with our soul, Eliza," Black Elk explains to me. "But anyway, you will learn more about sharing soul energy as you move forwards on your path. For now, just know that Little Buffalo shares soul energy with John's soul, and so it was possible for Little Buffalo's soul to impress upon John and determine John's spiritual knowing if you like. Do you understand?"

"Aye, I think so . . . it's like when Uncle Gerry was able to speak to me from the spirit world. I could *feel* him, almost like I can feel you."

"That is correct. So John was feeling Little Buffalo, and in this way he brought Little Buffalo's energy into my life."

"Oh, aye!" I exclaim, "And when Uncle Gerry came to visit me when I was ill he was bringing *your* energy into *my* life."

Black Elk gives me an ethereal hug. "Exactly like that" he agrees. "Now to the vision, Rose; I had that vision when I was very ill. I was lying on skins in the tepee and I saw quite a lot that you in particular will be interested in knowing."

"Oh, yes?" I am intrigued already.

"Do you remember when you were nine years old and I showed you part of the vision? Do you remember when we entered a tepee wherein a little boy lay sick?"

"Aye, I remember that. I remember the boy changed into the little girl from Mexico, Maria, and then into me at the age I was then. You told me there was no separation between us."

"That's right. Well, when I was a child lying sick in that tepee, and I was unconscious of course, you understand . . ."

"Of course."

"I saw two people step into the tepee. It was a man and a strange looking little girl. At the time the man looked familiar to me, like I knew him but couldn't recognize him. It was me as a man, and the girl was you, or rather it was our *spirits*. When I took you on that journey and we stepped into the tepee, we actually stepped into that very moment, and the unconscious child,

149

Eliza White Buffalo with Nicholas Black Elk

who was me, saw us. He saw us because he was in the world of spirit. It was only his conscious mind that was asleep, not his spirit. You see how all is in the now; there is no linear time, not in spirit?"

"Wow! I do . . . I can see that," I agree. "It all makes sense to me, all these lifetimes that you showed me really *are* in the present moment. It's all now, all happening now. And the reason I could see you lying on the bed and then see you change into Maria from Mexico, and then into me, is because all these people are part of the one original soul, which is whole. The different people are the different splintered parts of that soul."

"Well done, Rose," Black Elk says with a grin. "That's it. So, there I was lying on that bed and I was seeing with my spiritual sight because I was in the spirit world; my body was asleep on the skins. All of a sudden you were there with the man that I would grow into. I didn't know that at the time of course and I thought you to be very strange."

"Me?"

"I was an Indian boy, remember, I had never seen a white girl before never mind a girl from a hundred years in the future."

"Tee hee, hee, hee" I giggled "I must have seemed very strange indeed."

"Ha ha, okay. I guess you understand then how it is in the spirit world?" Black Elk asks me.

I sum up what he's told me so far, "Okay, the spirit world is the real world and in reality time does not *really* exist. The present moment is all there is, so when I travelled in spirit to the time in your life when you were a little sick boy I was actually not moving *back* in time but entering a reality where all time is now. In this way I was able to see you as a child, and you as a child, were able to see me."

"Exactly, well done!" he replies. "And this is how it was when I was given my great vision. I was lying on the skins, in my parents' tepee, and I saw those guardian spirits coming from the sky."

"Were they angels do you think?" I ask.

"Some may like to think of these messengers as angels or spirit guides. The truth was they were spirit in a form that I could relate to according to my belief system. If you believe that angels carry messages to us then angels is what you would see in that situation. With you, for example, you already saw spirit people around you; people who had passed into spirit, and so when you first saw *me*, your spirit guide, you saw me as I was on earth, an old Native American man with a worn out bible in his hands. The white cross on the cover was *my* idea," he added with a grin.

"Genius," I declare. When I was a kid and I met with Black Elk in the spirit world, in the place called The Green, he would have been holding a black book in his hand and on the cover was a white cross, a symbol of the two roads which he explained to me.

"Okay now, Rose, we must move on with the story or we shall be here when you too are ready to pass into spirit," he says now with a cheeky glint in his eyes. "These two messengers were coming for me to take me on a journey, just like I would do for you. They were bringing the wisdom of Grandfather Spirit or Beloved Source of All That Is. You call it God but for the ease of simplicity I will call it Source. So these messengers had come from Source carrying great wisdom. They each carried a spear and each spear had lightning coming from its point. It seemed to me then to be lightning but in essence was that which gives us life, that which becomes the very spark of our being. I'm talking about pure life force from Source. It is when that essence is brought into the realm of the material that it becomes a spark, for when you marry a positive life-giving charge to a negative receptive charge, that action creates a spark just like lightning. So the messengers were bringing the Source of life to me so that my body could be well again, you see?"

"I understand," I reply "please, go on."

"Those messengers had been calling me for some time, and as they touched the ground they called me again. They told me to listen because my grandfathers were calling to me. What was happening was Source was calling to me; I was hearing the voice of Source calling me to wake up and listen. So I got up and I saw that my body was lying there still. And I walked right out of that tepee and stepped onto a cloud that the two messengers had come to earth on. Then the cloud hurried back into the sky with me on it and the two messengers flying ahead of me leading the way. Do you understand what was happening, Rose? When I was going up into the sky, do you understand what was really happening?"

"Aye, I do, your consciousness was being hiked up. The spirit guides or messengers were hiking your awareness up," I reply.

"That's correct," he tells me, "I was going into the world of my higher consciousness or awareness . . . yes, I was becoming more aware of spirit, of Source. All around I saw many clouds that seemed to whisper to me. They were the whispers of my soul reminding me of who I was, of who I was in many lifetimes on Earth, and of who I was yet to be. My entire existence was there among those clouds in the world of spirit."

Eliza White Buffalo with Nicholas Black Elk

"Was it like what you doing with me here today?" I ask. "Did you see your soul's journey like you are showing me?"

"No, it was like a moment of knowing. I heard those whispers and I knew, I remembered."

"Wow, how amazing!"

"Source never ceases to be amazing to those below, Rose. His greatness gives a feeling of awe to those who only touch upon a tiny part of Him, so you can imagine the awe I felt while I was so much closer."

"Indeed."

"And when those two spirit messengers spoke to me the awe I felt was great. I admit I was afraid. They told me to listen to The Red Stone of Power."

"Aha! The Red Stone of Power!" I exclaim.

"*It dwells within your heart space,* they told me. *It is the prophecy that will be shown to you.* In that moment I felt a tiny leap of joy in my heart. It was a familiar sign that I was hearing or feeling truth."

"I feel it too," I tell Black Elk.

"I know you do," he replies. "So there I was and the messengers were telling me that I was to be shown a prophecy, and I knew what they were really saying was that I was to be shown the truth of who I am, *all* of who I am, *and* what was to be. *Are you ready to see your truth, Black Elk,* they asked me. And they showed me a bay horse standing some distance away from us. Now the bay horse is a being with four legs and this was important because it was meant to represent to me a being with four aspects to its nature. These aspects are represented in my Lakota tradition as west, north, east and south, and in some traditions as body, mind, spirit and emotion. In some traditions they are the elements of all life; earth, air, fire, and water. So this bay horse stood before me then representing the source of life, Beloved Source. It turned to the directions, which as I said, represented the four aspects of its nature. It turned to the west first and there I saw twelve black horses with buffalo hoofs in their manes and thunder in their nostrils. They represented the aspect of Source that brings life in abundance, hence the buffalo hoofs, for the buffalo was a source of abundance for the Indian people. And the thunder represented the aspect of Source that brings death, hence the storms that come and destroy life on earth. Are you following me?"

"I am, Black Elk," I answer. "It is the aspect of Source that gives life and takes it way also. It is death and rebirth?"

152

The Four Ascents

"Exactly, so the bay horse then turned to the north and what I saw there was twelve *white* horses. They had snow in their manes and wind in their nostrils. And all around the white horses I saw white geese flying. White, white, white; why was it all white, Rose?" Black Elk asks me.

"Because all that comes from the north is white?" I guess.

"Yes, the white wind of the north is cleansing and healing. It blows away all shadow; and the snow that comes in the winter clears the earth of all disease. White, white, white; Spirit is in all things and all things are in Spirit. And I say white is in all colours and all colours are in white. Ah white! White was all around; all was spirit, all was whole. And the bay horse was facing this white and he told me to pay attention because it was my truth, the truth of who I was, who I *am*. Now, the bay horse then turned to the east and told me the same, to watch and see my truth. I saw in the east twelve *red* horses this time. They had elk teeth hung around their necks and the light of dawn shone in their eyes. This light is the power that makes all things renewed. It is rebirth, if you like, the light of understanding, the light that dispels the darkness just as daybreak chases the night."

"You have often told me that whoever sees the daybreak star gains much understanding, Black Elk," I tell him. "That is one of the reasons I like to get up early and witness the dawn."

"And you are a good student, my white buffalo woman. You listen well. I am proud of you."

"Thank you. I love you and I always try to listen at least."

"I love you too, White Buffalo, Rose. So tell me, when the bay horse turned then to the south, what did I see there?" Black Elk asks.

"Twelve yellow horses with manes that were alive and growing," I reply.

"And why was this?"

"Because the south represents Earth and it is the aspect of Source that makes things grow?"

Black Elk smiles and says, "You are partially right. Yes, it is the aspect of Source that brings growth, but I will explain more in a bit. So, let me recap, there I stood in a world of white, before this bay horse who not only represented Source but also who I was, a spiritual being with the Source of All Things dwelling within my highest consciousness. It had shown to me four aspects of Source and told me that I would come to know them as four aspects of my *Self*. The next thing that happened was the bay horse told me that my grandfathers were meeting and that all those horses were going to take me to them. I understand now that it meant that all the four powers,

153

Eliza White Buffalo with Nicholas Black Elk

four aspects of Source, were coming closer to me, or rather that *I* was coming going closer to *them*. I say that because the horses represented four aspects of my higher Self. I was to become closer to them by becoming more aware of my Self."

"Isn't that the part of the vision when the horses began to dance?" I ask.

"Yes, they did," Black Elk replies. "They all began to dance. They were showing me what was really happening within me, which was that I was becoming more aware of the four powers of Source that was my higher Self. As they danced, coming together in one dance they were showing me, that within and without, the four powers of my Self were coming together in response to the call of Source. As I watched that thunderous display of power I was in awe of it because I knew that they were dancing my truth in that world of Spirit. All that is in Spirit is reflected on Earth, so the dance of power was being made manifest in my earthly self. It was no wonder I was in awe of what I was seeing and feeling."

"So, you mean you were becoming more powerful on Earth?" I ask.

"Yes, I would never be the same again. My earthly being that was Black Elk would have power dancing within him that would bring him closer to his higher Self."

"I see. You were becoming closer to your wholeness . . . just like I am now," I add, hoping I'm correct.

"Yes! Well understood, Rose. Let's move on now . . . the dance was over and the horses all changed into birds and animals of all kinds. That showed me that I was all living things. There they were showing me that I was these four aspects of Source coming together in wholeness as you say, and they were then showing me that this wholeness was all living things. Therefore, they were showing me that *I* was all living things, *I* was the Source of All Things. My spirit grew brighter and stronger then and it seemed to encompass all that was there. The dance was gone and the animals and birds were gone but I knew that all was within me. And I turned to the bay horse that represented Source for even more understanding. We walked in that world of white, me and the bay horse, the bay horse representing Source leading the way. Soon, I saw a cloud that was shaped like a tepee. It was almost exactly like a tepee. The tepee shape looks like a triangle with three equal sides. Do you understand, Rose, that it meant that Source has three faces?"

"Well, it seems to me that everything in the vision was a representation of Source. So I guess it meant that Source has three faces or three main parts, yes."

154

The Four Ascents

"Well understood, Rose. That is exactly what it represented. Everything in the vision represented the *I* within, the Self within, or Source. So the Self has three faces, three parts of the one source, and these are the male part, the female part, and of course, the marriage between the two which is the child part: three supreme beings in one Source. And this is how all things are created, in three stages." As I listen to Black Elk saying this about three faces of Source and three stages of creation my heart begins to throb and I know that I should understand. However, I'm not altogether clear on Black Elk's wisdom.

"I'm not sure I know what you mean," I tell him, "but my heart is throbbing. The Red Stone of Power is telling me that I *do* know, but you'll have to enlighten me."

"Okay, Rose, consider this . . . Three supreme parts of the one being is the Source of All Things. That is creation itself. The Indians believe in Father Sky, Mother Earth, and us as the children. And the Indians see *all* life as belonging to north, east, south . . . are you with me? I'll give you a hint: Spirit, enlightenment, growth . . ." He stops speaking there and waits for me to understand.

Hmm, I am thinking . . . *Father, Mother, Child, and north, east, south,* and *spirit, enlightenment, growth* . . . "I know!" I suddenly say with a grin. "The Father sends forth the word . . . that is the North bit. And the Mother gives birth to the word making it flesh . . . that is the east bit." I wait for Black Elk to speak and when he doesn't I go on, "And the south bit is the growing bit. Therefore, the word grows with the child; the word *is* the child."

"Ha, ha, well done, Rose," Black Elk replies triumphantly. "All creation is made up of three parts; it begins as nothing with Father Spirit, it is but desire. Desire becomes thought which is sent forth as light and becomes flesh through Mother Earth. It then grows into fullness of being, balanced between Spirit and Earth; it is the marriage of the two; it is the Child. Or another way of saying this is it is creation. I am telling you that all creation is the Child of Source."

"Right," I nod, biting my lip. "What about west?"

"All creation comes full circle and dies to its earthly body. From the west of its life it goes back to Spirit in the north only to be reborn in the east; and so all of life is eternal."

"Okay," I grin, "*Now* I'm satisfied, ha, ha!"

Eliza White Buffalo with Nicholas Black Elk

"Good, well I like you to ask questions; although you know you really do understand . . . you just like to speak it out loud, don't you?" Black Elk says grinning back.

"It helps me to be clear on what I'm feeling," I explain. "When I hear it spoken I can make sense of it."

"Oh Dear Rose, do you think I don't know that? I know everything little thing about you," he tells me lovingly.

What a great feeling his words give to me! My heart is filled with the warm security of knowing that I am completely safe because he loves me and is always one step ahead of me, always aware of my needs.

"Now that we have understood the three supreme beings in one I will carry on with what I saw in the vision," Black Elk continues after I cry a few tears, tears that release me from any tension I am holding in my body. "So I was looking at this tepee and I saw that a rainbow was the open door of it. As I came closer to it I saw that six old men were inside it. The many horses were all standing around it. The blacks were in the west and the whites in the north and so on. So here is another part of the truth: the horses were each in their quarter around the tepee which was representing Source with its three faces. There were twelve horses in each quarter and in the centre was one being with three faces each with four aspects to it. And this being represented my Self remember; this was who I was, my truth. So we have one being which is three, and we have four times three which is twelve. Source is twelve then; that is why there were twelve horses in each quarter. So this represented who I was, who I *am.*"

"And who *I* am," I add.

"Yes, we are all one in Source, and Source is the Self within. And here we understand the Self is one, yet it is three, and it is four times three which is twelve. And we could go on and on because I was shown twelve horses in each aspect of Source, therefore each of the twelve is twelve which makes one hundred and forty four and so on and so on. You see how Source is endless, Rose?"

"Yes . . . infinity; they say God is infinite."

"Exactly, so I was shown that my higher Self, my Source is infinite and at the same time is one being."

"As you say, there is no separation . . . mitakuye oyas'in . . . all are relatives"

"You understand well, Rose," replies Black Elk. "Now, I was shown that the Self is twelve, Source is twelve; that is why there were twelve horses in each quarter. As well as this there were six old men within the tepee. Now, since Source is both male and female then each of those old men also represented a female component which made them twelve instead of six. I was being taught that the Self is twelve. I am the Child and I am the Father and the Mother, and I am all four aspects of each, I am infinite, the Source of All Things."

"Just like the soul, Eliza, understood at the beginning, you know, when she was in Atlantis," I say now, "She understood that she was the Child of the Sacred Parents and that she was one with them. In fact, she was told that by the golden being who gave her the Red Stone of Power. He told her all would know that they were one with the Sacred Parents in Heaven."

"And that is part of the prophecy which we will get to later," says Black Elk. "For now let us continue with the six old men. In fact, those old men were the grandfathers that the messengers said were calling to me, and the reason was to tell me of the prophecy."

"And to tell you who you were, who *I* am" I add.

"We need to understand who we are in order to *awaken* the prophecy," he explains. "So there I was, before the tepee, and one of the grandfathers spoke to me telling me to enter within. Actually, he told me not to be afraid to enter within, which is true of all people. You do not have to be afraid to go within yourselves and face the unknown. When you do you will find that you are never alone and that all you need, all knowledge, all help, is within. The thing is, *until* we go within we constantly search for the unknown outside of the inner Self."

"And that was in the story of Atlantis too," I note. "Eliza wandered the difficult path searching for the light but could never reach it, not until she went within and came to the centre where the two roads meet."

"I have taught you well, Rose. Well understood."

"Thank you, Black Elk."

"And so, these old men told me not to be afraid to enter within. They represented the six powers of the universe, powers that are found only within the divine centre. There are seven directions in the universe, Rose. These are north, south, east, west, above, and below. And these first six directions or powers are found in the seventh which is within. So the grandfather that spoke to me first was the one that represented the power of the west. He told me to look to the west, and when I did I saw thunder beings there. These beings or power of the west were to give me their power and also take me to the centre of the world and to the east so that I could understand more of the great revelations. And as the old man was saying all this I understood that

Eliza White Buffalo with Nicholas Black Elk

I was to go right within the Source of my being to be shown who I was and that I would be given full understanding of what I would see. You can imagine I was of a very high consciousness to enable me to understand these things. And as I understood the grandfather's words the rainbow above the door leapt into flames, and it was oh so brightly shining with seven colours. These seven colours of the rainbow also represented the Self and they represented the six powers as did the grandfathers, but with one power in the centre that was the oneness of all powers combined, one colour that represented oneness of Source. Do you understand, Rose? Just as the cloud tepee represented oneness of Source with the six grandfathers as the powers, so too did this one central colour of the rainbow represent Source with the six other colours as the powers."

"I understand," I tell him. "By coming to understand who you are and by the fulfilment of the prophecy that we have yet to discuss, you will come to be inflamed with light just like the flaming rainbow in the vision."

"That's right, well done. So there I was with the rainbow in flames above me and the grandfather of the west was not finished with me yet. He gave me a cup of water and in the water I could see the sky. It was the power to make live. And he gave me a bow which was the power to destroy. Understand that these are powers of the west, the aspect of Source that gives life and takes it away. This was the power given to me and in fact, it was the power that I was representing so strongly in that spirit world. The old man pointed to himself and told me that his power, the power of the west was very much the power of my spirit then. And he told me that this spirit was given a name and the name was Eagle Wing Stretches."

"Your spirit was called Eagle Wing Stretches?" I ask just to make sure I understood.

"Yes, just as I like to call you White Buffalo Woman, these great powers of the universe were calling *me* Eagle Wing Stretches. So, that was my name. Now, this grandfather, he got up and run off. Suddenly he was a very sick horse. And the second grandfather, he told me then to go after the horse, and he gave me a coloured herb. When I held this herb to the horse it became well and came back to the tepee where suddenly it was the old man again. Do you understand this, Rose?" Black Elk asks me.

"I think so," I reply. "The horse or the grandfather rather, was representative of your body which was lying sick on earth. You healed it with the power that the second grandfather gave to you. I imagine it was the power of the north, the power that clears away all dis-ease. So you used the power of the west to destroy the sickness and the power of the north to clear it all away and bring new life to your body."

"Very well put, Rose. I am proud of how much you understand," says Black Elk. My heart throbs quickly in response to the love that is washing through me in this moment.

And Black Elk goes on, "The grandfather of the north also gave me a cleansing wing. You understand he was giving me the power to heal, and not only to heal my own body but heal an entire nation on earth. This was displayed then as white geese from the north began to wheel and dance with the beings from the west. They danced and danced and were becoming manifest within my being so that on Earth I would be able to dance out these powers too. On earth I was to destroy all dis-ease and make live again in pure spirit."

"An entire nation?" I wonder.

"You will see how that is later," he tells me. "For now, let us talk about understanding. The third old man, the third grandfather which was the power of the east, spoke then to me. He pointed to the east, to the daybreak star there, and I saw two men coming flying towards me. I was told that these men would give me power and that this power was enlightenment, understanding. Now, there were two men that flew from the sun. They were representing two sources of enlightenment. These are the outer source which is the sun, and the inner source which is the awareness of the higher consciousness."

"The divine heart," I say.

"The divine heart, the Christ consciousness, the Buddha . . . let us call it the Christ Consciousness. So this is the source of enlightenment within, the Christ consciousness. You understand that this is the Red Stone of Power, don't you?" Black Elk asks suddenly, wanting to ensure that I was following the story.

"Aye, I do," I tell him.

"Good. So the grandfather of the east was holding a pipe in his hands. On the stem of the pipe was a spotted eagle with his wings outstretched."

"Eagle Wing Stretches, I wonder?" I ask and Black Elk smiles in response.

"You know, the peace pipe was given to the Sioux a long time ago by a divine being called White Buffalo Calf Pipe Woman. She was an avatar of sorts, a kind of messiah. She taught that the stem of the pipe was representative of the male part of Source, and the bowl the female part; the marriage between the two, represented by the rising smoke would bring harmony, hope and peace to the Indian people, to the world really. So there

Eliza White Buffalo with Nicholas Black Elk

was this old man with such a pipe in his hands who was telling me that I would heal a nation with it, on Earth. In a way he was saying that I am the smoke, the Child of Source, and I would bring that harmony, hope and peace to the world. And to prove this I saw a red man that was me. The red man ran to the east and turned into a fat buffalo. You see, he had become a source of plenty for the people because the buffalo is all good things to the Indian people. Also, by giving of myself, of the understanding that I gained, many others would come to know the truth and understand too."

"And you did do this, didn't you?" I ask Black Elk enthusiastically. "You taught many people about truth through the knowledge of your vision and through the knowledge of your Lakota and Christian understanding."

"I did Rose, but it meant much more than that. Can you understand that if all beings are really one being in Source, then if I heal my own self, my own soul, I will essentially be healing all beings?"

"Oh gosh, yes I understand that!"

"Okay, so the first three grandfathers had spoken to me and then it was the turn of the fourth one to speak. He was pretty much saying those very words, that by healing my own self I would heal the world. He said that I would walk with the powers of the four aspects of Source alive within me. He gave me a bright red stick and told me that it would stand in the centre of my being. With the powers given to me and the understanding of them I would make this stick grow and blossom into a glorious tree, a living tree."

"The living Christ?" I suggest.

"The living Christ, yes. The rainbow colours of my being would be so bright and inflamed with light that the centre, which is the Christ Consciousness or the divine heart centre, would grow and blossom and heal so that all would heal, all would be alive in the awareness of Source. Oh Rose, to feel that awareness is to be so happy; happiness beyond measure. And for a moment in my great vision, as I stood there looking at this bright red stick that had turned into a blossoming tree with birds singing in its branches and great peace all around it, I felt such happiness. And the grandfather was feeling it too because he was quiet for a bit so that he could hear the birds singing. Then he spoke again, and he told me to look to the earth. So I looked towards the earth and there I saw the two roads crossing over each other and where they crossed stood the living tree with peace all around. The great hoop of my people lived in harmony below the tree. It was such a beautiful sight there in the centre of the two roads. Of course, one of the roads was black and went from west to east, and the other was red and went from north to south."

The Four Ascents

As Black Elk pauses from speaking for a moment to contemplate the two roads I feel such a memory stirring within me. The Red Stone of Power seems to be throbbing in my heart centre. It is shining from within and I feel its glow filling me with clarity and knowing. Black Elk is aware of how I am feeling of course, and so he tells me, "Rose, let us leave the great vision for a while. Come with me to another vision."

He takes me to a world where I see the two roads stretch out across each other and I am standing in the holy place where they meet. I seem to recognize a place from deep within my soul's memory although I cannot say where or when. Before me stands the golden being that I saw in the video about Atlantis.

"My child," the golden being says, "I am so proud of you. The Red Stone of Power lives within your centre. It is the centre of you and it is the centre of all things. It is the centre of a great nation."

"And the living tree?" I ask the golden being.

"It is the centre of all things. It is the meeting place of two roads that you walk. For four ascents you have walked the earth in this fashion, each ascent bringing you one step higher on the stepladder to Heaven. Soon, you will be with me in Heaven and all beings shall know that they are with me in Heaven."

"Who are you?" I ask.

"I Am That I Am," replies the golden being.

"Who am I? I then ask.

"You are I and I am you," answers the I Am that I Am. "You are my child, known as Eliza upon the earth. Have faith and listen to the Red Stone of Power; when it sings the prophecy will be on Earth as it will now be made known to you."

And with that the golden being vanishes and I am back in my room, lying on my sofa, and talking with Black Elk.

"Oh! Black Elk, that was amazing!" I exclaim.

"You were simply reminding yourself of the purpose of the two roads, which is to learn and grow and rise four steps of awareness back to the wholeness of your soul, Eliza, and so back to the lake which is Source," he tells me with a warm glow. "Rose, the living tree is the centre of your being, your Christ Consciousness. As you rise up the four ascents it will continue to grow and blossom until all is in the wholeness of your soul, in peace and harmony."

Eliza White Buffalo with Nicholas Black Elk

I remain silent for a while, feeling the peace within me inspired by my vision and by Black Elk's wisdom. But I am aware that we ought to continue with the great vision.

"Rose?"

"Yes, Black Elk?"

"Are you ready to resume our story?"

"Aye, I am," I say dreamily.

"So I am looking down on the earth and there I see the two roads. I was told that I shall lead a nation on Earth and that the nation shall walk the two roads. One road, the black road which goes from west to east, is a road of difficulties yet it would give me the power to destroy any enemy. This is the earthly road, you understand Rose, and the power gained from it would be mine as I climb four ascents. This is what I was told. And also that the other road, the good red road that ran from north to south, I was to walk that road too with my nation. The good red road brings abundance of all kinds through communion with Spirit. So I was to walk two roads bringing death to my enemy and making all live in harmony. This is what the grandfather told me, I was to have that power as I walked the two roads. But you must understand that it was not only *me* that would have that power for the Grandfather had also said that the nation was to walk with me. All beings are my relatives, all are my nation, and since the Source of All Things is the higher Self, then all things walk within. We climb the four ascents with the power we gain on the two roads and we make a good life in this way. We make this prophecy grow until it is complete on Earth, all beings within the one higher Self that is Source. This is what the golden being meant when he said by walking the two roads over four ascents of consciousness, you will be in Heaven, and so all beings would know that they are in heaven."

"That gives great hope to be sure, for that means that by lifting my own consciousness up I am actually lifting everyone up, right?"

"Right; and hope is what makes things grow, you know. When the fourth grandfather had said those things to me about leading the nation on the four ascents he got up and run off to the south. There he turned into an elk and all the yellow horses there were elk too. You see, he had turned into the power of the south, the power to make everything grow; he turned into an elk, a proud majestic animal that has the ability to bring dreams and the seeds to make them grow. So then it was the turn of the fifth old man to speak. This old man turned into a spotted eagle and said that I would go across the earth with this power. Well, you know the eagle represents the highest consciousness so that spotted eagle there in the world of white was representing the highest consciousness within *me*. As the spotted eagle hovered there I felt incredibly powerful. You see, the grandfather was giving me the power to see as an eagle sees, from the higher realms of spirit. I would be able to see all below and all around. This is the power the grandfather gave me, the power with which I would go across the earth in four ascents. It is the power of spiritual sight and knowledge.

"Now, the last grandfather spoke to me and he told me to be brave because I was to have great troubles on Earth and I would need his power. This old man represented me as I would be when I was an old man. He grew young in front of my eyes until he was the boy that I was then. Then he grew old again and I could see how many years I would live on Earth. So really, this grandfather was telling me that the power gained from walking my life's two roads, was really already mine, for he had given it to me. Do you understand?"

"I think so" I reply. "He was giving you courage by telling you that you already had all the power you need to walk the two roads and climb the four ascents. You would do it because you could see that you had already done it."

"That's right, Rose, and what I am about to tell you is another example of how we know we can achieve because in reality we already have achieved; we already have the power needed to do so."

"It's like a journey of empowerment but in reality we are already fully empowered," I suggest.

"Exactly, ha, ha," laughs Black Elk.

"So now, Rose, I will tell you of the four ascents and how it was shown to me in the prophecy. But first you must understand just what the four ascents of my vision represented. What do you say they represented?"

"Four steps in consciousness, I think. But also four stages of your life that was to come, almost like four generations of your family you would see on Earth. Isn't that what it says in Black Elk Speaks?" I say cheekily.

"Ha, yes, all correct. And so much more than that too, though the four ascents that I want *you* to understand is four lifetimes on Earth used to represent the four ascents of awareness. If you can understand that mine is the first in this example and yours is the fourth then you will understand that there are two more in between us. You shall hear me speak of these, mine, yours, and what is in between, in relation to what is going on spiritually. After I'm done I will continue with the video of the journey of the soul, Eliza. So I will be showing you two more lifetimes in between yours and mine. Okay?"

"Okay, I see that . . . and Mexico must be one of them, it has to be," I insist, feeling the peace within me stir somewhat like ripples in a lake.

"Ah!" says Black Elk "I see I have dropped a pebble into the still waters. This is good because it shall reveal much truth to you. And I want you to pay heed to what you are feeling now. Listen and be aware for what I am about to reveal to you will teach you so much more about who you are, who we all are, many souls with one being."

And as Black Elk begins his story I try my best to focus on what I am feeling, though it is not easy for me; Mexico is a memory that is hiding great reluctance for life. I shall have to try harder than ever before to stay aware of the strange sensations in my body.

∞∞∞∞∞∞∞∞∞∞∞∞∞∞∞∞∞∞∞∞∞∞∞∞∞∞∞

And so Black Elk speaks . . .

"My Dear Rose, you have heard how the earthly soul is so close to wholeness, to the Father, to Beloved Source. How near Source is to all! It is the breath you take and yet it is the life that breathes. It is the vision and yet it is the visionary. It is the prophecy and yet it is the prophet. You have witnessed how the soul was risen up from the depths of the earth to be one with Source in the crystal heart. You have heard how my body lay sick on Earth and how I came before Source in the white world. I have conveyed to you much truth of who you are and the knowledge that lies within your crystal heart. And you will hear how this knowledge is revealed many times along the four ascents. This was the truth that was shown to me. I am of the soul, which was risen up from the depths of being and shown a great prophecy that is to be on Earth. Remember, as above so below. What is in Heaven, so shall it be on Earth."

CHAPTER NINE

Death and resurrection

"And now I will tell you how it was for me in that great vision," Black Elk says to me with a kindness such as that that can ease any unrest within. My heart slows to a peaceful rhythm and the stirring memories of Mexico fade into quiet. "Rose," he says "just listen to my voice and if you feel or hear other than what I am giving to you, relax with it; accept it and relax. Do not think on it at all; rather, focus on my voice. There I was looking down to Earth and to the two roads that I could see there. In the centre, where the two roads met stood the flowering tree. I suddenly found myself on the bay horse's back. Remember, the bay horse represented Source, so that means I was representing Source. I turned to the west, to the twelve black horses there and a great voice came from within me telling me of what had happened so far. It told me of the cup of water and the bow, the power to make live and to destroy; and when the voice had said this all the black horses came to stand behind me four abreast. The voice spoke of the sacred pipe and the power of peace, and it spoke of the sacred stick and the nation's hoop. And when it had spoken these things all the yellow and red horses stood behind me four abreast. You see, I was calling upon these powers and in answer to the call all the horses were coming behind me meaning that I had accepted my powers. The horses stood four abreast behind me displaying the truth of four aspects of Source, with three rows representing three supreme beings of Source. And I understood that the cleansing wind was my power too and I had that too in that world of white. So I was looking at the two roads and I knew I was to go there and learn how it would be for me on Earth. I knew that I was to walk the two roads then, and as I walked all nations of the earth would be afraid of me. This was because I was going to Earth with the power of the west. They would fear me for I would come from the west as thunder storms. So I began my journey on Earth. I rode towards the east to the fearful black road with all the horses behind me. The sun was just beginning to show so everything was still a little dark. The earth was a sickly green and the grasses, hills, animals and birds were all frightened. I felt like I was the chief of everything, like the ruler of the world and the chief was riding over the earth with all below in awe of him. I really was a thunderstorm and the rain was coming hard and the wind was blowing. It was a big thunderstorm."

"Now, I will tell you about the blue man. This is very important, Rose. In the river I saw huge flames and in the flames was the blue man. And the Earth around him was in drought. Everything was dying. I could see that the blue man was powerful indeed and I understood that he was representing a part of me that had shown itself as I had ridden over the earth. What I want you to understand Rose, is that he was representing a part of me that was my lower self as opposed to my higher Self. If you remember, I felt so special and important and I admit that it felt good to me, but that it is not the way of the Christ Consciousness; rather it is the way of a much lower consciousness. It is the way of the ego, a part of humanity that is merely man and that loves to feel important. I wish to make it clear to you that this way of being is not a choice that leads to self fulfilment. It is not a choice that arises out of a higher awareness. And as far as the soul Eliza is concerned, do you remember how Demetria discovered that this lower choice leads to a limited world, a world that appears to burn with the flames of suffering? In this world one does not know the joy of spiritual sight nor does one know the gift of enlightenment."

"So, how was I ever to bring about the prophecy? How was I ever to lead my nation to peace and harmony if I had limited myself in this world? No, this is not what I chose to create for myself and it is not what I wish for you. And I understood that, there in the great vision. I understood the choices I had. And I decided to destroy that blue man that brought drought and bring forth the sacred waters of the good red road to quench the drought. In that way I was making the world alive again. And I didn't succeed at first but I kept trying. I tried to destroy him with the power of the bow, the power to destroy. That was my first attempt and it seemed the obvious choice but it didn't work, the blue man was still there. Then I tried with the herb, the power to heal and transform but that didn't work either. And then I tried with the power of the south, which was not a good idea because the power of the south makes things grow in strength. I wonder do you see what it was I was doing, Rose? At first, like all people who are faced with a problem, I tried attacking the problem head on, but that energy never works because it is aggressive and only results in creating more fiery energy, represented by flames. Then I tried a gentler approach by trying to cool the flames and transform them with the power of the north, the power to transform; but that only resulted in fanning the flames for it is a wind that power. I tried the red

The Four Ascents

power; I tried to understand this blue man and I reckon I did understand him a little. But what I did not fully understand then was that he was a reflection of my Self; he was only a reflection, an illusion; he was my lower self, my earthly ego. Because he was a reflection of my Self he too had all the power that I had. It was futile trying to destroy him with one of these powers when he had the full strength of all of them. This I understood finally when I tried the last power, the power of the south, the power to make things grow."

"All people do this, Rose. They try to beat a problem first by hitting it head on, and then they try a different approach; maybe they pray. Then when prayer doesn't work they try something else and something else. The last power, the power of the south helped me to understand that as long as I was not using all of my power in a centred and whole manner the problem would always be, growing and growing the more I focused on it. Understanding is key; as I always say to you, it is by knowing the enemy that we conquer the enemy."

"So I understood then what I had to do. I heard all these powers call to me and they called to Eagle Wing Stretches, my spirit, and not Black Elk, my earthly ego or self. I understood and so I charged upon the blue man again, but with all my powers this time. I was bringing to him the light of Source itself since all these powers combined are the light of Source. And I'd like you to understand too, Rose, by deciding to bring my whole power forwards like this I was essentially saying hey! This is who I Am. The blue man had to listen because first of all, he was part of me, and of course, through choosing with my highest consciousness, the highest awareness of who I was, then my lowest consciousness had no choice but to align with that awareness. So I declared who I was and the blue man was destroyed, the lower ego was destroyed. Suddenly, the sacred waters flowed putting out the flames and bringing a quench to the whole world. All was lifted up and renewed in pure spirit. The blue man became a turtle to show me that he still existed but in a very gentle and harmless way. The turtle is balance indeed for it lives on both earth and in water. It this way it taught me that balance between the powers of Heaven and the powers of Earth will bring about harmony and wellness for me on Earth, for me and for my nation, which is all beings."

"So what wonderful things I was shown then! What wisdom the prophecy contains! I had brought death to the blue man; to a part of me that leads to limitation and suffering. I washed that part clean with the sacred waters of the good red road, which was the light of Source. In doing so, I brought new life, resurrection. It was the power given to me by Source, by the aspect of the

Eliza White Buffalo with Nicholas Black Elk

west, the power to destroy and to make live. I was about to embark then on a journey along the fearful black road of difficulties. I was going to need this power to destroy all that was in disharmony with my higher Self and resurrect it with the sacred waters of the good red road."

"There I was on the bay horse and the four troops of horses behind me, and we came to a village of tepees. I understood that this village was my nation that I was to walk with. The Source of All Things dwells within. It is in this reality that what we see before us is who we are, and with every moment we are displaying this reality outside of ourselves. So it was clear to me that the nation before me was who I was, and because we were supposed to be on Earth then, the nation was actually representing my earthly being. It was my body. As I rode quickly into the village I saw that it was indeed my body for all there were sick and dying, just as my body was lying in my parent's tepee. Well, I rode around that village and made them all well again. And this I did with all my powers centred in the Light of Source. I was healing my body in that spiritual world knowing that the healing would be reflected on Earth. I was creating my earthly experience. All our experience is created in this way: first in spirit and then it is reflected on Earth. I was full of joy in that moment, Rose. I knew I had healed my body and that I would live to be an old man. Besides, I had seen it when the sixth grandfather had grown young and old again before my eyes. So I already knew it. I was so overjoyed and I heard the great inner voice again saying that I would make the nation's hoop live. I had that sacred red stick in my hand, Rose. I could feel its power in my hand, in my being. I knew it was true that I would bring the nation to harmony in one beautiful hoop of peoples. That stick was to become the flowering tree that would shelter them all. I carried it to the middle of the village and thrust it into the ground, and it grew and grew as I focused on spreading the powers that I knew right around the nation's hoop so that each person there would have these powers too. I was there in the middle but I wasn't a great chief. I claimed not the greatness of chief because I was simply being and every living thing there in that nation was but a part of that being. What I felt in that instance was self-empowerment and not self-importance. This is very important, Rose, you will be challenged on this many times and you must know which is true; you must know where the power lies."

"So there the people were all around me and the stick had grown into the flowering tree. Everyone was filled with great joy. I laughed and cheered with the people for I was so happy to share in their joy. Well Rose . . . you know only too well, how joy raises the vibration of your being and makes

168

you soar into the higher realms. In this instance that joy brought fourth the power of the north in abundance. It came in and swept throughout the entire nation and when all was lifted up by pure spirit the power of the east was all around. Peace, peace, everywhere. The sun rose and I gazed upon it. The inner voice said that whoever sees it shall be enlightened and whoever does not see shall live in darkness. And because I understood this the whole nation looked to the sun shining there and they were lit up with enlightenment. You see, Rose, the daybreak star is a representation of the wisdom of inner Source. As I said before there is an inner representation of Source, which is the Christ Consciousness, and there is an outer representation of Source, which is the sun, Wakan Tanka. It dwells in the east for it is there the light of understanding comes into the world. The great inner voice meant that whoever shall look upon the star shall come to acknowledge this outer reflection of their inner Self, their Christ Consciousness. Essentially they would receive the light of wisdom. Whoever does not receive the light of wisdom shall remain in the dark. And that inner voice spoke more wisdom then: the circle of the nation's hoop is holy because it is endless, and it is in this way that all powers within shall be one endless power in the people. A circle *is* endless, containing all things. It has no beginning and no end, just like Beloved Source. That is why all life comes in cycles like the seasons. There is no death, Rose, only constant rebirth in cycles of growth. So the voice said that the nation was holy. That meant that the nation that was me was in its wholeness and was endless in its being. It wasn't limited by one village of people but was comprised of all things, all places and all worlds. Yet all was contained within the holy circle of one being. Tell me Rose, how do you understand what has happened in the vision so far? Tell me in a few words what you understand."

Oh my goodness, I think . . . how to capture it all in a few words. "Okay," I tell Black Elk "you were sick on Earth and your spirit was taken up into the spirit world to be shown the truth of who you are. You were shown how you represent Source within your Christ Consciousness and you were given all the powers of Source to take with you to Earth. With these powers you not only healed your body but you also gained tremendous insight into how all things that appear to be outside of you are really a reflection of what you have created within, what is true already in the spiritual realms."

"Well done Rose," replies Black Elk. "That is a pretty fair summary of what I have told you. Also, remember what I said about the blue man, the ego, the part of you that is the exact opposite to the truth of who you really are.

The ego is a powerful entity but only exists according to how you understand it to be. If you understand it to be an enemy you will always be challenged by it. On the other hand, if you understand that it is a *reflection* of you, then it is easy to understand that it is not real. Because it is not real, merely a reflection of what *is* real, and through being centred in the wholeness of your power, you can align the ego in balance with your power, thus creating harmony on Earth."

"By knowing what your enemy *really* is, you can conquer your enemy," I say, showing that I understand Black Elk's teaching to me before.

"Exactly! Now this is important to understand because when I resume the other lifetimes of the soul you will see how the ego appears as a very real and threatening entity. Only now, you will understand how illusionary it is. I shall go on. Relax again, Rose, and listen to what I have to say. So yes, I had come to Earth and healed the nation that was my body and I had raised it up to be one with Source in the centre of all things, in my crystal heart, the Christ Consciousness. So then I was to walk the good red road with the nation. I was to walk in wholeness as I made the four ascents, for the four ascents can only be made in wholeness, in empowerment. Oh, the procession that started out on that journey! There were the four troops of horses in front, first the black, then white, then red, then yellow. And the reason for the order of their going is this: it represented to me the cycle of death and rebirth. All things are complete in the west. Even a man's life shows this truth for he comes from spirit in the north to be born with the power of newness in the east. He grows from a boy into a man with the south and then to the west where he becomes an elder and eventually dies. His body is returned to the west, and his spirit is returned to the north and on to the east again for rebirth in a new body. And so the cycle continues, just like our seasonal Mother Earth who withers and rests, renews and grows and withers again."

"The people came next in the procession, starting with the children in first place and finishing with the elders in fifth place. I was in sixth place but I wasn't the last. Behind me as far as the eye could see was an endless stream of people. I gazed far into the distance behind me and I felt the power of the south strong within me. It was the power to make things grow and it was stretching out over the numberless people and even beyond them. These were the generations that were to come; the children and the children's children that would be of my lineage. And not only were these numberless people of my earthly lineage but they were the countless spirits that would spring from my soul. They were to be the known and the unknown to me."

The Four Ascents

"So we began to walk like that in a very holy manner. Up ahead, stretching out before me were the four ascents. It was clear to see that they were the four steps I had to take so that I would be in Heaven, and the four steps you are taking to Heaven to be with the golden being, the I Am That I Am. Now you understand the golden being's words with greater depth. I was to rise each ascent of the stepladder to Heaven. This I would do over four lifetimes including the one I was then in, and when I had risen all four ascents all would know that they were in Heaven. I took one last look far ahead to what was prophesised to be on Earth. The Red Stone of Power glowed and pulsed quietly within my heart space. The four ascents awaited. It was my truth which I had created in Heaven, and as it is in Heaven so shall it be on Earth."

Black Elk pauses now and for a very long moment we are both quiet. I know he is talking about the four steps of consciousness that we all must make in order to realize the power of Heaven on Earth. But I also know that his great vision was also showing him how his soul, Eliza would reflect this on Earth. I am in the last lifetime. He is in Heaven. He played his part on Earth beautifully. I remember just a few weeks ago, how he lifted me up with him in spirit and we flew over the forest on a cloud. It was the moment when everything made sense to me. I knew who I was. I was Eliza, at peace in my heart at last, and I was in balance with the Father aspect of my soul. It was represented by Black Elk. All my life he worked to guide me, to console me, lift me up into the awareness of my higher Self so that I would not forget who I was. He is doing it still, from the heavenly realms of spirit. And I remember what he said to me when we sat on that white cloud together; he told me that the heart of the child is whole and can never be destroyed. I had thought my heart *was* destroyed, but it had been washed clean by the waters of the good red road. For a while then, I was a child again sitting on my Indian's lap, fully aware that all was perfect in love and peace. He had shown me part of the vision when I was nine years old, and now he is showing me so much more than that, and telling me great things about how I would lift myself up to Heaven. And all people will know that they are one in Heaven. This is the final ascent, the fourth lifetime revealed in the vision. It is up to me to reflect the soul's truth on Earth. He told me that the middle world, the world on Earth, was my decision. The choice is always mine in every moment how the soul's truth is played out on Earth. I hope I make it beautiful. I smile at him now . . .

"And so it shall be on Earth," I say.

Eliza White Buffalo with Nicholas Black Elk

∞∞∞∞∞∞∞∞∞∞∞∞∞∞∞∞∞∞∞∞∞∞∞∞∞∞

And so Black Elk speaks . . .

"My Dear Rose, my sweet white buffalo child, I am proud of you. As I relate to you the journey along the four ascents know that Beloved Source is therein with all the powers that is one power. It is the source at the centre of all things. You are created in Its likeness, the crystal heart. Yes, the Red Stone of Power is present always. As it is in Heaven so it shall be on Earth. The soul, Eliza, once climbed the first three ascents only to fall into the depths of being. Reaching towards the light Eliza has returned to this place. Here the journey begins. Now the journey begins. It is here and now that the journey begins. Here in this place of creation; now in this moment that exists. This is the time and the place where all things are created. So dear Rose, listen closely to the journey of the four ascents and know, as the soul walks the four ascents that it is the soul's creation and that in each moment that exists the soul creates."

And Black Elk says . . .

"I Am that I Am! Go forth now in co-creation with Beloved Source."

CHAPTER TEN

The four ascents

"The first ascent was long but not very steep. It was familiar to me and this was because it was the life I had then. Everything seemed calm and peaceful, well and happy. Well Rose, it was good for me then . . . when I was a child and the world was at peace. Remember also, that my body was healed and my spirit was free, so it is how I saw the first ascent. For a fleeting moment I had recognition of many lifetimes that have gone before. That was powerful; The Red Stone of Power was glowing strong in my heart space and its peace was filled with knowledge of other times, other experiences. And the four lifetimes ahead would be filled with more valuable experience; experience that was to lead me onwards along the four steps of the stepladder to Heaven.

Be awake! whispered the Red Stone of Power to me, *On the four ascents you shall walk both roads. Be aware of what it is that you create along the way because the black road of difficulties shall challenge you greatly. Always remember to come to the centre where the two roads meet. In this way you shall make your choices in clarity and with the powers given to you by your grandfathers.*

"My dear Rose, do you understand what this means to you?" Black Elk ask me.

"I think so, Black Elk," I reply. "The Red Stone of Power meant that the black road could have thrown you off the path, and although you would still have been walking the four lifetimes you would not be focused on rising up the stepladder to Heaven. I guess the blue man which was the ego self could have caused you to forget that you create your truth as you go along. For me then, and I understand that I am part of your original soul that remains in wholeness . . . for me, the ego self would likely have me believe that life is chaos and I have no control over what happens. But if I stay centred in the powers of the spirit like the Red Stone of Power has advised, then I will be aware at all times of what I am creating and of the spiritual path ahead." I look at Black Elk hoping that was correct.

He smiles sweetly. "Well understood my little calf," he says.

"You haven't called me that since I was a child" I tell him, my heart soaring with love for him.

Eliza White Buffalo with Nicholas Black Elk

"You'll always be my child," he adds. He doesn't have to say anything more. I feel his heart energy within me growing and expanding, bright and powerful.

"And so there I was on the first ascent," he continues, his words resounding powerfully in my being. "The people were happy, happier than ever. They were giving thanks for the good red day that was theirs. Always give thanks for your blessings, Rose, that is important. So the sky was filled with blessings that day. I could see baby faces in the clouds, always a blessing. It seemed to me that the first ascent would be blessed with new life and blessings. It felt good to me. I was happy for it meant that I could expect great things on Earth. Amidst the faces, just for a moment I thought I saw the face of the boy, Little Buffalo. He was reaching out to me with his fat little hands, his face smeared with the juice of wild plums. And the Red Stone of Power said to me, *He shall walk alongside you; a voice for many to hear."*

"When I came to the end of the first ascent I was still happy. The people were still happy and the world seemed calm and happy still. They made their camp as they did before, in the sacred circle, always in a circle. I saw the flowering tree was in the centre and it was healthy and happy too. As I watched from upon the bay horse, the four legged being that represented the four aspects of Source in one, I knew that this was a good life and that it would be blessed with spiritual wellness. I knew too, that Little Buffalo would bring great hope to me for he would be a voice that expresses my truth for the ears of my people. In that way, many would understand the truth that I had been shown; that the human soul is co-creator with Source, the very essence of our being; and that by walking the two roads with the powers of Source the human can ascend four steps to be one with Source in Heaven."

"*You see said the Red Stone of Power to me, the first ascent of the stepladder is fullness of Self expression. When you come to the heart space in the centre where the two roads meet, you come to the awareness of the Christ Consciousness. You remember who you are; not just Black Elk, but pure spirit in an earthly body. You remember that you are co-creator with Source. The four ascents begin there and the first is this expression of the Self. Now the second ascent is beginning so stay awake."*

"And then I could see the second ascent, Rose. It was very close to me then, and it looked good too, although it seemed to get steeper as it went on. The people were all changed from human beings into all kinds of animals and birds. And even I was changed then, I was the spotted eagle, I was Eagle Wing Stretches. And just as the fifth grandfather had displayed, I was flying high over everything and I saw much and understood much. Understand this

174

The Four Ascents

Rose . . . this is the ascent of spiritual sight and higher knowledge. It is the ascent into seeing and knowing all things as they really are which is pure spirit. All things are spirit and all spirit is of Source, thus all things are of Source."

"I looked down at all those beings that were all part of Source and I saw that they represented the many qualities of Source. I saw winged beings with the gift of sight and knowledge and four legged beings with the gifts of strength and endurance, freedom and abundance, wisdom and transformation. That ascent too would be wonderful. But listen to this, Rose . . . listen carefully . . . There seemed to be trouble among the animals and birds. Suddenly, they were panicking that they did not seem to be what they once were. I hovered high above them listening to their cries for help. As the people made their camp at the end of the second ascent the flowers and leaves on the holy tree begin to fall one by one. I felt the peace within me stir but I could not waver in my knowing and understanding that I represented Source or indeed, that as a human soul, I was a co-creator with Source. My people would walk in difficulties thereon. As long as I would stay aware of the four aspects of power that is the Self and come to the centre where the two roads meet, I would be making wakeful choices with clarity and understanding of the challenges presented to me on the fearful black road of difficulties. I had to stay awake. I gazed down upon the troubled camp below me, at the many creatures in distress and I felt no sorrow for what I saw. Even though I knew that it represented how I would be in the second ascent I felt neither apprehension nor pain. I hovered there, a spotted eagle within that peaceful awareness of the Self. Nothing on Earth could say to me that I was anything less than that. Nothing on Earth could disturb me. But as I gazed upon how it would *be* on Earth it was clear to me that on the first ascent I would live a long life and that I would not lose faith in the powers of the Self. However, it was clear that on the second ascent I would begin to disconnect with that knowing. It was evident in how the nation was panicking. They simply did not remember who they were."

As Black Elk takes a pause in his story to express the sadness he had felt then for his people I too relate to the emptiness that comes from not knowing who you are.

"Black Elk?" I whisper softly.

"Yes, Rose?"

"When I didn't know who I was . . . I mean, before . . . y'know . . . when I was aged between thirteen and thirty six, before I became aware again of your presence in my life and you helped me to see who I was . . . well, during that time I think I was really frightened like the nation in your vision. And I really believe that what caused that deep fear was not the stuff in my life but rather, the absence of light. I couldn't see the light and therefore I couldn't see Beloved Source. It is in Him that we find our source of strength, of knowledge, of security; it is in Him that we discover our true selves. But we must come to the centre of our beings to find that awareness."

"Well said, Rose. It is true: Beloved Source is the centre of all things. You had shut your awareness of spirit down and you had gone into your head energy, constantly thinking and I may add . . . thinking you were in control. But once it became clear to you that you were not what you once were, you panicked. Great fear set in. So, Source is the centre of all things; the centre of you. By coming out of your heart and into your head you felt the absence of your only source of well-being. You were aware of the absence of Source, the absence of love, which is fear. And that is what happened to the nation in my vision. The people had lost their awareness of spirit. They were on the second ascent of spiritual sight and higher knowledge. By shutting off the awareness of their centre they began to panic. The flowering tree had begun to wither and die."

"So, I saw they were breaking camp again for the third ascent. How reluctant they were to do so for it was the black road then that lay before them. They ran around in different directions, each one desperately seeking their own identity, their own truth. I noticed the storm clouds up ahead. They did too, and they knew it would be powerful and they were frightened, yet they knew they had to go onwards. Off they went and I followed. I felt great compassion for them for I knew that they would be fine. I was there and I would never leave them."

"And you represented Beloved Source" I add.

"Exactly! The ascent was frightening indeed for them and they were so reluctant to see their wholeness. Should they have come to the centre and made the holy tree bloom again they would have been safe but they were reluctant indeed. And instead of coming to the centre where the holy tree would bloom again they wanted to cling on to what they knew before, but it no longer existed. Yet all was well; there I was in the fullness of my being. I was the Source within, and the third ascent was the step into communication with Source. They would have the gift of being able to communicate with me, but yet, that communication would have to be made through the centre. I breathed deeply and exhaled a peaceful sigh. *Oh my beloved nation*, I tried to communicate to them, *what an illusion this is that blinds you from my presence!*

The Four Ascents

Onwards the nation went. By the time we reached the top of the third ascent the nation's hoop was very much scattered. The flowering tree no longer flowered. It was dying, and all around the black day was terrible. The camp was made but the circle was broken. I looked up ahead to where the fourth ascent was looming and I saw that it would be terrible. Where I was it was light but over the camp darkness rested. I sighed long and deep, the peace within me was stirring like a low rumble of distant thunder."

"Black Elk?" I interrupt again to ask him a question. I was thinking of all the pain that my lifetime, the fourth ascent, had held up until I healed.

Black Elk answers my question without me asking it, "Rose," he says with compassion, "you must not hold on to what is past. Yes, the fourth ascent was terrible . . . and you know it was for you lived it. But do not hold on to what is past for it does not exist; it is the here and now, this moment that exists, and therefore, it is now that you find your only source of power. All else is fear."

"I understand" I utter.

"It will always be a part of you," he adds, "a part of your life that brought you to where you are now. All experience is valuable. Lessons are learned thus and they colour our decisions in the present. But you know who you are, Rose."

"I do," I tell him with truth warming my heart.

"Okay, let us return to the four ascents," he says positively. "I was looking at the fourth ascent and I could see how dark it would be. The nation was getting ready to move onto it but they were still in the third ascent. And they were so ill, thin and pitiful. The holy tree was gone, the great circle of the nation, broken. Disharmony prevailed. Compassion flooded from my heart like the sacred waters of the good red road and tears rolled from my eyes to see the nation's plight. Ahead, the fourth ascent was looming darkly—the fourth lifetime and it was to be terrible. I wept, though my crystal heart was glowing. In my heart The Red Stone of Power whispered gently to me, telling me to use the powers I was given by the grandfathers to fix what was broken. I was to heal the nation and make the holy tree bloom again. Just as I had done for my body on Earth, only this time I would be doing it in the fourth ascent. And that is why I came to you in this lifetime, Rose; that is why I raised you up into your awareness of your Self. I had already done it in spirit, in my great vision."

"Oh my goodness, I can see that! As it is in Heaven, so shall it be on Earth," I state.

Eliza White Buffalo with Nicholas Black Elk

And Black Elk goes on, "And as I understood that I was to heal the nation I saw in the starving camp below, a vision of hope. On the north side of the camp stood a red man. He walked into the centre of the nation with a spear in his grasp, and there he lay down and rolled. When he got up again he was a fat red buffalo which symbolises plenty. Beneath him, there in the centre of the camp where the holy tree had been, was an herb growing. From the one stem grew blossoms of four colours: blue, white, scarlet, and yellow, and they each glowed and sent forth a ray that reached the sky. You see, the bison symbolises the people's strength, their abundance. What better strength for them to receive then than hope, and this was brought to them by a good red spirit bearing the light of Beloved Source. Understand Rose, the fourth ascent is the connection to the star origins where all things are one with Source; and Source is one being, thus all things are of one being. It is the ascent into the awareness of oneness of time and space where all experience of all lifetimes may be recalled. So, I understood, and I realized that in the fourth ascent I would recall the experience that was mine then. I would recall the vision of knowledge and prophecy. And it was to be me, Black Elk, or Eagle Wing Stretches that would walk among the nation in the fourth ascent. I am that good red spirit and it was I that brought hope that was the four-rayed herb. With that hope the nation would be healed and nourished and abundance would once again flow to them. I was to make a good red day for them for I represented their Source and I loved them greatly."

"The people seemed better after the red man had come among them. Throughout the camp I heard the north wind breezing and where it blew light appeared. Suddenly the flowering tree was back and was standing there at the centre of the camp whence the four-rayed herb sprang. You see what this means; I had brought hope to the nation in the fourth ascent; and the north wind, which was one of the four aspects of my being, had breezed among them and cleaned away any disharmony that was there. As a result the light of pure spirit prevailed among the nation and the living centre blossomed once again."

"Then I was on the bay horse again; the representation of Source with its four aspects. I was Eagle Wing Stretches and I had come to Earth in the fourth ascent to make a good nation. And I saw you there."

"You saw *me?*" I gasp, wondering how that could have been.

"Yes, you were a big black stallion, but it was you all the same ha ha!" he laughs.

"Oh, remember that black stallion out on the mountain the other day?" I blurt out suddenly. I had been out on a mountain top with a friend just a few days ago and she had introduced me to her horse, a beautiful big black stallion called Dancer.

"Aha!" exclaims Black Elk, "and how did you feel with that stallion, Rose?"

"I loved it. It seemed so free; a free spirit running wild on a sacred mountain high," I reply.

"It was your own spirit that you felt, Rose. Horses are beautiful beings, and powerful too. Dancer reflected your own freedom of spirit. What do you think of that eh?"

"I think I love him, Black Elk. I think he is the most wonderful animal I have ever met. And I can totally see how he reflected my inner self; I understand that we are all really only one being, all people and animals, and birds and trees; all beings are really only one being. We are Beloved Source *being* on earth."

"I'm glad you feel like that because it will help you to accept what I am about to tell you," replies Black Elk proudly. "In the vision I saw a black stallion. He represented the soul on Earth, my being, your being, the being of my Lakota nation, all beings really. The black stallion represented all expressions of being, Earth herself even. But for *your* sake, and for the understanding I wish for you to have concerning my being your helper in this life, let's say the stallion represented *you*."

"Ok"

"So this horse was ill, very ill. It was so ill that its coat was a dull brown and its bones were sticking out. Well, I knew I had the power to do something to make this poor beast better."

"Hey, less of the beast," I tease.

"Sorry. Ha, ha! So this poor creature was ill, just as you were once. And the people were praying for help, which means that you were praying for help."

"Too right I was," I tease again.

"Ok Rose, let me tell the story," Black Elk says strictly, though with a slight grin.

"Sorry, go on."

"And I was on the bay horse, so I rode around the stallion and made it better with the four aspects of Source I had been gifted. Well, that stallion got up and was as good as new again. Light shone from it as bright as a star. It was *filled* with light. So you see, when you prayed for help I came and I healed you and you were filled with light."

Eliza White Buffalo with Nicholas Black Elk

"I was that to be sure," I grin joyfully.

"This is the same for *any* being that makes the call to spirit, Rose. Spirit will always answer with healing opportunities that dispel darkness and lighten the being with the pure light of the soul. But the being must pay attention and be ready to receive that healing."

"I was ready, Black Elk."

"Indeed you were my little calf," says Black Elk. "Well, that stallion was so well and healthy and filled with divine light that it ran about to all quarters snorting and kicking up dust. And from each direction came the powers of Source galloping in until that once ill being was a mighty display of all the powers of Source in one being. In other words, Rose, we had done such a good job of healing you that you danced and danced the good dance and it resulted in you remembering your wholeness, your soul which is a child of Beloved Source."

"As I have danced upon the earth, so must you. You said that to me once, remember?" I ask.

"Yes, and do you remember me telling you that when the Red Stone of Power should sing, then the prophecy would be released?"

"Aye," I utter, wondering where he is going with this.

"Well, that stallion was so well it sang and sang. Its whole being was so full of light that its crystal heart sang crystal clear. It is the same with all beings, Rose. When the being is filled with light, the crystal heart begins to sing. Its song is magical and entrancing. It pulls other beings into its power and reminds them that they too are crystal light. This is how the prophecy shall come to be: as hearts sing and awaken other hearts the whole world becomes filled with light. So, the stallion sang and sang until the whole universe was filled with its song. All was in peace and harmony with a beautiful rainbow of light displaying the perfect harmony, burning brightly with the powers of Source. In the centre of the nation stood the holy tree and it was filled with birds and blossoms, and the seven rays of the rainbow lit up its beauty. Oh Rose, my heart soared with joy at such a beautiful display. And I want you to understand, Rose that you are like that black stallion, you are the centre of your nation, and the Red Stone of Power therein is singing, releasing the prophecy. The world around you is in harmony with you, all humming in one voice, one note. And the rainbow of your light burns brightly. Remember the rainbow over the white tipi, the one that represents the six aspects or powers of Source with the one colour in the centre that

The Four Ascents

represents all powers in one? It burns brightly for you are in your wholeness. The Red Stone of Power has sung and the prophecy has been released."

"But this is in spirit, Black Elk, not this reality; not yet for there is still darkness in this world," I add feeling a slight pang of unhappiness within me.

"It is as it is in reality, Rose. What is in spirit is the real world; this is but a reflection of that which you *believe* to be."

"So that means that I will know peace and harmony on Earth in due time, for I do believe that what you say is true, that in reality we are whole, we are pure crystal light."

"Yes Rose," Black Elk replies, "And when you experience less than wholeness it is because you have made an error along the way. Remember what I taught you about the difference between truth and error?"

"Truth is our essence, our true selves, which is love; error is when we fail to recognize that. When we acknowledge and express our truth we experience Love and Joy, but when we express less than our truth we experience the absence of love which is pain and separation from God."

"Well done, that's correct," Black Elk says and quickly moves on to the rest of the story: "Now listen carefully, Rose. This is a very beautiful and important part of the vision . . . The stallion being had sung and the world was in harmony with it. So there the nation was, going over to the top of the fourth ascent. I guess in your case we could say that this is the elder part of your life. This going over the summit of the ascent represented the beings return to Source in Heaven. Remember what the golden being said to you, Rose? He said: *for four ascents you have walked the earth in this fashion, each ascent bringing you one step higher on the stepladder to Heaven. Soon, you will be with me in Heaven and all beings shall know that they are with me in Heaven.*"

"And when the nation had climbed the summit I was *taken* to that place which you call Heaven. I was taken to the centre of the earth. Now, this was a high mountain in the Black Hills because that is where we Indians knew to be the centre of the earth. But really it was my crystal heart that I was taken to, the place where the two roads meet. I was riding on the bay horse still and all the horses were coming after me representing that I was in my wholeness with all the four aspects of Source within. We were riding eastward from whence comes understanding. There was more for me to understand you see, much more. Well, I stood there on high and I was like that black stallion, filled with light. I saw all things as they should be, Rose: filled with light. I saw all things as all things truly are: light. I see that now, Rose. I see all things in truth. I see *you* as light just as I saw on that mountain high. I saw many

Eliza White Buffalo with Nicholas Black Elk

circles of peoples from there, many circles that were really one big circle of peoples, one being. And I watched as they all merged together to form that one circle, and in the centre was the holy tree, more beautiful than ever. I had reached the summit of the fourth ascent you see, Rose . . . and now I was in the fifth world where the child, the soul, Eliza, is one with the Sacred Parents, the Mother and Father supreme beings of Source. Remember I said Beloved Source is three supreme beings each with four aspects to itself? And that each soul is a representation of the whole on earth? Well, I was then in the fifth world, the *fifth* ascent which is the ascent where the being is aware of the oneness of its true Self. I had come to be one with the soul in Heaven, not just the temporary soul that was Black Elk, but the original soul, the lake."

"The lake, yes, known as Eliza," I add.

"Known as Eliza upon the earth, yes," he answers. "Do you remember what Eliza means?"

"One who climbs the heights of Heaven reflecting the mind of God," I state.

"So there you have it. One who climbs the heights of Heaven reflecting the mind of God . . . this is done on Earth. In Heaven, the soul is but one lake of countless other lakes, a droplet from the ocean which is Beloved Source, just as you are a droplet from the lake which is Eliza."

"Wow! That is so beautiful . . . and mystical," I exclaim.

"I aim to please," teases Black Elk. He pauses a while and then continues, "And so there I was in Heaven. All hoops of people were one big hoop with one glorious holy tree in the centre. Heavenly music was playing in my ears; it was the harmonics of that world. I hear it yet, Rose. The prophecy is complete for me, for you too, for all though they are not all aware."

"When I talk to you I can feel it, I think," I tell Black Elk. "And when I am in meditation I touch on a feeling that must be it, a feeling of bliss, like everything is Love."

"Yes, you do, darling Rose, though nothing will prepare you for the rush of being free from duality . . . completely free." There is another pause while Black Elk allows me to contemplate his words. Then he goes on, "So . . . Rose . . . do you remember I explained about the two men from the east, the inner source of understanding and the outer source? Well, they came back. They came back then and they spoke to me telling me that whatever I undertake to do on Earth I would succeed with. They gave me a sacred herb, the daybreak star herb which is the herb of understanding, and they indicated that wherever I plant a seed of this understanding there it will grow. And

182

that, dear Rose, was near the end of my great vision. But it wasn't the end yet, for I was brought back to the grandfathers then. The grandfathers were very pleased with me for what I had achieved. As I greeted each of them I received again all the powerful gifts that they gave to me. And each time I received a gift I felt more and more close to my body. When I came out of that tipi for the second time all beings that were cheered me for what I had achieved. I got closer to the ground and soon I was back in my parent's tipi and back in my body. I saw then, just for a fleeting moment, the little girl and the man standing there looking at me. And I didn't know that the man was me. He was me, Black Elk as the good red spirit who would bring hope in the fourth ascent, and I didn't know that the little girl was you. How would I have known? A grandfather spirit spoke then. No-one heard him but me and the little girl. The grandfather said, "Welcome back my child. You were gone a long time."

"Just like I heard when I was there, when you took me there," I say solemnly.

"You were nine years old, Rose; the same age I was when I had that great vision. I showed you much then, but I didn't show you it all for you would not have understood. I hope you understand now?"

"I do, thank you for relating it to me. And thank you for showing me the other lifetimes too."

"Do you know why I took you to that moment, Rose? The moment when I was just back from the vision?" he asks. "I took you back to that moment to teach you what it felt like to recognize that there is no separation."

"I remember you took me there," I reply. "We stood outside the tepee and a little boy came out to greet us. We followed him inside where I saw him lying ill on a bed of furs. The boy was you, but suddenly, he was not you. He was Maria from Mexico. And when you told me *there is no separation* I could feel it. And even when the grandfather said *welcome back my child. You were gone a long time*, I knew that he was talking to the child on the bed but also he was talking to me. It's as if I was away for a long time and then I was back."

"You were away in that your awareness of yourself was separated from the awareness of the soul and then you remembered again. You felt the oneness with me and with Maria, didn't you?"

"I did"

"Good, and so it is."

∞∞∞∞∞∞∞∞∞∞∞∞∞∞∞∞∞∞∞∞∞∞∞∞∞∞∞

Eliza White Buffalo with Nicholas Black Elk

And Black Elk Speaks . . .

My Dear Rose, I speak to you *now* from the realms of the spirit, through Eliza. And now you know who Eliza is. Eliza is a child of the Mother and the Father, and she burns brightly with them as a three-fold flame of Source. Some people like to call this the soul. I wish to speak with you now about the journey of the soul. As you know, my soul, like all other souls, lived on Earth for many lifetimes. Each lifetime the soul sent a droplet of itself to Earth as a temporary soul. Each time it created a new body, a new person. This lifetime you live now, Rose, is the fourth lifetime that we saw in the great vision, the fourth ascent. I lived as Black Elk and in that lifetime I enjoyed the knowledge and peace of the Christ Consciousness within. This I have done through the awareness of the vision and the gifts given to me therein. And even though that lifetime appeared to be filled with mourning for the broken hoop of the Lakota nation, I knew within that all peoples were my nation. It is in the centre of *that* reality that the holy tree blossoms. And so it is now too, through *your* being as Eliza White Buffalo, that the holy tree is blossomed and the prophecy is complete. Three lifetimes on and three ascents climbed. Your soul is in the fourth ascent on Earth, and at the summit. The Red Stone of Power that is your crystal heart, your Christ Consciousness, sings with wholeness. As it is in Heaven, so shall it be on Earth. The prophecy was shown to me in Heaven and it has been reflected on Earth throughout the four lifetimes. In the first ascent I expressed my higher Self, my higher truth, through the way I spoke and the way I lived, and also through the means of the book written by my friend, John. That is my lifetime as Black Elk, the first ascent of the vision. It is the ascent into expression of one's truth. The second ascent is the ascent into higher knowledge and spiritual sight. As I continue to show you what you have called the video you will learn how the soul made the second and third ascents, for the next two stories are the stories of the second and third lifetimes. In the second lifetime you will see how the soul's new expression on Earth, its new personality, and I shall tell you now that her name is Gabriella . . . you will see how Gabriella gained much knowledge and awareness. You will see how that lifetime was filled with panic and loss of identity. You will see how Gabriella was reminded of who she was and to stay focused in that knowledge if she was to succeed in her divine life's purpose. The third lifetime I will show you, and you will learn how the great reluctance to go on was reflected on Earth. You will see how at the end of that lifetime the soul's expression, this time—Maria, was given hope for the

The Four Ascents

fourth ascent. You will understand the great terror that *your* lifetime held and you will see how the soul travels over the summit of the fourth ascent and returns to oneness in Heaven."

"The Red Stone of Power has sung, Rose. The prophecy is complete. But my dear, this prophecy was given not only for me or for you, but for all peoples. Each and every one of you has a crystal heart wherein rests the Christ Consciousness, the spark of Source. Each and every one of you is a child of Source. Each and every one of you is climbing the four ascents of the stepladder into Heaven. Each and every one of you is creating Heaven on Earth. It is the prophecy that is given to all beings of one being. So before I show you the second ascent, Rose, I wish for you to be clear of the journey so far. The soul has ascended the first step of self expression. Through my lifetime as Black Elk, the soul has been expressed on Earth in the beauty of imagery and the written word. The soul is now walking with the rainbow staff of light, The Beloved Source's truth for all to witness. Yet, the soul stands now facing the second ascent, and there is much yearning ahead, yearning for a sense of wholeness, for completion."

Part Three

SO SHALL IT BE ON EARTH

CHAPTER ELEVEN

The second ascent

And the video begins to play again. The story continues . . .

<u>*I am in Paris France, 1306.*</u>

"Gabriella, Gabriella, wake up!"

I'm not an easy person to stir from sleep. I love to dream, mostly about far off places, places where everything is perfect and everyone lives together in peace. Sometimes I dream about places I've been in other lifetimes; places of great mystery and beauty. Just now I was about to discover the secrets of the pyramids in Egypt, but my husband was shaking me just at the crucial moment, ending my dream abruptly.

"Pascal," I moan, "leave me alone. Let me sleep."

"My dear, Esme is outside," he tells me.

"Esme? Why would Esme be here at this time? Where is she?" I rub my sleepy eyes and glance at the window. It's still dark; can't even be close to daybreak.

"She's in the street. Listen!" says Pascal pulling back the curtain. The glow of the streetlamp lights the room.

Esme can be heard calling up to us. Her voice is low and distraught. "Pascal! Gabriella!" she calls urgently, trying not to make too much noise lest she wakes the entire street. "Pascal, is that you? Let me in, quick!"

Pascal opens the window and leans out. "Give us a sec," he whispers down to Esme.

I get out of bed and wrap a shawl around me. "Is Pierre with her?" I ask, realising that I am wearing my thinner nightgown.

"No, she's alone I think," replies Pascal. "What on earth does she want at this time? Doesn't she ever sleep?"

Our ten year old daughter, Madeleine comes sleepily into our bedroom with three year old Clairose close behind. "Papa, Maman, there's someone outside calling. I think its Aunt Esme," she says yawning.

"Oh for goodness sake Pascal, now she's woken the children," I moan. "Go back to bed children."

Eliza White Buffalo with Nicholas Black Elk

"But I want to see Aunt Esme," pouts Clairose.

"Bed, now!" I insist. "You can see Aunt Esme in the morning. But now, its sleep, go!"

Off they patter with their little bare feet. I smile after them. They're good children really. Madeleine, whom we call Maddy for short, can be a bit scatty sometimes, especially when she's given a chore to do; always day-dreaming, just like her mother I suppose. And dear sweet little Clairose follows her everywhere. He wants to play but he bothers her so. Still, she doesn't chastise him. She'd do anything for him. She's such a good girl. Esme is my sister, older by two years and has five children of her own, all girls. I'd swear she'd keep going until she has a boy. Her husband, Pierre would be so happy. Not that he's not; I'm sure he is, but I have heard him so many times lament that he doesn't have a son to carry his name on within the order. Both Pierre and Pascal have been in the Knights for twenty years now. They were sworn in together at the age of seventeen. They grew up together. The two families are not blood related but are as close as any kin could be, closer likely. Pierre and Pascal are like brothers. They did everything together, even ended up marrying sisters on the same day.

I wonder if everything is alright with my sister's family. I hope it's not one of the children. With lamp in hand I follow my husband down the stairs, and whilst he lets Esme in through the front door I set a light to the fire. "Gabriella, be a dear and make me a hot drink," says Esme as she takes a seat by the fire. She blows on her cupped hands and rubs them together, shivering with cold.

"Is it that cold?" I ask playfully, "October's not normally that cold at night. Anyone would think it was snowing the way you're behaving."

"Sister, let me tell you. If it was you standing out there yelling your guts out for over ten minutes you'd be freezing too," she replies without a hint of being amused. Only now do I notice that she too is in a nightgown and shawl.

"Why are you not dressed Esme? Surely you didn't walk the full length of the street in your nightgown."

"I did! And what of it?" she snaps. "Besides, I had to come straight away. Pierre is already gone and the girls are preparing to leave."

I hand her a bowl of hot herbal infusion. "Leave for where? What on earth is going on Esme?"

She sips at her drink, her hands still shaking with the cold, or is it fear? I take Pascal's hand as he sits down beside me. "What's going on Esme?" he asks her. "Why has Pierre not come? Where is he?" Pascal looks very anxious,

The Four Ascents

angry even. I wonder did he know that something was wrong. Most of the time he doesn't tell me what is going on. I usually find out from Esme.

"Pierre's gone to Claude's place," she answers him. "He told me to come straight here and tell you that the king's men have destroyed everything. The king is very angry apparently at being refused so bluntly. There was no stopping what he wanted to do."

"Which is to make sure that he gets it all, regardless," Pascal adds. He gets up and paces the room. "The tyrant!" he shouts angrily, "the greedy bastard!"

"Shh" I whisper to him, "*the children*. Oh no! The treasure! He won't have got the treasure, would he?" The wealth of the order is one thing but the real treasure is priceless. Its whereabouts must be kept secret always.

Pascal gives me an irritated look. "No, don't be stupid" he snaps angrily. "He wouldn't even know what he'd be looking for never mind find it."

"Pascal, keep your voice down. You'll have the children up. I was just thinking the worst case scenario I suppose."

"The children have to get up anyway," interrupts Esme, blushing awkwardly. "I really must go, and so must you. We're all to leave immediately for Claude's. Pierre has informed him by now of the situation. He will be expecting us. Pascal, he wants you to meet him at the place you dropped him off yesterday afternoon. It's all kicked off, he said and the studio is too risky. He says you'll know what he means."

"Blast!" rants Pascal, "Gabriella, hurry! Get the children up and dressed. Take as much as you can carry and meet Esme at hers. You're both to stick together. And go to Claude's the long way . . . don't look at me like that now—the long way is safest and that's that."

"Yes Pascal."

I know when I shouldn't argue with my husband. He uses that tone of voice that means 'this is not up for dispute' and I do exactly what he says to the letter. Besides, we wouldn't be ordered to go to Claude's in the middle of the night unless we were in grave danger. This is no time for arguments.

"What about Amelie?" I ask Esme, quickly dampening the fire.

"Pierre says to leave her and Jacques and Michel will come fetch her," she replies. She seems even more upset talking about Amelie, her closest friend. Amelie's husband, Henri is in the order also and they have a little baby girl. They will need a safe place.

"Why Jacques and Michel?" Pascal demands to know stiffening, his face as white as a ghost.

And it suddenly occurs to me: Henri would have been on watch tonight. The king's men will have stopped at nothing to get into the headquarters. What if . . . ? Esme hangs her head and sobs. I'm right. I must be. Henri must have been killed. I look at Pascal questioningly. The anger is so evident in his ashen face. He shakes his head at me as if to say 'we're not talking about this now' and storms upstairs to get dressed. I look back at Esme. She is still sobbing as she wraps her shawl around her.

"Hurry," she mutters before opening the door.

As if in slow motion I watch her make her way up the street and around the corner. I close the door softly and look back into the room where just moments before I thought she had come to tell me that one of the girls is sick or the baby is in need of a potion. Trancelike, I lift the bowl with the still hot drink in it and take a sip. I go to the stairs and look up. I can hear Pascal swearing loudly as he dresses and the children stirring in their beds. I put one foot on the bottom stair. Can this really be happening? We're to go now? What if we never come back?

"Gabriella!" shouts Pascal from above, "what are you doing woman? Get the children and get going." His shouting startles me out of my dreamy state and I hurry up the stairs to the children's room.

"Maman, what's the matter? Is Papa alright?" whispers Maddy, a little scared.

"He's fine dear. Worried that's all. Listen up now, something has occurred in the city and we must go now to Claude's home. You know the man that has been teaching me all about the potions? Yes? Well, he knows we're coming and he's happy to let us stay with him at his chalet for a while; at least until all this blows over." My voice sounds strange, as if it it's not me talking.

"All what Maman? What is going on?" Maddy asks.

"Hush, I'll explain later. Now I want you to get dressed. Put as many clothes on as you can and take what you can carry. I must see to Clairose. Be a big girl now dear, and do as I say."

As Maddy busies herself with her clothes I pack as many of Clairose's as I can fit into a basket. Thinking again, I take half of them out. Maddy's stuff will have to go in there too. We must travel light, and no doubt I will have to carry Clairose. Maddy can take two baskets only and I need to bring some of my own stuff.

"Clairose, Clairose," I say shaking his shoulder. No time for our usual waking routine of me tickling his little face and ruffling his curly blonde hair.

The Four Ascents

"Oh yes, you sleep now when I need you awake, yet when I want you to sleep you won't" I say to my little boy, my voice sounding normal again.

"I'm awake Maman," Clairose giggles, "I want you to tickle me."

"No time for tickles baby. Let Maddy dress you because we're going on an adventure. Hurry up now, out of bed."

"An adventure, yippee!" he squeals, jumping up and down and making his blonde curls dance. He's such a cutie. Pascal has the same blonde curly hair though his eyes are blue. Clairose' eyes are grey like mine.

From downstairs the bang of the front door slamming shut tells me that Pascal has left and is on his way to meet Pierre. He didn't say goodbye. I hope it won't be long before he joins us at Claude's. Gosh! What am I doing, sitting here day-dreaming when I should be getting a move on? I dash into my bedroom. Pascal's nightgown is lying on the floor where he dropped it. I try to ignore it and begin throwing some of our clothes into a second basket. I pause, wondering if I should take my warm cloak with me. I decide to wear it. It's likely I'll be too hot but at least it's easier carried that way. Besides, we may not get a chance to come back here and the days are getting colder. I wonder did Pascal take his cloak with him. I run to the children's closet and pull out their warm cloaks also.

"Put these on too children," I tell them, "no arguments please. Hurry up now. Maddy, what on earth have you got there?" Maddy is stuffing some paper down the bodice of her dress.

"My drawings Maman."

"Leave them dear, you have enough to carry."

"But Maman," she complains, "Clairose is taking Mister Ted. Why can't I have my drawings?"

Looking at her forlorn face, how could I refuse her? Besides they'll not be a burden stuffed in her dress. "Okay dear, just put your cloak on quickly. Good! Are we ready then? Let's go."

I carry Clairose down the stairs, followed by Maddy struggling with the two baskets. Such a good girl! She rarely complains about anything. It will do no harm to let her take her precious drawings with her. She's quite promising as an artist actually. As for me, there's not a lot in this house that I would miss. Oh, the many happy years spent here yes, but not things. Things are things! Family is what is important. And right now the safety of our family is in jeopardy. Closing the front door I glance up and down the still dark street. All is quiet. No-one is about. "Quietly now" I whisper to the children, "no talking." We start walking and my eyes are stinging with tears and my heart

193

Eliza White Buffalo with Nicholas Black Elk

hurts. No time for saying goodbye or looking back. I keep my gaze ahead and hold Clairose close to me as we go.

"Maman," he chirps, "why can't we talk?" I don't answer him. My throat is full with tears.

"Shh, Clairose," whispers Maddy, "we're secret explorers and we must be silent lest we are discovered."

Bless the darling child. She's so good. It's strange though how her words reflect my dream in which I was a secret explorer searching for knowledge and trying not to be discovered. This isn't the first time I wonder if she possesses the gift. Ever since I was a child myself I had the gift. Maman said I was destined to do great things. I always seemed to know things about people that seemed impossible for me to know. Like the time my mother's friend was crying because her husband was very sick, and I said that she ought not to upset herself because her baby would need her to be happy. They thought it was a strange thing for me to say then but they didn't realise that the lady was with child. She had a little baby boy eight months later and named him Charles after his dead papa.

We reach the end of our street and turn the corner into Esme's street. This street too is deserted, dimly lit by the streetlamps along its length. It looks exactly the same as our street; lined on both sides with tall city houses all in darkness except for Esme's which has a lamp lit in the front room it seems. Reaching the door I find that it is ajar. We enter and I thankfully put Clairose down on the floor.

"Getting heavy?" Esme asks indicating my son.

I notice that her face is red and puffy with crying. She and Pierre are very close to Amelie and Henri. She became best friends with Amelie when she and Henri were posted here five years ago. I must admit, even though they live beside me I don't know them very well. Henri is quite thick with Pascal but my lessons take up most of my free time so I rarely see him or Amelie. I wonder if Henri really is dead. Did the king's men kill him in cold blood just because they wanted into the headquarters? He would never have permitted their entry despite the king's wishes. I suppose as long as the treasure is safe then that's the main thing. Though I'm sure poor Amelie doesn't see it that way at the moment. She will though, in time. Henri gave his life to the Knights and swore to protect the treasure under pain of death if necessary.

"Thank goodness Pascal and Pierre weren't on duty tonight," I say to Esme who nods and wipes another tear from her cheek.

Esme's girls are all ready it seems. Charlotte is the eldest at almost fourteen years old. She is quite a handsome girl with milky white skin and sandy coloured hair like Esme. Next is Maia who is twelve. Then twins Nicole and Gabbie are nine. Gabbie was named after our grandmother like I was. There was a long gap after the twins until they were seven when Esme lost one, another girl. Then came little Marie who was one year old just last week. We all had a picnic party down by the riverside walk, not far from Claude's place. Amelie and Henri were there too with their little girl, Henrietta. It was a good day, and with all those little girls laughing and playing about Pascal and I felt really blessed to have Clairose, the only boy among them. Esme would have loved to have had Claude at the picnic. We have grown so close to him these past few years during which we both have learned much from him. We've known him for much longer than that though, but we have to keep his life as separate from ours as we can. He's connected with nobility you see. His father is the Noblesse de Cloche, the noble mayor of Paris and his brother is a self professed lord, Sieur de Paris. He is a doctor, for the wealthy and noted I believe. Claude is not Claude's real name. I don't even know what his real name is but we know him as Claude to keep his work a secret from his family. He's an extremely gifted alchemist; has worked with herbs and elixirs ever since he was a young man. Thirty years ago he came back from his travels around Europe full of excitement and enthusiasm about the knowledge he had uncovered. He began to build up a store of various minerals, stones and herbs. I have no idea how he came to be involved with the Knights. He isn't one of course, but he does liaise with some of them. That is how he came to know about my gift. Pascal told him that I was interested in herbal remedies and that I had the natural gift of inner sight and healing. He set up a meeting between us and ever since Claude has been my master teacher. He teaches me the sacred art of alchemy which comes naturally to me as does herbal medicines and hands on healing. Together, Claude and I discuss spiritual matters. He never grew up with the knowledge of the ancients, not like us; for generations the secrets of the ancient knowledge has been passed down in our families. Very few have been allowed access to our circle of trust. It must be this way, especially since all this business with the king. If it were out about our families' ancestry we would all be branded as heretics and tried for crimes against the church. Worse still, rumours lately have filled us all with the fear of death upon discovery. Anyway, it seems Claude is a natural mystic and the knowledge unfolds within him like a rose unfolding its beauty. He is so happy that I have come into his life, saying that I am a heavenly messenger. In return

Eliza White Buffalo with Nicholas Black Elk

he passes to me all his secret potions and elixirs. I have been an eager student and already I have reached mastery.

There are some things I don't tell Claude though. Some things I like to keep secret, like my dreams and visions. I haven't even told these things to Pascal. My favourite one is a dream I have been having ever since I can remember. I am standing in the meeting place of two long roads. A golden being appears to me and says, "Eliza, my child. I am so proud of you. You stand in a holy place. Stretching ahead of you is the good road of abundance. You will know this road and be blessed with all things good. But you must also walk the fearful road of difficulties. It is only by walking the two roads that you will create this holy place on earth. From here you climb the four ascents. You have made the first ascent with humility and with power. Now, in this second ascent you remain balanced and at peace. The difficult road is ahead. Go forth with courage and remember who you are."

"How will I know the way?" I always ask.

The answer is always, "In the centre where the two roads meet, the prophecy lies within the Red Stone of Power. It is from here that your crystal heart shall guide you, and when the fourth ascent is made the Red Stone of Power shall sing and the prophecy will be released. As it is in heaven, so shall it be on earth."

This dream is so precious to me. I think about it a lot, especially when I am worried or unsure of my choices. In the dream my name is Eliza. I don't know why that is but it feels right to me somehow. I believe that the Red Stone of Power is my crystal heart, so called because it vibrates at the rate of crystal. Plus I often dream of another holy being that surrounds me with a red crystal light. In that dream I am two parts, one male and one female. The male part leaves me and I am given a prophecy that I must manifest on earth. In order to fulfil the prophecy I must reunite with my male counterpart bringing balance to all aspects of myself. It's all very ethereal really, and is complicated I suppose, and I know that there are those within the knowledge who could tell me exactly what it's about. But it is so precious to me that I do not wish to share it with anyone just yet. Besides, I feel strongly that I am doing what is expected of me by the holy beings and that a time will come when I must speak of the prophecy. That time just hasn't come yet. I have four ascents to make. I don't know what that means but I do know that this is only the second. I know that my quest for knowledge is powerful and I would give anything to travel. I have always wanted to go east, to the lands that the Master Jesus walked. I would dearly love to find proof of His life, of who

The Four Ascents

He was, of the reality of the treasure. I would love the world to know the truth of humanity as I know I know it deep down within my soul. I guess that's what I was looking for in my dream about the pyramids. But alas! It is not to be, not for a long time I think. In the meantime, it is the work of the families to keep the ancient knowledge secret and to maintain the survival of the treasure.

∞∞∞∞∞∞∞∞∞∞∞∞∞∞∞∞∞∞∞∞∞∞∞∞∞∞∞∞∞

It's the thirteenth day of October. We have been here at Claude's chalet for a week now and so far it seems we are safe. The king has set himself up at the Knight's headquarters. I think even he didn't bargain on the wealth of the order. The word is he has decreed that all Knights are to be apprehended and tried for heresy. Anyone connected with them will get the same treatment. If it wasn't for the children and Pascal's dedication to the order, I'd be well gone from here by now. I hate hiding. I hate having to look over my shoulder every time I go into the garden to gather vegetables for the table. I can't help but feel that as long as I must live like this then I could be using my time in the quest for knowledge. I could be following my dreams instead of spending day in day out cooped up in this small chalet. Pascal spends most of his time away from us. I've seen him only once since our flight and even that was just for a few minutes. Sometimes I wonder if he resents me and perhaps the children as well. I know I often wonder what my life would be like if I were not their wife and mother, but I love them dearly and never want to be without them. With Pascal it feels different. He loves me. In fact, I don't think I've ever known a man to love his wife so fervently. But it feels as if he has dedicated himself to me in the same way he is dedicated to the order. It is a choice he has made out of a sense of duty, destiny even. Though, he seems so innately angry and resentful of me that it tears him apart inside. Heaven only knows why he is like this. Perhaps I have wronged him greatly in another life. My grandpapa always said that the wrongs we do to others will always come back to us, even it is in the next lifetime. He says we reincarnate over and over until we amend our mistakes and fulfil our reason for being. He also used to say it is what we do here and now that counts and that every moment is an opportunity for forgiveness. Heaven knows what forgiveness I must seek from Pascal but it doesn't seem forthcoming. I guess I haven't earned it. I'm always day-dreaming which he doesn't agree with. He says I should be more mindful of my family rather than trying to be alchemist of the year. Sometimes I think he feels angry that I spend so much time with Claude. But then, he often says how he admires my convictions albeit that I should come down to earth a bit more. Oftentimes I wonder which one of us is right. Should I indulge my dreams and visions, or should I focus on more practical grounded things? Either way, the issue at the moment seems to be staying alive regardless of what that means. I just wish Pascal would be more open with me about what is going on in the city. Claude has been absent for the past week also. He has been spending most of his time with his mother, Madame Antoinette de Paris. Apparently her younger son, the doctor has expressed to her that he fears his brother may be consorting with witches. There has been a poisonous notion going around for a while now that the use of herbs and potions denotes a tendency for witchcraft. Somehow, the doctor has come to hear of Claude's interests outside of the family. Thankfully he can't have any proof given his brother's alias and the fact that he keeps all his work safely hidden away at this secret chalet on the outer edge of the city. The only people who know of his work are the Knights and their families, and none of us would dream of speaking his name publicly. In fact, very few of us know of his true identity as a member of one of Paris' most noble families. Heaven knows how the doctor came to have his suspicions but he did. That is why Claude is spending so much time with his mother. It will put her mind at rest that the doctor is mistaken. Why if she knew of her son's activities she would exile him from the family immediately. She may even have him assassinated in order to keep the prestige she has become accustomed to.

Today is Friday. Claude said he would come back this morning and spend the weekend with me and the children. We have no idea when we will get to see Pascal again. He needs to keep moving around, more to keep the trail away from us than anything else. I worry about him all the time. Just this morning before dawn I mixed a potion that will carry him safely back to us. The children joined with me in sending it forth with the river. We are sitting here on the bank of this gorgeous little stream that runs into the River Seine closer to the city. We decided it would be nice to have our breakfast here as well. The sky is heavy though and there is a horrible sense of dread in the air.

I smile reassuringly at the children. All wrapped up in blankets, they look like babes in the wood. "Your nose is pink, Clairose. Do you wish to go indoors?" I ask my son.

"No Maman," he replies, "I wish to wait here for Papa."

"But it could be all day before he comes, Baby. Are you going to sit here all day?"

The Four Ascents

"He's coming soon, Maman," he states with certainty.

"What makes you think that, Baby?" I ask amused at his grown up little voice.

"Maddy told me. She said Papa's coming after breakfast."

I look at Maddy who seems a little uncomfortable with her little brother's disclosure. "Why would you tell him that, dear?" I ask her kindly, "it will only get his hopes up."

"But Maman." She stands up and faces me, holding her blanket tightly to her body for warmth and maybe courage. "Maman," she almost cries, "Papa *is* coming this morning. I dreamed it last night and I know it's true, but . . . oh Maman!"

The child bursts into tears and throws herself into my arms. I hold her tightly, rocking her back and forth. She used to love this when she was little. Bless her, the poor child! She's been under such strain lately. I think sometimes we adults forget that she's growing up and is aware of what is happening, even if we don't talk directly to her about it.

"There there, dear, don't fret," I croon. "Tell me all about it now. What can be so terrible to upset you like this?"

"Well" she sobs . . . "I had a dream, and Papa came back after breakfast, but he was very scary."

"Scary? Papa? Surely not" I reply attempting to ease her worry.

It doesn't work though, for Maddy is inconsolable. "But he *was* angry and wasn't making any sense," she wails. "He said that we had to run away and never come back. He said that he would come find us when the coast was clear and that we ought not to worry about him. He said that people are saying that we are witches and that we worship the evil one, and that if we are caught we will surely be killed. Oh Maman, I'm frightened. You don't think he's right, do you?"

Heavens, the poor child! What a dream to have! Sometimes this gift is more of a curse than a good thing. I wish she didn't have to know these things. So, the situation in the city must have gotten worse then. Will Pascal really show up this morning and tell us to run away? But where would we run to? Who would help us? Surely not Claude—he has too much to lose. I must tell Esme of my daughter's revelation. We ought to be prepared just in case she is right, as well she may be. First though, the children need me to be positive and strong.

"Hush now dear," I croon to my daughter, "It will be alright. Chances are it was just a bad dream, and if it isn't then we shall all go on a lovely

Eliza White Buffalo with Nicholas Black Elk

adventure, into the country probably. We could find a sweet place with Esme and Pierre and the girls . . ."

"And Papa?" squeals Clairose.

"Yes, and Papa," I laugh. "There will be lots of good things to eat and lots of great places to play. Now I want you to go up to the house and wash up. If Papa comes he will want to see a clean little boy. Run along now."

"Yippee!" Clairose squeals again and runs off to the house clapping his hands together.

"Maman?" says Maddy freeing herself from my embrace.

"What is it dear?" I ask.

She walks over to the stream and kneels down there, letting the water trickle through her fingers, just like I did a million times in my childhood. I get up and sit down on a rock beside her.

"That's not the only dream I had," she tells me. "I've dreamed lots of things since we've been here. Some of it was a bit bad but some of it was nice, in a way."

"Oh! really? That's interesting dear. What are the dreams about?" I ask, aware of her need to be heard.

"Well, it's mostly about you and Papa," she replies.

Maddy seems happy that I am not dismissing her gift. I remember when I was a child and my parents listened to me. It meant the world to me because most others thought I was just weird and some called me a liar. There's no way I'm going to give my daughter cause to doubt herself.

"Go on dear," I encourage her.

"Well it's about Claude too and Aunt Esme and even Clairose," she says decidedly.

"Clairose?" I ask surprised.

"Yes, he's very smart you know. He knows a lot of things. He's a bit like you and me in that way but different, you know?"

"I don't know dear," I say. "Why don't you tell me? How is he like us but different?"

"Well, it's like he's not really a regular boy," she begins, and I smile because if there's one thing Clairose is not then it's regular. Maddy goes on, "He's knows things about . . . well I don't know . . . about space and that; the stars."

"He certainly loves to talk about the stars," I confirm. "You know what he said the other night? He said, when Papa comes back he is going to take him to the stars and that they will light the sky for me." I laugh though

The Four Ascents

Maddy doesn't find it amusing. "He said that I am to stand out in the garden where he can see me and wave to me." Still she doesn't even smile. "Maddy dear, please don't be sad. Everything will be just fine, you'll see."

"No Maman!" she yells to my utter surprise, "it won't be fine. Don't you see, that's just why Papa is angry at you. You always think everything is roses when it's not. You must face reality Maman, and be responsible. You're always telling me to be responsible but you never are yourself. You think tinkering with potions will fix everything; well it won't, it just won't, Maman."

"Goodness child!" I gasp trying to hold her again, but she pulls away from me.

My goodness! I had no idea that she was this frightened. And *she* also has noticed her father's resentment towards me. I must get her to talk some more. It will do her no good to harbour such emotions.

"Maddy dear" I begin carefully. "I'm sorry that you're upset and I'm truly sorry if I've let you down in any way, but please, tell me what you want me to do to make it up to you."

She sighs impatiently and says, "You need to listen to me Maman. I tried telling you before, but you wouldn't listen."

"Tried telling me what dear? What wouldn't I listen to?"

"To my dreams about Papa and that."

"But isn't this what we're talking about?" I ask reassuringly.

"I suppose," she sniffs.

"Well then, let's talk. Tell me about these dreams."

Taking her hand out of the water she dries it on her skirts, then plonks herself down flat on her back and stares at the sky. The ground is cold but I follow her lead and lie on my back too. It looks like a storm coming.

"Okay," she begins matter-of-factly, "in my dream there's a bad man who wants to destroy us, you and Papa, and Aunt Esme and me and even Claude. As long as we hold hands in a circle the bad man can't get to us. He's powerless to do anything to harm us at all. But there are two more people in the circle that don't wish to hold hands and it is up to us five to keep the bad man away." She pauses for a bit, thinking of what she will say next.

"Okay," I say" encouragingly, "and who is this bad man?"

"He's not really a man," she says screwing up her face and biting her bottom lip. "He's more like something bad that will happen if the circle is broken."

Eliza White Buffalo with Nicholas Black Elk

"I see," I reply, deciding that the dream appears to be just that, a bad dream." I ignore the throbbing in my chest and the strange feeling in my middle that says otherwise.

"Anyway," she goes on confidently, "you break away from the circle because you are attracted to the tricks that the man is playing to tease you away. Claude is very frightened and Papa tries to stop you going but you go anyway. And then the bad man unleashes his terror. He kills Aunt Esme and Papa, and by now Claude is so angry and distraught that he can barely look at you. It seems I am the only one that is not angry with you, but there is nothing I can do to change things."

"Oh my! That seems like a terrible dream indeed," I tell her acting shocked. "I'm sure I was very sorry for breaking the circle."

Although I say these words purely to appease my daughter and not because I want to believe that the dream is real, I can't help but feel guilty and my thoughts turn to the circle of trust between the families of the knowledge. I would never do anything to endanger the circle, would I?

Maddy goes on, fuelled by my attentiveness, "You *are* sorry Maman, soulfully sorry, but along comes Clairose and makes you feel better again. He is a big man in the dream and he says that you ought to follow his guidance if you want to be safe. Claude is still frightened and Papa is so angry with you that you can feel his wrath beyond the grave. But Clairose says that you can make everything good again by walking the two roads and then we shall all be happy."

I sit up startled by the mention of the two roads. "What did you say? The two roads? Did you say two roads?" I coax her gently.

"That's what he said in the dream: two roads, and something about a red stone, but I suppose that's silly really."

Maddy skips a stone into the river, happy now that I've listened to her dreams.

I can hardly believe my ears. "Clairose said that?" I ask her in disbelief.

"Yes!" she looks at me oddly, "In my dream" she adds.

I decide to play this thing down, "Okay then dear. That's very interesting. And so Clairose is my guide then. What does he say I should do next?"

Maddy is pleased now that I am so interested in her dream. She smiles for the first time in days and says, "He didn't say this but I know: if you want to make things alright then you do what Papa suggests when he comes today. If you're not sure that you are doing it right then you must ask Clairose what *he* wants to do. He will give you the right answer."

"Maddy, Clairose is three years old. How could I ask a three year old what is best to do in a situation like this? Now be reasonable dear."

"I know Maman," she says skipping another stone, "but he really *will* give you the right answer. He will know it from the stars. The stars will tell him. I know it sounds crazy but I just know."

"Okay, okay dear. I believe you" I say wanting to put an end to this conversation. "And if we are in a quandary as to what to do then we shall ask Clairose his opinion."

I say that but at the same time I make up my mind exactly what I'm going to do. I'm going to prove to Claude and to Pascal and Esme and even to Maddy and Clairose that I *do* know what I am doing. I know exactly what I am doing and that my potions *can* make a difference, especially to this situation.

∞∞∞∞∞∞∞∞∞∞∞∞∞∞∞∞∞∞∞∞∞∞∞∞∞∞∞∞

The video comes to a stop. And Black Elk speaks . . .

"My dear Rose, the difficult road looms ahead for Gabriella, and the storms can blind her from faith in her path. The second ascent is the step of spiritual sight and knowledge. The quest for knowledge is strong yet Gabriella does not seek it within. Oh that she would come to the centre where the two roads meet and listen to the guidance of her crystal heart! That she would feel the wisdom of the one who stands humble in her midst, Clairose. It is in the innocence of a mere child that we find our answers reflected before us, guiding us and leading us into wholeness. She is loved greatly by Beloved Source. He will never forsake her. Oh dear, Gabriella! Remember who you are!"

CHAPTER TWELVE

A quest for knowledge

And so the story continues . . .

Esme is going frantic, waving her arms about like a mad thing and trying desperately to keep her voice low so as the children won't hear us. "You can't be serious Gabriella," she insists. "It's complete madness to attempt such a thing."

"I *am* serious Esme," I tell her. "I *can* do this. Wait until Claude comes later and he will tell you of my ability to do it. If you won't listen to me then maybe you will listen to him."

"And what if it goes wrong? What do you think becomes of the children then?" she demands to know.

I don't need this hassle. If Maddy's dream is real, which it very much seems to be, it is my responsibility to prove myself to the others in the circle. I have a lot of faith in dreams, especially the sort Maddy and I have, and I believe in myself.

"For goodness sake Esme, you don't seriously think I'd put my children at risk, do you?" I ask her. "They shall be with Pascal or with you. All I need is to get close enough to headquarters, take the potion, get in, get the key and get out."

Claude and I have been working on the potion for years. It was my idea that we concoct a potion that would assist us in our search for spiritual truth. He was very keen to get started when I told him that it is possible to raise one's consciousness to a height that would leave one vibrating at such a quick rate that one would literally be invisible. We began immediately experimenting with all sorts of hallucinogenic plants. Some of them served the purpose of getting very 'high' but made us violently ill. We discarded them very quickly and kept trying. Eventually we concocted a blend of two plants that gave the desired effect. Claude has witnessed me actually vanishing for moments of time.

"It's as if you are tuning in and out of this world," he had told me red faced with excitement, "like a flash of light you think you see out of the corner of your eye but when you want to look at it it's gone."

204

The Four Ascents

Esme knows we've been doing it; Pascal does too, but neither of them witnessed what Claude did.

"You'll be seen," stresses Esme now.

"I won't be seen," I retort. "I don't think you understand Esme. I *can* do this. I'll take the potion. It'll only take a minute to kick in and I'll consciously raise myself into the higher realms and stay there. No-one will see me because there won't be anything to see. I'll be pure light. For goodness sake, I've done it loads of time in our experiments. I can do it for longer if I take enough potion."

She doesn't believe me, "Maybe, but nobody's seen you disappear, have they?"

"Claude has. Well, for flashes anyway. Why can't you accept that we've actually done it? It really works."

Esme looks at me doubtfully but nods as if she has accepted that we did do it. "We've been meaning to experiment with a stronger potion but the time never seemed right . . . until now," I add. She doesn't respond. "You have to trust me."

"Trust you with what?" comes Pascal's voice at the door. I turn to see him standing there. His face is pale and stricken with fear.

"Tell him!" says Esme folding her arms and leaning back against the kitchen wall, "go on, tell him."

I tell Pascal my plan. I tell him how I will get into the headquarters this way and retrieve the key to the treasure, thus quelling any fear that the treasure will be discovered.

"Nonsense," he snorts, "as if I would permit you to do such a thing. Besides, the key is fine where it is. Who knows what it is for? No-one even knows that the treasure exists never mind that that key would lead them to it. And it's in a very safe place. If it *was* found, which is highly unlikely, it would just seem like a key that could be for any lock anywhere. And anyway, the treasure will be moved as soon as it is safer to do so."

I try to argue my case but he gives me that look and I know it's pointless. I shall just have to wait my moment. They shall see eventually that it's a good plan. Feeling somewhat dejected I tell Pascal, "The children are out back. They'll be overjoyed that you're here. They did their own little ritual this morning to bring you here. Please don't crush them by saying it didn't work."

"Okay," he says much more calmly. He looks at me with sad eyes. "It's good to see you" he says kissing me on the cheek.

Eliza White Buffalo with Nicholas Black Elk

I put my arms around his neck and hug him tight. I love him so much. If only he would believe in me. I wish that just once he could look at me and really see me; not just Gabriella but all of me in my full power. He goes out into the garden. I don't follow him. Let him enjoy the children on his own for a bit; then we shall talk.

Several minutes later he returns, "I take it Claude isn't here?"

"He said he would be here," I reply, "but I don't think he will."

I look into Pascal's sad eyes. I want to help him, beseech him to have faith in me but I don't know what I can say that will change his mind. "Everything's ready to go" I say despondently, "but must we leave right now?"

Pascal seems surprised that I am one step ahead of him. Then he shakes his head feigning amusement. "I should have known you would predict this," he says trying to please me.

"I didn't. It was our daughter who told me," I say flatly.

Silence; he has no answer for that. Oh why does he have to question everything that I know to be real? He should know that these things are possible. After all, his own mother was a healer and seer. If he can't accept it for my sake then why can't he for his own child's sake?

"What of Pierre?" asks Esme, ignoring the tension between me and Pascal.

"Pierre's fine, Esme," replies Pascal, "but things are hotting up. It's no longer safe for any of us. That's why we must leave immediately." He avoids my gaze when he says this.

"But I don't understand," says Esme. "I thought we were safe here. Pierre always said that we would be alright here if things should get a bit tricky, and the girls are settled now. I really don't want to move them again."

"It's not as simple as that anymore," he tells her. "Why do you think Claude hasn't returned? They're watching him closely. They know he's been harbouring us, don't ask me how but they do. It's only a matter of time before they discover this place," he says desperately. Up until now I have been quietly listening to this news I knew was coming; that we are to flee further. It never occurred to me though to think what could have jeopardised our safety here. I wonder if Claude is strong enough to remain silent about us. I pray he is but somehow I don't think so.

"How did they find out about Claude?" I ask Pascal suspiciously.

"You must understand what it's like in the city Gabriella," my husband replies irritated by my tone of speech. "Everyone's panicked. Everyone's saving their own skin, and anyone could have dropped him in it. No-one's safe you know. Even the Roman Catholics are being tortured into admitting heresy."

"What?" Esme and I gasp in unison.

"That's how bad it has got," he goes on. "Every day is worse than the previous. People are being killed, some burned at the stake for witchcraft." He flinches at our shocked faces. "It's crazy I know but that's the danger we face."

Poor Pascal! Now I see our full plight I realise how much stress he must have been under. He covers his face with his hands, sitting down at Claude's big kitchen table strewn with potions and herbs that I wanted to take with me. How selfish I am to want to prove myself to him when all along I would be adding to the grave danger that we are in. I don't think I realised until now the enormity of this danger. I sit down on a chair beside him and put my hand on his arm.

"My dear," I speak softly, "I'm sorry. You're right. Esme and I will fetch the children and we'll go with you right now."

He lifts his head to look at me. He is crying. My lovely handsome, brave Pascal is crying. He puts his arms around me and pulls me close, weeping into my neck. How awful it must have been for him this past week! How selfish I have been!

"We'll meet Pierre down by the river, where we had the picnic last week remember?" he says dejectedly.

"Yes, Pascal," Esme and I reply together.

He wipes his nose with the sleeve of his blouse, the same blouse he wore when he first left our home. It was little more than a week ago but it seems like forever.

"And from there we go east," he continues. "We don't stop until we're out of the country, yes?"

"Yes," we agree. He looks at us with pity. It will be near impossible. The poor children, how will we manage?

"There's no choice," Pascal goes on despondently, his voice breaking with more tears. "If we stay in France we are surely dead, all of us!"

There is a long pain-filled silence after which Esme utters, "What of Amelie?"

"Don't know," says Pascal shrugging his shoulders. "I haven't seen Jacques or Michel at all. I only hope they shall do the same as us. You must concentrate on the children, Esme. Pierre shall be waiting."

So it is that with great fear of discovery and the prospect of weeks of running Esme and I gather our belongings and round up our children. We tell

Eliza White Buffalo with Nicholas Black Elk

them that we are meeting Pierre by the river and that we shall go from there to another safer place. We don't bother to close the door behind us. Through the back garden we go and make our way along the stream. We can mostly stay out of sight with the high growth along its bank, and when the hedges and trees get sparse Pascal goes a little ahead and checks that the coast is clear to go on. At this rate it will take all morning to reach the river. Esme has a basket in her arms, full of provisions that will last a couple of days at least. I am carrying Marie and Pascal carries Clairose. Funny that Maddy's dream says I ought to follow him. What exactly does that mean? Am I to let him lead the way out of Paris? Of course not; that would be preposterous. What could it possibly mean? I keep my eyes fixed on Clairose.

"Papa is coming to take me to the stars," he had said to me yesterday. What could he have meant by that? He said I was to wave to him up there but Maddy said I ought to follow him. I reach my hand into my apron pocket and close it around a tiny little glass bottle. I have the potion should I need to use it.

∞∞∞∞∞∞∞∞∞∞∞∞∞∞∞∞∞∞∞∞∞∞∞∞∞∞∞∞

It is already afternoon. We have been waiting here for an hour with no sign of Pierre. This part of the river is beautiful, peaceful and alive with river life. I watch an otter dive into the water further along from us. It doesn't seem to mind that we are here or that all hell has broken out in the city beyond. Even from here we can hear the gunshots and explosions. Black smoke is rising in the distance and sometimes I think I can hear the screams of frightened city folk. The otter paddles passed us sending its quake to the river's edge. Clairose and the twins are racing twigs there. No-one can see us unless they happen along the path themselves, but everyone is too concerned with the riot to spend time down by the river. The other girls are huddled around Esme. Poor things; they are so afraid. Esme is nursing a sleeping Marie who was crying very loudly before we got here, but has been fed since and is now blissfully unaware of any danger, safe in her mother's arms; unaware too of the worry for her father's whereabouts. Pascal is franticly pacing up and down the path near to them, muttering under his breath. I get up from my seat on the river bank, and checking that Clairose and the twins are safe I walk over to my husband.

"My dear" he says decidedly, "we can't stay here all day. Pierre shall have to come after us."

The Four Ascents

Just as he speaks Pierre comes running along the path towards us, his hair and blouse soaked with sweat. Stopping to catch his breath he is bombarded by the twins, Nicole and Gabby. Their excited cries cause Esme to look up from her seat on the ground, her back resting against a stone wall. When she sees her husband she gets up and runs to him with Marie in her arms. Flinging against him she sobs uncontrollably until finally Pierre manages to prise her off him a bit so he can talk. With an arm around her waist and the other around Nicole and Gabby, he receives hugs and kisses from his two eldest daughters.

Pascal patiently waits for Pierre to greet his family whom he hasn't seen in over a week. Then he inquires, "What news brother?"

"Ah Pascal. It's gotten worse," puffs Pierre shaking his head in dismay. "I don't know. Do we stay where we are and go under cover of darkness? We'll be risking capture every minute we are here, but they're everywhere. There's no way we could walk out of here in broad daylight."

"But where *were* you?" Pascal wants to know. "Why did it take so long for you to get here?"

"I saw Claude. I'm telling you brother, that man is falling apart. If he stays in that chateau for much longer he'll spill his guts for sure. I tried to get him to come with us and I think he would have. He was talking about arranging transport but then that brother of his showed up. How in the hell he knew where we were, I don't know. He must have followed Claude. Then the weirdest thing happened. He saw me. I'm sure he did. Of course I ran like a mad thing but he didn't come after me."

"Perhaps he didn't see you at all," suggests Esme.

"Oh he saw me alright but why did he let me go?" Pierre asks.

"He needed to get to Claude more?" I suggest.

"Maybe," he says. "I didn't stick around long enough to find out. Anyway, I'm not sure that Claude will stay quiet now, and that brother will have the whole squad looking for us by now. I say the women and children lie low here and you and I try to get to Claude again" he says to Pascal. "Let's see about that transport. There's no way we'll make it on foot now. Besides, if we're smart we can manage some provisions and blankets as well. Claude's our only hope out of here brother. We need him."

"Agreed!" says Pascal.

When the men tell us what the plan is Esme and I are scared, not for ourselves but for them. We don't like the idea of them going back into the city. However, the thought of transport sounds good and we don't have much of a choice really. Once again we must pin all our hopes on Claude. There's no time to waste so the men give hugs and kisses all round and run off towards the city. The rest of us wait. At dusk there is no sign of their return, or of Claude. The smaller children are asleep on their cloaks spread out on the grass. Esme and I had thrown our own cloaks over the top of them and now we are praying for the safe return of our husbands.

"Heavenly parents," Esme prays, "please guide our men safely back to us. All their lives they have strived to be good men. They have risked their lives and the lives of their children to protect your holy truth. Send them your power. Send The Angel of Earth to guide our feet to safety."

"So be it!" I add looking up along the river where I had seen the otter earlier today. In the quiet of the moment my heart beats softly speaking to me. It says, *Gabriella, this night you will be with me in the heaven world. Fear not for all shall be revealed to you.*

"Back in a bit" I mutter to Esme. "Watch Clairose for me, will you?" I walk off along the path. When I come to the place where I had seen the otter earlier I stop and sit down on the bank hoping to see it again.

"May I join you Maman?" asks Maddy quietly. I didn't realize she had followed me.

"Of course dear," I smile.

She sits down and I put my arm around her shoulder pulling her close to me. Neither of us speaks for a long time after which the otter shows up again. It dives into the water from the opposite bank. We hear the splash first before we see it because the light is dimming fast. Thankfully it will be a clear sky tonight and the moon is full. The otter is swimming directly across the river in our direction. Maddy points to it silently so as not to scare it away. It swims right to the bank and comes out of the water close by us. We watch it play about on the muddy bank for a bit before it suddenly realizes that we are here. It stays perfectly still for a moment staring at us as if trying to work out why we are here. Then it turns swiftly, dives back into the water and swims back where it came from.

"Wow Maman!" exclaims Maddy, her mouth hanging open with surprise.

"Shh!" I whisper to her, "let's wait and see what it does next."

When I was a child moments like this occurred often. I grew up in the country where all kinds of animals were much more trusting than in the city outskirts. My grandparents taught me that animals are our teachers and that each kind offers us insight into our relationships with each other and with the Divine. Otters, as far as I remember are about the feminine essence within us and they teach us to bring balance to our lives by trusting and going with the flow of events. I guess I shouldn't be so driven to prove myself to others. Perhaps I ought to flow with the water like the otter does and not try to control what is happening to the families. Trust that all is in divine order and that as my intuition has said, all shall be revealed. A splash tells me that the otter has just dived into the water again. I strain my eyes to see but it is so dark over there on the other bank. Soon I see it swimming down river close to where the others are. Maddy has seen it too and is being very quiet. We watch as it climbs out onto the bank and dashes up towards where the children and Esme are. Unbelievably it goes right up close to Clairose's feet and then dashes back in a flash and disappears into the water. Good heavens! Is it telling me to trust Clairose?

"It likes Clairose, Maman," giggles Maddy. "Do you suppose it wants him to play?"

"Don't know sweetheart," I reply, my heart thumping inside my chest.

A thought has just occurred to me. What if Maddy's dream isn't just about the circle? What if it also means that I should listen to what Clairose has said to me about the stars? If indeed that is so, it means that tonight he and Pascal are going to the stars. Are they to die tonight? Something tells me that they will and that I am to follow them. Does that mean I must take the potion? Or does it mean that I am to die also? What will become of Maddy, and what of the others? Will they get away or will they perish too? My heart is thumping wildly and I can scarcely breathe with fear of what might be. I must get to Pascal. It has been too long. The men should have been back by now. Something is wrong, I know it.

"Esme!" I almost shout as I hasten back down the path towards her. Maddy comes running after me. She must think I have gone crazy. "Esme" I pant anxiously, "I must get to Pascal. Don't ask me how but I know he needs me and he can't get to me. I'm going now." I start to gather up my belongings.

"Wait!" exclaims Esme grabbing my wrist. "Don't do anything rash. They could be here any minute now. Gabriella, if you go you could be walking straight into disaster. And the men said to stay together. Just stop and think about will you?"

"I'm decided," I insist, "and I'm going now. I'm not sticking round here any longer waiting for my man to be killed out there while I'm sitting watching the river flow past."

"Maman, you're scaring me. I don't want Papa to be killed." Maddy's face is white with fear.

Eliza White Buffalo with Nicholas Black Elk

"I want Papa, I want Papa," wails Clairose.

"It's alright dears," I tell them, "Hush now, we're going to go get Papa right now. I know where he is. Esme, what are *you* doing?"

She pulls her little ones around her in a huddle and adamantly states that she is going nowhere.

"Fine," I relent. "Bless you sister. Bless all of you." With that I pull Clairose onto my hip and kiss my sister on the forehead. "We'll be back with the men. You have to believe that," I tell her.

It's near dark now. The city will be in chaos. If I'm careful I can make my way to Claude's family home without drawing attention to myself and the children. We've been walking for ten minutes and we are coming to the end of the riverside path where it meets with the outer pathways of the city. Suddenly I stop and caution the children to be silent. I think I hear a noise. It sounds like a horse whinnying. Yes, there it is again. "Stay here and don't move," I whisper to the children putting Clairose into Maddy's arms. Creeping noiselessly onwards I spy the wheel of a buggy behind a huge hedge. There is someone here in a horse and buggy.

Whoever it is realizes that I am here too because a voice whispers quietly, "Is that you, Madame Pommier? Gabriella, are you there?"

I don't answer, trying to figure out who owns the voice.

"Madame, it is Richard De Boir, the brother of Claude. He has sent me to fetch you," continues the whispering voice.

The doctor? Le Sieur De Paris? Surely he wouldn't be willing to help. But then, how did he know we are here if Claude did not tell him so, and how does he know Claude's alias? If Pascal and Pierre are with Claude then it seems possible that what he has said is true. Pierre was pretty sure that he saw him today and chose to let him go. Besides, we're not going to get past him without being seen and he knows we are here. I have to take the chance.

"Madame," he continues after a while, "I know your husband is not with you. He is with Claude at my chateau. He has told me to tell you that you must come immediately for he cannot get to you."

Still I remain silent. My heart is thumping madly. I can hear it in my ears. I close my hand around the little bottle of potion in my pocket. What if? No, he knows my children are here at least. There's no way *they* can get past without being seen. I shall have to trust him. I creep back to the children.

"There is a man here who says he is Claude's brother and that he will help us," I whisper to them. "We may have no choice but to trust him. But

212

The Four Ascents

if you wish we will return to Esme and walk in the other direction and try to find a way back to Claude's chalet."

"But Papa said we're not safe there," says Maddy in a tiny voice. Poor child, she is terrified. My heart aches that I can't protect them but I can't let them see that or that I am terrified too.

"I know dear," I tell her, "but it may buy us some time and if Papa doesn't find us here then he will find us there." Pray heaven that I'm right.

"It's alright Maman," says my brave little boy, "Claude's big brother is kind. He will find Papa for us."

Looking into my son's eyes at this moment I see a wisdom there that I hadn't seen before. Just like Claude describes it, it's like a flash of light that you think you see but when you want to look at it, it is gone. But Clairose is three years old.

"*Trust,*" I tell myself. "*Listen to him.*"

I have no choice really. The doctor knows we are here. If he wanted to he could have us captured right now. Before I could think again though, the doctor is coming walking up to us. He stops a respectful distance away.

"Madame Pommier, you have no reason not to trust me," he says. "I have spoken to my brother and I know of your friendship. He holds you all very dear and I have no desire to bring him any pain. He leaves Paris tonight. If you come now you may go with him. He shall see that you get out of the country safely."

"And my sister's family?" I ask.

"Them too," he adds after a moment's thought.

"I'll run and get them, Maman," offers Maddy excitedly. She starts to run off up the path.

"No stop!" he says loudly, "There's no room in the buggy for such a crowd. It'll be a squeeze as it is."

But how can we leave Esme and the girls? I search his face for answers. He seems like a kind man.

"I shall return for the rest of your party," he adds. "Now, let us go for time is running out."

And so I put my trust in this man. We go with him and climb up into the buggy. There really is barely room for the three of us as the horse trots along the outer path of the city. There is not as much noise now that darkness has fallen but I can see several fires from the seat of the buggy and every now and then a gunshot rings through the night. I hug my children close and shiver. I pray I've done the right thing.

Eliza White Buffalo with Nicholas Black Elk

After about ten minutes silence the doctor speaks to me. "So how long have you known my brother?" he asks without turning to face me.

"About ten years," I reply hoping that I'm not saying too much.

"And did you teach him everything he knows? I understand he is very gifted."

He must know all about us. It seems Claude has spoken after all.

"*He* taught *me*," I reply angrily.

"I'm going to show Claude my drawings," chirps Maddy proudly. "I have them right here, in my dress."

"An artist eh!" the doctor says amused at the child's pleasure amongst all this gloominess.

"I can draw horses," she says hoping to please our rescuer. "And when we get to our new home I'm going to draw the circle of people from my dream. Claude is one of the circle you know, and me and my maman and papa and even my Aunt Esme. There are two more and I'm going to draw them in a picture all happy and smiling. Claude will be very happy to have such a drawing. He will be happy that the circle is complete."

Suddenly the doctor stops the horse and buggy and turns around to question Maddy. "What do you mean?" he asks her very interested. "You dreamed about a circle? What circle?"

Before Maddy could speak I answer him, "Pardon me sir, but my child is a dreamer. Pay no attention to what she says. It means nothing."

"But Maman," begins Maddy.

"Shh" I tell her, putting a finger to my lips.

The doctor moves on and I wink at my daughter to let her know that I still believe her but that it's a secret to be kept by us alone. I wonder why on earth the doctor reacted to a child's dream like that. I can't see the doctor's face from where I sit and so I can't see the bewildered expression on his face. I don't know that he is thinking of his own dreams; dreams in which he is a member of a circle of people and that if he doesn't join with that circle terrible things will happen; if he doesn't keep every single member of that circle safe then terrible things will happen. I don't know that at this very moment he is wondering if he should let us escape from Paris with his brother after all. He has it all set up and ready. Word has gotten out about his brother's involvement with the witch and he has arranged to secrete him out of the country before his mother can do any more harm. He is his big brother after all. He loves him, but what if he ought to help him save the others in the circle. If indeed it is the same circle from his dreams. He is thinking all this

The Four Ascents

and I have no idea. I can't see the indecision in his face and I don't know when he decides: No, the witch must be destroyed.

∞∞∞∞∞∞∞∞∞∞∞∞∞∞∞∞∞∞∞∞∞∞∞∞∞∞∞∞∞∞

Pascal lifts his head painfully. What happened? Oh yes, he was running to catch up with Pierre. They had got separated when the explosion went off. He remembers he had just caught sight of him across the street when the men came from nowhere. There was a lot of shooting. He was running and suddenly he felt as if something had whacked him hard in the chest. He had fallen backwards onto the ground. He remembers nothing after that except coming round to find himself lying here with his chest pouring with blood. The street is quiet now. Pierre is gone; Pascal hopes he got away. He thinks about Gabriella and the children. He can't leave them. He can't leave Gabriella. She needs him. He shivers. It's so cold. *Please someone*, he thinks, *help me!* But he is alone. No-one will help him. The sound of crackling wood can be heard coming from the burning headquarters. Should he have trusted Gabriella? If he had he may not be here at this moment. He tries to speak. He wants to whisper that he is sorry. He could have believed in her but she is so vulnerable, and dangerous with it. He parts his lips to speak but all that comes out is a bloody gurgle. As his body shudders uncontrollably a memory flashes through his mind; a glimpse of lying like this once before, alone and cold in a rocky cave, with only angry and regretful thoughts of Gabriella, of his soul mate, to pass the endless moments before death. The cold wells up within him and the shudder stops. He closes his eyes letting go off his last breath. At last, the cold is gone.

∞∞∞∞∞∞∞∞∞∞∞∞∞∞∞∞∞∞∞∞∞∞∞∞∞∞∞∞∞∞

Clairose holds his sister's hand tightly. She's running too fast for him and his little legs can't keep up. He stops and wails, "I want Maman. Why can't I stay with Maman?"

"Hush Clairose," sobs Maddy. She is crying too but she must get him as far away from here as she can. The doctor said to go to back to the river. If they stay here they will be caught.

"No. Maddy bad. I want Maman," the child screams stomping his little feet on the ground. "I want Maman! I want Maman!

Eliza White Buffalo with Nicholas Black Elk

Poor Maddy, what is she to do? She wants her mother too but she knows that it is too late for her; she will be killed for being a witch. The doctor said so, and he said that if she doesn't run back to Aunt Esme immediately she will be killed for being a witch too because like mother like daughter. He said he might be a witch hunter but he is not a child killer. Maddy had been sure he was a kind man but she had been wrong. But now all she can think about is getting to Aunt Esme. Papa is gone . . . she feels it . . . she knows it . . . and now Maman. Aunt Esme is her only hope. She must get Clairose to Aunt Esme.

"Please Clairose," she begs the little boy. "We have to go back to Aunt Esme. Papa will be looking for us there," she lies.

It makes Clairose move again. He takes her hand and sulks, "Just don't go too fast."

Maddy sighs with relief and hitches Clairose up on her back; she has no baskets to carry now anyway. She even left her drawings in the buggy.

"Giddy up horsey," shouts Clairose just before he falls to the ground.

What was that? Maddy had heard a loud bang. Several people are running across the path they had just come along. She pulls Clairose by the arm.

"Hide baby, quick!" she urges him, but Clairose won't move; his blonde curls are red with thick warm blood and his little body is motionless. All hope leaves Maddy and she throws herself over her brother and waits to be found.

Clairose is floating high above the ground. One moment he was going to get a horsey back ride and the next he is up here. He can see Maddy below him lying on top of something on the ground. He calls to her but she doesn't hear him. Suddenly he feels someone with him and he turns to see his papa smiling at him. He is reaching out a hand for him to hold.

Papa!" he cries with excitement. He takes his papa's hand and off they go together on a journey to the stars.

∞∞∞∞∞∞∞∞∞∞∞∞∞∞∞∞∞∞∞∞∞∞∞∞∞∞∞

Richard De Boir takes leave of his brother and almost runs out into the courtyard of his family's grand chateau. He can't face him any longer. He had shown no remorse for his actions and didn't even correct him when he said the witch had learned it all from him. Doesn't he realise what this will do to the family, to his poor mother?

The Four Ascents

"Ah!" Richard cries angrily, lifting an axe that was thrown haphazardly against the wood pile. He swings it high above his head and brings it down hard into one of the logs. Wood flies everywhere and a huge splinted piece strikes his thigh cutting into the flesh. Blood seeps through his pants. He drops down to his knees on the grass.

"Ah!" he grunts again. He knows he messed up. His brother is lost to them now. And he can't get that damn dream out of his head. The guilt is overwhelming and the sense of responsibility to this *circle*, whatever it is. Should he really have saved the witch and sent her off with his brother? Should he have let them do whatever they want, as long as it is not in France? What about the other one, the one still at the river? And he has sent the witch's offspring back to her. Maybe he could salvage something out of all this. Maybe if he tells his brother where to find them. Maybe, just maybe it will appease his conscience and these damn dreams will stop.

∞∞∞∞∞∞∞∞∞∞∞∞∞∞∞∞∞∞∞∞∞∞∞∞∞∞

Claude prays for guidance. He was too late for Esme. They were gone by the time he got there. Several baskets of food and clothes were sitting neatly beside discarded cloaks on the verge of the riverside path. If they had moved on they would have taken them with them. Pierre and Pascal must not have been able to return to them. He had been doubtful all along. It was much too risky to try to go right into the city streets. They wouldn't listen to him. He had tried to tell him how bad it was but they wouldn't listen. What on earth were they trying to accomplish?

"A fat lot of good the order is to them now," he mutters to himself. "Damn stupid idiots!"

He shall have to go on. There's nothing left here for him now. Richard was very happy to report the news that his secret chalet has been discovered and destroyed. His life's work is ruined. He can't stay in France now anyway. If he does it won't be long before it all comes out. If that happens, even his parents would be prosecuted. Best that he leave and never come back. He stops the horse and dismounts, staying close to the shadows. Something moved up ahead, on the outer path. He would have thought this area would be deserted at this hour.

Can't afford to be seen by anyone, he thinks wondering if it is a person at all. Whatever it is it seems to be low down on the ground. Perhaps it's a dog? He waits for a bit until he is confident whatever it is poses no threat.

Eliza White Buffalo with Nicholas Black Elk

"Must be a dog, wounded maybe," he tells himself.

He creeps nearer keeping close to the hedge so that he can hide if necessary. The bulk on the ground doesn't move again but is perfectly still. A few more steps and he realizes it is a child lying there.

Poor thing, he thinks, *must have been hurt.*

He glances around quickly for any sign of an adult close by. There is no-one. Approaching cautiously he asks, "Hello, can you hear me child? It's alright. I won't hurt you."

The child sniffles and lifts its head. It's a little girl and there appears to be another smaller child beneath her. She looks up at him standing in the moonlight and begins to sob. "Claude?" she utters in a tiny voice.

"What? Who is it? Oh my goodness, Maddy, is that you?"

The child's sobs turn into a high pitched wail. Shocked, he lifts her up and holds her close. His eyes are drawn to the other child lying motionless on the ground. Nausea waves over him when he realizes it is Clairose.

"Maddy dear, I want you to wait here while I check on Clairose," he tells her softly whilst lifting her up onto the horse's back. She says nothing but continues to sob.

"Damn you Richard," he mutters under his breath.

Clairose is dead; shot in the back of the head it seems. But he can't leave him lying here. Numb with shock, he lifts the tiny little body and lays it across the back of the horse behind Maddy. With just enough room for the three of them he starts off. He shall have to get as far out of Paris tonight as he can. As they go his thoughts wander to Gabriella and Esme and all those little ones. What is their fate? He can hardly bare the images that come into his mind.

∞∞∞∞∞∞∞∞∞∞∞∞∞∞∞∞∞∞∞∞∞∞∞∞∞∞∞∞∞

The video comes to a stop. And Black Elk speaks . . .

"My dear Rose, you see how the soul, Gabriella, stands now on the summit of the second ascent, the step of higher knowledge and spiritual sight. The fear is great and reluctant to move forwards along the black road, yet it shall be a great servant. If only she would listen to the Red Stone of Power. If only she would listen to her crystal heart. It is calling out to her from the depths of the soul: *Remember who you are!*"

CHAPTER THIRTEEN

Remember who you are

And so the story continues . . .

Thank heavens the doctor let the children go. I can only pray that they make their way back to Esme. Oh what will become of them? I have failed them miserably. If only I had gone the other way. At least we would have had a chance. Or if we had stayed at the chalet, would we now be well on our way out of Paris? What has become of Pascal and Pierre? And Esme and the girls; are they safe? Are my children with them? Oh Heavenly Parents, please let them be alright! My head is pounding. The potion is starting to take effect but I don't know if I can maintain a good enough focus to raise myself into the spirit world. I am standing on a wooden platform. My hands and feet are bound and tied to a stake and below me huge flames are almost reaching the platform. Beside me, tied to another stake is an old woman. She stares at me, her eyes wild with fear. I watched them carry her up and tether her to the stake. Her screaming came at me from all around, sounding over and over in my head until I hardly knew if it was her screaming or me. My breath left my body several times only to come flooding back, awakening me to the full horror of my plight. Then, as the potion began to warm my insides and I began to feel that lightness of body I accepted my fate. The potion is strong and it blocks out the fear. Waves of clarity are washing through me now. I think that if I can gulp in enough of the black smoke then I will pass out before the flames engulf me. That is what I am trying to do. And as the old woman watches me it seems she is doing the same thing. I can no longer feel my legs or my middle. The potion is so powerful I cannot feel my body. Good, that will help. I've got to focus harder though.

Focus Gabriella, focus, I tell myself. *I Am Light! I Am Light!* Flashes of purple light streak before my eyes; I close them softly. I am in a world of purple haze. I feel my body swaying. *Stay with it. Light, light, light!* The purple brightens and alternates with pure white light. A high pulsing tone rings in my head lifting me up and up. I can hear music . . . almost there. The smoke is swirling around me, thick and black, but I don't notice it. I am tingling all over in a world of white. Waves of ecstasy fill my body. Soon, every cell feels to be floating in sensuous rapture. All awareness of my surroundings becomes dream like. I open my eyes. Below the platform the flames are raging and reaching upwards. Soon they will reach the platform and it will be engulfed in fire.

On the ground beyond hundreds of people rant and cheer. Their words are distant and detached from my reality. "Burn witch," they are shouting.

The lightness in my body becomes more and more. Waves of pleasure swim throughout me and I seem to float in pure consciousness. As I do, I observe the mob below. The jeering is stopped. People are pointing upwards. Some are screaming and running away. Others are staring speechless. They cannot believe their eyes. Their witch has vanished.

There is silence now. For a few blissful moments of sheer existence I float. I am aware that I am and I am aware that I am that I am. The platform, the stake, the old woman writhing in agony next to me, the mob below, the flames licking around my feet; I am all this. I am all that is. I think of my dream, the dream I dreamed of the quest for knowledge and suddenly I am there . . .

. . . I am an explorer. I am amongst the pyramids in Egypt. The sun blazes down from a cloudless sky and I am happy that I am here amongst these ancient monuments that hold the secrets of who I am. For a long time I have searched for the truth. For a long time I have felt that I am not what I was, what I truly am. I feel like a charlatan among charlatans. We walk as if in truth. We talk as if in truth, but we are not truth. We are not who we were before our truth was stripped away from us. But here in this ancient landscape the truth has lain hidden for generations. Here I am about to discover at last the truth of who I am, *what* I am.

A bodiless voice speaks to me powerfully. It seems to come from within my heart. The voice glows outward from my heart with a red crystal light and it sounds with golden musical tones. It is great and it is soft. It is mighty and it is gentle. It is awesome and it is love. It whispers and it directs. It sings and it throbs within my chest. It takes my breath away and it fills me with the breath of life. I listen to it as I move effortlessly through this sandy land.

I see before me a great pyramid. Around it four winds are blowing. They meet in the centre and swirl around the pyramid surrounding it with a light brighter than white.

The Four Ascents

"I am the Red Stone of Power," says the red golden voice. "Behold my truth for it is your Self that you shall know."

I look and the pyramid is shining with a light brighter than white. "Go within," the Red Stone of Power says to me. "Much you shall know."

As I walk towards the pyramid the four winds conjure up a storm and now around the pyramid four clouds of sand are blustering. Just for a moment I imagine I see the heads of many different horses and I imagine I hear the sound of thunderous hoofs galloping. In the west I imagine I can see black horses there. And in the north, amidst the cloud of sand I imagine there are many white horses. In the east I think there are red horses there and in the south they appear to be yellow. All around the pyramid horses of four colours appear to be. And although they seem to come from my imagination a strange memory is pulsing in my mind. I seem to remember from somewhere or some other time, perhaps in another dream, I seem to remember the sight of four teams of horses, twelve in each team. I seem to remember that I was riding a pony with four teams of horses coming after; twelve black horses, twelve white horses, twelve red horses and twelve yellow horses. The horses vanish now and a door opens up in the pyramid inviting me to enter, which I do. Inside there is a long corridor with four doors. I assume they lead into four chambers within the pyramid.

"Go through the first door," says the Red Stone of Power.

I open the first door and there before me is a white landscape. In the distance are snowy hills and all around a wind whistles through snow laden trees. A frozen lake glistens in pale crystal sunlight and from the sky large snowflakes are softly falling. They are perfectly formed and tinkling like glass. I reach my arm through the doorway and catch the snowflakes on my open palm. They feel warm to the touch and as each one falls and melts into my palm I find myself going deeper and deeper into the landscape. Such a winter wonderland I have never seen before. Its beauty compares to no other. As I walk further along a white path I notice that I leave no footprints; behind me the snow lies perfect as before. I close my eyes and breathe in the cleanness of the air through my nostrils. Exhaling, I twirl myself around and around smiling with the sense of rest that this world fills me with.

"Eliza," a gentle voice utters from beyond the hills; it has been some time since I heard that name.

I respond eagerly, "It is I."

I notice that nestled in the snow at my feet is a medium sized white box.

Eliza White Buffalo with Nicholas Black Elk

"Eliza, my child," the voice continues, "Open the box and behold the power that is yours."

Doing as I am bid I open the box. Inside is a wing with beautiful white feathers. I lift it out of the box and to my surprise a flock of white geese appear and soar above my head. They fly off to the north where they stop and hover there.

"They are the power of the cleansing wind," says the gentle voice.

Now I see that also in the box is an herb. It is brightly coloured and seems to glow with all the colours of the rainbow. I take it from the box and hold it up to look at it.

"Yours is the power to heal my child" says the voice. "It is my power which has been given to you."

And when the voice had spoken these words I look to the hills and there I see a vision. In the vision there is a small boy. He is lying in a coma and he will surely die if I don't help him.

"Hurry!" the voice says, "take the herb."

I take the herb and run towards where the boy is lying. As I near him he gets up and smiles at me and he is well.

The voice speaks again saying, "Look on him whom you have made well for he is your Self."

I look again at the smiling boy and I recognize that he is a part of me that I had forgotten. With that the vision is gone. Now the empty box is before me and as I look it disappears.

"It is no more" says the gentle voice from the hills. "Go forth now with my power what was given to you and remember who you are."

Now I am once again in the corridor with the four doors there for me to see, and I stand before the second door.

"This power also you shall know," says the red golden voice that is the Red Stone of Power.

I open the second door and there stretched as far as the eye can see is a morning sky. Lit with golden reds and warm blues, and with the sun rising majestically above distant black hills yonder, it is the most beautiful dawn I have ever witnessed. I walk slowly into this fiery world and as I walk the sun shows its full face and smiles down at me. Heavenly music chimes all around and birds chirp and sing in the wondrous glory. Happiness floods through me with the highest joys. I think that should I lift my arms I would soar into

The Four Ascents

the sky like an eagle. And as I once more hear that gentle voice my happiness soars from my chest and dances over the sky like a hummingbird's wings.

"Eliza, my child," the gentle voice says, "Look and see what is."

Coming flying from the sun is an eagle. It comes directly towards me and now it is a pipe floating there in the air before me. It has a long stem with feathers hanging from it and the bowl is made from bone. On the stem is an eagle with outstretched wings. This pipe is strange indeed, none like it have I seen yet it seems familiar to me. I take it in my hands and suddenly the world is filled with deep peace.

"It is the power that is knowledge and understanding and it is the power that is yours now" says the voice.

And as I hear these words I rise up into the sky and hover there with invisible wings. I look across the sky and I look down upon the earth that I now see. And what I see there on earth and in the sky I know to be part of one being and that I am that one.

"With this power, on Earth where there is despair you shall bring hope. Where there is unrest you shall bring peace," says the gentle voice.

Now I am on the earth again where there are many animals of all kinds and they are happy and peaceful; and in the sky birds of all kinds are happy and peaceful.

And the voice says, "Go forth now with this power that is I. It has been given to you. Remember who you are."

Once more I am in the corridor and this time I stand before the third door so I know that I will open this door and what I will see beyond I will understand for I have been given the gift of knowledge and understanding. I put my hand on the door and before it opens the Red Stone of Power leaps within my heart and sings. The music is full of joy and deep peace.

And when the Red Stone of Power has sung it is quiet for a moment, and then it says, "Eliza, what you shall see is my truth. It is the prophecy that rests in peace within. When the four ascents are made and the prophecy is released all shall be in joy and peace. You shall be with your sacred parents in Heaven and all shall know that they are in Heaven. Go forth now with courage and remember who you are. The fearful black road stretches ahead and the third ascent shall be difficult. As long as you remember who you are you shall not fall."

With that the door opens. Before me is a world no different than any world I have known on earth. I walk through this world and I see people

Eliza White Buffalo with Nicholas Black Elk

going about their own business, making their homes and raising their children as best they can. They have enough to eat and clothing to keep them warm. All around people are busy doing their own thing. Occasionally, they come together in little groups and communities. They search for meaning within their groups and each group claims to have the answers to their questions. But no-one is happy. All are afraid that they are not what they should be.

I raise my hands to the sky and pray for them, "Oh gentle voice! You have given to me the power of understanding and knowledge. These people need my help. Speak to me now through that power and tell me how I am to help them."

And the voice comes from the far distance, "Eliza, my child. I am proud of you. Here you see how it shall be in the third ascent. Have courage child. I love you and I shall never forget you."

At once the white geese of the first world come; flying about the people, and a breeze is blowing from the north. It blows its way throughout clearing all traces of despair from the many groups. And as I marvel at the power that is given to me I see that in my hand I hold the pipe of understanding and knowledge that brings peace. With this I walk throughout the groups and they are renewed with this deep peace.

"See the world that is yours to make," says the gentle voice.

Now as the many groups of people begin to join up and make one grand community of people there is in the centre of this community a tree that is growing. It grows fast and blooms with sweet smelling blossoms. In its branches birds are singing and below its spread the entire community lives in peace and joy. A light rain falls from a sun blessed sky bringing thirst quenching freshness. Happiness dwells throughout the world and all the people sing with one harmonious voice, giving thanks and praise. I gaze upon this world that I have made well with the power of the cleansing wind and the power of knowledge and understanding that brought newness in peace.

And the gentle voice says, "With my power that I have given to you, you shall make this grow. Go forth now and remember who you are."

And as the voice speaks there appears above the central tree, a rainbow so beautiful that it shines with heavenly light. And as I marvel at the beauty that is shown to me I see that the tree stands in the meeting place of two roads. Towards the north a good red road leads and from west to east is a black fearful road. I understand that these are the two roads of my dreams and the flowering tree stands in the holy place wherein the prophecy is held. It is the

The Four Ascents

holy place that is my crystal heart and the Red Stone of Power is that which guides me from therein.

Now the gentle voice speaks again saying, "Go forth now with courage, my child and remember who you are."

Now I see that I am at the fourth door. I pause to think about the powers that I have been given; the power to cleanse that is the power to heal, the power of knowledge and understanding that brings peace and rebirth, and the power to make these things grow in oneness and beauty. Now the fourth door opens and beyond it the world is terrible indeed. I feel reluctant to go forward but the Red Stone of Power sings to me again, encouraging me and I gain great courage.

And the Red Stone of Power says to me, "Eliza, do not despair for this is the fourth and final ascent before you will know oneness with your sacred parents in Heaven. Remember the powers given to you by the one that is your source; the one that is the Source of All Things. Take strength from the knowledge that you are not alone, you were never alone, and you never shall be alone. The One is with you, bringing balance in all ways. Trust in the One and the One shall bring you home."

And so it is with courage and hope that I step forth into the fourth world, the fourth ascent. How dark it is; a world of darkness and agony! It is more terrible than any nightmare I have known, yet I know that I shall be alright. I have the powers given to me by Source, the gentle voice. He has declared that with these powers I shall make a good world on earth. I walk on past screaming demons and tortured people that hold out their hands to me in despair. I want to help them but their pain fills my being so that I feel only helplessness, only disempowerment. It is not long before I am on my knees with agony. Around me fires blaze painfully hot and thick black smoke obscures my vision so that all I see is hopelessness; all I feel is abandonment. A cold black alien presence slivers its way around my body and enters my middle. The terror is great and I scream for salvation but all hope is gone.

From within my mind the alien presence makes itself known. "You have fallen once again from your heights of self-delusion," it sneers. "Here, this that you see around you, this is who you are. Ha ha! Did you think that you could delude yourself forever? Is it not I that has pulled the blindness from your eyes and revealed to you the truth of who you are? How far the mighty has fallen!"

Eliza White Buffalo with Nicholas Black Elk

"No!" I scream. "This is *not* who I am. Get behind me and know that I am light," I cry out in my defence.

"Light?" the alien presence derides me. "Ha ha! Look around you. Do you see light? No, because it's not real. This is what's real; this is what you are."

"Oh Gentle Voice," I cry desperately. "Why have you abandoned me?" I listen for an answer but none comes. I will not give up though. I look behind me for the door of this world but it is gone. All that is behind me now is pain and anguish. The memory of anything else is fading rapidly. I lie down upon the scorched earth and with the last remaining whisper of hope within my memory I open my heart to receive it.

"I am light, I am light," I utter in my submission. I make my decree over and over until the agony subsides and I begin to feel an inkling of joy once again. I focus on this sliver of joy with everything I have and very soon it begins to grow until once again I hear that gentle voice.

"Welcome back, my child. You've been gone a long time," it says.

Now the joy flows within me and I cry out, "Father, Mother! Hear my voice. Give me the strength to walk the fearful black road."

And suddenly the alien presence is gone and I am standing in a still dark world. The fires have cooled and the demons are licking their wounds. The many unfortunate people lie about in sickness and they beseech me once again.

"Help me," they beg.

In the darkness before me I see a light beginning to glow. The light grows and grows until the world is now visible and I see that the light is a good red spirit of a kind and loving man. He holds his arms outstretched to embrace me and when he wraps them around me I am filled with hope and love. We two stand now in this world that is brightening fast and I feel that he is a part of me, a very ancient part of me.

And from the brightening sky the gentle voice of Source speaks to us, "Eliza, my child, I am proud of you. I am the power to destroy and to make live, which is yours now. With this power you shall crucify all that is separated by despair and resurrect it again into wholeness."

Now the fearful road stretches out before me and in the distance I see the place that is holy. I start off on the road and as I walk all around me lightens. Before long I find that I am standing in the holy place and the good red spirit is standing with me hand in mine. He is so much a part of me I cannot tell where my hand ends and his begins. He is my right hand and together as one

The Four Ascents

we are one being known as Eliza. The world is bright and happy now and the people are well and at peace.

And the gentle voice of Source speaks again saying, "Eliza, in balance shall you walk now and where you go all shall follow. I send a messenger to you. He shall ascend the four steps to Heaven walking alongside you; a voice for all to hear and a light to light the way. You will know him by his sound and his sound is Artamor."

"Artamor," I echo loudly. Immediately the sky is filled with faces and many of these faces I know, and many of their names I remember from a deep sense of other times when I have lived in other worlds. I know the man that is known as Jason and the little boy that is known as Little Buffalo. I see a boy that shall be known as Pedro and a man that shall be known as Stephen. All these people and many more are Artamor, and amongst them is a face that I know now. It is the little boy with dancing blonde curls and laughing grey eyes. He is such a huge part of my heart now. He is Clairose.

"The soul is infinite and its journeys can be long and arduous," says the gentle voice of Source. "As you behold the many earthly temples of Artamor, know that it is so with Eliza. Go forth now with courage and remember who you are."

Now the fourth world is gone and I find myself outside of the pyramid, in the desert once again. The gentle voice has ceased to speak and the white light of the pyramid is lessening even as I watch. It is just an ordinary pyramid now standing on a sandy expanse. The day is over and the sun is low in the desert sky. I feel I am all alone in this world.

And then the Red Stone of Power speaks to me saying, "Eliza, all over the universe you have been searching for truth. You have gone deep within the sacred being that is three beings in one. You have discovered that the four powers are to be found therein. You have found there the power of the cleansing wind which clears away all that is diseased and brings the gift of life. You have found the power of knowledge and understanding which brings peace and you have found the power of growth that will aid you in bringing the prophecy to completion. And you have discovered that you have the power to crucify and to resurrect. All this you have learned. You have learned also that the voice you listened to is the voice of Source; the three supreme beings in one. It was the voice of the Father being that spoke to you teaching you faith in who you are. I am the voice of the Child being that brings you hope and joy. All along you were held by the Mother being. It was She who

Eliza White Buffalo with Nicholas Black Elk

sheltered you with Love. And just as the inner world is no longer visible, so too must you leave the outer world. Have courage for you are now on the threshold of the third ascent, and although your reluctance is great may you walk in balance, always coming to the holy place within that is the crystal heart. There you shall hear my word for I Am the Red Stone of Power."

"What of the good red spirit?" I ask.

"He is an infinite part of you. He is your right arm, your male counterpart. You shall know him in the fourth ascent and his name shall be Black Elk. With him you shall walk in balance."

"And Artamor?"

"Artamor shall walk alongside you as he has always done. He will be known in the third ascent as Pedro." And the Red Stone of Power continues, "There is one other, The Crystal Keeper. She who was known as Esme; she is the third point of a sacred triangle that is Eliza, Artamor and The Crystal Keeper. She will be known in the third ascent as Catherina. Walk in balance and in harmony with the sacred triangle. In this way will the prophecy be complete."

. . . And with that the desert vanishes. I am on the platform. My body is engulfed with fire. I feel nothing. I hear nothing. Above me the smoke clears to reveal a star lit sky. In my heart a gentle voice is silently speaking. It says, "Eliza! Come home!"

I rise up again; this time right out of my body and onwards into the mystical yonder. The stars get closer and closer and a tunnel of light appears before me. I drift on into the tunnel and upwards towards two beautiful happy spirits. They stand at the end of the tunnel, hand in hand, waving to me and encouraging me forwards. They are Pascal and Clairose.

∞∞∞∞∞∞∞∞∞∞∞∞∞∞∞∞∞∞∞∞∞∞∞∞∞∞

And Black Elk speaks . . .

"My dear Rose, you saw how the way forwards looked steep and full of challenge for Gabriella. And you saw how she was reminded of who she was by The Red Stone of Power. She was the soul's expression in the second ascent. And now I will show you the third ascent, the third lifetime, which I explained to you through the vision. This is Maria's lifetime. Dear, sweet little Maria. You love her so much . . . I feel it from your heart. I love her

The Four Ascents

too, Rose. The children are so pure and so close to Beloved Source. Maria came to Earth, an expression of the soul, Eliza. She came with awareness of Gabriella's story and she feels the desire to escape the physical reality. But the fearful black road runs into the far distance. The reluctance is great yet when Maria comes to the holy place in the centre where the two roads meet she finds her respite. She came to show great courage. This is the third ascent, the step of connection to Beloved Source."

CHAPTER FOURTEEN

The third ascent

And so the story continues . . .

I find myself in Mexico

"Found you," I squeal running for home base as fast as my legs will go. I am playing hide and go seek with my best friends in the whole world, Eduardo, Pedro and Catherina. It is Eduardo who I've just discovered in his hiding place. He is five and a boy so he can run really fast, and I am only four and a girl but my legs are strong and I have a head start so I should get to the tree before him. I do, and I laugh and laugh as he comes after me pretending to have gone over on his ankle and making a face like he's just eaten a sour grape.

"That doesn't count," he says grimacing with feigned pain. "I hurt my ankle and couldn't run, otherwise I would have beaten you."

"Eduardo Raul Del Ortega Perez!" I exclaim in a voice very like that of my mother. My friends and I love to call each other by our full names. They call me Maria Olivia Del Santiago Lopez. We pretend that when we're grown up we will be very important people and everyone will want to know who we are, and since our names are so hard to say then we should get plenty of practice in now. When we are grown up we shall get married and live in a house in the country. I will marry Eduardo and Catherina will marry Pedro. We shall live side by side and keep chickens and ducks and grow all sorts of vegetables and lots and lots of pretty flowers which we will water all day long in the summer and never ever forget. It wasn't so long ago that my mother gave me a right telling off for forgetting to water my flowers and letting them wilt in the hot sun.

"What?" Eduardo asks now, eyes wide and innocent.

"You *know* what," I chastise him, hands on my hips like my mama did when granpapa had been smoking his pipe in the house and she had smelled the smoke still hanging in the air long after he put it out. "There's nothing wrong with your ankle. You're a sham . . . sham, sham, sham!"

"There is plenty wrong with it . . . it hurts, so there" he argues.

The Four Ascents

"No it doesn't. You're just making it up."

He can't really argue with me because sometimes I just know things and that's that. And this time, I know he didn't hurt his ankle. He doesn't say anything else which says it all really, doesn't it? Instead, he folds his arms and pouts in that irritating manner that he does when he doesn't get his own way. I told Granpapa about Eduardo's pouts ages ago and he said that I can do my fair share of pouting too and that I ought to be more forgiving of Eduardo. I replied that if Eduardo was going to be the papa when we're big then I ought to start behaving like a mama and my mama would never bow down to my papa's pouting, so why should I put up with Eduardo's pouting. And would you believe it? Granpapa laughed at me . . . he really laughed at me. I was so mad that I pouted all afternoon but that made him laugh all the more. Every time he saw me for the rest of that day and the next he laughed and laughed. I told Mama to chastise him for it but she said that sometimes I can be so funny and aren't I cute when I'm angry? My granpapa is great. He's the best granpapa in the whole world . . . when he's not laughing at me that is. His name is Miguel and he's lovely. His hair is long and white and he wears it in a pony tail tied with a red and white bandana. My mama, his daughter, whose name is Alma, hates the pony tail and swears that one of these days she will cut it off with the kitchen scissors. But Granmama loves it. She has long white hair too and she loves to give it fifty strokes with the hairbrush every night before bed. She would brush Granpapa's hair too if he'd let her, but he won't. Granmama is called Rosalina. I think it is the nicest name in the whole world. I have three dolls and I named them all Rosalina. Juan says that it's confusing to name them all Rosalina.

"How will I know which one is which if they're all called the same name?" he asked me once.

Juan is my papa but I call him Juan because that's what my mama calls him. Juan works all day long in a very special place. Sometimes Granpapa works there too, and the man that lives next door, Eduardo's papa. Eduardo is an only child like me but both Pedro and Catherina have big sisters who never let us play with them. Once, they were teasing us and saying that they were going to go see their papas' work and that we were too small to go. My papa, Granpapa, Eduardo' papa next door, Pedro's papa and Catherina's papa all work in the same place. I will tell you the story that Granpapa told me. Once upon a time there was a city. It was a very special city with temples and monuments and plenty of market places and lots of houses. In the city lived very special people. They are our ancestors and they are called the Aztecs.

231

Eliza White Buffalo with Nicholas Black Elk

These people knew lots of stuff, far more than we know now, mostly stuff about the stars and the planets. But something happened, and bit by bit, over many years the ancient city disappeared under the ground.

Now, a very clever man has come along and said "why don't I dig down into the ground and uncover the city; this way many people can look and see how our ancestors lived hundreds of years ago." He is a very rich man and pays lots of money to men to come and help him dig up the city. And that is Juan's and Granpapa's very special work, digging up the city.

Anyway, when the bigger girls went to the work place that day they were told off and were sent packing with their tails between their legs. It's very dangerous you see. Granpapa told me never to wander over there with my friends or he will give me a right earful and my mama will keep me inside for a whole day to punish me. I love my Granpapa. He is the best fun in the whole world. He is thrilled to be working at the work place but he can only go in the mornings. In the afternoons he needs his nap because he is an old man. If he doesn't come home on time for his nap Mama chastises him. Mama chastises him a lot. I think he is sad about that because sometimes when he thinks I'm not watching, he stares wistfully at the sky and I know he is just thinking, *if only I could turn into a great big bird and fly away to the sky and not have to be old and tired all the time. I could go where I want and do what I want. I would be free.*

Sometimes I think that if *I* had wings instead of the smallest legs in the family I would be free to go where I want and do what I want. Granpapa knows a lot about the sky. He knows a lot about the stars too, but not as much as the ancient people I think otherwise folk would just ask him what he knows instead of going to all that trouble to uncover the knowledge of the ancestors. He talks to me about the sky and the stars when the sun has gone down and it's nearly time for my bed. It's a very special time and Granpapa says it's a magical time. He says that the sun knows secrets that we can only dream of knowing and that at this time it gives us little clues to the secrets.

"What clues, Granpapa?" I once asked him. He pointed to the beautiful colours in the sky.

"Those clues, Poppet," he replied softly. When he speaks to me of the sun's secrets he always speaks in a hushed voice and I always get so excited at the mystery of it all. "See those colours, Poppet?" he said. "My papa once told me that in God's kingdom there are seven worlds and each colour of the rainbow represents one of the worlds. When the sun is rising and going to bed, it is much easier to look at it without hurting your eyes. And when you look very closely you can see all seven colours pulsing around it. At this time it spreads the colours all across the sky. Look and tell me what colours you can see."

"I see red, Granpapa, and I see orange and purple. Purple is my favourite," I replied.

"If you look really closely you can see all the colours of the rainbow there," he said, and he made a rainbow arch in front of him with his hands.

I'll never forget what Granpapa told me that night. Nearly every night this summer he and I talked about the sun and the stars. He told me about the constellations and that many believe that we come from there and when we die we will return to there. I told him that I reckoned that is true and that when I go back to the stars I will wave to the people on Earth just so that they know I am okay.

Sometimes Granpapa looks at me with sad eyes and I say, "Don't worry Granpapa. I won't go back to the stars for a very long time yet." Once I overheard him telling Granmama that I'm too precious for this world and that I'm living on borrowed time, whatever that means. He told her he reckons I'm only here to give him joy in his old age and what a selfish old man that makes him. But I told him that night when we were having our star time . . . I told him that he's not a selfish old man . . . he's the best granpapa in the whole world and how else would I know how to get back to the stars if he didn't tell me? But then he just looked even sadder and held me so close on his lap that I thought he would never let me go ever again.

I told my friends about me living on borrowed time and giving Granpapa joy in his old age in return for his stories about the stars. I tell them all about the stars and the secrets of the sun. I tell them all about the seven worlds of God's kingdom and the seven colours that represent them. For the past month or so we have been playing a great game. We call it the stars game. Each one of us is a different colour of the rainbow and we have to pretend that we are going on a trip to that world. Earlier this week I was blue and I had to go to the blue world. I told them all about the many wonderful things in the blue world, like poetry and songs and bird's singing. One time Eduardo was red and he had to go to the red world. He told us about seeing trees that were alive and could talk to him and all sorts of animals that could talk. I think I would like that world very much because trees are my favourite thing in the whole world, next to the sun and the stars that is. When I grow up I will have a whole forest of trees around me and I will talk with them all day long. Sometimes when Eduardo and the others aren't looking I try talking with the

Eliza White Buffalo with Nicholas Black Elk

trees. There is a particularly big tree in my back yard. It is the one that we use as home base.

I said to it, "If you can talk then tell me how I can get to the purple world." And it answered me, not with words of course, but it dropped a lovely leaf right on top of my head and the answer came right into my heart and whispered to me there.

"Open the way through the top of your head and you will know the heavenly world," I felt it say to me.

Today we didn't play the stars game. Eduardo wanted to play hide and go seek. He pouted for a long time until we said that we would play it. And since we played the stars game nearly all summer it seemed fair that we play Eduardo's favourite game for a bit. Catherina, Pedro and I simply love the stars game. We would play it every day for the rest of our lives if we could. So far I've been red, although my red world was a lot different from Eduardo's red world; and I've been orange and yellow and blue and indigo and green. I've still got to be purple and since that's my favourite colour it seems a bit unfair that I haven't got to be purple yet. So we've been playing hide and go seek all morning and it's nearly lunchtime now. Granpapa will be coming home soon for his lunch and a nap. He said this morning that after he has his afternoon siesta he will sit on the terrace with all four of us children and tell us a very special story about a young man a long time ago who went on an adventure across the seas and fell in love with a beautiful Grecian girl. I can hardly wait for the siesta to be over so that I can find out all about it. Plus my friends' parents have all agreed that my friends can sleep at my house tonight just for fun. We will have our supper on the terrace with Granpapa and we can look at the stars and tell stories of our own adventures to him. I imagine he will love our stories just as much as we love his.

Catherina is getting bored with playing hide and go seek now and she wants to take time out and sit at the bottom of the yard under the big tree. "We can play the star game" she suggests hopefully.

"Yes please," I reply, "let's do that. Here Eduardo, sit beside me. It's nice and cool here." I pull Eduardo's hand so that he sits down under the tree beside me. I like Eduardo best despite his pouting. And since he can never be cross with me for long he gives me an extra special smile, the kind of smile that makes his eyes shine like sunlight on a glass window.

"Okay, Maria," he says, "but it's your turn to be the adventurer. Which colour star are you going to be today?" he asks me trying his very best to please me.

The Four Ascents

I don't have to think about, "Oh, may I go to the purple star? Please may I go to the purple star?" I plead.

"Yes, you do purple," replies Pedro in a big brotherly voice. Pedro is seven and Catherina is six. I am the baby because I'm only four and sometimes Pedro acts like he's my big brother. I guess he likes doing that because he always seems pleased when I listen to him and do what he says. Anyway, he is much bigger than the rest of us and should be the boss really. "Okay now," he directs us. "Catherina, take Maria's hand, and Maria, you take Eduardo's hand and . . . yeah, that's good. Everybody close your eyes."

We all close our eyes tightly. I peek a bit to discover that Eduardo is peeking too. I shake his hand in mine. "Keep your eyes shut, Eduardo" I complain.

"You had yours open too," he retorts.

"Shut up!" snaps Pedro and Catherina together.

I keep my eyes shut as tight as I can in case I am tempted to peek again. I know that Eduardo is doing the same. Neither of us utters another word. This is my turn now. So I ought to be quiet and use my imagination. Granpapa says that I have the greatest imagination he's ever seen in a child. He says that I ought never to change because my imagination is my greatest gift from Heaven. I focus on using it now as I tell the others what it is like in the purple world.

"The sky is a bright purple," I tell them beginning to make a picture in my mind. "There are lots of white fluffy clouds with golden dust sparkling inside them. On each cloud sits a little magical girl with long white hair and a beautiful purple dress that goes right down passed her ankles so that I can't see what her shoes are like. I think she must not be wearing any shoes at all for she can just fly from cloud to cloud when she wants to and doesn't have to use her legs. I guess she must have a pair of fairy wings underneath that long white hair."

"Are all the little girls the same?" asks Catherina who would dearly love to have a pair of fairy wings.

"Every one of them," I reply decidedly, and I go on with my story: "Now I hear lovely music in the sky. I can't see the ground at all. I am floating high up in the sky where I can see everything clearly. When I look around I see the six other stars dancing about in the universe. Look, I can see the blue star smiling at me and all the children on it are laughing and playing. They are so happy to be playing. Over there is the indigo star and the children there are sitting on clouds too and waving up to me. The purple star is the highest star

Eliza White Buffalo with Nicholas Black Elk

in the sky and all the rest can see me when they look up. Down there I can see the green star. It is a very beautiful star, more beautiful than the time I went there. There are hundreds and hundreds of children there and they are all holding hands in a circle like we are too. They are singing a song and dancing. They seem very happy to be doing that. Beyond that star I see the yellow star and the orange star and all the children on them look very happy also. And now I can see the red star. It seems so very far away and I can hardly make out the children playing there. But I can see a little man . . . oh, how odd!" I stop for a bit to giggle because the little man looks so very odd indeed.

"Don't you dare stop," demands Pedro, "tell us how the little man looks."

"W . . . ell" I giggle, "He's not really a man. He's even shorter than me. He looks like a dwarf with a long white beard and a pointy red hat. His cheeks are fat and rosy and he has a little shovel over his shoulder like the one Juan uses at the workplace."

"What's his name, Maria? Go on, tell us his name," giggles Catherina. By this time I am giggling so much that I fear I might not be able to say one more word. I take a deep breath and settle myself. What is the dwarf's name?

"Okay," I decide after a moment's reflection. "His name is Treebeard."

"Treebeard, ha ha!" laughs Eduardo.

"Well he lives in the trees," I say explaining his funny name. "But I don't want to talk about Treebeard now. I want to talk about the pretty girl with long white hair and the purple dress."

"In the purple world," adds Catherina.

"Yeah, and her name is Sera. She is singing a song, a very special song about messengers from Heaven. It goes like this: There is a messenger from Heaven that would tell you wondrous things. She would fill your heart with music and give you special wings; so that when you feel afraid and you don't know who you are, you just fly up to Heaven towards the purple star."

"Is she really singing that?" gasps Eduardo with amazement. "Why that's just like the poems in my bedtime story book."

"It's like a real song," says Catherina.

"Like a prayer," adds Pedro.

"Well, it *is* a kind of prayer and a song at the same time," I tell them feeling very clever that I made up such lovely words. But I didn't really make them up from scratch I think. I seemed to hear them first and then I just repeated them, exactly the same thing as with the tree that spoke to my heart and dropped a leaf on my head.

"Tell us more about the purple world, Maria, please," asks Eduardo.

236

The Four Ascents

"Yes Maria, please go on," begs Catherina.

I think for a bit, then shake my head, "Nope" I say, "Sera tells me it's your turn Catherina."

"Does she? Does she really?" Catherina asks excitedly.

I open my eyes, "Yes, you have to go to the green star and tell us what it is like there."

"Okay then I will," Catherina decides.

We are so excited by now with the magic of the purple world that we can hardly keep our eyes closed for the green world.

"You're right, Maria," Catherina says after we all settle down and be quiet. "The green star is beautiful. I see all the children holding hands in one gigantic circle. They are singing and dancing just like you said they were. Now they are all falling down in a heap like when we play ring a ring of roses. Some of them are changing into birds and flying about in the sky with me. I can fly after them like I have wings too and I can dip and swing about amongst them. This is great fun. I might never come back again."

"You must come back," I complain beginning to feel afraid that she might fly away and I will never see her again.

"Don't worry. I'll come back," she reassures me. "Now look here. There is a tree in this world. It is huge with giant spreading branches hung with blossoms of all colours; the birds are all sitting on the branches now and singing at the top of their little bird voices. Two of them are looking at me as if to say listen to what I am telling you."

"Will you listen?" I ask eager to know what the birds say.

"I *will*," says Catherina impatiently. "They are going to show me a story. Okay, be quiet everyone because I don't want to miss this." We are all quiet whilst Catherina watches the story, giggling at some parts and gasping at others. After a while she speaks again. "The two birds are sister birds," she tells us. "They chirp and sing and fly around together very happily until one day a great big black crow comes and chases them. It catches them and is about to eat them for its dinner when it bursts into flames and all three are burned up. The sisters turn into white doves and fly away to the Heaven worlds. Then they come back and they are two little chicks once again. They are so cute and have beautiful voices that sing with songs they learned whilst they were in Heaven. But one day before the two could grow up to be grown up birds, the black crow comes back and jeers at them. The strongest chick flies away and mocks the crow saying that it cannot touch her this time, but

Eliza White Buffalo with Nicholas Black Elk

the other little chick is so badly hurt by the crow that she cannot fly away and very soon she is trapped in its clutches."

"Oh my gosh! Does she get away?" I gasp.

"Shh," insists Catherina, "Let me finish. The poor little bird is caught in the black crow's clutches and it is afraid that it will die in flames like it did the last time. It struggles and it struggles but the more it does the tighter is the crow's grip on her. Now this is a lovely part that I know you will all love. A golden eagle comes from Heaven and speaks gently to the poor little bird saying, *little bird, please do not struggle. Trust me and you will be safe.* Well . . . the poor little bird is tired struggling now and she thinks, *why not trust this golden eagle? He seems to know what he is doing which is more than I can say for myself; for here I am for the second time in this terrible crow's clutches.* The little bird lets go of her struggles and immediately the crow opens its talons and drops her into the sky. Then the golden eagle picks her up and carries her to safety. But it is too late; the little bird has died of shock and once again flies away to Heaven." With that Catherina pauses. The story is done.

"Wow," says Eduardo in awe.

"So sad," adds Pedro.

I say nothing. I can't help thinking about the little bird and what it meant to it not to burn in flames again but to go to Heaven with its little wings as perfect as the day it was born.

"Why are you so quiet Maria?" asks Pedro. "You usually have much to say about our adventures in the star game."

"Well . . . I can't help but wonder if it did any good," I reply sadly. "I mean, the poor little bird still died, didn't she? Didn't the eagle make any difference at all?"

"Of course it did," replies Catherina with a big smile to make me feel better. "She didn't burn in flames did she?"

"No, but . . ."

"But what . . . what do *you* think should have happened?" she asks hoping to hear a nice ending to her story.

"W . . . ell . . . I think she went to Heaven, okay?" I say beginning to imagine a happy ending to Catherina's story.

"Okay," agrees everyone.

"And then she comes back as a little chick once again. Only this time her wings are magic wings which means she can fly off to heaven whenever she wishes and not have to stay there." I am pleased with my version of the ending. I shoot Eduardo a big grin.

The Four Ascents

"And she can get away from the crow very easily should he come after her again because her wings are magic and they can go with super speed," he adds with an even bigger grin.

"Yeah!" squeals Catherina and Pedro at the same time, Catherina clapping her hands together excitedly.

∞∞∞∞∞∞∞∞∞∞∞∞∞∞∞∞∞∞∞∞∞∞∞∞∞∞

It is way past bedtime but we are still giggling and chatting and Mama is getting very cross with us. We can't help it; today was such a wonderful day. We have discussed in great depth already, the adventures to the purple world and the green world and we have discussed Granpapa's amazing story about the young sailor who sailed away across the seas. He sailed to Greece and fell in love with a beautiful maiden who loved him back. But alas, their love was not meant to be because she was betrothed to another. He gave her beautiful gifts and riches to keep her by his side but she would not give her heart to him nor would she give it to her betrothed. She dreamed of being a goddess you see and wanted nothing more than to serve in a beautiful temple. Then one day she was taken by a monster that lived in a cave. The monster took the maiden to its cave and kept her prisoner there for hundreds of years. When the maiden was finally rescued by the young man her betrothed had died of a lonely heart and she vowed never to love another man again. The young sailor sailed away into the distance but he never forgot the beautiful maiden. Each night after the sun went to bed, the young man gazed at the stars and vowed that as long as he exists he will strive to bring about her dream of becoming a goddess. It was such a beautiful story and I cried when the maiden was captured by the monster.

"It's just like the nasty crow in the green world," I had sniffed when the story was told, "the one that killed the little bird."

"But the maiden got away from the monster and she didn't die," Catherina had smiled reassuringly.

"Well," Granpapa had said when I still felt sad, "It is but a story and sometimes stories can be told with our own lives."

"What do you mean, Senior?" Pedro had asked him.

"Well, take my precious Maria here," he said taking me on his knee and giving me a big squeeze to make me feel better. "She's *my* little goddess and I will stop at nothing to make sure that all her hopes and dreams come true."

Eliza White Buffalo with Nicholas Black Elk

"And *I* will stop at nothing to make all *your* hopes and dreams come true Granpapa. You're the best granpapa in the whole world and I love you very much" I said giving him a kiss on his white hairy chin. It had struck me then how much he looks like Treebeard . . . long white hair and two big rosy cheeks. Plus Granpapa loves trees nearly as much as I do.

"I really like your granpapa Maria," whispers Catherina after my mama shouts up the stairs a second time.

"Will you children for the love of God, go to sleep," she shouted.

"Yes," I whisper back to Catherina, "I think Granpapa is really a magic being from the stars. Don't you think he looks like Treebeard?"

"A bit I suppose," she replies.

"I think you're very lucky to have a granpapa like him," whispers Pedro. "My granpapa died before I was born so I never knew him."

"That's very sad," says Eduardo much too loudly.

"Children!" shouts Mama from the kitchen. "Go to sleep or I will come in there and march you all back to your parents."

We don't dare utter another word. Within minutes I am fast asleep, tired out from the excitement of the day. In the morning it is me who wakes first. I have always been an early riser, Mama said. I jump out of bed and tip toe to the shutters. I don't want to wake my friends since it was very late when we finally went to sleep last night. Opening the shutters I get my first glimpse of the sun rising above the horizon yonder. Granpapa loves the setting sun best but I love the rising sun even more. The horizon is a kind of purple with a big white glow just where the sun is. I am just in time. As I watch, the white glow rises up and then I see the sun itself going up and up . . . faster than it comes down at night. I smile and nod to myself . . . another gorgeous summer morning. Soon it will be fall and the mornings will get colder and then I will have to go to school too. Juan says that he will take me in his truck and pick me up. He says that things at the workplace are not going so well now but it means he will have time to take me to school and back which is something at least. I don't want to go to school. I'd rather stay here and talk with Granpapa all day long about the stars and the sun and stories about young sailors and beautiful maidens. But Mama says that I have no choice now that I'm nearly five and besides, school will be fun and I will meet lots of new friends. I don't need any new friends. Catherina, Pedro and Eduardo are all the friends I want. The only good thing I can see about school is that I get to see them all day. This last year was awful during the mornings when Eduardo went to school

The Four Ascents

too with Catherina and Pedro. I missed him terribly and was bored all the while he was gone.

"Good morning," yawns Catherina behind me. I turn around to see her stretching and yawning. "What day is it today?" she asks.

"Saturday," I tell her.

"It's Monday silly," yawns Pedro stretching too. "What do *you* know, you're only four."

"I'm nearly five," I tell him, hands on my hips in disgust.

"Of course you are, but this is Monday and I'm going with my mama to the store this morning to get some new shoes for school," he says leaping out of bed and starting to put his pants on. He whistles a tune loudly pretending to be grown up.

Eduardo is awake now and he never wakes until at least six thirty. I glare at Pedro. Sometimes he can be a very tiresome big brother and not very helpful at all.

"Now you've gone and woken Eduardo," I moan at him.

"Hey, chill out baby!" he grins cheekily. "What are *you* gonna do today then, besides hang out with Eduardo that is."

Why is Pedro being so irritating? I don't like him when he's like this . . . teasing me just because I am the smallest. "Me and Catherina and Eduardo are going to the creek for a splash," I huff.

"Sorry Maria," says Catherina, red-faced, "Mama says I need new shoes too. We're going this morning. But I'll see you after lunch."

"But that's Granpapa's time," I wail.

"I'll go to the creek with you," says Eduardo grinning.

"I've changed my mind. I'm going to tell Mama that I'm going to see Granpapa at the workplace," I tell him, more to make the others jealous than anything else. "I want to ask him about Treebeard and he will have left for work by now. He always goes before sunrise when it's nice and cool."

"Can I come too?" Eduardo whispers almost afraid to suggest such a thing.

"If you're big enough," I tell him giving Pedro my best glare.

"And what if your mama says you can't go?" Pedro asks in his big brother voice.

"Then I'll just turn into the bird with the magic wings and I'll fly to the workplace to see Granpapa."

"Will you fly away to heaven?" gasps Eduardo.

Eliza White Buffalo with Nicholas Black Elk

"I might do. But I will certainly come back again in the evenings to see Granpapa."

"And me?" he asks, eyes wide with amazement.

"I shall be very busy I think, what with flying around the sun and that but I reckon I will come back to you some day."

"Promise?" he begs me.

"I promise Eduardo . . . some day!"

∞∞∞∞∞∞∞∞∞∞∞∞∞∞∞∞∞∞∞∞∞∞∞∞

The video comes to a stop, and Black Elk speaks . . .

"And so it is, my dear Rose, that the reluctance to walk the black road grows. You saw how Maria desires to walk the good red road but it is by walking both roads in balance that she will find freedom. Yet she has made her choice and so it shall be. May she go forth now in courage and fortitude and remember who she is."

CHAPTER FIFTEEN

Escape from the black road

And so the story continues . . .

Mama was against it from the start. She knew Juan and Granpapa would be angry with her for taking me. She knew it was a bad idea even for her to go to the workplace, but to bring me along would be madness. Eduardo's mama didn't think on it for a second. She said *no* and that was it. Mama nearly did the same and would have if I hadn't cried so much, more than enough to get her to change her mind. "But I want Granpapa," I had roared at her angrily. Eventually I cried and roared enough and so here we are at the workplace.

"Just wait here for a moment, Maria," Mama says.

She grips my shoulder with her hand so that I can't go even a little bit further. We are standing just outside the workplace. There is a big gate in front of us and there is a long fence that runs the whole way around the entire site. I scan the fence close to me. It's in need of repair in several places and there are holes on both sides of the gate. I can fit through those holes very easily, so if I have to I will get in through one of those holes. Through the big gate I can see lots of interesting things. There are huge big things called pyramids that have steps going all the way to the top of them. Everywhere there are lots and lots of stones; some great big ones and some little ones. Hoards of men are working in there. All of them seem to be covered in the same dust that Juan and Granpapa drag into Mama's clean house every day after work.

Oh, I see Juan with Eduardo's papa, and there's Catherina's papa with them too. They are all sitting down under a canvas shelter. I expect those are cups of coffee they are drinking.

"Look Mama!" I exclaim, pointing a finger towards the shelter. "There's Juan."

"Yes, I see him darling," she replies. "Now where is your Granpapa?"

"Let's go in and ask Juan," I suggest, eager to get inside the workplace.

I don't understand why we have to stand here and peer in, especially when Juan is so close. But Mama clearly has a good reason and I find myself

Eliza White Buffalo with Nicholas Black Elk

thinking it's because she has changed her mind. I study the fence again so I can pick a really good hole should I need it.

"Shh Maria," says Mama quietly. "Your papa won't be very pleased with us for coming here. No, we'll find Granpapa and get his attention." She kneels down beside me and takes a good strong hold of my arm. "Look," she says pointing with her finger, "there he is over there; see by that high wall?"

I follow her direction, looking for the high wall. It isn't hard to see; it's the biggest wall in there. And there's Granpapa standing alongside it, resting on it with his elbow and holding a cup of coffee in his hand.

"Granpapa!" I yell at the top of my voice. I wave madly at him with excitement.

"Maria, shh," says Mama.

Granpapa heard me; he puts his coffee cup on the wall and makes a gesture as if to wave us away. "Go on home now," he shouts coming towards us. "Alma, for the Lord's sake . . . what were you thinking about."

Juan has heard his shouting and is coming towards us too.

"Come on now Maria," Mama says to me. "I told you he'd be angry. Come on home now."

"But I want to ask Granpapa about Treebeard," I wail struggling with her attempts to pull me away.

"You can ask him when he comes home. Look, there comes your papa. He will be very angry with you," she says trying to persuade me to leave.

"Maria, go home with your mama now" Juan shouts to me from beyond the fence. Then he shouts at poor Granpapa and shoos him back to his work. Sometimes my papa gets cross with him too. "Miguel" he shouts at him now, "I'll deal with this."

Papa is near the gate now. Soon he will come out and tell me and Mama off. He will make sure we go back home and I won't get to see Granpapa in the workplace and ask him about Treebeard. Mama let's go of my arm and walks through the gate to talk with Juan, so I take my chance. I dash to the fence and am through the biggest hole within seconds. Both Mama and Juan shout to me to stop but I won't. I keep my eyes on Granpapa who has gone beyond the big wall now and is sitting with the others in the shelter.

"Granpapa!" I yell, running as fast as my stupid short legs will go. If I had magic wings I would be there in an instant.

Granpapa heard me and is running towards me. Suddenly it seems everything is happening slowly. Are my legs actually getting slower and slower? Everything seems so weird; silent and strange like it's not really happening. I hear a dull rumbling sound like thunder and dust falls around me making it harder to see Granpapa through it. I can just about see the other men coming slowly towards me. They seem to be racing each other but in slow motion. Catherina's papa has a red bandana around his head and Pedro's papa has a blue one. The blue one is winning, just out in front. His coffee cup goes flying to the dusty ground, the coffee already spilled out. The blue bandana reaches me first, just as I feel a heavy blow to my shoulder. I fall slowly to the ground and fix my eyes upon the coffee cup just feet away. Pedro's papa backs off from me as several heavy blows strike me painfully on my back. There is a loud swishing noise in my head and I can hear Granpapa's distant voice shouting my name. The coffee cup blurs behind the dust, and now everything is dark.

∞∞∞∞∞∞∞∞∞∞∞∞∞∞∞∞∞∞∞∞∞∞∞∞∞∞∞

"How long will she be like this doctor?" I hear my Mama ask.

"Senora," a strange man's voice replies. "I am sorry . . . truly I am but there really is no hope. I told you and your husband, the spinal cord has been too badly damaged. She will never have any movement below the neck. Nothing short of a miracle will change that."

"Does she know we're here?" comes Granmama's voice.

"I don't know," is the doctor's reply. "Perhaps she does. Some people believe that."

"But when she comes out of it we will know for sure," states Mama.

"Senora, your daughter is very sick. The chances of her coming out of it are slim to none. I am sorry, but I really think you ought to prepare yourself for the possibility that she will never come out of it."

Come out of what? I wonder. *Doesn't Mama know that I am right here? I can't see her, but I can hear her and she's right next to me.* "I'm right here Mama," I say amused at the game she seems to want to play.

"She can't hear you Eliza," says a voice from somewhere. I can't see who owns the voice. I can't see anything at all. Perhaps I have a blindfold on. That would be a fun game. I go to lift my hand to see if I'm wearing a blindfold but my arm won't work. I try again but it still won't work. It just stays there by my side. I try the other arm but it won't work either. What is going on? This *is* a strange game and I'm not sure that I like it. I attempt to get out of bed but my legs won't work. Why won't my legs work . . . my stupid short

Eliza White Buffalo with Nicholas Black Elk

legs? Why can't I move my legs? I can't move any parts of my body. I can't move at all. Why can't I move?

"Mama!" I cry out, "Why can't I move? I don't like this game. Mama!"

"She can't hear you Eliza," repeats the voice.

"Who said that? I'm not Eliza. I'm Maria. Who said that? I can hear *you* so why can't Mama hear *me*? Mama! Granmama! It's me, Maria. I'm here and I can't move."

"It's alright Eliza," says the voice. "I am here."

I see a funny light flickering in the dark and soon it becomes a girl . . . more like a fairy. She becomes clearer and I see that she is Sera from the purple world. She is so pretty and is much bigger now that when I first saw her. Her long white hair is so beautiful that I want to reach out and touch it but I still can't move my arms. I feel like crying but immediately she smiles at me and I feel instead a warm loving feeling filling me up like when Granpapa tells me his stories about the stars. Sera is wearing the purple dress and I still can't see any feet.

"Do you have magic wings?" I ask forgetting all about not being able to move.

"I do Eliza," she smiles.

"Why do you call me Eliza? My name is Maria."

"Come with me," she says, "let me show you."

And in a magic moment I am standing beside her, holding her hand. She is really big now, much bigger than me and she has a nice Mama kind of feeling. My bed is in front of us and Mama, Granmama and the doctor are there talking.

"Mama!" I say excitedly, "look at me and Sera."

"She can't hear you Eliza, or see you," says Sera softly.

"Why do you call me Eliza," I ask again.

She points to the bed, "Look, *there* is Maria; *you* are Eliza."

On the bed, to my complete surprise and confusion I see myself lying there. I am so still and pale. My head is wrapped up in bandages and my body looks really tiny under the blanket.

"How can I be there and here at the same time?" I ask Sera.

"Because this is the real you known as Eliza, and that you is just a body that keeps you on Earth."

I think about this for a bit. "What's wrong with me; am I sick?" I ask.

"At the workplace a wall fell on top of your body. It is hurt very badly and it can't move," Sera replies.

246

The Four Ascents

"Oh!" I think about this for a bit too . . . "But I *am* moving."

"Your body isn't moving, Eliza. This is your spirit, the real you, and you're not in your body right now. That is why your family cannot see you or hear you."

"But Mama couldn't see me before either. She kept saying that I was away somewhere and was wondering when I was going to come back," I say a little confused.

"Your body is in a coma," Sera continues. "That means that you cannot communicate with those around you. To them it's as if you are asleep, as if you have gone away somewhere in your mind."

"Do you mean that Mama can't ever hear me?" I want to know wondering if I just go up to Mama and touch her would she turn around and see me.

"There is a way but they don't know how," Sera tells me.

A thought just occurs to me, "Am I going to Heaven like the little bird did?" I ask her.

"Not if you don't want to, Eliza," she replies. "Here, let me introduce you to someone."

Suddenly, just like magic, Treebeard is here with us. He is smaller than me and so cute. His beard and hair are as white as snow and his little red pointy hat sits comically on his head. He has left his shovel wherever he came from but I reckon he doesn't need it here. Perhaps he just needs it for his workplace. He bows low to me and I giggle as the point of his hat touches the floor.

"Hello Eliza," he says with a funny little voice.

"Hello Treebeard," I say and I give him a little curtsey.

"Treebeard is keeping your spirit here close to your body," explains Sera. "He belongs to the earth too you know. Look at the doctor."

For the first time since leaving my body I take notice of the strange man talking with my Mama and Granmama. He is a short man with a white beard like Treebeard and white hair like Treebeard too only his hat is flat and black and he carries a black case instead of a shovel. I go closer to get a better look and I see that his cheeks are red and shiny just like Treebeard's cheeks are.

"He looks almost the same as Treebeard," I tell Sera.

"That is because he *is* Treebeard," she says smiling. "At least, that is Treebeard's body."

I may not be five yet but I'm big enough to understand what she means: Treebeard is the spirit and the doctor is his body just as I am the spirit called Eliza and that is my body lying on the bed sick and not able to move.

"Is Treebeard sick too?" I ask.

Eliza White Buffalo with Nicholas Black Elk

"No Eliza," Sera laughs politely. "Treebeard is not sick. He is a very clever doctor and he is looking after your body whilst *it* is sick."

I find this explanation perfectly okay. I reckon that if I'm not in my body then it's a good thing that Treebeard is looking after it, so I give him my best smile and tell him, "I'm glad you are looking after my body Treebeard; it looks very poorly, doesn't it?"

"It is very poorly indeed, Eliza," he replies in his funny little voice.

I bite my lip and study him for a bit. *I wonder* . . . "You look like my granpapa," I tell him.

"Well, we *are* brothers," he replies with a wink making me giggle. "And you are our sister," he adds with another wink.

"Silly Treebeard. I'm just a little girl," I tell him with a snigger. I like Treebeard. I like him being silly.

He waits till I stop giggling and gives me another bow right down to the floor. "*Maria* is a little girl," he says correcting me. "And the doctor is an old man just as your granpapa is an old man. But your spirit as you know is called Eliza. You are from a constellation far away and there you are known by another name. There you are my sister Osiah and I am your brother Amir."

"And Granpapa?" I probe, feeling a rush of energy like I do when I go on my star adventures.

"And Granpapa is our brother Amir also," Treebeard confirms, grinning from one pointy ear to the other. Well, I really must have a long think about this one. Imagine Granpapa . . . my brother Amir . . . and Treebeard too. And I am their sister Osiah . . . and Sera . . . well she's . . . who is she?

"Are you our sister too, Sera?" I ask her excitedly.

"In a way," she replies kindly. "I am from another constellation called Pleiades. But I am your sister in the great oneness of all things. I knew you once when we all were together in one place on Earth. In earthly time it seems so very long ago but in reality it is not so far away. In fact, it is here right now. Would you like me to take you there, Eliza? Would you like to see your brothers and sisters?"

"Oh yes please!" I exclaim jumping up and down and clapping my hands with excitement. I take her offered hand, all the time chattering away about how I love to go in my mind to the stars.

"Yes, I know Eliza," she tells me. "I saw you there remember, in the seventh world."

"The seventh world?" I ask screwing up my nose.

"The purple world," she explains.

248

The Four Ascents

"I love the purple world. You were sitting on a cloud weren't you? Do you really have magic wings? Do you have feet?"

Sera is laughing at my many questions. Sometimes Granpapa laughs at them too. It's just that there is so much to know about the stars. They are much more interesting than the ground, except maybe for the trees. Treebeard would agree with that.

"You like trees too, don't you, Treebeard?" I ask him. "I love trees. They can talk to me you know. Are we nearly there yet, Sera?"

"Look around you Eliza," she says smiling.

I keep hold of Sera's hand as I look around me. We are standing in a green meadow that is absolutely covered in daisies and buttercups and other sweet smelling wild flowers; not like the ones Mama and I grow in the pots. Huge big stones are standing up tall and proud in a circle around us and a cool pleasant breeze is gently tickling my face and moving my hair. I can hear music and singing as it blows gently about, in and around the stones and meadow flowers.

"This is Atlantis, Eliza, where we were all together a long time ago," says Sera. "You can let go my hand if you like, Eliza. Go and play. Your brothers and sisters shall be here soon and they will all be happy to see you."

"Are they big too? Will they play with me?" I ask.

"If you want them too," she replies. "And yes, they are big for they wish to talk to you about something important."

"What do they want to talk about?"

"You'll see," says Sera kindly.

I accept that and go about the important business of playing. I start by counting all the stones in the circle . . . one, two, three, I count. But then I get to ten and I don't know my numbers after ten so I have to start all over again. After the third count I hear people coming. A long path leads downhill and into the distance and I can see lots of people coming walking along on it. They are all chatting merrily to each other. I think that they must be the prettiest people in the whole world because they all have lovely yellow hair and they all are wearing long white dresses, even the men. And to my utmost surprise I discover that I am all grown up too with yellow hair and a white dress. I take Sera's hand again as the others approach and stand a little distance from us, smiling at us.

Sera leads me gently over to them. "Good day, Sisters . . . good day, Brothers," she says bowing her head.

"Good day, Sister," they say together, "Good day, Eliza."

249

"Hello," I reply in awe of them.

"Eliza, these are your family in spirit," explains Sera. "There are fifteen spirits here counting you and me, and we are all sisters and brothers."

One very pretty lady comes to me and takes my hand. She holds it warmly in hers and smiles at me. "Hello Eliza. Do you recognise me?" she says.

I look into her smiling face and somehow I do feel like I should know her very well but I can't remember her. "Kinda," I tell her.

"Let me put it this way," she says. "Sera showed you how your body is in a coma yes?"

I nod. The lady's hand is getting warmer and it feels really good to be touching it. Suddenly I feel very happy and not one bit shy at all.

The lady goes on, "And she told you that your body is called Maria but that your spirit which you know now is Eliza, yes?" I nod again. "Well, I am not in my body, just like you. Can you tell what my body is called? Do you recognise me?"

"Kinda," I say honestly. "You remind me of my granmama."

"So now do you know who I am on earth?"

I nod amused and excited. This is a fun game to play. "You're my granmama. You're Rosalina," I tell her with a giggle.

"Oh well done, Eliza. That is very clever. Yes, I am known as Rosalina. And although I am your granmama on Earth, I really am your sister. I'm from a constellation called Sirius. You and I were great friends when we were here in our bodies."

"Is that my star . . . Sir . . . ius?" I ask, struggling with the name. I realise that Sera didn't tell me the name of my constellation home.

"No, you are from Serabe," the spirit that is my granmama says. She notices my surprise at the name that is so like Sera's name. "Like Sera," she adds smiling. "Would you like to meet some of your family from Serabe?"

"Oh yes please," I reply.

She moves away for a yellow haired man to come in her place. His hair is not as long as the lady's hair but it is still down to his shoulders and it is very yellow and curly. He has a lovely kind face and nice white teeth that twinkle when he smiles. "Hello Sister," he says, smiling and twinkling brightly.

"Hello," I reply.

He too takes my hand and it is every bit as warm and as nice as the lady's hand. "I am Amir from Serabe, and you are my sister, Osiah. Do you understand?" he asks me.

The Four Ascents

I nod quickly, not wanting to waste one single glorious moment here by going to the trouble of having to speak words. A nod is much quicker.

"I am one that challenged you and assisted you with the four ascents. I am the one that loved you in Greece and who believed in you when you had your mighty vision," Amir says.

I don't understand most of what he says but I think he means that I was the beautiful maiden in Granpapa's story and he was the young sailor. I smile and nod anyway, just to please him because he is too nice to upset.

"Do you know who I am known as now, Eliza? Do you recognise me?"

"You're the young sailor," I tell him hoping that's the right answer.

"Yes, I was once the young sailor, and who told you that story?" he probes.

"Granpapa," I reply shrugging my shoulders.

Amir looks at me smiling with his white teeth and shiny eyes. "Granpapa" he repeats. "I'm Granpapa on Earth . . . Miguel."

"You're not old like Granpapa," I say, though I know that he is indeed Granpapa because I can see Granpapa is his eyes.

"And you're my little granddaughter, Maria," he adds explaining it to me more.

"Granpapa . . . I mean Amir . . . Is this how you know so much about the stars?" I ask him. "Do you come here and learn it all?"

"*Remember* it all," he says correcting me. "I come every night when my body is asleep."

I have lots more questions I want to ask Amir and so we chat back and forth for a very long time. We talk about stars and stories and the workplace and Treebeard. "Would you like to see what Treebeard looks like when he's not a gnome?" Amir asks me. He introduces me to another yellow haired spirit "This is Amir too, our brother from Serabe," he tells me.

The second Amir smiles and says hello and I say hello back. "Eliza" he says, "I am Amir also because I am from Serabe. Do you understand?"

"Yes," I reply as a matter of factly, "The boys are Amir and the girls are Osiah."

"That is correct. Well done. Do you see who I am now on Earth?" he asks.

"Treebeard?" I make an educated guess based on the fact that no-one is who they appear to be in this world and the fact that Granpapa's spirit wanted to show me Treebeard.

Eliza White Buffalo with Nicholas Black Elk

"That's correct," he giggles, and I take to him warmly. "I am Treebeard, Eliza. And on Earth I am the doctor who is tending to your body . . . and I was once your earthly brother in Egypt. I reminded you then of our home on Serabe. I was your servant in Greece when you needed my help then too. I am always near to you Eliza. It was I who named you Eliza right here in this world. It was I who tended your sick body when it lay in a coma; and at another time too, a time when you were a very sick little Indian boy. That was when you had your mighty vision."

"What's a mighty vision," I ask.

"It's when you see something in this world that tells you great truth," answers Amir.

"Did I have a mighty vision? How come I don't remember it? How come I don't remember any of this stuff?" I ask.

"You will," he replies. "Now, how would you like to meet some more of your spirit family?"

One by one the many spirits come before me, take my hand in theirs and tell me who they are. One is Juan, my papa. "I was always your colleague in the many lifetimes we knew," he says. "But this time I chose to be the father, and because you needed to follow your grandfather's guidance more than your father's Maria calls me Juan instead of Papa. She feels I am but a colleague."

Two more of my spirit family are Pedro's papa and Catherina's papa. "We were never meant to get to you before the wall fell," they tell me, "and so it is as you chose it to be. Your body rests while you are here preparing for the next stage."

My favourite spirit is Sera who has been waiting patiently for the first six spirits to explain their relationship to me. When the two that are Pedro's and Catherina's papas are done talking Sera bids them to hold hands in a circle.

"Make a circle with them, Eliza," she bids me.

I hold the hands of Granpapa's and Granmama's spirits and we make a lovely circle with the others who have made themselves known to me. Sera steps inside the circle and says to me "Remember this circle, Eliza? Remember how you seven made a vow to be a sevenfold expression of Beloved Source? Remember how I stood in the centre like so and how I swore to assist the circle in any way necessary until you all return to Beloved Source having fulfilled the Father's Dream of Heaven on Earth? Oh dear sweet Eliza. I have watched over you always, just as I have watched over the others here. I knew you after you had your mighty vision and I helped you overcome the great fear you felt when you thought of it. And when you make your next brave

The Four Ascents

journey to Earth I shall come to you and remind you who you are just as I am reminding you now."

As I stand in the circle holding hands and listening to Sera's words I know in my heart that she speaks the truth. I *was* here like this with all these souls and we did indeed make a vow to stick together as one. Slowly, the recognition and memory of other times is seeping into my awareness. And although I know that I am Maria now on earth the awareness of her is just like a story I have been telling. I look around at each member of this circle and the memory of them comes fleeting back to me. One by one, they break hands and come to embrace me. I love each and every one of them and my heart is full of gratitude and admiration for all the wonderful ways they each assisted me in my many times on Earth. And now it is the turn of the remaining seven spirits to make their relationship with me known. A young man with extra long yellow hair takes my hand and walks me to the opposite side of the meadow where many more of the tall stones stand silent and knowledgeable.

"I am Artamor," he tells me. "These members of your spirit family form a second circle. Here, where we now stand, this second circle was formed. The meadow holds the memory of how that was. And now, each will come forward and present themselves to you."

"Hello Eliza," another yellow haired man says with a smile. "You do not know me yet in this lifetime, but I chose to be a teacher for you, should you decide to remain as Maria. But you have known me many times before. I was the High Inquisitor at the temple here in Atlantis. You came to me for help and guidance. I was your High Priest in Greece when you reached this stage for the first time, before you fell from grace. I was your teacher in France when you sought to know the earthly art of alchemy. It was of great advantage to your spiritual alchemy. You see, I have served the circle well in my capacity as a mentor and teacher. You have done this also and will continue to do so."

"Eliza, dear sister," says a lady with very long yellow hair and kind blue eyes. "I too have not yet been made known to you in this lifetime. I am a friend of your mother's who will love her much when she prepares to leave her body. But I was once the one in France who commanded my son to put you to death for your gifts. You see, it was your choice and I in my infinite love for you ensured that you had your desire. I love you greatly and will continue to assist you through the heart no matter the consequence to my earthly being."

"And I am that son, Eliza," adds a young man. "I followed her wishes for I knew them to be for your highest good. I was a doctor then but I followed my heart and not my head though my head troubled me greatly because of it. And now in this lifetime I shall be a doctor again though I am but a child yet. It is often my choice to practice earthly medicine for there is a great need for it."

The young man steps aside for a lady to speak to me. She seems so beautiful to me and I feel her to be my mother now. "I *am* your mother now," she tells me. "I have been your mother many times but sometimes *you* chose to be the mother. I was your daughter in France and in many other lifetimes. Next time I will be your daughter again and it will be very exciting for we have great achievements to make together."

"Will your name be Rosalina?" I ask her. "I . . . I mean Maria loves the name Rosalina. She named all her dolls that." I am very much aware now that I am Eliza and Maria is but my body on Earth. I am beginning to feel grown up and less like Maria but that feels ok to me.

"No," the lady replies, "I would very much like to be called Grace because it is with the grace of the Mother's Love that you and I shall achieve great things."

I have met another four beautiful and amazing spirits, all who have assisted me many times and in so many different ways on Earth. There are three more left, a man and a woman and the young man who called himself Artamor. Artamor introduces me to the other three.

"Eliza, these two spirits you have known always," he says. "Here you see the one that is sworn to be your union in body so that other souls may come to earth. He united with you here in Atlantis and in Egypt. He was the one who loved you in Greece, the one you betrayed. And in France he united with you again though he fought the constant memory of your betrayal."

"You were angry with me," I say to this man, suddenly realising that this is true and feeling a memory of what it was like.

"Yes," he replies. "Although I didn't know it, I was still affected by how I died in Greece, alone and angry. I needed to forgive you and you needed to forgive yourself so we created a similar situation so that we could bring that energy in. But it turned out on Earth that we were not aware of our plan and we blamed each other. As a result I died alone and angry once again and you died believing I had deserted you."

"And will we do the same thing in this lifetime?" I ask him. "When Maria grows up will we create another similar situation so that we can forgive each other?" I have a deep desire to make it right with this spirit. I feel a lot rides on it. But his next words sadden me a little.

The Four Ascents

He says, "For the first time since we made our betrothal I have not come to be with you. I am elsewhere on Earth, with a young woman who is teaching me the power of forgiveness."

"And who shall teach me?" I ask him.

"His earthly name is Eduardo. He shall teach you how a free spirit holds no residual energy from what is past."

This makes perfect sense to me: Eduardo, my lovely Eduardo next door. We already said that we would marry and have children and animals and vegetables and even flowers. I think about this for a bit and the others are quiet while I do. Before long I decide that it is a good plan and I am happy that it was our choice this time. I nod to the one who is my union and he smiles back. We are both happy with the plan. So, I look to the lady now that is standing by the union's side.

"Greetings sister," she says with a bow. "I am The Crystal Keeper. Together you and I had the dream of this second circle. I am the one on Earth now that you call Catherina. We are sisters you and I . . . always. We were sisters in the temple in Greece and we were in fact earthly sisters in France. But most importantly, I am one third of a triangle of power that is you, me and Artamor."

"A triangle?" I repeat feeling something powerful moving through my being. In an instant a picture of a triangle flashes into my mind . . . a white cloud shaped like a triangle that changes into a pyramid with three sides. The picture goes as rapidly as it came.

"Yes," The Crystal Keeper says. "With Artamor's faith, The Crystal Keeper's love and Eliza's hope we are a trinity of power that is insurmountable to any darkness. Thus we shall remain until the Red Stone of Power sings and the prophecy is complete."

Artamor steps forward now and bids me and the others to make a circle, holding each other's hands which we do. Into the centre of the second circle he walks and speaks to me from there. "I am Artamor" he says. "I have been known to you many times on earth. I was sent to walk alongside you, a light for you to follow. That is why I watch over the circle."

"And do I know you now on Earth?" I ask him.

"You know me as the one called Pedro," he replies. "Before that I was Clairose, and before that I was Little Buffalo. I was with you in Greece when you fell from grace. I was known as Jason. I rescued you from the flames of your own demise and lighted the way for you to come home. Now, once more

Eliza White Buffalo with Nicholas Black Elk

you have made the first three ascents on that stepladder home. You are ready to make the final and last ascent."

Pondering Artamor's words about the ascents I look around the circle at the many spirits I have known for lifetimes. Snippets of emotion flow in and out of my awareness; fleeting moments of past relationships, pains as well as joys. I see mothers and fathers, brothers and sisters, friends and colleagues. Many who have assisted me in the ascents of the stepladder home; role models and adversaries No matter which role they played or which role I played, every relationship had been co-creative, providing me with valuable experience that assisted me on the journey home. And I know that what Artamor says is true; I have made the third ascent into the seventh world. I think about the tree at the bottom of the yard that told me to open the way through the top of my head so that I could reach the heaven world. This is it, the third ascent . . . connection to spirit. And I also know now that the fourth ascent shall be amazing. It is the connection with the heavenly home, the stars . . . to Beloved Source. I think about the many roles I played on earth and I think about Maria still living and breathing and I realise . . . I have a choice to make.

∞∞∞∞∞∞∞∞∞∞∞∞∞∞∞∞∞∞∞∞∞∞∞∞∞∞∞

The video comes to a stop, and Black Elk speaks . . .

"My Dear Rose, Beloved Source is so proud of the child, Eliza. Twice she has fallen and twice she has picked herself up, centred herself firmly upon the path and risen again to the heights of Heaven. She fell first at the original incarnation to Earth . . . remember the story of Atlantis? Then she fell again at the first challenge in Ancient Greece . . . remember dear Demetria? The reluctance to walk both roads in balance has been full of difficulty. But you understand through Maria's story, how the great reluctance has now been matched by great faith and love in Beloved Source. Maria has risen up the ascent to connection to Source. She is a child and close to Spirit. And you saw how she creates a magical means of making sense of her world. It is when the reluctance is so great that the child finds a way to escape the black road. I want you to understand something, Rose. Before I continue with the video I want you to remember the part of the vision at the summit of the third ascent. I want you to remember how the good red spirit came into the camp and brought hope and understanding to the nation. So you see, Maria is

The Four Ascents

experiencing that hope and understanding. She is being filled with the light of her soul, and so soon you will see how Maria makes a choice to step forwards on the holy path of the soul once again. Soon you will see how she makes that brave step onto the fourth ascent."

CHAPTER SIXTEEN

The choice

And so the story continues . . .

It is almost night here in this ethereal Atlantis. The sun is low in a purple sky and the stones are glowing violet and gold. From time to time they hum quietly to each other. The atmosphere in the stone circle is electrifying, intense with anticipation. All fifteen spirits gather here, laughing and chatting about past experience. I am sitting cross-legged on the grass with several of my spirit family. What fun we are having, drinking cool spring water and eating fresh sweet strawberries. The spirit Amir who is my granpapa now reaches out his hand to me offering me a few more of the delicious berries. "Here, Eliza, share what is left," he says. He drops into my palm some of his own portion. "You taught me how to do this you know. Now you give an extra berry to every one here."

"Did I really teach you this?" I ask happily sharing the berries with the others in our little group.

"It was down yonder in the lower meadow where we first formed our group," he replies pointing far down along the steep path that runs along the meadows.

"And that is where Eliza was first spoken. It was I who did that" says the other Amir, the one that is Treebeard. "Since then I have been called many names, but you know me best as Amir the Prophet."

"Amir the Prophet . . . my star brother from Serabe," I muse out loud.

"Yes," says Amir the Prophet smiling.

As I study him, looking deep into his eyes I find myself wondering about something. I am thinking that I have seen Amir the Prophet in spirit here before. "Did we speak here before, you and I?" I ask him, "In spirit like this I mean, not when we actually lived here on Earth."

A wide grin covers his face and he throws his arms into the air in an exuberant manner. "Ah Eliza!" he says merrily, "your awareness is becoming sharper with every moment. Soon you will be ready for the alignment."

"What's the alignment?" I ask feeling that I already know the answer.

The Four Ascents

"You will know when you get there," he replies. "But to answer your first question; yes, we spoke here in spirit. It was during the lifetime in Greece before you fell from grace. I was known as Eusebius upon the earth and you were known as Demetria."

"Ah yes! Eusebius" I exclaim finally recognizing the servant who taught me so much. "He was a wonderful healer," I add.

"That's true. Remember the olive leaf?" he asks laughing.

"I do. Ah, Eusebius and Demetria had many wonderful times together," I say remembering with great pleasure the special relationship we shared.

"And we met here as Amir and Eliza," Amir adds getting back to the original subject. "We spoke of the great challenge that was ahead for you and I reminded you of our conversation in the temple yonder." He points to a temple, the top of which can just about be seen beyond the meadow, nestled between tree covered hills.

"And that conversation was?" I encourage him to continue. I am fascinated in how intricate and wonderful my journey has been.

"About the prophecy," he states nodding. And then, seeing that I am still unsure of what he is talking about he goes on, "This is why you call me The Prophet; I was the first to speak of the prophecy you hold in your heart space. We all hold that same prophecy, Eliza. It is a prophecy of wholeness, of harmony and balance. It is the Father's Dream, the reason why we make the journey on earth. It is the place that is reached when we climb the four ascents bringing the awareness of Heaven into the heart space."

He stops speaking for a bit while I ponder his words. I place my palm across my heart and close my eyes feeling the energy there. After a few moments The Crystal Keeper speaks softly to me saying, "The crystal heart is where the three-fold flame of Beloved Source burns infinitely. You call yours The Red Stone of Power. You named it thus because it is the powers of Faith, Hope and Love."

"The trinity of power!" I exclaim with sudden understanding, "That is what you, Artamor and I are representing. That is why we do so much on Earth as a threesome; we're reminding ourselves who we are.

"Exactly," she says. "The trinity is three supreme beings or highest expressions of the oneness that is Source. We remind ourselves of this truth by bringing our earthly awareness into the crystal heart where these three flames burn as one; and from there we make the four ascents."

Eliza White Buffalo with Nicholas Black Elk

The Crystal Keeper smiles broadly at me and I feel my heart burn brightly in truth. "The Red Stone of Power always reminds me of who I am" I tell her warmly.

And she goes on, "The crystal heart guides you upwards towards full awareness of the Self. The fourth ascent is where we reconnect with our heavenly origins and bring that awareness into the heart space. It is The Father's Dream . . . Heaven on Earth."

"The Father's Dream," I affirm.

"And the vision?" encourages Amir the Prophet. "Do you see it now?"

"I do," I smile, gently sighing.

What peace I feel in my heart space as we speak this truth! What utter knowing that all is as it should be! And the vision . . . Oh yes! I see it so clearly: the two roads and the flowering tree. I see the four ascents, and me on the back of a horse with four troops of horses and riders behind me. I see the spotted eagle flying high over the long procession of the nation's people and I know that it is my highest Self, Beloved Source and the nation is my child, my creation known as Eliza.

"I see it all," I tell Amir the Prophet. "I was a male manifestation in that lifetime. My name was Black Elk given to me by my father and I was also known as Nicholas. But why was I male? I can hardly remember any other lifetime when I wasn't female."

"It was your choice, Eliza," he tells me. "You chose to experience male sexuality in order to understand what happened to Demetria. It was the pivotal point at which you plummeted to the lower worlds, so it was advantageous that you conquer that adversity."

"And did I? Conquer it I mean? I don't think so. I feel that even now with Maria, sexuality is an aspect of myself that is misconstrued, controlled even."

"That is so," confirms Amir the Prophet. "Yet you learned much of your sexual energy in your last lifetime in France and you learned what you must do to alchemize that energy. You chose to be Maria purely for reasons of resting in the balanced love of your parents and grandparents. It is essential to connect with the Sacred Parents within that is the male/female aspects of Beloved Source."

""I have a choice to make then," I state knowingly.

"It is so," he replies.

I turn my attention to Sera and I say, "Sera, you said it to me when we stood before my damaged body. You said that I could go to Heaven if I so wished."

The Four Ascents

"And it is so," says Sera.

"Then I can choose to go back to Maria and grow up with my parents and grandparents resting in their love. I can choose to make a union with Eduardo just as we planned?" I ask her laying out my options.

And Sera replies, "That is what you *chose* to do Eliza. And now that your body is so badly damaged it seems an ideal scenario to express unconditional love and forgiveness, yet the union with Eduardo is greatly jeopardised."

I explore another option, "Or I can choose to integrate my experience as Maria into my energy and take a different role; perhaps one that will challenge me to conquer the base sexual energy that resulted in my fall from grace. I mean, now that I have made the third ascent would it not be good if I go forwards on the path and make the fourth ascent without the heaviness of the base energy dragging me down?"

"I see what you mean," says Sera thoughtfully.

"You are Maria's mother," I say to the one who is Alma on earth. "How will it affect you if Maria dies?"

"It will bring Alma closer to the Mother's Love. In fact it is an essential reason for my experience now . . . to express the Mother Energy on Earth," she replies lovingly.

"And how shall it affect the rest of you?" I ask looking around my company.

"I shall show great patience," says the one who is Juan. "It is something Juan is having difficulty with."

"Miguel shall learn to rest his body in preparation for the fourth ascent," says the one who is Granpapa on earth.

"And I shall express great wisdom," says the one who is Granmama on earth. "Through Rosalina's past experience with death she will teach Alma that wisdom. It shall lift *Rosalina* closer to the Mother energy also as well as serve Alma."

"Then it seems I have made my choice," I declare. "What say you all?"

"It is so," they all reply in unison.

Artamor speaks now and he says to me, "And now you are ready for the alignment."

∞∞∞∞∞∞∞∞∞∞∞∞∞∞∞∞∞∞∞∞∞∞∞∞∞∞∞∞∞∞∞

It is night now, though the sky is clear and the stars are shining brightly upon us. I am full of anticipation for what is about to be. I feel that I have stood

Eliza White Buffalo with Nicholas Black Elk

here many times before for the alignment. And even though I cannot say for sure what the alignment actually is, I know that I shall feel my way through it, recalling it as I go along and accepting that whatever transpires shall be for my highest intention of making the fourth ascent on earth. There are fifteen of us in all gathered around in one big circle.

The Crystal Keeper speaks to us, "Sisters, brothers," she says, "the stars are in the correct configuration and the moon is full in a clear sky. The alignment shall be tonight." The Crystal Keeper stands behind a plinth in the centre of the circle. I hadn't seen this plinth before now and I can hardly take my gaze from it as it glows with a white light. It hums loudly and seems to pulsate with the energy of the light. As The Crystal Keeper touches the plinth with her two hands the light seems to vibrate through her being which glows now too. Suddenly, there on the plinth is placed a huge quartz crystal. I intuitively know it is The Focus Stone. The Crystal Keeper takes her hands off the plinth and her being stops glowing.

"Is everyone in their correct position?" she asks loudly, looking around at us all. I hadn't realised up until now that we had a position to take. I look around at the others who seem to be happy that they are in theirs. "That's it" The Crystal Keeper goes on, "and Serabe? Yes, that is good Eliza. You are where you should be?"

Obviously, those from Serabe are to position themselves here on this quarter of the circle. I am sandwiched between my two brothers Amir. Across from me, on the opposite quarter of the stone circle I see the one who is usually my union on earth. I wonder if he will unite with me in this next lifetime.

"Silence now!" cries the Crystal Keeper as she takes her place in another quarter between Artamor and Granmama's spirit. Everyone is silent as the loud hum of the central plinth gets even louder. I look up into the sky and there I see that the lights of the stars are emanating down and into the Focus Stone which is now humming as well. The humming seems to fill the entire circle causing each outer stone to glow and hum also. My being is vibrating with power and as I glance around at the others I see that they are also vibrating. The great humming increases even more and I realise that my being is making that very humming sound as it vibrates. I can feel my brothers Amir beside me, their hands holding mine. Our feet are touching the ground but it seems that we are lifting up into the air. I feel my crown at the top of my head open wide and then it seems that there is no separation between my being and my surroundings at all. The stars, the Focus Stone, the plinth, the many standing stones and the fourteen people here with me are all within my own being. They *are* me and I am them. For what seems to be one eternal moment of completeness, a blissful awareness of home, I float. The humming deepens and the vibration slows and I seem to come back down onto my feet. I wriggle my toes feeling the grass between them and I squeeze my brothers' hands. They squeeze back. The alignment is done. The humming slows even more until it eventually stops. The Focus Stone still pulses and glows and the stones seem to sing to each other softly. We all remain silent until the Focus Stone stills and then we turn to embrace each other. If everyone here is feeling the Parent's Love as much as I am then I cannot imagine how more perfect it could be. There is no need for words. They would only shatter the blissful quiet. Besides we have no need for words as our thoughts project esoterically.

∞∞∞∞∞∞∞∞∞∞∞∞∞∞∞∞∞∞∞∞∞∞

Back on Earth in Mexico

"Here we are Eliza," says Sera. We are back in my bedroom, standing where we stood before. My body is still lying like dead on the bed. My parents are gone and the doctor too. I can hear them talking in the next room.

A touch on my hand causes me to look down and there is little Treebeard. He takes my hand and tells me, "You must go back to your body for now. I shall stay with you until it is time to leave. It won't take long but your parents should see that you are gone. Quickly now, they are coming back."

With that he lets go of my hand and I find myself entering my rigid body. The body gives a shudder as I come right in then stills again. I see nothing because the damage to my brain has failed my sight organs, but I can hear; I hear the parents come back into the room. I hear the curious machine beside me bleeping and whirring. And I hear the distant hum of the purple world as it keeps the connection open for me to return. Mama is here, and Juan. I hear them talking but I cannot see them. I try to hear their spirits in their voices but what I hear sounds raspy compared to the beautiful sounds of their spirit voices. Granmama puts her hand on my head and utters a prayer for me. She doesn't know that I am fine and happy. She doesn't know that I am leaving to embark on another adventure and that it is her that she ought to pray for. She will need all the help she can muster if she is to express wisdom and strength for poor Mama. I cannot hear Granpapa but I feel him close by. I know he is here.

Eliza White Buffalo with Nicholas Black Elk

"Oh Granpapa! I loved you best," I silently project to him. "You taught me how to make the third ascent. When the time comes I would like it to be you who makes the transition with me to the fourth ascent."

I try to feel Eduardo's spirit. I know he wasn't in the purple world. He's not one from the two circles of sisters and brothers but I know that he has a spirit and that it is likely a member of a different circle altogether. I want to say goodbye to him and tell him that I'm sorry I won't be his union. I try to feel his spirit but I cannot. I wish he was here to say goodbye.

"Maria my child," Mama is saying to me. She is weeping. Poor Mama! I wish I could tell her how happy she really is that I am moving on but she wouldn't understand. Some day when she makes her own journey back to the purple world, she will know then that it is for her highest intention. "Maria my child," she says weeping, "I am so sorry that I took you to that terrible place. Please wake up my dear, please wake up."

It is time to go. Treebeard is gone and Sera too. I wonder who will bring me back to the purple world. I don't see anyone or hear anyone but I won't be afraid because I know that someone will come for me. They all know I am coming. I hear my heartbeat slow and steady. The machine beside my bed bleeps with each beat. I must slow it down now. I am not afraid. I concentrate on the humming of the purple world. It is not so distant now. My heartbeat slows and stops. The machine makes one continuous bleeping noise. Mama gasps and cries out in fear. Juan shakes my body attempting to make my heart start again. Granmama and Granpapa hold on tight to each other and look on with sadness in their hearts. The doctor pushes Juan away and pumps my heart but I do not respond to it. I am standing by the bed holding Granpapa's hand. I wonder if he can feel me. Squeezing his hand tightly I focus on sending as much love as I can to him.

"Goodbye Granpapa," I am saying, "I loved you best." He looks down at me and although I know he can't see me, he does feel me.

His eyes well up with tears and he whispers "Bye, bye, Poppet! Have fun in the stars."

Now I really must find Eduardo before I make my return to the purple world. I run off quickly to the yard but I don't see him. I look in his yard but he isn't there. The humming from the purple world is loud in my ears now and a bright light opens up in front of me. From the light a beautiful spirit steps out into the yard. He is wearing white clothes like the others and his white hair is glowing like the focus stone. He smiles brightly and holding out his hands to me he says "Come now, Eliza, it is time."

The Four Ascents

"But I want to say goodbye to Eduardo," I tell him.

"You shall, at another time," he replies kindly. "You have a contract with him that will be fulfilled then. But for now I shall take you to see your mother."

And taking his hand I find myself back in my room. I look to the bed to where I expect to see my body lying dead but instead I see an old woman there. Around the bed are people I don't know but one old woman beside the bed is familiar to me. Studying her I realise that she is the spirit from the second circle, the one that is to be a friend to my mama and help her prepare to leave her body. The old woman on the bed is my mama preparing to leave her body. It will not be long before we will meet again in the purple world.

Mama can see me for she is looking right at me and she says, "My darling Maria, I swear that one day I will bring life back to you so that you may be the beautiful woman you were always destined to be."

Ethereal Atlantis

I am in the upper meadow once more. The sky that was purple is now white. The stones are white and the central plinth is white. Everywhere I look there is white. I am alone with the beautiful spirit who brought me here. "Eliza," he says, "I am the Master Hilarion. I have brought you here so that a record can be made of your experience as Maria and you can choose your next role."

And with that the stones disappear, and in their place is a huge white hall with many doors. People are going in and coming out through these doors. I don't ask where they lead to because I know that they are transition chambers. Hilarion and I enter one of the chambers and greet the many spirits who are waiting for me. All of the members of the two circles are here and many more. I need no instruction. I have done this process many times. I am to be a female. I shall be born into the country called Ireland. I meet with the two spirits who are to be my parents and the spirits who will be my extended family. Then the members of the circles speak to me one by one. We make pacts and agreements that will aid us in our next role. Our goal is to make the fourth ascent into the star origins. We shall raise our physical bodies into that awareness and balance it in our crystal hearts. The Father's Dream shall be realised and the prophecy will be fulfilled . . . Heaven on Earth.

Eliza White Buffalo with Nicholas Black Elk

The one that was Granmama's spirit speaks to me first. "I shall be a loving friend to you," she says. "I shall teach you about the feminine energy for you will need it to lighten your sexuality."

"And I shall work with you at the moment of your transformation into the fourth ascent," says my brother Amir, the one that was Granpapa's spirit. "I shall come with the one called Sera for she is to help me much in this role."

Amir the Prophet speaks next and he says, "I shall be the door through which you will come to know your true Self on earth."

"And I shall open that door," adds the Master Hilarion.

The spirit that was Juan comes to me and he says, "I shall remain in Mexico and earth the energy of our story there for you and for the others."

"I shall be a link to Mexico also," says the one that was Pedro's papa, "a physical reminder of our plan."

"And I shall go before us all and prepare the earth for the holy path," says the one that was Catherina's papa. And when all these members of my first family circle have spoken and made their vows the six members of the second circle come to me.

The one that was to be a teacher for me in Mexico comes to me first and he says, "Eliza, I shall show you the art of alchemy. It will not be difficult because you already have done this but it will remind you to transmute that sexual energy into the light."

"Eliza, dear sister," says the one that helped Mama's spirit prepare to leave the body, "I shall come to you when you most need me and I will prepare the way for the alchemist."

"I shall earth the circle as usual," says the one that was to be a doctor, the one that ordered my death in France. "I shall not forget the stones."

"I shall be your child," says the one that was Maria's mama, "the earthly wound that reflects your inner hope. I ask that you name me Grace for it is with the grace of the Mother's love that you and I shall achieve great things."

Now the one that comes to me next is the one that is my union on earth. "We agreed to express the aspect of forgiveness on Earth," he says. "I shall unite with you again as your partner. Once again I shall be a plinth for you to stand on but also so that we both may embrace each other on Earth in full awareness of that forgiveness."

And then the Crystal Keeper speaks, "Sister," she says lovingly, "the triangle of power is to be known on Earth. I shall come to you first before Artamor."

The Four Ascents

"And I shall walk alongside you," says Artamor. "You will know me by my sound."

I take all their hands and with much hope all around I say, "I shall clear the path in preparation for your coming. The experience of the mighty vision and the man called Black Elk will be re-presented in this lifetime; in this manner shall I express my truth clearly and powerfully."

"And the energy of Black Elk shall light the Mother/Father Flame in the crystal heart," encourages the Master Hilarion. "The doors of the temple I shall open and when you come to me in balance the Red Stone of Power shall sound for all to hear." And having said this, the Master Hilarion is silent for a moment and then he adds, "When you make the fourth ascent, the great energy of Serabe shall welcome you home as It sounds Na-ther-n-a."

"And so it is," I declare.

"And so it is," declare the many spirits.

∞∞∞∞∞∞∞∞∞∞∞∞∞∞∞∞∞∞∞∞∞∞∞∞∞∞∞∞

The video comes to an end, and Black Elk speaks . . .

"Rose, my beloved White Buffalo, my story is done. I will not show you any more because as you know, the fourth ascent, the fourth lifetime begins with your birth into the world. You are the expression of the soul, Eliza, here on Earth now in this lifetime. The journey of the soul has yet again reached the fourth ascent. I say yet again because the four ascents are not made over merely four lifetimes, as you may think from this story. But the four ascents are reached over many hundreds of lifetimes of experience. I have used my vision and the story of the soul, Eliza, which I have shown you, to teach you the four steps and how the soul falls three times. This is the journey of all souls as they follow the holy path back to harmony of the One Beloved Source."

CHAPTER SEVENTEEN

The fourth ascent

"Rose?" Black Elk says now.

"Yes?"

"Why do think you fell three times?" he asks me. He obviously is teaching me yet more amazing truths.

"Did I fall three times?" I ask. "I know that Demetria fell from grace in Greece when I was in the Order of Delphi. That was the second fall. I realise that the first fall was the original fall to Earth. That makes sense to me Black Elk, but when was the third fall?"

"What do you think you did when you were thirteen, when you *shut down* as you like to put it? You fell into your lower body then did you not? You described it yourself as being but a shadow of your Self." Black Elk is talking about that terrible night when I was thirteen, when Grace was born, when I was so overcome with fear of the black road that I shut away all conscious awareness of my life up until then. For the next twenty years I was surrounded by a thick fog of pain that I had shut myself off from. Eventually I clambered up into my heart and it was as if I woke from a nightmare. I began to climb the four ascents and as I climbed I healed in the Light of Heaven.

"I was in darkness, to be sure," I answer Black Elk's question. "Yet, I do not have any memory of it like I do from the time in Greece. I mean . . . it wasn't the same . . . I didn't have any great visions of hell or that."

"Rose!" he laughs. "Have I taught you nothing? As it is in Heaven so shall it be on Earth."

"Oh I see," I reply laughing at his manner. It has *always* been my manner to laugh at myself. I reckon it's what kept me sane through years of mental anguish. "The years of pain were a reflection of the darkness of my being," I say. It is more a statement of truth than a suggestion.

"That is so Rose," Black Elk confirms. "Oh! You think I forget what it's like to be in a solid form, but I don't. I understand how difficult the black road can be. And here you are, on the crest of the fourth ascent. Our grandfathers have given us all the power to make over and that is just what you did. You walked the two roads, climbed the four ascents and . . . well, is it not reflected in the oneness of our being?"

"It is Black Elk, it is," I reply feeling the Father's Light sweep through my being, *His* being.

"So will you answer my question?" he asks.

"What question?"

"Why do you think you fell three times?" he asks again.

"I don't know," I reply.

"Who else do you know fell three times before being crucified and resurrected from the dead?"

"You mean Jesus Christ?"

"Yes, I mean Jesus Christ. Why do you think He showed us that?"

"I don't know."

"That is something you could think about," he says. Black Elk often leaves me with food for thought like this. "Feel the answer," he adds.

I will too . . . eventually I will.

"Do you feel this Rose," he asks me indicating the ecstatic feeling of limitlessness I am now experiencing. My awareness is sharp and expanded so that I experience all things like it is all part of my being. "I Am Eliza," he continues. "I Am the Flame of Source."

"I Am Eliza," I repeat, "I Am the Flame of Source."

And Black Elk continues teaching, "Rose, remember the vision when I was told, *your grandfathers are having a council*?"

"Yes," I reply.

And Black Elk explains, "It means that the truth that is my spiritual awareness is meeting with my earthly awareness. I was shown the truth of my heavenly being so that I could raise my earthly being into that truth. When you lift your awareness into the higher realms and meet with all those spirits that really are us for there is no separation, then you are doing that very same thing."

"I understand," I tell him, "It's what I've been doing all my life."

"Rose . . . our grandfathers . . . or I should say grandparents are having a council. They are our male *and* female energy."

"Or in other words, our spiritual reality shall be made known to me and I will raise my earthly reality up to meet with it," I add.

"Exactly," he says with great joy. "As it is in Heaven so shall it be on Earth. Today, our grandparents are having a council. I will take you there and you shall know our truth. So now, I am not going to show you a video. I am going to take you to a place within you right now, in the spiritual realms. And having witnessed and understood the many lifetimes I have shown to you, you will no doubt recognize this place as the meadow in ethereal Atlantis."

With that I find myself in a world of white light. A wide crystal meadow spreads throughout the world and a circle of standing crystal stones is here, lifted from the ethereal world of Atlantis. I stand in the centre of the circle and watch as the two groups of souls come walking up the long hill to the stone circle. I am Eliza, male/female as one. Black Elk is within.

"Hi family," I project into each of their minds as they approach.

"Hi Eliza," they project back, smiling.

One by one they take their positions around the circle, sitting on the crystal meadow. Their beings are translucent, both male and female, and are glowing with crystal light. Without another word we take each other's hands making one continuous circle and we begin to sound. The sound is a low humming noise that gets louder and louder, increasing with intensity and becoming clearer until it stops suddenly and is a silent vibration holding us all in the awareness of Source. We start to move; up and down at first like we are sitting on the crest of a gentle wave. Then we begin to move forwards and backwards, rocking and swaying in a sea of pure consciousness. I feel myself to be all that is, constantly swaying to and fro. I exist as this sea of consciousness. There is nothing only I. I begin to feel desire, desire to be. Images float into the sea. Three sided shapes. One is made of stone and as its image comes closer the waves begin to lessen and I feel like I am stepping back and looking on at my creation. In this vision, on a stone plinth lies a male body that is my right arm. I also lie on another plinth, a female body. A red crystal light is placed within us by the Mother Being and we are separated. My right arm vanishes and I fall from the great heights of Heaven to a world between Heaven and Earth. There I am addressed by a golden being that tells me of the prophecy and gives me the Red Stone of Power. I take the Red Stone and place it in my heart space. Almost at once, I find myself in a dense world. I am rock. I feel myself ascend into lesser density over and over, becoming grass and animals and birds until finally I am a human being. I am in Atlantis where I first began my journey on Earth. I am sitting in the upper meadow within the stone circle. It is daytime and the sky is blue with a bright sun shining down on my head. I am with this large group of souls that are here for the same reason I am, to set down their intentions to create the Father's Dream, Heaven on Earth. These are the very souls I knew first on Earth, the souls I incarnated with into many lifetimes. This is our very first lifetime on Earth.

I am the first to speak, "We are here to establish a group of souls that will be a seven-fold expression of Beloved Source," I proclaim. "One such group has already been formed and shall be from hereon known as The First Group. This new group shall be known as The Second Group. Brother Amir shall now speak of how it will be."

Brother Amir speaks now and he says, "Brothers and sisters, a short time ago in the lower meadow seven of us made a union as a sevenfold expression of Source. Each of us re-present on Earth the energy of the seven points of power that connects us to Source. Yet in an outer unification the display is even more beautiful, even more potent for it reflects the unification within as well as being a reminder of truth to those who succumb to the earthly maladies of separation."

A sister from the Pleiades speaks now. "Good morning family," she says smiling at everyone, "I have vowed to assist The First Group on their journey of the four ascents. This morning they honoured me with a naming ceremony. So from hereon I shall be known as Sera. Now the seven members of The First Group shall present themselves before us all."

Sera stands up and walks to the centre of the circle where she invites each member of The First Group to join her one by one. Firstly, Amir joins her and introduces himself, "I Am Amir from Serabe," he says.

At once I remember who he is. He is my star brother, Amir the Prophet and I am Osiah, also from Serabe. It was Amir who named me Eliza just days ago in Atlantis time, down yonder in the lower meadow. The memory of the establishing of The First Group is clear to me now. It seems that no time at all has passed since that day. Yet I know that I have incarnated many times. The journey, the four ascents has taken me right back to the beginning, to the star origins. Now, it seems that I am re-running the screenplay, only this time I am fully aware of the Father's Dream being *here* and *now*. I look at Amir the Prophet and I think of the many embodiments he has experienced. I see Ames, my brother in Egypt and Eusebius, the slave in Greece and I see the man that he is now on Earth, a man I know and love called Jonathan Kane.

Amir is talking about his position as the sixth point of power, "The sixth point which is higher knowledge and understanding," he says. "With this knowledge on earth I shall heal by bringing disharmony back into balance."

"It is so," I say to him, "you *are* a healer *now*, in many lifetimes." Standing up, I address everyone here, "Dearest family, I have been given a wonderful gift, the gift of awareness," I tell them. "It seems that we are establishing a second soul group. Yet through the awareness what was given to me I tell you

Eliza White Buffalo with Nicholas Black Elk

that both groups have already made the four ascents. My Sacred Parents have told me that when I make the four ascents I shall be with Them in Heaven and all shall know that they are with Them in Heaven. In this eternal moment of *now* the Father's Dream is complete. I am sent to remind you to step out of the illusion of time and separation and into the reality of Eternal Oneness with Source." My whole being almost sings with joy as I relate the good news, "The Father's Dream is here and now. The illusion is gone and I am awake." I throw my arms around Amir, my wonderful star brother Amir. "Oh Amir" I cry, "The long sleep is but a moment. It's all now. We just need to step out of the illusion of time and realise the truth on earth; that there *is* no journey, there *is* no others . . . there is no . . . Oh Amir, the truth is there is only Source, there *is* only I."

"And we," adds Amir indicating the many individuals, "are an illusion of separateness for *we* are One in reality. *We* are I."

"Yes," I reply in blissful holiness, "I Am that I Am. Here, let us form the two groups for I Am the Father *and* the Mother."

And so The First Group members come and stand in a circle with me holding hands. And I say to them, "you are my family. In the illusion I have a saying and it is 'Mitakuye Oyasin'. It means all are relative; you are all relative to I, you are a reflection of I; that is I the Source, not the female body you see before you." And I go on, "We all reflect the wholeness of Beloved Source on Earth, but individually we reflect one aspect of the seven aspects of Source. We reflect that aspect more than the others for that is our gift to the group. That is the part we play that fulfils our contract with the group."

And to the first member I turn and say to him, "you reflect the seventh point of power, the crown. That is why on Earth in the very lifetime I know now you are James, the one who channels from Beloved Source through the seventh point of power."

The one that is James now acknowledges my words as his truth by bowing his head and saying, "So it is."

"And you reflect the sixth point of power, the third eye," I say to Amir, the prophet. "That is why you are the healer and a teacher of ancient knowledge, Jonathan on earth."

He bows to me also and says, "And so it is."

To the third member I turn and say, "You reflect the fourth point of power, the heart. That is why on Earth you love so purely and unconditionally. You are an earthly reflection of peace and harmony and you are known as my dear friend, Gertge."

272

The Four Ascents

And she bows her head to me and says, "So it is."

Now to another member I turn and say, "You reflect the third point of power on earth, the solar plexus. In this way you have gone before us always clearing our path and preparing the Earth for each ascent. I know you on earth now as Robert."

The one who is Robert on Earth bows to me and says, "So it is."

"And you reflect the second point of power, the sacral," I say to another. "That is why on earth you are Davy, a creative and sexual human being."

The one who is Davy on earth bows and says, "So it is."

To the last member but one I turn and say, "You reflect the first point of power. That is why you ground our energies so well on earth. I do not know you on Earth but I know that you are a man called Juan and that you connect us all through the earthly domain of Mexico."

And the one who is Juan now bows and says, "So it is."

"That leaves one more," I tell them, "and that is me. On earth I am a woman called Rose, and I reflect the fifth point of power, the throat. That is why I express the Self, my truth through the written and spoken word."

And they all speak as one saying, "So it is." And now that I have said all this, I invite The First Group to close their eyes.

"Remember in the lower meadow, how we lifted each other up in joy and aligned with each other?" I ask them. They say that they do. "In this eternal moment of *now* the oneness that is I exists. Through the Father's Dream we have manifested that oneness on Earth. Let us raise ourselves up once again in the same way, only this time we know that The Father's Dream is complete. We have walked two roads climbing four ascents into the awareness of Beloved Source. Let us rejoice for Heaven is on Earth."

Immediately we begin to sing the song that we sang in the lower meadow. The one who is Sera comes to the centre of the circle as before and reflects back to us our love and light. And as we experience that oneness as before, we lift up into the air and one by one, starting with the crown we vanish into the sea of consciousness.

And in the eternal moment of *now* The Second Group is holding hands in a circle. In the centre of the circle stands one who is contracted to assist us. The crown who is known as Hans on Earth speaks first of his contract with the group. Then the Third Eye, known as Georgina speaks. Next speaks the Heart known as Lisa and the Solar Plexus known as Roger. The Sacral, known as Grace, speaks, and then the Root known as Jack. Finally, I speak. I am the Throat, the one who is known as Rose.

And I say, "This is The Second Group that is a reflection of Beloved Source on earth. And in this group is reflected the Holy Trinity, the three supreme beings in one, that is The Mother, The Father and the Child." To the one who is Georgina on earth I say, "You are The Crystal Keeper. You have been given this name here in Atlantis because you are the keeper of the focus stone and this is how you are known in the oneness of all things. You are the Love of The Mother." And to the one who stands in the centre of the circle I turn and say, "you are Artamor. You are the word that is sent forth, a light to follow and a voice for all to hear. You are The Faith of The Father." And then I say to them, "I am Hope. I am the Child, known as Eliza. I am the prophecy that is complete *now* in the centre of all things. I Am Heaven on Earth." And when I have said these things The Second Group sings and Artamor reflects our joy back to us from the centre of the circle. Aligned in oneness, The Second Group rises up and vanishes into the sea of consciousness.

∞∞∞∞∞∞∞∞∞∞∞∞∞∞∞∞∞∞∞∞∞∞∞∞∞∞∞

The vision comes to an end and I find myself back in my body, still lying on the sofa. The time is almost seven am. And Black Elk Speaks . . .

"My Dear Rose, what a morning you have had! I have explained to you the soul and how it experiences many lifetimes on Earth by incarnating many droplets of itself. And I have explained to you how the droplets live life and come back to the wholeness of the lake, the soul, so that they may bring that valuable experience back too. Know that these experiences teach those on Earth who they are, and about the journey of the soul, the two roads each must walk, and the four ascents of Spirit each must climb in order to bring the awareness of the heavenly soul right onto Earth through the crystal heart. I have shown you the journey of your own soul, known as Eliza. And I have shown you how you grouped together with two soul groups in order to assist each other on the path. Just now, I brought you to the awareness of the eternal moment, wherein you experienced the Oneness of Beloved Source. You were able then to voice this truth out into the universe which you understood to be *your* creation. Essentially, you have brought all awareness of your journey throughout your many lifetimes on Earth together into one realization . . . that Heaven is, and always has been, present on Earth through the crystal heart. And Rose, that realization that is in Heaven shall also be on Earth. Enjoy your special day, Rose . . . and welcome home, my child."

CHAPTER EIGHTEEN

Heaven on Earth

The ceremony is over. "Wakan Tanka, The Great Spirit has blessed us with gorgeous weather," I say silently to Black Elk.

"This is a holy place, Rose," he replies. "It is a reflection of your heart where all is in the peace of the prophecy."

We had the ceremony outdoors in a huge white tepee I had erected in the south east corner of the garden. On the outer canvas of the tepee I painted scenes from Black Elk's vision; the flaming rainbow, the four troops of horses, the cup of water and the bow, the cleansing wing and the healing herb, the pipe that is peace and the sacred flowering stick. On the inner canvas I painted the nation's hoop with the flowering tree sheltering all peoples of one Father and one Mother. Grace looked so beautiful when she accepted her name. She shone with happiness. With new life too as it turned out. She took me aside after the ceremony and told me that she is pregnant.

"Why didn't you tell me before?" I almost squealed in excitement.

"I wanted to wait," she replied. "I wasn't feeling too perky when I came back from my holiday in Mexico. I'm twenty weeks gone now and feeling much brighter" she told me.

So now I am to be a grandmother! Now, is one continuous day of blissful happiness. Grace's fiancé, John has been running around with his professional camera since early this morning. He must have snapped a thousand pictures by now. He is trying to get us all into one picture.

"Squeeze in everyone. You there, come to the front. I can barely see you," he yells from behind the camera.

My dear friend Lisa from Holland tiptoes to the front of the gathering and sits down on the grass beside Georgina. Almost everyone is here that was invited. Lisa has been here for weeks staying with Gertge. They arrived early this morning armed with gifts and well wishes for me and Grace. Hans, who is also from Holland, has been staying with Georgina in England and the two of them have come especially for the ceremony. A new friend of Georgina has come with them; a man called Stephen. I find him very interesting and Black Elk has been so excited at his arrival. He's been going on all day about who he is and the great energy he brings with him. What with all the other stuff going on I have had to put it aside until this evening. Black Elk's news will just have to wait. There has been so much to prepare and so much more to do now that the celebrations have begun. Roger lives just up the road from here so it was easy for him to be here today. He's been a blessing these past few days, helping to get everything ready. Today though, he was only to be found in some corner or other deep in conversation with Hans over the fact that they were brothers in the past life in France. A darling friend and soul brother of mine, Robert is here too. He has enjoyed talking with Davy, another dear friend. Both men are fascinated by alien life and have been swapping stories all day. What with talks of flying saucers and crop circles, past lives and prophecies, I think Grace's John reckons we are all mad. I suppose taking countless photographs is his way of avoiding the eccentricity of the colourful gathering.

"John darling," Grace says to him when he starts rearranging the gathering yet again. "Can we get this one done already? Don't know about you but I'm ravenous. Let me at that buffet."

"Nearly there," he replies getting Lisa to shuffle on in a bit more. "Ah! Perfect. Now, smile everyone." At last the great photograph is taken and we can all relax again in each other's company.

Grace walks with me to the house. I want to check the telephone to see if there are any messages for me. "Have I told you about James and Jenna?" I ask Grace as we walk.

"Yes," she replies. "I think so. They're the couple from New Mexico aren't they?"

"That's right. They wanted to be here but they already booked a Buddhist retreat in a place in Colorado. They'll be there now, but they said that they would spend some time today connecting with us all here in Ireland. And then there's Jonathan. I don't know if he will have much free time today. Do you remember him?"

"Think so," she replies. "Jonathan Kane . . . he's the guy in Brazil isn't he?"

"Aye, he's over there for the full summer working with a bunch of healers from around the world. Apparently they see hundreds of people a week. There are so many people over there that need healing and most of them can't afford to pay so Jonathan and the rest are basically giving their whole summer for free."

"What kind people!" adds Grace.

"Exactly! Anyway James, Jenna and Jonathan can't be here, and then there's Juan in Mexico. I would love to go to Mexico some day," I tell my daughter,

The Four Ascents

"Not just because of our connection there but it would be nice to meet with Juan." I have wanted to go to Mexico for years now, ever since I first recalled the past lifetime there when I was a little girl and Grace was my mother. And now, thanks to Black Elk, I have witnessed that lifetime for myself. I take a moment to hug the memory of sweet little Maria to my heart. What a gift it is that Black Elk gave to me this morning!

"I talked to Juan last week you know," Grace says interrupting my thoughts. Juan is the only member of the two soul groups that I haven't met in this lifetime, but Grace and John met him when they were on holiday in Mexico. "I told him all about you," Grace says. "Well, he had an idea that something other worldly was going on with me. He said he thought about our meeting for weeks . . . kept having dreams about being my husband in Mexico."

"Aha!" I exclaim. "And did you tell him that he was?"

"I did, much to John's horror," she says laughing.

She is still laughing as I pick up the phone and dial the message line. "You have two new messages," the automated voice says. I put on the loud speaker so that Grace can hear them too. "First new message," says the voice . . .

"Hi Rose," comes Jenna's voice over the phone. "We're just taking our breakfast out on the terrace overlooking the mountains. We're really high up so the views are breathtaking. Won't stay on too long my love, just want to say good luck for today. I suppose it's nearly over by now . . . silly me . . . but I hope you had a lovely time and all went well. Say hello to Grace for us. I hope we get to meet her soon. We intend to connect with you all this lunchtime; we have like a kinda siesta then so that's what we'll do. At least we'll be there in spirit. Love ya lots, byeee!"

"Second new message," says the automated voice . . .

"Rose, how are ya?" comes Jonathan's voice to my delight. "Oh you wouldn't believe how much I have to tell ya when I get back. Anyway, everything here is going well; lots of good healing and people getting well. I'm off on an excursion this evening as ways of a wee break. There are a few of us going. So I'll find a nice quiet spot and tune in with ya all . . . . hope ya had a great day and all went well. Say hi to Jack and the boys for me. Hi to Grace also and I'll see ya soon. Bye, bye now!"

"End of messages," comes the automated voice. I put the receiver back on the stand.

Eliza White Buffalo with Nicholas Black Elk

"You know such nice people Rose," Grace says still on a high from the ceremony. She just hasn't stopped smiling all day.

"Oh it's been a long journey, Grace," I tell her. "I feel so blessed now. Ever since the accident . . ."

"Did you really die in the accident?" she asks interrupting.

"I believe so," I reply. I had a car accident years ago in which I believe I died and went into the light. My life was transformed as a result.

"You're lucky to be here at all. And I'm lucky for I might never have known you," says Grace taking my hand.

"I was never going to die then," I tell her. "It was a way of jolting me awake . . . reminding me of the work I had yet to do. And now I've gotten to know all these wonderful people; my soul family."

"The woman that was talking just now, Jenna . . . is she part of the soul groups?" Grace asks.

"Black Elk told me that she is a very special soul called Sera," I tell her. "She was always meant to assist the group, he said. James, her husband has been with her many times. Black Elk says that is because he is the crown of the group and Sera is the guardian of the crown."

I think back to this morning when I rose into the spirit world and had that vision in the ethereal Atlantis. A lot was revealed to me this morning. Lots of pieces and answers had come together for me. I really *know* now that the prophecy is complete and that it is being revealed on earth. But I won't say anything to anyone about it just yet. Besides, they will come to realise that in their own way for we are all connected. The prophecy is complete in them just as it is in me.

"I understand that," says Grace meaning that she understands about Sera. "Don't ask me how I do, but I do." And then she asks, "If Sera is the guardian of the first group then who is the guardian of the second group, the group I'm in."

"His soul name is Artamor."

"How do you know that?" she asks. I don't really want to tell her about my spirit journey this morning.

"I just know," I reply, then decide to tell her what I know of Artamor to date . . . "Black Elk once asked me, where is Little Buffalo? I knew he meant a little boy that was in his story, his lifetime. He showed me a picture of him. And I knew something else . . . I knew that in that lifetime in France I had two children . . . a girl of about ten years old that was you and a boy of about three that was Artamor. Recently, I have discovered that Artamor, like all the

The Four Ascents

rest, has been in my life all along. He was a priest in Greece, and was the very soul that pulled me up from the depths I had fallen. And in Mexico he was a little boy that I played with. Always, it seems he was much wiser than me. I think he always had a strong connection with his star origins and it was that strength that I followed on the four ascents."

"Wow," amazing stuff indeed" says Grace.

"Well, I've spent my life remembering these things," I explain. "To me this is normal everyday stuff. It's my truth."

"And it's Black Elk's truth," she adds.

"He calls it The Two Roads Truth, The Journey of the Soul," I say noticing the change that's just come over her. The light of understanding is shining in her eyes.

On the way back down to the garden she asks me, "Do you think you will ever meet Artamor?"

"I think I already have," I reply to her surprise.

"What? When? Who is he?" she asks with great interest.

"Okay, don't say anything to him now," I warn her playfully.

"My lips are sealed."

"That guy Stephen that Georgina brought with her. Black Elk has been saying all day: it's Little Buffalo . . . it's Little Buffalo."

"And is it?" Grace asks.

I don't answer her but give her a wink instead. Stephen and Georgina are walking straight towards us.

∞∞∞∞∞∞∞∞∞∞∞∞∞∞∞∞∞∞∞∞∞∞∞∞∞∞∞

It is nine thirty and the sun is low in the sky. It is a very special time, a time when the veil between the world of spirit and the physical world is at its most permeable. I have always loved the sunrise but sunset also holds a special place in my heart. Many of the guests have gone home. All of those that are members of the groups are still here though. We have special plans for tonight. And now that Artamor is with us, it will make it even more special. I am sitting in the shade of a beautiful beech and talking with Stephen and Georgina whilst everyone else is entertaining each other with singing and guitar playing. A group of my mates are singing a rhythmic African chant whilst beating on Djembe drums.

"Sounds great" remarks Stephen.

Eliza White Buffalo with Nicholas Black Elk

"They're available for bookings," I joke. The sound is intoxicating indeed and as the momentum increases it seems to take us into a groove of heightened consciousness. *Perfect place to be speaking from the heart,* I think to myself. "Stephen, are you aware of the reason why I am known as Eliza and not Rose?" I ask him.

"It's your soul name, is it not?" he replies.

This is good; he may know also that *he* is known as Artamor. Happily, I don't even have to ask. "*My* soul name is Artamor," he tells me to my utter delight.

I look at him and for the second time today I feel a love for him that really surprises me. Even though I know he is the Father part of a triangle of energy that is Artamor, The Crystal Keeper and Eliza; even though I know that he has protected and guided me for lifetimes on Earth and that in this very moment in spirit he is one with Georgina and me; even though I know these things I am surprised at the depth of love I feel for him. I feel protected by him, loved by him. I feel safe in his presence. I have never felt such a powerful connection with another human being since I met Jack and instantly recognised him as my earthly union.

"I *thought* you were Artamor," I tell him whilst grinning profusely. "I hoped it was you. I mean . . . Black Elk has been saying it's you since you arrived. I have been waiting to meet you for years."

"I met Georgina just a few weeks ago," he tells me. "We felt an instant connection, didn't we?" he asks her."

"We did," she agrees nodding at me.

And Stephen goes on, "And then when you started speaking about your work with Rose I knew I had to meet her too. You said it too, didn't you?" he asks Georgina.

"I said I felt that you had worked with her before and that you will again," Georgina replies.

My thoughts instantly shoot to a scene in another lifetime in which my soul was incarnate as Black Elk and the energy sitting opposite me now was listening to me tell him of the great vision. Once again a wave of love sweeps through me for Stephen. He feels to me like a father, only no father that I have ever known on Earth.

"Why is this feeling so strong?" I inwardly ask Black Elk.

"You are more aware of oneness with the Father," he replies. "How does Georgina feel to you at this moment?"

I switch my focus from Stephen to Georgina. "Like a Mother, only no mother I've ever known on earth," I silently report, describing the wonderful feeling of motherly love emanating from Georgina.

"And Eliza is the Child, the Holy Flame; the Fruit of Their Essence," states Black Elk peacefully. "Rose?"

"Yes my love?" I reply feeling a sense of overwhelming peace within and without.

"Heaven is on Earth!" Black Elk's statement fills me with peace. It brims over and spills from my eyes, cascading down my face; a river of peace where once there ran a river of sorrow.

"What is happening Rose?" asks Georgina who is well accustomed to knowing when I am deep in conversation with Black Elk. "I can feel it," she adds, "yet I wish to know that which has been revealed to you."

Stephen sits quietly, bathed in the holy energy that is. I take his hand and I take Georgina's hand. "Firstly, let me tell you what is in spirit," I say to them. Black Elk is very present within me. He speaks through me, in balance with me. "Early this morning," I tell them, "I travelled in spirit to the star origins. In oneness with all there is I rose into the sea of consciousness."

"Source!" utters Georgina.

"Yes," I respond. "I cannot describe how that experience feels only to say that I am constantly in motion. All that is, all that ever was, and all that ever shall be is pure thought that springs from my inner well of desire. I am desire. I am Father. I am other, I am Mother."

"And so the Child is born," interjects Georgina.

"Exactly; and this is creation. Essentially, it is the three supreme beings that are the Father, the Mother and the Child, or the creation," I add. "This truth was revealed to me as if in instant replay, I descended onto Earth and the very first lifetime I created through my imagination."

Now up until this moment Stephen has been silently listening to my story. Now he has heard enough, felt enough to know that his presence here today and particularly in this little meeting is significant to what I am saying; that it reflects what I am saying in a visible and tangible manner. "Rose" he says to me now, "When Georgina asked me to come with her to Ireland I didn't hesitate because I felt strongly that the three of us should meet and talk. What you are saying . . . about the three supreme beings in one . . . I know that to be the threefold flame in my heart that is Faith, Hope and Charity."

Eliza White Buffalo with Nicholas Black Elk

I nod in agreement and he goes on, "Now that I am here I feel a connection between the three of us that is very much to do with that. I don't quite know what it is but I feel that we three are a reflection of that Holy Trinity."

The river of peace is still flowing from within me and as Stephen speaks about the Holy Trinity it gushes forth with tremendous power. With its flow comes the knowledge born of spirit. I open my mouth and it floods from there with melodious sound. "All over the universe I have made a good red day," I say. "The prophecy is complete on earth."

And putting my hand on Georgina's chest I say to her on Earth as I said to her in Heaven, "You are the Crystal Keeper. You are known thus in the oneness of all things for you are the earthly Mother that holds the focus of the Father's desire in her crystal core. You are Love." I lift my hand from her chest and put it on Stephen's chest, and I say to him, "You are Artamor. You are the Light we turn our faces towards. You are the voice we hear. You are Faith, the Father." And having said this I put my hand on my own chest and I say, "I am Eliza. I am the prophecy that is Heaven on Earth. I am the holy Child one with the Father and the Mother. I Am Hope." And taking their hands again so that we three form an unbroken circle I smile lovingly at Georgina and Stephen and I add "And so it is that the prophecy is complete on Earth as it is in Heaven."

"And so it is," echoes Georgina.

"And so it is," says Stephen too.

∞∞∞∞∞∞∞∞∞∞∞∞∞∞∞∞∞∞∞∞∞∞∞∞∞∞∞

It is ten pm now. The sky is ablaze with gold and purples streaked across the cloudless canvas by the setting sun. Wakan Tanka, the Great Artist has painted the sky in heavenly colours as a backdrop to the earthly display of oneness my guests and I are performing tonight. The two groups of my soul family are mostly here. Jonathan, James, Juan and Jenna are with us in spirit. We are holding hands, forming one great circle of unified souls. I find myself looking around the circle into one face after another. As I look into one pair of eyes at a time I see the spirit that in the eternity of *now* is holding hands in the star origins. It is a holy spirit; holy in the sense that he/she is whole, complete with the Mother and Father within. One by one I see them. On my right is the one known as Jack here on earth. Next to him is the one known as Grace. She has reflected my inner child to me many times. Next to Grace is

The Four Ascents

John. I gaze into his eyes, into the spirit that he is and I see that he is equally beautiful; deep behind the eyes of my future son-in-law is a powerful spirit that reflects Grace's spirit so splendidly. She couldn't have chosen a more perfect union. I look from John to Hans next. There I see the spirit that has reflected my power of alchemy, the ability to transform my base energy into the golden heights of my heavenly consciousness. Next to him is Georgina, The Crystal Keeper. She is a sister, a mother. She is all things female, reflecting the Love of my Mother Flame. And beside her stands Gertge who holds the hand of Davy. Robert is next, holding Lisa's hand. Lisa is holding Roger's hand. Next is Stephen. Looking through his eyes I see the one called Artamor. He has been a voice and a light for me to follow. I am so happy to have his physical presence with us tonight. Having looked into the eyes of every one I hang my head in quietude. I am so grateful for their presence in my life; for the roles they played on my journey home. I love each and every one of them with a love that is infinite.

"Eliza!" calls a voice in my heart. It is the Red Stone of Power. "Eliza," It says, "Embrace the beauty that you see before you, for it is your Self that you know." And I know that every one of these beautiful spirits here is part of my Self, part of the holy being within me that is the Flame of Source. I embrace the truth revealed on Earth as I proclaim, "I Am That I Am!"

And each member of my Self proclaims in unison, "I Am That I Am!"

Now, the plan was that we would sound The Great Om four times and then Georgina would lead us on a guided journey to The Centre of All Things; to our hearts, the holy place where we are connected as one. As she begins to speak her voice takes on an ethereal quality. It sounds more like music than speech and quickly becomes a song. Georgina is humming and sounding heavenly notes that sharpen and heighten with every moment. What beautiful sound! It fills my being with its beauty. It lifts me gently and carries me off to even more beautiful awareness of it. With my body as light as a feather suspended in air by a warm caressing breeze, I look around the circle of souls and I see that they too are feeling this wonderful music. Georgina has her eyes softly closed. They all do. I know that should I close my eyes and allow the music to carry me off I would melt away into the sea of consciousness, and I don't want to do that just yet. Something is to be done here on Earth first. I glance around at each member again, looking for a sign, some clue that will tell me what is to be done. I let my eyes rest for a while on Grace. She looks peaceful. Her eyes are softly closed and her lips part slightly. On closer inspection I see that they tilt upwards in a Mona Lisa smile. Beside

Eliza White Buffalo with Nicholas Black Elk

her, John appears to lean towards her as if some invisible force is pulling them together to be one body. He is smiling too. I wonder what he is thinking. My eyes go around the circle until my gaze once more falls on Georgina. Immediately I see that the aura around her has lightened so that it is glowing with what looks to be crystal light. Her aura is so wide that it touches the entire circle. I see now that everyone's energy is melted into the group so much that instead of individual auras I see one large aura around the group. Instead of individual energies there is one energy, one consciousness. As I watch the crystal light swirls around the circle. In it flashes orbs of colour: blue, yellow, green, red, and violet. They flash and spark as they spin around the circle in the stream of crystal light. Georgina has ceased singing now, but the music can still be heard. Her mouth is hanging open and her head is slightly tilted forwards. I glance across from her to Stephen. He too is rapt in ecstasy. It is now that I notice the cyrstal cord streaming from his heart. It shoots straight across at Georgina, connecting up with the same crystal cord emanating from her heart, then both shoot the cord slantways to my heart forming a triangle of golden light. Closing my eyes softly I begin to rise. The stream of crystal light spins around us carrying us onwards to our destination. The cyrstal cord connecting the trinity is within the circle. And in this way we all rise up and up. I look down to where we come from and I see there many more circles, hoops of peoples that spin and rise to follow us. I see hoops without number and all around them spins the crystal rainbow light. Above the house we rise and above the hills. Down below, the world is alive with crystal light. We rise and rise until I no longer see the ground and we are standing in the crystal stone circle in the stars. All around us the many hoops of people are. There are numerous hoops, too numerous to count, but as they begin to merge together they become fewer and fewer until there are twelve circles of souls standing here; each circle surrounded by a swirling crystal light and each with an inner triangle of crystal cord. And as we marvel at the beauty of it all, each crystal cord of each triangle pulls towards the centre and the three souls that hold it merge into one being. Georgina, Stephen and I merge into one. The others start to spin towards this one and soon there is one being in each hoop. Twelve now stand here. We are twelve. The twelve begin to merge into four groups of three. Now we are four times three. Each three merges as before into one and we are four. One stands on the North side of the crystal stone circle and one on the South side. One stands on the West side and one on the East side. And as the four merge it seems I am standing on two worlds. One world is in darkness and one is in Light. And as the two worlds merge I melt away into the sea of consciousness and I am desire existing there without expression. Ebbing and flowing I move in infinite awareness that I am nothing.

∞∞∞∞∞∞∞∞∞∞∞∞∞∞∞∞∞∞∞∞∞∞∞∞∞∞

High in the mountains in Colorado James and Jenna finish their lunch quickly. They want to get off by themselves before it is time to rejoin the others in the retreat centre. "It must be night in Ireland by now" Jenna says to James as they walk along the mountain trail towards the pool they spotted the other day.

"It'll all be over," replies James. "It would have been nice to celebrate with them."

"I've always felt a deep connection with Rose," says Jenna choosing a rock to sit on. The pool isn't very large but its crystal cool blueness is very welcome in the heat of the afternoon. Jenna removes her sandals and dangles her feet in the water. "I mean, ever since we met her I've felt that I've always known her."

"Me too," James answers her. "You know what she says is real, don't you, that we all are connected as this group? That we all have a part to play in manifesting the group's purpose?"

"To bring about The Father's Dream," Jenna says nodding in agreement.

"I wonder how it will go tonight," says James lying down on the ground and putting his bare legs from the knees down in the water. "I wonder if they will know that we're connecting with them."

"Let's get on with it anyway," says Jenna. "We have to back in the retreat centre in half an hour."

"Okay." says James pulling himself into a sitting position. "Oh I wish I hadn't eaten so much. I can hardly bend in the middle," he groans.

And so they begin: James and Jenna, sitting thousands of miles from the others high on a mountain in Colorado. They close their eyes and centre their awareness in their hearts. Then as one, for they do everything as one, they bring their focus to the group of people standing in the white tepee in Rose's garden. The many sounds of mountain life fade away from their awareness and before long they are surrounded by a swirling crystal light that flashes with sparks of rainbow colours. They feel themselves rise as they become lighter and lighter. They go with it; for they always go with the flow of events, even those unexplained. They find themselves in a crystal meadow with a standing

Eliza White Buffalo with Nicholas Black Elk

crystal stone circle. They are holding hands in a circle with the others and all around are many more circles of people too numerous to count.

∞∞∞∞∞∞∞∞∞∞∞∞∞∞∞∞∞∞∞∞∞∞∞∞∞∞∞∞∞

In Brazil, Jonathan steps from the bus thankful to be on terra firma. The bus driver was tipsy enough when they started out this afternoon but he had more to drink when they stopped for lunch at a little tapaz bar. It was just before they really came into the rainforest. Almost buried beneath a mass of thirty feet bougainvillea trees with their hot pink blossom scent weighting the already dense air, the clammy little bar was just off the road but close enough to be spotted by hungry travellers. The proprietor was happy to see them and by the obvious absence of cooking smells in the place he hadn't seen anyone all day. Still, within no time at all hardly he put a spread before them that was fit for a king. Jonathan ate his fill, not knowing when they would get back to the healing centre. They may not get back at all was what he thought then watching the bus driver knocking back glass after glass of red wine.

"Thank heavens we're here in one piece," laughs a fat American woman over Jonathan's shoulder. She had sat beside him on the bus the whole way from the bar and she hadn't stopped laughing since then. All Jonathan wants is a bit of silence; get his mind off the centre and off anyone connected with it. The American woman is pleasant enough and a good healer but all Jonathan wants now is to get away on his own where he can switch off. He telephoned Rose earlier this morning and told her he would tune in with her and the others when he got a chance. He looks around him, ignoring the American woman's incessant chatter. They had driven into a public park on the edge of the forest. Jonathan is standing in the middle of a huge dirt car park. All around the edges of the car park are dense trees reaching high into the cloudless sky. Looking up into the trees he can't spot any birdlife but it is there all the same, for the air is filled with the sound of squawking parrots and toucans. The sun is beating down and he decides to get under shelter quickly. Checking in his back pack for the extra bottle of water he packed at the bar he makes his way over to a big sign. On the sign is a map of the park and a big red arrow that says *you are here.* Various little recommended pathways are traced out on the map but Jonathan decides to take the less trodden path up the side of a steep rise.

"This way I'll be alone," he tells himself. But it's not to be. He hasn't gone far along his chosen route when a voice calls from behind him.

The Four Ascents

"Cooee! Jonathan! Wait up dear." It's the American woman.

"Ah!" he mutters to himself. "So be it!" The American woman catches up with him panting. He waits while she hokes in her oversized bag for a bottle of water. She takes a long drink and then, out of puff says how glad she is that she caught him.

"All the others are going on the flat trail," she informs him. "I reckon a climb will do us no harm at all. Besides, it's nice to have a bit of peace and quiet," she pants. Jonathan wonders if she is fit to climb at all and decides not to go too far up the rise in case he has a casualty on his hands.

"I thought I'd go up just a bit," he tells her, "high enough to see about me."

"That sounds perfect," she says smiling at him with bright blue eyes and perfect white teeth. Jonathan thinks that she reminds him of someone but he can't quite put his finger on who it is.

Off the two of them go, up the side of the rise. The trail is very steep in parts and they have to stop talking, or at least the woman does, until it flattens out again. The roar of running water can be heard and as they get higher the sound gets louder. Jonathan listens. He learns a lot about his companion on the way up but none of it sticks with him. He can't help feeling that this is someone he knows. Only he doesn't know her, she *reminds* him of someone he knows. Suddenly it's clear to him: Rose; the woman reminds him of Rose. Oh, she doesn't even look like her, not really; this woman is blonde and her skin is a golden brown. Rose is auburn haired and pale skinned. This woman is big across the middle; Rose is a slight thing. Yet something is obviously telling him that this woman resembles Rose. He studies her face; it isn't that. He listens to what she is saying; it's not that either. Yet when she smiles, her eyes light up and all of a sudden Rose is written all over her face.

"Ah well now," he tells himself, "We're all connected." And he contents himself with that knowledge.

The roar of water is great now and the next turn on the trail shows the source of the roar in majestic splendour. Jonathan and the woman turn into a clearing where there is a pool of water being filled by a huge waterfall. The water tumbles off the peak and falls into the pool only to fall away again into the hidden depth of the trees. Spray from the waterfall soaks them in moments as they stand stunned by the unexpected sight.

The woman is the first to speak. "We didn't expect to see this, did we? The others will be livid when they realise what they've missed."

Eliza White Buffalo with Nicholas Black Elk

Jonathan says nothing. He has spotted a way into the back of the waterfall and is losing no time in getting in there. The woman follows him. "Good idea Jonathan," she says.

Jonathan looks at her. Again he sees a glimpse of Rose in her face. It strikes him that he doesn't even know the woman's name but he doesn't wish to ask. He would rather see her as Rose. Behind the waterfall the sound of the water takes on a different quality. It feels to Jonathan like being in a gigantic box with the entire sea roaring all around. There is just enough room to stand and look out through the veil of water. Not much can be seen except a blurred idea of the shapes and colours of things in the forest. Jonathan is thankful that the woman is silent for a while. He uses the time to think about what the others might be doing now. The naming ceremony will be long over no doubt, but the group alignment may not be.

They may be doing it right now, he thinks glancing at his watch.

"Time has no meaning in a place like this," remarks the woman. Jonathan looks at her. She's not smiling now. "In here, in the womb of our Mother Earth . . . time doesn't exist, just the essence of life willing itself into form."

Jonathan wants to say yes, I agree with you and what an appropriate thing to say, but he can't speak. He would rather she be quiet, not say another word; yet he feels pulled towards her. It's not her words that entice him but the sound of them. The woman continues talking about time, about creation, about the deep rhythm of Mother Earth's heart as she brings life to her children. And all the while Jonathan listens to the sound of the words. They're not English, certainly not English. He doesn't speak any other language yet he understands these words that are being spoken and he feels himself melt with their sound. The woman's face is changing. It is Rose's face that he sees now before him. It is Rose who is saying those beautiful words with their amazing sound, telling of creation. And he knows: this is the sound of his star origins. It is the sound of Serabe, the star where he *is* creation and from where he creates. And Rose is his sister soul speaking to him now through the voice of another. The sound of Serabe fills the womb of the earth. He can feel the roar of the water inside him; a river of power. Crystal droplets of water cascade from the rock above his head and dance through the air. Their tiny particles hit his body and swirl around him, joining with the crystal river within. Where they there all along? He hadn't noticed. The veil of the waterfall has shifted form now as well. The water has become a stream of crystal light and on the other side, the forest glows with white light. He reaches out one arm and gently leans it into the fall. It's not wet. He doesn't retrieve his arm but

The Four Ascents

keeps it there in the stream of crystal light. The river within him quietens suddenly and the light from the fall merges with it until he is entirely made up of this light. Feeling himself swirling and rising he becomes aware of the sound of Serabe increasing in intensity. And as he rises higher and higher the sound rings out like a grand orchestra. It plays the most beautiful music imaginable and Jonathan feels every note, every tone, harmonize within his body. When he stops rising he discovers he is standing in a crystal world. A glistening crystal meadow spreads all around and standing with him amongst a circle of standing crystal stones are the others. Rose is here, Jack, James and Jenna, everyone.

∞∞∞∞∞∞∞∞∞∞∞∞∞∞∞∞∞∞∞∞∞∞∞∞∞∞

Juan steps onto the balcony of his sixth floor two-room apartment in Mexico City. He likes to stand out here after his morning shower. The city is still cool from the night this early in the morning and he can dry off whilst enjoying his first coffee of the day. He scans the view. This is the good part of the city, not so touristy. He deals with tourists all day long at Teotihuacan, the ancient city where he works as a tour guide. Not that he doesn't like tourists, they're alright he reckons but he much prefers the company of Mexicans, particularly the elder folk. He could listen to his old grandpapa harp on forever about the good old days. Sometimes Juan reckons he was born too late. He should have lived fifty years ago when his grandpapa was a young man. At times he wonders what it was like before then even. What would it have been like over a hundred years ago for instance, when the ancient city was excavated? Apparently his great, great grandfather was actually involved in the project. How great would that have been? He often asks himself that question, but he contents himself with working at Teotihuacan. At least it makes him feel more alive, more in touch with his history. He left his position as a nurse in the city's main hospital five weeks ago and he never regretted it for one second. Plus, the tour guide job pays much better and he gets extra for working Sundays. He could never have afforded this apartment on his nurse's salary. He loves his work; being with the ancient monuments, wondering what it would have been like for his great, great grandpapa uncovering the secrets of the past. If he listened to Lissy talking about him having been her husband in a past life . . . one in which he did work on the dig, then he could satisfy himself that at least he's been there, done that, got the t-shirt, even if he doesn't remember any of it. He met Lissy last June. She had come

289

Eliza White Buffalo with Nicholas Black Elk

to the ancient city with her fiancé John and he met her there. They had . . . well, connected he supposed. At least that's the word Lissy is using these days. She had fainted on the steps of the Temple of the Sun and he had gone to her rescue. She'd had some crazy dream or vision or something about being there in a past life. He was her husband and he had deserted her after the death of their daughter or something. All Juan knew was that the very presence of Lissy was doing something to him, shaking him from the inside out. If it wasn't for her he would never have had the courage to leave the hospital. They kept in touch. Every so often he would ring her or she would ring him. Her fiancé John thinks it's all a bit far-fetched but . . . well, there's just something about what she says that rings true. Now she is talking about her long lost psychic mother and how she has remembered so much of her past life experience and how we are all connected. She says that he is one of a group of souls who have been working together for a single purpose over many lifetimes. Juan doesn't know about that. He reckoned at the time Lissy told him about it that this Rose person must be a mad woman. At least that is what he thought then. After last night, he's not so sure. He leans his elbows on the balcony railings and thinks about his dream. Last night he woke several times. He was spooked. He couldn't help feeling that there was something or someone there. When he eventually slept he dreamed. He dreamed he was holding hands with a big group of people. Lissy and John were there and he felt that the rest of them were the others in this soul group that Lissy talks about. It was the strangest dream, one of those dreams when it feels real, as if it's really happening but you know you're dreaming. The group was standing in the centre of a stone circle that was entirely made of quartz crystal. The meadow that the stone circle was in was crystal too. Thinking of it now Juan reckons the entire scene consisted of crystal or crystal light. Weird things were happening yet he never felt afraid or curious even. It was as if it were all perfectly normal. Three people in the circle began to merge with each other until they were one soul. Then the rest of the group merged into each other until there was only him. All the others were part of him. That was when he noticed that many other soul groups were standing alone having merged into one soul. They merged with each other into four groups of three and then into two and lastly into one and that one was him. That was when he vanished completely and although he had no form and there was no form about him, he was still aware that he existed. It was as if he was floating in and out of an invisible sea. There was rhythm . . . just that—rhythm and a desire to be.

Oh and love, he thinks to himself now as he watches the sun rise over the city. It was as if love was all around or within . . . no, it was as if he *was* love. "It's a dream" he tells himself. "But it felt so real . . . much more real than standing here" he says. The sun casts its light across the tops of the city buildings and reaches his face. He lifts it to the light, his eyes softly closed. Tears roll from them onto his cheeks and fall the six floors to the pavement below. The dream had felt so real and it had been so beautiful. The oneness, the love, the awareness of simply being in nothingness, it was all so real.

He screams out across the city, "I want to go back. I want to go home." His words sound like a distant echo in a far off dream and Juan hangs his head as his heart feels fit to burst wide open and the tears stream like a river of pain from his chin into an abyss. He drops to his knees wrapping his arms around his naked body as it shudders, though not with cold or fear but with the exodus of years of yearning; yearning to be real, to be complete. "It wasn't a dream," he wails, "It wasn't a dream." His body stops shuddering as the river of tears runs dry. After several minutes in which he seems to drift away to the peaceful feeling of the dream once again, he opens his eyes and smiles. Gently he picks himself up from the balcony floor and scans the city again. It looks different, as if someone turned on the beauty switch. Juan never felt so high up before. Now he is soaring above it all. In his heart he is a thousand feet tall and he has just woken up from a long sleep. He had been dreaming; he still is; the city, the balcony, his body . . . it's the *real* dream. The one he thought he had last night, the return to oneness . . . *that* is reality. "This is all my imagination," he tells himself. "Take a long look at your creation, Juan," he says sweeping his arm before him in a dramatic gesture to take in all his surroundings. "*This* is the dream. Only thing is, now you have woken up from the long sleep . . . now you *know* you are dreaming."

In the beginning there is nothing . . .

I Am nothing

Yet . . . I Am

Table to show the many incarnations of each soul within the story

The first column lists the characters from book I The Two Roads.

Book I The Two Roads	Ancient Atlantis of book 2 The Four Ascents	Ancient Egypt of book 2 The Four Ascents	Ancient Greece of book 2 The Four Ascents	France of book 2 The Four Ascents	Mexico of book 2 The Four Ascents	Ireland of book 2 The Four Ascents
Rose/Eliza	Osiah /Eliza	Pheonix	Demetria	Gabriella	Maria	Rose
Lissy/ Grace				Maddy	Alma	Lissy/ Grace
Carlos					Eduardo	
Jack	Soul mate from Pleiades	Seth	Philo	Pascal	Spirit that is the earthly union	Jack
Davy	Brother from Sirius				Catherina's papa	Davy
Jonathan	Amir The Prophet	Ames	Eusebius		Treebeard/ Amir	Jonathan
Francie			Lord Percius			
Gertge	Sister from Sirius	Elmara			Rosalina	Gertge
Glenda			Thucymus			
Lisa					Sister in Spirit World	Lisa
Georgina	The Crystal Keeper		Eumelia	Esme/The Crystal Keeper	Catherina/ The Crystal Keeper	Georgina/ The Crystal Keeper
Hans	High Inquisitor		Hermetius	Claude	Brother in Spirit World	Hans

Eliza White Buffalo with Nicholas Black Elk

Roger				Richard De Boir	Brother in spirit world	Roger
James	Amir	Rhatu	Duncan		Miguel	James
Jenna	Sister from Pleiades				Sera	Jenna
Juan					Juan	Juan
			Jason/ Artamor	Clairose/ Artamor	Pedro/ Artamor	Stephen/ Artamor

ABOUT THE AUTHOR

Eliza White Buffalo has been a shaman from birth. In her childhood she made thousands of out of body journeys into the spirit world. She travelled with a spirit lady called May, who took her to an imaginary place called The Green. It was in this place that Eliza met with Black Elk who taught her much about who she is, who he was, and the divine purpose of her life. He showed her much of the great vision when she was nine years old. He taught her how to survive the difficult black road and how to be happy from within. Eliza had a near death experience in 2002 due to a serious road accident. She believes she died for three minutes, and was sent back to do the divine work she had come to do. For the past eleven years Black Elk has been guiding Eliza in fulfilling this divine life's purpose. The Two Roads Trilogy is a story based upon Eliza's experiences in the Spirit World, her experiences with Black Elk and other spirits, and her many past life memories. She lives in Ireland with her husband and sons.

For further information see Eliza's website www.elizawhitebuffalo.com

Also by Eliza White Buffalo with Nicholas Black Elk

The Two Roads
Part One of The Two Roads Trilogy

Born with amazing paranormal abilities, Rose survives her terrible life with the help of her spirit guide, Black Elk. Using his world renowned vision of spiritual truth, Black Elk teaches Rose who she really is and the divine purpose of her life, transforming it into one of unbelievable joy . . .

Lissy was born in a hen shed, torn from her 13 yr old mother, Rose, and secretly adopted. Having traced her birth mother's identity, she uncovers a heart wrenching secret which propels her forwards on her own journey of self discovery . . .

Featuring past life regression, astral travel, and spirit communication, *The Two Roads* is an incredible dark to light story of survival that can teach us all how to transform our lives through our shamanic nature.

Praise for *The Two Roads*—

"Eliza is one of the bravest new spiritual voices around. Her story is captivating and her wisdom will truly touch your heart. Many people send me their books to read and review, few are as well written and captivating as Eliza's book. You really will be engrossed in the power of her story. I give it my highest endorsement."
—Jonette Crowley, *The Eagle and The Condor*.

In part I of *The Two Roads Trilogy* Eliza White Buffalo weaves a fascinating and enthralling story of the immense pain and suffering of an abused child and her escape into her spiritual Self where she meets one of her spirit guides, Black Elk, who helps guide her intuitively out of the dark existence of her childhood. The mixture of suffering, hope and, ultimately, redemption makes this *all too real story* a must read.
—Tommy Suggs—*From a Student's Notebook* series and founder of *Sweetwater Education Foundation*.

"*The Two Roads* will change you. Embrace this truth and drink it in. It is a journey across the 'fearful black road,' the painful path of the physical realm. It is the sacred walking grounds of the wounded shaman."
—Cathleen Hulbert, *The First Lamp*

"Eliza is a true healer. Her warmth and compassion for others is apparent. Her amazing journey is meant to be shared with the world and we are so happy her story is being told and enlightening others at the same time. Wisdom is the knowledge that comes from understanding one's true nature with the Divine, and knowing how to share that knowledge. Thank you, Eliza, for the gifts you are bringing to the world."
—Cindy Lora Renard and Gary Renard, *The Disappearance of The Universe*

"I had a wonderful meeting with Eliza in beautiful Sedona. She reminds me of a beautiful flower on a South Dakota prairie. Her wisdom and authenticity is apparent from the first meeting. Her story is truly amazing and inspirational, and I am so happy that it is shared with the world."
-Grand Chief Woableza of the former *Spiritual Elders of Mother Earth Council.*

Coming soon

The Childhood Diaries
Part Three of The Two Roads Trilogy

Lightning Source UK Ltd.
Milton Keynes UK
UKOW051520100713

213527UK00002B/142/P